CHINESE

VISIONS

OF WORLD

ORDER

*

CHINESE

VISIONS

OF WORLD

ORDER

Tianxia, Culture, and World Politics

Ban Wang, editor

*

Duke University Press * Durham and London * 2017

Designed by Courtney L. Baker
Typeset in Garamond Premier Pro by Westchester Publishing Services

Library of Congress Cataloging-in-Publication Data
Names: Wang, Ban, [date] editor.
Title: Chinese visions of world order : tianxia, culture,
and world politics / Ban Wang, editor.
Description: Durham : Duke University Press, 2017. |
Includes bibliographical references and index.
Identifiers: LCCN 2017015436 (print)
LCCN 2017019412 (ebook)
ISBN 9780822372448 (ebook)
ISBN 9780822369318 (hardcover : alk. paper)
ISBN 9780822369462 (pbk. : alk. paper)
Subjects: LCSH: China—Foreign relations.
China—Civilization. World politics—1989–.
Classification: LCC DS740.4 (ebook) |
LCC DS740.4 .C354549 2017 (print) |
DDC 327.51—dc23
LC recordavailableathttps:// lccn.loc.gov/2017015436

Cover art: *Ch'onhado* (Map of all under heaven), mid-eighteenth century.
Heritage Image Partnership Ltd. / Alamy Stock Photo.

Contents

Introduction ⋆ 1
Ban Wang

Introduction / Ban Wang

As China is becoming a major power in the world, thinkers and writers are debating the implications of a Chinese vision of world order. The classical idea of *tianxia* has become the focus of debate in scholarship and public discourse. Literally meaning "all under heaven," tianxia refers to a system of governance held together by a regime of culture and values that transcends racial and geographical boundaries (more on this later). This new interest in tianxia calls to mind a similar focus half a century ago. In *The Chinese World Order: Traditional China's Foreign Relations*, edited by John K. Fairbank in 1968, scholars examined imperial China's trade and ritualistic relations with the adjacent regions of East and Southeast Asia under the rubric of the "Chinese culture area." In his introduction, Fairbank claims that the Chinese concept and practice of an international order flourished over two millennia "until the Western powers intruded into East Asia in the mid-nineteenth century."[1] Such investigations of a Chinese world vision, he cautions, would have to confront the challenge of the concepts of nation, sovereignty, and equality of states, which are ill equipped to deal with the body of thought and practice associated with tianxia. This challenge persists today and reflects the confrontation of two worldviews. Recent scholarship continues to address the gap between the Western interstate concepts and Chinese world visions. Taking issue with the entrenched model of balance of power in interstate relations, David Kang discerns a broad pattern of diplomacy, ritual, and hierarchy as the condition of peaceful coexistence among Sinicized East Asian countries.[2]

Despite economic globalization and interdependence, despite the flow of capital, commodities, media, and culture across borders, geopolitical conflict and economic competition by powerful nations continue and often flare up. Interstate conflict, unequal development, neoliberal agendas, and environmental disasters are tearing the world apart. The divided world seems to have an increasing need for a cosmopolitan ethos, leadership, and cooperation.

As China has risen among the global powers, it has come into more direct confrontation with the international system rooted in "nation, sovereignty, and equality of states." Since joining the World Trade Organization (WTO) in 2001, China has gained a firm foothold in world institutions and has exercised increasing leverage. All signs point to China being in a position to claim global leadership and reshape the economic order. While some see this claim as imperial hubris, others view it as beneficial. But where does this ambition come from? Many have argued that the rising China cannot be understood without tracing its roots in ancient history.[3] With power comes responsibility, and China's strategies are derived from an ambition from its past in which China strove, in Joseph Levenson's words, to go "against the world to join it."[4] Its campaign of One Belt, One Road harks back to the ancient trade routes across Euro-Asian lands, and its Asian Infrastructure Development Bank recalls precolonial maritime trade networks. Chinese leaders and writers are fond of cloaking China's image in the time-honored mantle of its five-thousand-year history. Crystallized in the doctrine of tianxia, its ambition had remained submerged, but it has been raising its head in the last few decades. An examination of tianxia and especially its modern avatars—cosmopolitanism, Confucianism, socialist internationalism, and transnationalism—will offer a sense of how China draws on its past to advance a different worldview.

Taking issue with the current world system, Zhao Tingyang, whose work is at the center of the tianxia debate, invokes the idea of tianxia in opposition to the modern nation-state and related political theory. His story of tianxia's genesis focuses on the dawning of a vision that departed from the state-centered polity. In the fall of the Shang dynasty, the small kingdom of Zhou (ca. 1046–771 BCE) prevailed over the powerful Shang because Zhou had moral appeal and Shang was corrupt. But, vulnerable to Shang's remnants, the new kingdom of Zhou had to cobble together the fragmented areas by investing cultural authority in a framework capable of pacifying subversive forces. In a departure from state-centered politics, tianxia was born. Its mission is to win support from all populations, *de minxin* (得民心), and to provide a framework for social and economic life. Winning people's hearts and minds is pivotal to the legitimacy of tianxia, which is buttressed by a culture of morality, ritual, and rites. Sustained by affective ties rather than coercion, tianxia distinguishes the inside from the outside less by geography and ethnicity than by cultural competence. Boundaries are fluid and relational: whoever attains cultural norms can be an insider, and the outsider can move in on merit.[5]

Zhao Tingyang is not the first to pit tianxia against the international system. When China encountered the West in the nineteenth century, thinkers resorted to the classical tradition to question the unfamiliar world. Wei Tsai-ying suggests that Kang Youwei's mentor, Liao Ping, revamped the tianxia vision against the nation-state system.[6] Premised on the formal equality of nations, international law constructed a world prone to conflict, anarchy, and lawlessness. State sovereignty was a tool wielded by the strong nations to forge a power balance at the expense of the weak. Drawing from the Confucian classic *Spring and Autumn Annals* (*Chunqiu*), Liao Ping considered tianxia a corrective to crisis-ridden interstate relations. In view of the similar power struggle in the Spring and Autumn period, he found that the Confucian classics proposed a model of governance by two lords of the states of Qi and Wei: *ba* (霸) and *bo* (伯), referring to military domination and imperial authority. While he favored authority, Liao Ping sensed that a combination of domination and authority could work together to impose an order over lesser states. Instead of mere realpolitik, he envisaged a moral and formal arrangement anchored in family and kin. Access to the power center was based on cultural and ritualistic criteria that fanned out to the periphery. Through cultural transformation and instruction (*jiaohua* 教化), the Kingly Way (*wangdao* 王道), the compass of authority, held sway over the realm and knew no bounds.

Like Liao Ping's attempt to recover the past to inform the future, contemporary tianxia discourse stems as much from a sense of frustrated tianxia aspirations as from China's newfound position. Well received among intellectuals and academics, Zhao Tingyang's book *The Tianxia System* (*Tianxia tixi* 天下體系) has made a strong impact on popular culture and state policy.[7] Critical of self-seeking, expansionist nation-states, the book focuses on the conflict between a morally conceived international society and antagonistic nation-states.

Yan Xuetong, a professor at Tsinghua University, has also updated tianxia by critiquing the international system.[8] Yan deplores the current hegemonic system as well as China's deficit of leadership. In his book *Ancient Chinese Thought, Modern Chinese Power*, Yan revisits the pre–Qin dynasty thinkers and recovers interstate relations modeled on "all under heaven." The key to pre-Qin political philosophy is "humane authority," which includes ideals of social justice, public service, and moral leadership. Yan proposes combining a moral tianxia with strategic alliances for curtailing geoconflict. Advocating for leadership that is humane, moral, responsible, and capable, he prioritizes the common good over national self-interest.

The resurgence of tianxia has also met with some criticism. As William Callahan has noted, Zhao proposes "a system that values order over freedom, ethics over law, and elite governance over democracy and human rights."[9] Through the lens of the international system, Callahan views tianxia not as a regime of culture and authority but as the projection of a global hegemon. Callahan's view points to the tension between culture and power, ethics and law in the conceptions of tianxia. Despite its popular revival, tianxia has rarely been defined with rigor. According to the late Benjamin Schwartz, the concept presents "a notion of universal kingship linked to a widely shared sense of participation in a higher culture." Rooted in a religious and cosmic foundation, the idea embodies a universal authority and a sacred set of ritual and kin relationships as "the absolute criteria dividing barbarians from the men of the Middle Kingdom." But authority was achieved through "military-political consolidation over large areas."[10] For Yuri Pines, tianxia denotes an imperial culture "that looks like a classical hegemonic construction in the Gramscian sense."[11] The early empire builders, while developing military and administrative mechanisms, "formulated ideals, values, and perceptions that laid the intellectual foundation" for "the unification of All under Heaven."[12] As a cultural and intellectual construct, tianxia emerged as a centerpiece of Chinese political culture set in the framework of empire. Two aspects become apparent in the above definitions: normative appeal and realpolitik. For Zhao Tingyang and others, the normative ideal aspires to a worldview that transcends the differences in particular communities, nation-states, race, and ethnicity. "The entire world under heaven" yearns for a common world beyond the modern political landscape fraught with power struggle and rivalry, echoing Levenson's idea of "regime of value" as opposed to the *guo* (state).[13] A faith in common values privileges political unity over differences by virtue of shared culture immanent in the everyday lifeworld, customs, and commerce. Levenson wrote that the tianxia mind-set accepted cultural differences as the way of the world. Although they distinguished the civilized from the barbarians, Confucian thinkers were aware that "the barbarians are always with us." Tianxia was "a criterion, a standpoint, not a point of departure."[14]

Guarding against the use of tianxia as a sign of Chinese exceptionalism, we propose that the concept offers an alternative vision to the current international system. In contemporary discussion, its projection of a worldwide public is crystallized in a statement from the Confucian classic *Records of Rites* (*Liji* 禮記): "When the Great Way was practiced, the world was shared by all alike."[15] While the military and political consolidation of large areas and the related tribute system was common among ancient empires, tianxia insists on "the anchorage of a universal authority in the moral and ritualistic framework of a secular high culture."[16]

Some people's meat, however, is poison to others. Schooled in modern political thought, possessive individualism, and the doctrine of state equality, critics tend to see the Chinese worldview as presumptive and a threat, regarding it as an expression of nationalist hubris of a rising hegemon. The fault line of culture versus realpolitik threads through current debate, intellectual history, and the chapters of this volume. Indeed, as a body of thought and practice, tianxia has wavered between the normative claim to values and culture on the one hand, and coercive mechanisms of domination on the other. The concept has played out between an impulse toward universal principles and an ideological cover for power politics. In its modern avatars, the fault line parallels the divide between cosmopolitanism and interstate geopolitics. As changeable and varied meanings of tianxia reflect historical vicissitudes, a historical and interpretive inquiry into the concept may shed light on the tension between culture and power, and morality and politics.

Rather than disembodied metaphysics over and above history, the contributors to this volume rethink tianxia as implicated in historical contingency and political practices. By keeping an eye on the nexus of culture and realpolitik, we attend to the concept's rise and fall, its use and abuse, its mutation and metamorphoses in modern times. As a universal mandate, tianxia aspires to normative principles, and its validity rests not on the power to impose on others but on its potential as a critique of parochial interests and structures of domination. A coercive state may resort to it as an ideological alibi to disguise its private interests as general interests, but the normative thrust may also invoke universal principles to pit the public criteria of justice against such parochial agendas and abuse of power.

In what follows, this introduction provides context and analysis for the chapters, which are grouped under four themes. Beginning with the recent Confucian revival, part I revisits the Confucian classics and uses tianxia ideas to question nationalist historiography and the interstate system. Part II focuses on cross-cultural exchange, learning, and comparison of civilizations. Indebted to the tianxia worldview, this learning process embraces the humanist ideal of a common world. Examining tianxia's relation to socialist internationalism in Mao's China, part III traces the relevance of the classical vision to the socialist imagination, whereby working peoples of peripheral nations strove to emancipate themselves in a concerted struggle against colonialism and imperialism. The two essays of part IV are skeptical of the official version of tianxia and see its rhetoric as part of a state-sponsored ideological campaign. By supporting the critical stance of intellectual autonomy, the last chapter reaffirms the hopes of the Global South.

In general, the contributors trace tianxia's intellectual resources, track its historical mutations, explore its limitations, critique its abuses, rearticulate its worldviews, explore its manifestations, and reconsider its hidden links to China's rise. The four parts are interrelated, but each provides a reference point for reconsidering tianxia as an alternative vision of world order.

Tianxia, Confucianism, and Empire

In recent decades, a revival of Confucianism has sought to promote China's new image—its millennial culture, identity, and role on the world stage. The revival involves the government, institutions, popular culture, the media, and local communities. In small towns and villages, Confucianism is filling the vacuum left by the collapse of the dominant ideology and moral fabric. The intellectual goal of this new Confucianism, however, is to look to past resources to advance a new worldview to meet the challenges of the contemporary world.[17]

The revival of Confucianism is nothing new. When Confucian China crumbled before Western encroachment, Kang Youwei and Liang Qichao, while absorbing Western knowledge to strengthen China, wove the Confucian idea of tianxia into the nation-building project. Writing about his European trips, Liang proposed the idea of the cosmopolitan state (*shijie zhuyi de guojia*, 世界主義的國家). Inspired by the League of Nations, Liang saw the possibility of nation-states working together toward a world community.[18] Although China had yet to attain the status of a nation-state, all nation-states that committed themselves to the cosmopolitan principle could have a chance to reconcile their aggressive and self-seeking agendas.[19]

To Liang, nation building was only a way station to the cosmopolitan state. The *raison d'état* is not self-interested but entails a planetary ethic, which progresses in a spiral from the individual to the family to the nation-state, culminating in a united world. Drawing on the Confucian doctrine of *xiu qi zhi ping* (修齊治平)—cultivate the self, order family ties, govern the country, and bring peace to all under heaven—Liang envisions a self that is not self-serving but sociable, and a nation-state that is not aggressive but a team player:

> The ultimate aim of an individual's life is to make a contribution to humanity as a whole. Why? Because humanity as a whole is the upper limit of the self. If you want to develop yourself, you need to move in this direction. Why must the state exist? The reason is that with the state, it is easier to rally the cultural power of a national group; to perpetuate and grow it so that a country will be able to contribute to humanity as a

whole and help the world grow as well. Building a state is thus a means of advancing humanity, just as the coordination of a municipal government with self-governing local regions is a means of building a state. In this light, individuals should not rest content with making their own state wealthy and powerful, but should instead make their nation an addition to humanity. Otherwise the state is built to no purpose.[20]

Liang goes on to claim that contribution to humanity would require a synthetic convergence of Chinese and Western cultures to create a world culture.[21]

The contemporary scholar Wang Hui has built on Liang's claim on a Chinese vision of world order. His monumental work *The Rise of Modern Chinese Thought* (*Xiandai Zhongguo sixiang de xingqi*) links Confucian universalism to cosmopolitan ideals by reviewing diverse schools of thought in modern China. Weaving together classical resources, Western Enlightenment, socialism, and social democratic ideas, Wang analyzes the dialectic between culture and politics, the particular and the universal, the national and international. A history of Chinese thinkers in constant conversation with Western traditions, his book advances a critical mode of modernity against capitalist modernity.[22] As the Qing dynasty was swept into the system of nation-states, Liao Ping and Kang Youwei, through New Text Confucianism, provided strategies for thinking about world governance and nation building.[23] Deploying ideas of Confucian universalism or empire rather than tianxia, Wang refrains from elevating the Confucian view to a universal discourse. But empire serves as a substitute: it embodies a political culture that transcends the nation-state system. Wang describes the way the Chinese state evolved into something more than a nation-state. In the late imperial era, tianxia enabled the Manchus to shore up their legitimacy as a Chinese regime by incorporating diverse ethnic communities, populations, and religions "into a flexible and pluralistic political structure."[24] Although national knowledge and institutions helped China to become strong on the way to becoming an important part of the world, Chinese thinkers went beyond them and aspired to a different worldview.

The European nation-state, keyed to individual subjectivity, political economy, and legal institutions, imposes a global narrative of modernity. The cornerstone of the international system and historiography, the nation-state drives global capitalism and colonialism. Nationalist historiography deems imperial China to be devoid of history and lacking inner dynamics, languishing under the Mandate of Heaven. Discontent with that view compelled the historians of the Japanese Kyoto School to discern evidence of a proto-nation-state in the Tang-Song transition. The result is a reconstruction of East Asian modernity.

Wang Hui recasts this Asian modernity with a Confucian logic. Instead of national signs, the self-understanding of Song Confucianism recalls the unity of rites and music of the golden age of the Three Dynasties and the subsequent decay in the hollowing out of value from institutions.[25] Projecting a political vision broader than that of the nation-state, Wang overcomes the tired dichotomy between nation-state and empire. The empire embraced interregional communication, centralized political power, multiethnic demographics, fluid cultural identities, and varied regionalisms. It overlapped with the national form as China waded deeper into the modern world.[26] In Wang's version of Confucian China and its modern fate, Chinese modernity attests to the transformation of an ancient cosmology from the Confucian heaven (*tianli* 天理) to the scientific, public principle (*gongli* 公理).[27] Instead of the new replacing the old, Confucian universalism persists in modern thought in the articulation of a morally coherent, culturally meaningful, and politically integrative universe.[28] Wang Hui's work confirms Levenson's remark that Chinese historians harbor cosmopolitan aspirations in writing about China.[29]

The empire versus nation-state distinction also informs nation-centered historiography. In chapter 1, Mark Lewis and Mei-yu Hsieh question China's image as a timeless empire qua nation-state in terms of territorial integrity and ethnic homogeneity. Attentive to China's tenacious ties to the past, they trace the Han dynasty's road to empire through cultural interaction, ethnic commingling, and cosmopolitan linkages. This process bears witness to a shift from a ritualistic and shared culture to an entwined operation of diplomacy, alliance, population management, socioeconomic exchange, and military campaigns. From a limited polity besieged with pluralistic, decentering forces, the Han evolved into a tianxia polity governed by a single, supreme ruler. The pinnacle of the empire commanded the recognition and the services of the Han peasantry, the Indo-European oasis kingdoms, and numerous steppe peoples. Initially, the ruler asserted his superiority over his former peers through gift exchange and kinship ties with the Xiongnu ruler. Dividing the world between two masters, this balance of power allowed each to strengthen his power. The necessity of curbing local challengers and bolstering imperial authority brought ethnic minorities into the fold, as they were absorbed into and employed in the Han regime. This inclusive policy made imperial rule explicitly transethnic and transregional, setting the example for subsequent empire builders. The rise of the Han corresponded to the earlier vision of a single tianxia wherein all people, no matter how distant or alien, were brought together under the imperium.

This narrative challenges the image of a timeless China with a homogeneous Chinese people residing in a bounded place called the Middle Kingdom. To the contrary, the Han chronicles show that all parties, inside and outside, could promote the power and status of the ruling house, and cultural and ethnic differences were negligible. In this multicultural empire, very little evidence shows that different peoples must be folded into a common ethnocultural tradition. The Han managed to integrate diverse peoples of varied cultures and regions into the expanded state and constructed an interregional network connecting polities across the steppes.

In their contributions, Wang Hui and Prasenjit Duara retrieve ideas from Confucian sources. Reinterpreting Kang Youwei's New Text scholarship, Wang Hui in chapter 2 addresses the fault line between empire and nation-state. Treating culture as vital to political unity, Kang seeks to transcend conflicted feudal fiefs by means of a cultural politics that propelled Confucianism's rise to orthodoxy. From the competing schools of thought in the Spring and Autumn era, Confucianism emerged as a common culture and a regime of value. Kang draws a parallel between the rise of orthodox Confucianism and the clash of civilizations in the early twentieth century, when rival religions and cultures competed for supremacy. Here, the need for cultural authority amid political breakdown prefigures the importance of cosmopolitanism among warring colonial and imperialist states. Rendering the empire as a multiethnic state to combat divisiveness, Kang Youwei addresses the question of ethnicity by appealing to the notion of empire sustained by cultural authority and state religion, which transcends ethnic divides and cultural differences. As a civilization and empire, China encompasses loose social relations, multiple ethnicities, and heterogeneous cultures in a vast land.

Taking a leaf from the ancient doctrine of *tian*, if not tianxia, Prasenjit Duara in chapter 3 addresses the tension between the nation-state system and cosmopolitanism. Based on state sovereignty, self-other relations, and neoliberalism, the modern world has run into deep trouble. This calls for a cosmopolitan ethos capable of sharing sovereignty with regional communities and making decisions on matters of common concern.

The religious experience of transcendence points a way out by drawing strength from the Confucian ritual of self-cultivation. Self-cultivation not only trains individuals to develop spiritual wisdom but also encourages them to undertake a moral mapping of the world as the locus of the common good. Comparing Kant's kingdom of ends with the tianxia vision, Duara focuses on the Confucian trajectory of moving from the inner to the outer realm. While reserved for sage-kings in the past, the ethical life in tian—a symbol of transcendent moral authority—has played a significant role in sustaining social and moral bonds in Chinese society. In today's global societies, the ethical ideal could foster a sense of authority and sympathetic feelings. Cultivating righteous service and enhancing the unity of spirit and body, tian exercises moral authority over the power of nation-states and impels a habit of the heart that bears allegiance to ever-expanding communities. As self-cultivation spreads moral influence to both intimates and strangers, individuals could reenact past intellectual resources for a new universalism. Echoing Liang Qichao's above-mentioned moral progress of the individual through the ascending scales of family and community en route to cosmopolitan ethos, the transcendent authority represents a worldview that develops from the ground up, linking mundane experiences to the universal.

Tianxia, Cross-Cultural Learning, and Cosmopolitanism

Joseph Levenson observed that the historian of Confucian China was a cosmopolitan thinker in disguise. Although Confucian universalism was in retreat at the turn of the twentieth century, a "burgeoning cosmopolitanism" might rise "from the ashes of cosmopolitanism."[30]

Tianxia invites comparison with cosmopolitanism. Kant's universal rationality envisages that humans are bound by mutual obligations to arrange in concert their social and political life in order to realize a condition of universal justice and peace. Against humans' propensity toward sensuality and self-interest, Kantian ethics proposes that individuals and states must act on principles that are true and acceptable for all human beings. By curbing self-regarding and parochial tendencies, people across the world will learn to act as cultural agents by exercising their autonomy and creativity from the prior conditions of the natural world. The cultural agents follow a path from the particular to the universal: they lighten the burdens of history and tradition and fulfill what is distinctively human and universally rational.[31] In Pheng Cheah's analysis, as a passage to cosmopolitanism, culture involves learning, enlightenment, and the growth of arts and science, akin to the German ideal of *Bildung*. The cosmopolitan ideal finds a proper medium in the vision of "society of culture" that aspires to the universal community and promotes cosmopolitan sociality. Moving across national and territorial barriers, culture becomes cross-cultural exchange and learning, where "universally communicable pleasure, elegance and refinement" could overcome human limits inherent in our nature, which includes the primordial identities of race, ethnicity, and nation. "The moral progress of humanity," writes Cheah, "can be guaranteed only through cultural products that preserve for posterity all the significant achievements of humanity as a moral species beyond the lives of the individual actors."[32] Cosmopolitanism articulates the intellectual and ethical conditions for global politics, just as tianxia aspires to a regime of value and shared culture.

Both Kant and Kang Youwei, in Ban Wang's analysis in chapter 4, believe that moral and aesthetic experience could build bridges among peoples and nations. Kant's aesthetic notion of *sensus communis* resonates with Kang Youwei's vision of world community. While Kant focuses on cosmopolitan ethics, Kang Youwei explores how aesthetic experience promotes cross-cultural sympathy and communication. As an antidote to the warring states with their "unsocial sociability," Kant's theory of aesthetic humanity envisages a shared plane of sense and sensibility over and above self-interest and geopolitical conflict, proposing a cosmopolitan culture to heal the disjointed world. Aesthetic experience gestures toward a vision of rationally conceived society, enabling intersubjectivity and human sympathy. Similarly, Kang Youwei conceives of international relations in terms of morality and aesthetics. To him the aesthetic consists in learning from and immersing oneself in diverse cultures in a way that involves all the senses and the soul. Learning allows us to have intimate access to others and fosters sympathy and appreciation of pluralistic cultural forms, bridging the gaps among members of different nations.

Kang Youwei's worldview also contains a critical thrust embedded in the Confucian tradition. Vigilant about political corruption and cultural decay, the critique takes aim at the regime's immoral behavior as it falls short of the normative criteria embodied by the Kingly Way. The classic *Spring and Autumn Annals* stages a critique of the severance of politics from morality and of ritual from music (禮崩樂壞). This critique in the name of ethico-political integrity has encouraged generations of Confucians to remonstrate against moral decay and political atrophy in reforms. As the symbol of the sage-king, the Duke of Zhou occupied a position combining virtue with authority and was capable of implementing universal laws of the Kingly Way. This upholding of value against a fallen reality is well illustrated in the critique of the classic *Zuozhuan* (Zuo commentary). A narrative of the might-makes-right, winner-takes-all approach, the *Zuozhuan* implies a form of realpolitik rooted in political expediency and a concern with success and failure. In contrast, the *Spring and Autumn Annals* embodies ideas and beliefs that can be treated ahistorically by extracting moral precepts of perennial value. It treats historical events not as a gripping narrative of power and intrigue but as the transhistorical mirror of benevolence, righteousness, and justice.

The concern with universalism informs China's fascination with Greek antiquity in the early twentieth century. In chapter 5, Yiqun Zhou notes a blurred sense of differences between China and the West among Chinese admirers of

Greek civilization. Supported by the thinking of tianxia, they approached the civilization of the West as having universal significance for humanity's past, present, and future. The progressives embraced Greek antiquity and Western civilization as a beacon of enlightenment, modernity, and progress—a mirror that exposed the deficiencies and backwardness of the Chinese past. They believed China should strive to catch up and empower itself in order to survive and compete in the modern world. The conservatives, on the other hand, seemed more concerned about saving Chinese tradition in order to stand proudly on a par with the West. They combined the finest elements of tradition and modernity, East and West, in hopes that Chinese culture could contribute to a cosmopolitan world culture. To advance China in keeping with universal norms, they looked back and valorized the pre-Qin era as a civilizational embryo comparable to the most advanced of Western civilizations. Judicious borrowing from the West would also provide the new norms for world civilization. For all the varying mix of nationalism and cosmopolitanism, a persistent quest for cosmopolitan culture underscores the comparison of China and the West.

Riding on the wave of China's rise, however, contemporary writers, such as Gan Yang and Liu Xiaofeng, are pushing for Chinese leadership in propagating cosmopolitan culture—with a strong nationalist overtone. While their forebears looked to the West from the margin and appropriated foreign learning to strengthen China, Gan Yang has proclaimed that the age when the Chinese were pupils is over. With China's new power, Gan and Liu are more assertive and confident. Merging Greek antiquity with Chinese classics, they take a stance against modernity by advocating a meeting of classical minds with Western interlocutors. China has arrived and is poised to wield soft power to forge a new world order.

Could tianxia serve as a benign force in maintaining friendly and peaceful interstate relations? Daniel Bell in chapter 6 posits the idea of hierarchical foreign relations. Integral to tianxia, a hierarchy structured the tribute system for trade, peace, and prosperity in the precolonial era of East Asia. David Kang and Brantly Womack have studied the China-led hierarchy in regional networks in so-called Confucian Asia. Womack's *China among Unequals* accounts for asymmetrical foreign relations in Asia through a glimpse at its tributary system and foreign relations in East Asia.[33] Daniel Bell, in a more Confucian cast of mind, focuses on the complexity of a China-centered hierarchical Asian network, which flouts the sanctified principle of equality of states.

Questioning tianxia as a blueprint for world government, Bell argues that Confucian values limit our attachment and sociality to family, kin, and political community. This thick affective attachment becomes thin as we move beyond the circle of intimates to others. However, the classic *Great Learning* teaches us to extend our ties beyond family and nation by extending our kindness to others. In this widening gyre, tianxia would entail a moral attitude that resembles global ethics: a concern with obligations we owe to people living outside the territorial boundaries of our own community. Drawing on contemporary Confucian thinkers, Bell makes a case for the hierarchical arrangement of international relations—a proposal that may raise some eyebrows. Instead of domination by a handful of powers, hierarchy entails extra global responsibilities of a strong state. As China engages in economic cooperation with adjacent regions, a benign hierarchy would assign varying degrees of responsibilities and roles to states. An echo of tianxia, this structure may be conducive to solving territorial disputes and maintaining world peace, depending on the lesser states' readiness to accept their places and duties. For all its theoretical soundness, Bell questions the feasibility of this hierarchy, given China's insistence on sovereignty and its neighbors' unwillingness to pledge fealty.

Crucial to workable hierarchy are two related Confucian doctrines: meritocracy and harmony. Meritocracy selects the best and brightest and places them in posts of prominence. Combining virtue, talent, and expertise, this elite manages public affairs and performs administrative duties. With the greater good in mind, the leaders promote the well-being of all under heaven. The administrative hierarchy may even open its doors to talent and experts from foreign lands, like the multiethnic Han Empire. Harmony, on the other hand, brings together diverse ethnic groups to partake of a common culture without shedding their own traditions. Given much historical evidence to the contrary, it seems easy to rebuke hierarchy as authoritarian, meritocracy as elitist, and harmony as Sinocentric. But the rebuke may miss the heuristic value of these ideas in distinguishing liberal democracy from the Asian mode of governance. We may also note that the controversy about hierarchy and equality continues the opposition between nation-state and tianxia.

Tianxia and Socialist Internationalism

With the focus on classical literature and the Qing Empire's encounter with the West, discussion of tianxia tends to gloss over the long twentieth century. Marked by colonialism, the Cold War, decolonization, and socialism, the twentieth century requires a political worldview. Socialism, in its vision of a world run by the sovereign people and free producers, is inherently internationalist. Socialism seeks to go beyond the nation-state by transcending the capitalist world system. How does socialist internationalism relate to tianxia and by extension Confucian China? How does the Chinese Revolution break with the past while carrying on ancient aspirations? In 1938, Mao posited this link: "Contemporary China has grown out of the China of the past; we are Marxist in our historical approach and must not lop off our history. We should sum up our history from Confucius to Sun Yat-sen and take over this valuable legacy. . . . Communists are internationalists, but we can put Marxism into practice only when it is integrated with the specific characteristics of our country and acquires a definite national form."[34]

A continuous quest for tianxia has resurfaced over and over in new waves of Confucianism and, most notably, in recent accounts of the Chinese Revolution, Maoism, and socialism. Gan Yang's book, with its telling title, *Traversing the Three Grand Traditions* (*Tong santong*), sees a red line running from Confucianism through Mao's China to Deng Xiaoping's reforms.[35] Kun Qian's *Imperial-Time Order* brings to the fore a vision of imperial time in modern historical narratives, Chinese Marxism, nationalism, and socialist internationalism. As a response to historical contingencies, the vision "has always remained above and beyond" specific moments and places, haunting, as the "eternal return" of a persistent motif, intellectual discourses, cultural formations, aesthetic texts, and political practice.[36] This scholarship links the moral ideals of Chinese tradition to popular nationalism and socialist internationalism.

Joseph Levenson linked tianxia with what he called communist cosmopolitanism. But cosmopolitanism in the abstract must be distinguished from socialist internationalism. As a movement against the worldwide uneven and exploitive system, socialist internationalism entails a form of nationalism. As Pheng Cheah explains, Marx was unaware of the importance of the national question to internationalism in his presocialist thinking until he became interested in colonialism. The 1848 revolutions in Ireland and Poland against colonial rule provoked Marx to formulate a strand of socialist internationalism. Based on class analysis and emancipatory movements by the oppressed "class-nation" (a key term in chapter 8), socialist internationalism arose in a global condition of industry and trade that "created everywhere the same relations between the classes of society, and thus destroyed the particular individuality of the various nationalities."[37] Although the ruling bourgeois class adhered to national interests, "big industry created a class, which in all nations had the same interest and with which nationality is already dead: a class which is really rid of all the old world and at the same time stands pitted against it."[38] This worldwide class—the emergent proletariat—is stripped of national affiliations and identity, because it engages in economic activities and labor across national boundaries: workers have no country. But the nation becomes pertinent as the working class seeks to organize as a self-conscious subject against the oppressor. As in Mao's above quote, the Chinese Marxists must mobilize the toiling masses in the national liberation movement to achieve socialism. It was the same principle of emancipation that prompted Marx to "distinguish between the nationalism of the developed bourgeois states and the nationalism of oppressed, colonized people."[39] Self-determination and emancipation by worldwide working-class nations and their solidarity laid the foundation for socialist internationalism. As Cheah puts it, "proletarian emancipation necessarily involves the emancipation of the oppressed peoples elsewhere because the exploitation of other peoples through colonization is intimately connected to the exploitation of workers within the 'domestic' space of a colonial power."[40]

That national liberation is a vehicle for achieving socialism informs early Chinese thinkers such as Sun Yat-sen and Li Dazhao, who saw China as an actor in unison with other nations in shaking up the colonial and imperialist world. In his early years, Mao Zedong, admirer of Kang Youwei and Liang Qichao, proposed the union of great multitudes. In the war against Japanese imperialism, Mao claimed that communists are not only nationalists committed to national defense but also internationalists. Patriotism is congenial to internationalism because oppressed nations and peoples share a common destiny and should work in concert to change the world order dominated by colonialist nations.[41] In an interview about communism, Mao cited Kang Youwei's word *datong* (great unity), referring to internationalism.[42]

Just as revolutionaries on the periphery critique colonialism and imperialism by revamping indigenous traditions, tianxia may be a hidden weapon in socialist internationalism. In Viren Murthy's analysis in chapter 7, the ancient source has become a research method and an epistemology under the aegis of Asia as method or China as method. By tracing a genealogy of inquiry by Japanese Sinologists, Murthy delineates an East Asian vision for understanding Chinese socialism as a counterpoint to the capitalist system. Delving into past stirrings for a different future, Nishi Junzō and Mizoguchi Yūzō discerned Confucian features in Maoism. From the 1950s through the 1960s, Nishi envisaged an alternative socialist future based on China's revolutionary experience. Writing in a period marked by neoliberal capitalism and the decline of socialism in the 1980s and 1990s, Mizoguchi viewed China's connection to its past as signs of identity politics.

Rather than a statist mechanism, Nishi sees tianxia as a cultural unity based on a moral worldview. Its scope transcends emperors, people, and things, and its political compass presides over fluid boundaries. Its hierarchy of family bonds sustains loyalty and lineage but still leaves room for public morality. The public character hinges on tian, as noted above by Duara. Tian entails a relationship between the ruler and the ruled over and above the archaic relations—the "tyranny of cousins," a phrase that Francis Fukuyama borrows from Ernest Gellner to distinguish primordial ties from imperial administration.[43] Instead of small circles of loyalty and lineage, tian opens up a formal space for political intervention, in which the ruler relates to the ruled by virtue of broad moral principles, and political legitimacy derives not from the ruler's person, status, or power but from the Mandate of Heaven. Tianxia designates common property and culture, and has no use for private property. Instead of being governed by coercive power and rules, the individual lives in a society by obeying the norms common to all.

The public space inherent in tianxia provides an opening for participatory politics and popular initiatives. Nishi links this morality to the creative potential of a revolutionary people. In the encounter with the West, Asian regimes and foreign imperialism alienated people from their moral agency. The decline of imperial hierarchy unleashed popular potential and encouraged the people to rise up. And it is through this blank slate that the people are able to emancipate themselves from oppression.

By contrasting the state with tianxia, Mizoguchi locates legitimate power in the people. Drawing on Sun Yat-sen's writings, he distinguishes the people as a nation from the nation-state as a hegemon. The nation-state is legitimized by its benevolence in taking care of the people's needs, well-being, and prosperity. Loss of the people means loss of tianxia. On the other hand, when the state ignores and goes against popular interests, the people have the right to rebel as a revolutionary force. In linking tianxia to revolutionary China, Japanese Sinologists strive to find an alternative universal beyond the conventional narrative of capitalist modernity. China's ancient ideas and peripheral position in the world system offer possibilities for imagining a different modern path.

Although revolutionary discourse evinces traces of tianxia, it was Chinese socialism that actually brought some of its dreams to fruition. In the shift from empire to the modern world, socialist China became a sovereign nation-state. But does this shift retain traces of ancient thinking? Building a people's republic by appropriating the nation-state form, the Chinese Revolution is as much national as social, but did not, as Lin Chun notes in chapter 8, abandon the multicultural, multiethnic identity. Over millennia, intimate ties, interactions, and intermingling created overlapping and multiethnic horizons. This confirms Wang Hui's claims that socialist transformations "incorporate different ethnic groups, populations from different regions, and different religions into a flexible and pluralistic political structure."[44] The socialist state took over the conditions of diversity and transethnicity, which are at odds with the conventional definition of nation-state.

China's socialist stance, however, rests on another register of the universal: the worldwide struggle by working peoples against capitalist accumulation and expansion. Global capitalism created a world of uneven development and a massive underclass of laborers. Nations and societies are polarized into the ruling class in the center and oppressed communities in the periphery. The Chinese Revolution awakened the Chinese people into the self-consciousness of "class nation," in Lin Chun's analysis. As the people became aware and resentful of oppression, they sought to overturn their subordination and to emancipate themselves by standing up as an independent nation-state. This class nation sees itself as a natural ally with other colonized regions and communities, and is the key to understanding socialist internationalism.

Rather than a description of the preexisting strata, class functions as a regulating concept deployed to raise consciousness, forge solidarity, and mobilize political subjects. In this light, class analysis is integral to the project of self-emancipation aimed at orienting collective action. In solidarity and working in concert, the world's working classes strive to achieve independence and move beyond the rigid categories of ethnicity, nation, and local culture.

For Lin Chun, class nation not only presupposes the solidarity of colonized nations but also informs socialist China's domestic policy toward ethnic minorities. The Chinese Revolution brought numerous ethnic minorities into the socialist fold, because these groups belonged to the same oppressed class under the yoke of the ancient regime, parochial rule, and foreign imperialist encroachments. Socialist internationalism therefore has two faces: ethnic equality in domestic society against majority chauvinism; national independence and peaceful coexistence in the international arena.

Despite her reservations, Lin's account of socialist internationalism as a united front implies a tianxia premise: unity in multicultural, multiethnic, and multinational diversity. In the era of decolonization, socialist internationalism was built on the united front of the newly independent peoples of Asia, Africa, and Latin America as well as progressive movements in the first world. With Bandung, the symbol of an alliance of newly independent Asian and African nations in the event of the Sino-Soviet split, socialist internationalism transitioned to the third world movement, which forged a network of interdependence, mutual assistance, and cultural exchange among decolonized nations. This proto–Global South alliance worked for about two decades as a world-historical force, with the goals of overturning unequal development and achieving an integrated path of development.

Lisa Rofel captures tianxia's cosmopolitanism by considering the term "worlding" in chapter 9. Worlding refers to the project to envision and articulate a unified world. To engage in worlding is to aspire to a world built on the commonality of humanity, one that respects differences but also embraces universal values. Socialist internationalism, practiced by the former Soviet Union and embodied by the Communist International, promoted socialist movements against capitalism, supported decolonization, and assisted new socialist countries. China benefited from Soviet-style internationalism by receiving aid, technology, and cultural exchange. With the Sino-Soviet split in 1959, Chinese leaders were critical of the Soviets' increasing bureaucracy and hegemony—a big brother ruling over the socialist juniors. Mao shifted the internationalist focus from the Soviets to alliances with developing nations in Asia, Africa, and Latin America. With China in the lead, the third world movement projected a far-reaching vision to cover the Global South. The third world was launched on the basis of a shared history of colonial oppression, antagonism toward Euro-American powers, uneven development, and the need for national development.

Motivated by altruism and solidarity rather than self-interest, China's support for the third world exhibited elements of tianxia. But the split with the Soviet Union and military assistance to guerrilla forces diverted the third world to nationalist politics, which was the culprit in the decline of internationalist spirit. National self-seeking deviated from internationalism and became mired in the old interstate cycle of domination and subordination.

Returning to contemporary China, Rofel distinguishes socialist internationalism from capitalist cosmopolitanism. The former promotes solidarity and common purposes among disadvantaged peoples in their struggle against hegemony; the latter is a veneer of the neoliberal economy driven by consumption, fashion, and cultural industries. Although it is the ideology of private corporations and the financial elites, this cosmopolitanism operates under the banner of universalism and is touted as the only future for humanity, with no alternative. By riding on its wave, China's glamorous image today obscures democratic and popular modes of internationalism in the socialist past.

Tianxia and Its Discontents

Both Lin and Rofel express reservations about the contemporary revival of tianxia and newfangled cosmopolitanism in postsocialist China. Indeed, talk of tianxia is increasingly perceived as an ideology behind China's soft power offensive on the global stage. As mentioned earlier, tianxia has wavered between the quest for universal principles and ideological justification for domination. The political practice of tianxia evinces the entwined operation of consent and coercion. Instead of cosmopolitanism, critics see the rise of tianxia as the official ideology behind China's aggressive push into the murky waters of global competition and world politics. A looming Pax Sinica rivaling the Pax Americana, China is projecting its soft power and brandishing its culture around the world.

In Haiyan Lee's analysis in chapter 10, China's charm offensive for soft power—megamedia events and glamorous Orientalist shows—is falling far short of its economic power. Tianxia-related campaigns and discourse, redolent of authoritarianism, Sinocentrism, and imperial hubris, do not help. Lee suggests that we move from the spectacle to the authentic source of a society's universal attractions, which reside in everyday life, habits of the heart, and the moral qualities of integrity, constancy, and innocence. Steadfastly adhered to and practiced by individuals in a morally vacuous world, these virtues may be reenergized and become the real source of soft power that a national society may tap into.

By closely reading a wildly popular TV drama, *Soldiers Sortie*, Lee examines the domestic and international perceptions of the People's Liberation Army (PLA). The international media tends to view the PLA in terms of security threats and expresses anxiety about China's peaceful rise. But *Soldiers Sortie* provides insights into the PLA's special place in the dialectics of hard and soft power. Xu Sanduo, the principal protagonist of the drama series, is shown to be a paragon of moral virtue, innocence, constancy, and loyalty, resonating with the humanist values in the Hollywood film *Forrest Gump*. Xu's hard-nosed and earthy virtue, akin to Forrest Gump's humanist ethics, may well be mobilized to appeal to global audiences and win the hearts and minds of all under heaven.

In chapter 11, Chishen Chang and Kuan-Hsing Chen critique Zhao Tingyang's tianxia metaphysics as being out of touch with historical reality. Looping back to chapter 1, Chang and Chen trace the historically varied meanings of tianxia from the Western Zhou to the Warring States period, tracking the concept's genealogical mutations and political implications. The concept came to the fore as a floating signifier as well as a flexible political strategy. Rather than the inclusive embrace of others, tianxia refers to the varying scopes of bounded political community and graded spheres of cultural commonality. Fraught with paradoxes, tianxia's readings mix inclusiveness with exclusive policy, rigid territories with messy boundaries, ethnic homogeneity with racial heterogeneity, civilization with barbarism, insides with outsides. For example, inclusion of adjacent groups in the common culture could mean their subordination to a discriminatory hierarchy, and the apparent tolerance of cultural differences may mask a segregation of "us from them." A compelling analysis of the jagged lines of tianxia, this chapter questions Zhao Tingyang's critique of the Westphalian system by way of tianxia. Even more disturbing is the brandishing of tianxia for nationalist hubris and triumphalism. If tianxia means a Pax Sinica toppling the Pax Americana, people at the margins would have none of it.

For all their skepticism, Chen and Chang see in tianxia possibilities for a different world vision and a provocation for reflection in the periphery. Citing Japan's road to modernity, which was paved tragically with imperial hubris, colonial brutality, and militarism, Zhang Chengzhi, a paragon of self-reflection from the edge, sends a warning to tianxia ideologues. In his book *Respect and Farewell—to Japan*, Zhang lumps together Japanese expansionism, colonialism, and ancient Sinocentrism. Against these hegemonies, Zhang invokes socialist internationalism and the third world movement. The revolutionary response to Japan's catastrophic world making would be a renewed internationalist alliance among intellectuals of the south in support of victims of global capitalism. Antinuclear pacifism in Japan, support for Palestinian independence, Asian intellectuals against imperialism and chauvinism, and other grassroots activism—all these represent a groundswell of antihegemonic forces, reenergizing the forgotten sources of internationalism and third worldism. These intellectual legacies, suppressed and sidelined in capitalist globalization, need to be rearticulated against official ideology and imperial hubris.

Although the contributors disagree on some points, they share a discontent with the broken world system. Undergirded by nation-state doctrine, ethnicity, territory, colonialism, and interstate antagonism, the current system is plunging humanity into anarchy and chaos. A worldview like tianxia, looking to a world governed by moral norms and public principles rather than antagonism, may alert us to what is woefully missing in the status quo. Peace rather than war, unity rather than division, dialogue rather than conflict, morality rather than force, culture rather than domination, an embrace of differences with a sense of common purpose—all these are laid on the table as we envisage a better world.

NOTES

1. Fairbank, *The Chinese World Order*, 4–5.

2. Kang, *East Asia before the West*.

3. Recently, many works have considered China's links to its civilizational past. See, for example, Jacques, *When China Rules the World*; Hsiung, *China into Its Second Rise*.

4. Levenson, *Revolution and Cosmopolitanism*, 1.

5. Zhao Tingyang, "Cong shijie kaishi de *tianxia* zhengzhi," 44–84.

6. Wei Tsai-ying 魏綵瑩, "Liao Ping's View of China's Role," 54–119.

7. Zhao Tingyang, *Tianxia tixi*.

8. Yan Xuetong, *Ancient Chinese Thought*.

9. Callahan, "Chinese Visions of World Order," 753.

10. Schwartz, "The Chinese Perceptions of World Order," 277–278.

11. Pines, *Envisioning the Eternal Empire*, 2.

12. Pines, *Envisioning the Eternal Empire*, 2.

13. Levenson, "T'ien-hsia and Kuo," 447–451.

14. Levenson, *Revolution and Cosmopolitanism*, 24.

15. De Bary and Bloom, *Sources of Chinese Tradition*, 343.

16. Schwartz, "The Chinese Perceptions of World Order," 277.

17. See, for example, Billioud and Thoraval, *The Sage and the People*; Angel, *Contemporary Confucian Political Philosophy*; Bell, *China's New Confucianism*.

18. See Luo Zhitian, "Lixiang yu xianshi," 348.

19. Liang Qichao, *Liang Qichao quanji*, 2978.

20. Liang Qichao, *Liang Qichao quanji*, 2985–2986.

21. Liang Qichao, *Liang Qichao quanji*, 2986.

22. Wang Hui, *Xiandai Zhongguo sixiang de xingqi*.

23. New Text Confucianism refers to the study of the classical Confucian texts recovered after the Qin emperor's burning of the classics. The new text scholars defend the authenticity of Confucian doctrines in the new as opposed to the old texts. The themes relevant to Kang Youwei are the image of Confucius as a reformer, the valorization of the *Spring and Autumn Annals* over the *Zuo Commentary*, and transhistorical and normative principles over realpolitik. See Hsiao, *A Modern China and a New World*, 66–67.

24. Wang Hui, *The Politics of Imagining Asia*, 90.

25. Wang Hui, *The Politics of Imagining Asia*, 74–75.

26. Wang Hui, *The Politics of Imagining Asia*, 78.

27. Wang Hui, "Gongli, shishi yu yuejie de zhishi."

28. For a review of Wang Hui's book, see Ban Wang, "Discovering Enlightenment in Chinese History," 217–238.

29. Levenson, *Confucian China and Its Modern Fate*, vol. 1, xvi.

30. Levenson, *Confucian China and Its Modern Fate*.

31. See Kant, "Idea for a Universal History," 41–53.

32. Cheah, *Inhuman Conditions*, 97.

33. Womack, *China among Unequals*.

34. Mao Zedong, *Selected Works of Mao Tse-tung*, vol. 2, 209.

35. Gan Yang, *Tong santong*.

36. Qian Kun, *Imperial-Time Order*, 50.

37. Cheah, *Spectral Nationality*, 188–189; Marx and Engels, *The German Ideology*, 78.

38. Marx and Engels, *The German Ideology*, 78.

39. Cheah, *Spectral Nationality*, 188.

40. Cheah, *Spectral Nationality*, 189.

41. Mao Zedong, *Selected Works of Mao Tse-tung*, 196.

42. Schram, *Mao Tse-Tung*, 201.

43. Fukuyama, *The Origin of Political Order*, 54.

44. Wang Hui, *The Politics of Imagining Asia*, 86.

PART I. TIANXIA,

CONFUCIANISM,

AND EMPIRE

*

TIANXIA AND THE INVENTION
OF EMPIRE IN EAST ASIA

Mark Edward Lewis and Mei-yu Hsieh

*

Intellectual Background

The idea of tianxia (天下) has never been rigorously defined, but among modern scholars the primary dispute is whether it refers to a culturally specific realm without set political boundaries, or rather primarily to China. Thus, based largely on his study of Qing China, Joseph Levenson argued that tianxia primarily indicated "a regime of value," which he defined in opposition to a political unit, *guo* (國), that is, a state. Examining earlier periods, Morris Rossabi posited roughly the same distinctions, and for approximately the same period Peter Bol argued that tianxia should be defined as society in opposition to guo as state.[1] On the other hand, the authors of modern Chinese dictionaries such as *Cihai* (辭海) and *Hanyu da cidian* (漢語大詞典) assert that tianxia was a political unit essentially synonymous with Zhongguo (the middle states 中國), with only a secondary sense of "the larger world" or "civilized world." This is not a quibble, because for these and related authors the definition of the term is linked to the problem of China's modern entrance into the world of nation-states, and the relation of the Chinese nation to the earlier political forms that existed in the area the country now occupies. Light can be shed on this question not only by examining the functioning of the term in the late imperial period but also by studying the origins of the concept and the nature of the political entity to which it was applied.

The term "tianxia" as a major category of Chinese thought appears in political discourse relatively late in antiquity, not figuring prominently until the emergence of the *Zuo zhuan* (左傳) and, to a lesser extent, the *Lun yu* (論語).[2] Although both texts evolved over time and neither can be precisely dated, this would suggest that the concept was not prominent prior to the fourth century BCE, that is, the early Warring States period. The term has not been found in the surviving corpus of Zhou bronzes and scarcely appears in the *Shi jing* (詩經) and the reliably early chapters of the *Shang shu* (尚書). Even these few early occurrences do not seem to be an established compound, but simply an abbreviated form of the fuller *tian zhi xia* (天之下). The phrase in both forms seems to have referred to the territory ruled directly by the Zhou king (in his capacity as *tianzi* 天子), and even to have referred to a smaller territory when the power of the king declined.

In the *Zuo zhuan*, the term begins to achieve some prominence, appearing four times in the first half of the text and no less than eighteen times in the second half. For most of the text the usage supports Levenson's later generalization, featuring frequently in phrases indicating that a certain type of behavior would be either praised or condemned by "all under heaven," which in the context clearly indicates the part of the world that shares the values of the Zhou elite. In some cases, mostly later in the text, the term has a political meaning, referring to a realm that might be occupied and held. This usage comes largely from speakers from the southern state of Chu in discussions about the possibility of Chu's occupying the old Zhou realm. It also serves as what could be described as a term of "politicized culture," in which tianxia as the Zhou realm is specifically contrasted with the territory of the Rong (戎) or Di (狄) peoples. Both these political and cultural senses also figure in the *Lun yu*, but the term appears more frequently than in the *Zuo zhuan* (dramatically so in relation to the relative brevity of the *Lun yu*) and most often in the sense of a realm that could be possessed and ruled. This realm, as in the earlier texts, was essentially the core Zhou states, and most references to it being possessed or ruled attribute this ability to the ancient sages. In contrast, the present day is marked by the absence of a single ruler over all under heaven.

This shift toward a political sense continued into the later fourth century BCE. In the core chapters of the *Mozi* (墨子), which probably date from this period, the term "tianxia" appears more than four hundred times, even though the *Mozi* is only two and a half times the length of the *Lun yu* and much shorter than the *Zuo zhuan*. In the *Mozi*, "all under heaven" is treated primarily as a political unit, functioning routinely as the object of verbs such as "possess" (*you* 有), "rule" (*zhi* 治), or "be a king over" (*wang* 王). However, in contrast to the *Lun yu*, the *Mozi* not only cites the ancient sages but also indicates that any true ruler, including those of the present day, should unify and rule all under heaven. As in the earlier texts, this political unit should share a common set of cultural ideals. Thus the chapter "Unifying Upward" (*shang tong* 尚同) elaborates the argument that tianxia should be united through the establishment of a single criterion of duty or propriety (*yi* 義). Similarly, the text's repeated references to the "men of service and gentlemen of tianxia" (*tianxia zhi shi junzi* 天下之士君子) imply that tianxia possesses a single cultural elite who should share common values. The *Mozi* also sometimes identifies tianxia as an economic unit whose resources must be protected or properly exploited by the ruler.

Later Warring States philosophical texts such as the *Mencius* (孟子), the *Xunzi* (荀子), and the *Han Feizi* (韓非子) follow the *Mozi* in identifying tianxia as a territorial unit defined by common cultural ideals that would ideally have a single ruler. While the cultural aspect of tianxia as a unit of value figures throughout this period, the sense of it as a political realm continues to predominate. Moreover, as theorized by the modern scholars cited above, tianxia is routinely defined in contrast to guo, with the latter invariably being a political subdivision of the former.[3] The early difference between tianxia and guo was thus primarily one of scale rather than of kind. In this way it is clear that by the late Warring States period, as Yuri Pines has argued, tianxia was no longer simply a civilized world but also a potentially unified political realm, an imperium that transcended all existing state boundaries. It was first and foremost a place of political rule and only secondarily a regime of value or a normative society, as posited by Levenson and Bol for later periods.[4]

This shift of emphasis from culture to politics reflects the changing nature of the political order at the end of the Spring and Autumn period and during the Warring States. This period was marked by the decline and disappearance of the old Zhou nobility, whose shared ritual practices as reflected in archaeological remains were the clearest expression of the ideal of a world united by a common culture. (The same idea was also reflected in stories of poetic citation in diplomatic missions during the Spring and Autumn period that united a politically divided world through the performance of a common literary culture.)[5] As this old order was replaced by extended, ruler-centered states formed through universal military service and bureaucratic administration, the idea emerged that political rule extending across an ever larger and larger space, rather than any common elite cultural practice, was the basis for achieving a stable and enduring order. This ideal of peace through politics made sense only within a vision of a world that could be ultimately united under a single ruler. The diminution of appeals to culture was reinforced by the growing importance of states such as Chu and Qin that increasingly denied, seemingly in contradiction to their actual history, their strong cultural ties to the old Zhou order.[6] However, a residual appeal to shared culture as a background to the ongoing political competition, and to a vision of a possible future world unity, was perpetuated through increasing economic links, mutual borrowing of political institutions, and the flow of diplomats, political aspirants, and scholars across state borders.

A final change in the sense of tianxia during the Warring States period, one that is central to the subsequent historical discussion in this chapter, is its geographic extension. The ideal of a united world as articulated in the *Mozi*'s chapters "Caring for Each and All" (*jian ai* 兼愛) and "Unifying Upward" was universal, transcending the boundaries of the old Zhou realm. This is probably clearest in the text's discussion of the sage Yu 禹. When the text praises the sage for "bringing order to tianxia" by ending the great flood, it describes how his great work included the aliens on the fringes of Zhou civilization who benefited equally with the Xia people of the middle states. This discussion clearly sees Zhongguo as only one part of the broader, universal realm defined as tianxia.[7]

This extension of tianxia to include peoples beyond the cultural limits of the Zhou realm may in part reflect the *Mozi*'s rejection of the traditional emphasis on ritual and on the cultural superiority of the Xia people. At various places in the text, the authors of the *Mozi* equate the claims to ritual superiority of the middle states with other people's belief that cannibalism or the murder of first-born sons is proper conduct.[8] This shift toward a nascent cultural relativism that made possible the widening of sympathies and fellow feeling may well have partly reflected the increasing contact of subjects of the old Zhou realm with more distant peoples.[9] In particular, it may have been related to the increasingly important role of the southeastern states of Wu and Yue as political actors, military innovators, and masters of certain technologies in the late Spring and Autumn and early Warring States periods.

Whatever the grounds for the *Mozi*'s extension of tianxia to include more distant and exotic peoples, this idea came to dominate philosophical discussions of the question in the later Warring States. One of the most striking examples is the *Gongyang Tradition* (*Gongyang zhuan* 公羊傳), which pioneered a clear dichotomy between the Chinese (*huaxia* 華夏) and the barbarians (*yidi* 夷狄) but nevertheless describes a meeting in 576 BCE between the envoys of the alien state of Wu from the southeast and representatives of a league from several of the middle states in this way: "Why does [the *Spring and Autumn Annals*] emphasize a meeting with Wu? It considers Wu as external. What does 'external' mean? The *Spring and Autumn Annals* considers its own state [Lu 魯] as internal and all the Xia as external, considers all the Xia as internal and the Yi and Di [夷狄] as external. But the Son of Heaven wants to unite tianxia, so how can he speak of things in terms of internal and external? This simply means that he begins with what is close."[10]

Here the non-Xia peoples are treated as relatively exterior and inferior, but they are still part of the tianxia that is ideally to be united under a true Son of Heaven. Thus tianxia has come to include both what would be treated as the ancestral Chinese and the alien peoples who lay outside the middle kingdoms and the realm of Zhou culture. This or closely related ideas of a greatly extended state in which the majesty or virtue of the sage ruler extends to distant, alien peoples figure throughout the philosophical texts of the late Warring States period.[11] The term "tianxia" and related ideas come to function as the intellectual anticipation of the vast multiethnic empire that would emerge out of the unification of the old Zhou realm and its neighboring peoples.

Nor were these ideas of an empire limited to philosophical texts, for the stone inscriptions of the First Emperor incorporated the all-inclusive rhetoric of these texts in proclaiming that his might reached to the very edges of the earth, specifically locating his mountain inscriptions at the "extremities" of the land and stating that his beneficence reached "wherever the sun and moon shine, and wherever boats and carriages carry their loads," and later extended this to include "wherever human traces reach."[12] While Qin policies, such as building or connecting a "long wall" to the north, did not match these claims of universal blessing, the occupation of the Ordos in the north and the push into the south did indicate a commitment to extending the geographic range of the state and drawing in distant peoples as part of the desire to surpass earlier polities.[13]

The Early Han Empire as a Multiethnic Tianxia

Although the political philosophers of the late Warring States period developed a model of a polity defined by its vast extent and inclusion of alien peoples, more recent Chinese writers have produced a very different vision of the early imperial project. The grand narrative of China's modern historiography depicts the Han state, established in 202 BCE in East Asia, as a well-delineated block of territory ruled by a people called Chinese. These Chinese people fought along their northern border with another people from the steppe called the Xiongnu and conquered peoples in the Tarim Basin. The narrative also makes the unexamined assumption that little change has occurred since that time, so that the Han Empire can be regarded as the prototype of modern China. It attributes at least two modern concepts to the East Asia of the second century BCE: one people governs one state, and states are mutually exclusive in both political and ethnocultural terms. Consequently, this narrative assumes that both the core people and the core region of the Han state can be treated as a coherent unit that remained largely unaffected by its interaction with outsiders, and that this unit is fundamentally identical to the later Chinese state. The late imperial adoption of "Han" as a rubric for the newly invented ethnic group that supposedly defined a Chinese nation-state facilitated this conflation of the two realms.

Our research challenges this narrative and the ideology on which it is based, rejecting the received national narrative on two grounds. First, by conflating without question the organizing principles of ancient empires with modern nation-states, we lose the capacity to fully explore the nature of the Han state and imperial power. Second, the modern narrative depends upon ignoring substantial amounts of material preserved in the two Han chronicles, *Shi ji* (史記) and *Han shu* (漢書).

In this chapter, we aim to demonstrate that the Han Empire, and those that followed it, was something quite different from a modern nation-state, and that the Han polity as an imperial form can be usefully analyzed in terms of the category tianxia. We analyze alliance strategies and resettlement policies that promoted imperial authority and secured the existence of the Han state for four centuries. We begin with the first century of the Han, during which the state was transformed from a limited regional polity with multiple power centers to a cosmopolitan empire of multiple regions governed by one supreme ruler, something approximating the notion of tianxia. The Han court was able to strengthen its own position only by linking to the broader state-to-state networks in eastern Eurasia and incorporating diverse peoples into its state structure. While the Han did this first to block the power-building strategies of its challengers, above all the subordinate kings, and then to achieve superiority over the Xiongnu ruler in the steppes and Central Asia, in doing so it fashioned a vision of imperial authority that was multicultural and transregional. This definition of imperial authority shaped the thinking of all later state builders in

Chinese history and gave a specific political sense to the vague and moralizing notion of tianxia that had figured in political philosophy.

This chapter makes four major points. For about six decades the Han emperor operated in a triangular political network with the Xiongnu *chanyu* (單于, a peer emperor on the steppe) and with client kings in the Yellow River region. While these lesser feudal kings allied with either the Han emperor or the Xiongnu *chanyu* and occasionally switched sides, the two supreme rulers also negotiated alliances with each other against lesser kings in their respective spheres of power. The integration of steppe populations into the state was essential for the Han court to obtain new human resources to realize military expansion into unfamiliar regions in eastern Eurasia. By having peoples of varied backgrounds participate in the highest governing elite group and the state structure, and using such people to suppress their own ethnic peers, the Han defined the empire as a multicultural and cross-regional state that potentially incorporated all known peoples, and in which shared ethnicity was of no significance. Finally, after examining in detail the crucial involvement of steppe peoples in the early definition of the Han state, the chapter also quickly traces the pivotal impact of the reliance on steppe cavalry in the Eastern Han, the transformation of all the states that immediately followed the Han due to the dominance of steppe peoples in the military sphere, and ultimately the indispensable role of steppe peoples within the political structure of subsequent empires that emerged in what is now China.

A Limited Power in the Yellow River and Yangtze River Regions
(ca. 200–140 BCE)

From around 200 to 140 BCE, the Han was a limited state that struggled to secure its existence in the Yellow River, and to a lesser extent the Yangtze River, regions. The Han emperor faced two major challengers: the Xiongnu *chanyu* on the steppe and the subordinate kings in the east. Two phenomena were crucial in the dynamics of collaboration and competition among the three parties: ethnic and regional differences did not determine alliance decisions of the subordinate kings, and, for the Han emperor, forging gift-based alliances with the Xiongnu *chanyu* was an essential mechanism to strengthen himself in his contest with the subordinate kings.

The political landscape of eastern Eurasia had witnessed a dramatic change toward the end of the third century BCE. On the steppe, the Xiongnu ruler subjugated competing steppe powers and established a polity governed by him and lesser Xiongnu kings. As argued by Nicola Di Cosmo, this unification of the steppes was probably a response to the disruption produced by the Qin Empire's conquest of the Ordos steppe and the attempt to secure that conquest through building a great wall.[14] Shortly thereafter, in the Yellow River and Yangtze River regions, a military leader named Liu Bang (r. 202–195 BCE) and his coalition triumphed in the civil war that overthrew the Qin and established a new state, the Han. This nascent state interacted only with immediate neighboring powers such as the Xiongnu on the steppe. The Han was politically unconnected to interstate networks of other regions such as the Korean peninsula in the northeast or the Tarim Basin in the west.

After ascending the throne in 202 BCE, the first Han emperor continued to rely on his military coalition to assist him in managing the new state he had founded. He directly ruled only the western part of the Yellow River region, while entrusting most of the eastern region—the floodplain of the Yellow River—as well as the Yangtze River region to client kings. Although Liu Bang assumed the title of emperor, this highest governing elite circle of the Han state was essentially a group of peer rulers who had together emerged as military allies.

While reluctantly sharing power with client kings in exchange for their service, the first Han emperor started to elevate imperial authority by eliminating former clients and transferring feudal thrones to members of his own family. This process involved considerable brutality. For instance, after a client king named Peng Yue was killed in 196 BCE, his body was ground into minced meat that was then presented to all the client kings as a warning.[15] The emperor's violent approach to reducing rivals' power and asserting his supreme status rapidly dissolved his bonds with the client kings and, not surprisingly, provoked considerable resistance.

One of the clearest places to observe this was the Yellow River region near the southern edge of the steppe. Witnessing the ongoing persecution of their peers, some frustrated client kings switched their allegiance to the Xiongnu in search of alternative shelter or military support. From Liu Bang's ascent to the throne in 202 BCE to his death in 195 BCE, within only seven years, three kings (*wang* 王) and one lord (*hou* 侯) near the southern edge of the steppe either joined the Xiongnu or sought military assistance from Xiongnu forces to resist imperial intimidation.[16]

As indicated by the *Shi ji* and the *Han shu*, the first military confrontation between the Han and the Xiongnu was ignited by one client king who transferred his allegiance to the Xiongnu. The Han subordinate kings near the steppe had fought with steppe forces for some time, but the first Han emperor demonstrated little interest in any such direct confrontation with the Xiongnu until a client king in the Dai area joined the Xiongnu to escape imperial intimidation. The emperor led a punitive expedition against this client king and his new patron in 200 BCE. But the Han suffered a disastrous defeat and were forced to secure peace by sending a princess and annual gifts to the Xiongnu *chanyu*.[17]

The Han emperor's defeat sent a clear political message that this steppe polity was strong enough to be an alternative patron that could provide shelter from Han persecution. Threatened client kings in the Yellow River region did not have to submit to imperial intimidation, but could instead resist by choosing this new alliance option. The message was well received. For example, when in political danger, a lifelong friend of the emperor who was a client king in the Yan area also decided to take his entire family and thousands of followers to join the Xiongnu.[18] Even after feudal thrones all came to be held by male relatives of the emperor, these uncles and nephews remained willing to invite Xiongnu forces into the Yellow River region to challenge imperial claims to supreme authority.[19] These cases demonstrate that political collaboration and competition trumped cultural or regional allegiance. Once the emperor ceased to be a safe patron, subordinate kings in the Yellow River region simply renounced their allegiance to the Han and sought alternative options with the steppe empire to their north.

Han worries about the Xiongnu were thus a symptom of a larger problem—the clash between the subordinate kings' insistence on a power-sharing model and the emperor's attempts to move toward a more centralized state with a stratified political hierarchy. Although occasional conflicts with Xiongnu forces along the southern edge of the steppe were disturbing, more problematic for the Han emperor was the alienated client kings' renunciation of allegiance and recourse to Xiongnu protection.

In this context, the gift-based interaction between the Han emperor and the Xiongnu *chanyu* became more than a conciliation agreement. Its more important function was to provide a mechanism for both the Han emperor and the Xiongnu *chanyu* to claim a status superior to all the other kings as supreme rulers of their respective regions. This involved two methods. First, by referring to themselves as "two masters" (兩主) in communications, the Han emperor and the Xiongnu *chanyu* recognized each other as the highest regional representatives.[20] By the same token, this appellation transformed their gift-based connection into the highest level of interstate interaction, clearly distinguished from all other interactions between the steppe and the Yellow River region.[21]

Second, by excluding lesser kings from all exchanges with the *chanyu*, the emperor monopolized this highest level of interstate interaction. The sending of a princess and annual gifts was not mediated by any subordinate kings, nor did the latter participate in any manner in this presentation that defined the relations of the two empires. Instead the gifts passed directly from the Han court to that of the Xiongnu in a process that honored both participants at the expense of their erstwhile political peers. Also, the receipt of a princess-wife tied the Xiongnu *chanyu* to the Han emperor as kin. Such marriage alliances could discourage Han subordinate kings from considering the Xiongnu *chanyu* a reliable ally. This exclusive interaction between the emperor and the *chanyu* thus undercut and rendered illegitimate any attempt by the Han subordinate kings to establish independent alliances with the Xiongnu *chanyu*.[22] Any such unauthorized attempt could be deemed treason and should also have been rejected by the *chanyu*, whose own status was appreciably elevated through his unique ties to the Han emperor.[23]

In addition, this gift-based mechanism initiated a formalized communication channel for the previously unconnected Han and Xiongnu rulers to negotiate their respective spheres of power in the Yellow River region and the steppe. For example, the third emperor, Emperor Wen (r. 180–157 BCE), invoked the rhetoric of two masters to request an explicit division along the southern edge of the steppe between the two supreme rulers. He declared to the Xiongnu *chanyu*, "To the north of the long walls are the states of [those who] draw the bow, and [they] receive commands from the *chanyu*; to the south of the long walls are the households of [those who wear] cap and girdle, and I in parallel fashion control them."[24]

The model of the world proposed in this statement boldly ignored the ongoing competition between the emperor and the subordinate kings, let alone the existence of other states to the south of the Yangtze River region. In order to show his commitment to realizing this ideal, the emperor then issued an edict to Han officials that insisted on returning fugitives and captives who, based on this model, should be under Xiongnu control.[25] While this partition of the world would have represented a diminution of conventional Chinese claims in the eyes of later Chinese political thinkers, at the time it marked a significant inflation of Han sovereignty.

The series of alliances thus established between the Han emperors and the Xiongnu supreme rulers seem to have successfully restricted subordinate kings' alliance options. The war in 154 BCE between the Han emperor and the joint forces of subordinate kings, which marked the final collapse of the kings as a significant challenge to the Han court, is the most significant example. After ascending the throne in 157 BCE, the fourth Han emperor, Emperor Jing

(r. 157–141 BCE), duly dispatched gifts to the Xiongnu *chanyu* while taking more aggressive approaches than his father in suppressing subordinate kings.[26] His strict observance of established relations with the Xiongnu paid off when the increasingly desperate subordinate kings launched a joint military expedition in 154 BCE to challenge the imperial assertion of supreme authority. Although the subordinate kings allied among themselves, they failed to induce Xiongnu forces to intrude into the Yellow River region in support. The Xiongnu stayed on the steppe watching this warfare until it ended. Their forces were said to have made some moves on the steppe but halted due to rapid imperial suppression of the so-called revolt.[27] The ultimate inaction of the Xiongnu ruler could be understood as a reluctance, and perhaps outright refusal, to break the gift-based agreements with the Han court that had done so much to strengthen his own supremacy. This hesitation saved the Han imperial capital from the danger of simultaneous attack by the subordinate kings from the east and the Xiongnu forces from the north, and thereby facilitated the rapid and successful suppression of the military challenge.

Moving Away from the Two Masters Model (ca. 150–100 BCE)

As we have seen, from 200 to 154 BCE, generations of Han emperors had spent five decades blocking subordinate kings' attempts to seek support and protection from the Xiongnu. But lesser kings on the steppe had not until this point shown any interest in the Han emperor as a possible alternative patron.

The successful suppression of feudal resistance in 154 BCE marked a watershed, after which we find the first evidence of Xiongnu leaders shifting their allegiance to the Han. Late in the reign of Emperor Jing, eight Xiongnu leaders formally submitted to the Han court. This provoked a debate about granting these Xiongnu dignitaries the title of lord, which would have entailed incorporating them into the governing elite circle of the Han state. The prime minister objected to the idea of rewarding those who had "betrayed their master" (背其主). But Emperor Jing interpreted their switch of allegiance as a compliment to Han authority. He granted the title "Lord" to seven such defectors in 147 BCE and one more in 145 BCE.[28]

Two contrasting attitudes appeared here in the debate over how to define the role of the Han state in the political landscape of eastern Eurasia. By denouncing disloyal behavior, the prime minister essentially identified the Han as a limited regional state that should refrain from contesting peer rulers' control over lesser powers within their sphere of influence. On the other hand, Emperor

Jing, perhaps now understanding that there was no longer any real possibility of weakened subordinate kings allying themselves with the Xiongnu, embraced the idea of reorienting these kings' allegiance by taking them into the governing elite circle of the Han. That is to say, rather than adhering to the two masters model that focused on divided spheres of power, Emperor Jing evinced an ambition to replace the Xiongnu *chanyu* as the master of the steppe kings. However, just as in the preceding period, the newly strengthened emperor continued to define his power as much through the relations that he established with the steppe peoples as through his claims to command his own people.

Early in the reign of the fifth emperor, Emperor Wu (r. 141–87 BCE), court officials also expressed reluctance to disturb the status quo, instead insisting on clinging to the position of a limited regional state. As in the earlier cases, they recognized that drawing steppe peoples into the Han political sphere clearly exalted the position of the ruler and strengthened his authority in relation to his own people. The officials' reluctance became clear when Emperor Wu conducted two rounds of court debates in the hope of abandoning the gift-based interaction with the *chanyu* as a prelude to launching a military expedition against the Xiongnu. In the first debate, the imperial secretary supported the continuation of peaceful relations by arguing that the sphere of the Xiongnu since the earliest times had never been viewed as land for conquest and should be left the way it was. Court officials agreed, and on this occasion the emperor respected the majority opinion.[29]

At issue in this debate was supporting the established pattern of gift-based interstate interaction and rejecting a new expansionist policy. This connection implied that the officials understood the fundamental function of gift giving to be the negotiation of delimited power spheres with neighboring polities and the creation of a bond that obligated the parties to observe mutual agreements. Viewed from this perspective, sporadic conflicts along the southern edge of the steppe were a nonissue. The point was not whether conflicts occurred, but whether the Han court possessed the means to prevent random disputes from escalating into the breakdown of negotiated power spheres. As generations of Xiongnu *chanyu* had never shown any interest in conquering the Yellow River region, the gift-based interaction between the two supreme rulers could be considered effective from the point of view of the officials, and thus worth continuing.

But only one year later the same question was raised again. The detailed record in the *Han shu* makes clear that the real struggle in the court debates was between expansionism and anti-expansionism, with the former being identified with the emperor's assertion of his own power. In this round of debate, Emperor Wu no longer hid his intentions but started the discussion with a fixed premise: gift giving had never fully stopped conflicts, and thus war was to be preferred. A militant official proposed a plan to ambush the *chanyu*'s forces and thereby subjugate the Xiongnu with minimal loss of men and material. The emperor concluded the debate with the decision to carry out the scheme.[30]

The initial ambush failed, but the fragile balance between the Han and the Xiongnu continued until the emperor dispatched troops in 129 BCE to attack steppe peoples in trading posts along the southern edge of the steppe. This led to intensive state-level conflicts that stretched from the Ordos steppe to the Yellow Sea for more than ten years. Both sides enjoyed transient successes at the price of great losses in resources: soldiers, ordinary subjects, and livestock.[31] To some extent, relentless Han military expeditions did help loosen the bonds between the Xiongnu *chanyu* and lesser steppe kings, some of whom changed sides during the war. From 131 to 113 BCE, Emperor Wu granted the title "Lord" to seventeen Xiongnu leaders who surrendered to the Han, and celebrated the achievement of gaining such deserters by calling them "adherents to righteousness" (歸義), which implied foreign admiration of Han authority. They were then deployed to fight battles for the Han.[32]

By integrating surrendered steppe populations into the Han state structure and exploiting their service, Emperor Wu entirely abandoned the attempts of his grandfather, Emperor Wen, to negotiate with the Xiongnu *chanyu* an unambiguous division of the known world into two spheres through territorial markers and lifestyle attributes. Instead the Han increasingly came to act as a multiethnic polity in which peoples of different backgrounds were united under the authority of a single ruler who transcended all regional and cultural distinctions. One clear example of this was when the emperor stationed the surrendered king of Kunye, a powerful steppe leader, and thousands of his followers within the bend of the Yellow River, where at the same time Han immigrants were forcibly resettled from the eastern Yellow River region. The deployment of both populations to the same area created a buffer zone for the establishment of Han bureaucratic operations in the corridor west of the Yellow River, increasing the possibility of connecting the Yellow River region to the Tarim Basin. By abandoning attempts to fix clearly delimited spheres of power, the outward-looking Han state became an aggressive empire that mixed social groups of varied cultural and regional backgrounds for the purpose of expanding the imperial presence into the Ordos steppe and then beyond into the Western Region (modern Xinjiang).[33]

A Han-Centered Interregional Network in Eastern Eurasia
(ca. 100–80 BCE)

We have seen that from around 140 BCE, the Han started to incorporate Xiongnu leaders into its governing elite circle and steppe populations into its state structure. This transfer of the loyalty of steppe people from the *chanyu* to the emperor was crucial in transforming the Han state from a limited regional polity to a transregional power. First, the incorporation of such people into the Han state transformed it into a multiethnic, multicultural polity in which radically different people came together under the overarching supremacy of a single, unchallenged autocrat whose power imitated that of heaven in extending over all peoples.

Second, and on a more practical plane, these people from the steppe brought with them skills and knowledge that not only allowed the Han to fight battles in the formerly unfamiliar environment of the grasslands but also introduced the Han to previously unknown interstate networks that had developed between the steppe in the north and the Tarim Basin in the west. To the Han state during its first six decades, the Tarim Basin had remained an unknown land, whereas the Xiongnu had extended their dominant position on the steppe into the area. To assist the emperor in competing against the Xiongnu *chanyu*, some Xiongnu leaders who had entered the Han court suggested a new method that could supplement and strengthen military confrontation—cementing alliances with state rulers in the Tarim Basin who had submitted to Xiongnu power but resented this alien authority.[34]

The knowledge and expertise brought to the Han court and its armies through the incorporation of surrendered people from the steppes made it possible for the first time for the Han to contact and seek out alliances with polities in the Tarim Basin. As the king of Kunye and his followers shielded the northwestern side of the Ordos steppe for the Han, after 120 BCE Han emissaries were able to travel to city-states in the Tarim Basin without being obstructed by Xiongnu forces. In addition, the Han extended its bureaucratic operations into the corridor west of the Yellow River to facilitate the extension of imperial power into this previously unknown political web. Infrastructural support provided by Han garrisons and steppe allies guaranteed that large numbers of Han emissaries could move back and forth along the road to Central Asia without suffering major losses. It is said that from five to ten diplomatic teams were dispatched each year, indicating the intensity of Han activities within the newly discovered region. Large teams included hundreds of emissaries, small ones a hundred or so.[35]

But in the Tarim Basin the Han confronted multiple independent rulers who were either integrated into a Xiongnu-centered interstate network or strong enough not to join it. To maximize its capacity to exert more influence on the Tarim Basin than that of the Xiongnu in the shortest time possible, the Han deployed diverse approaches among the multiple steppe powers and city-states. While cementing a marriage alliance with a strong steppe power named the Wusun, the Han also used military threats to coerce reluctant city-states into cooperation, which was marked by the sending of royal hostages to the Han court.[36]

Through attacking selected targets, for instance, the Han successfully co-erced polities in the Tarim Basin into a Han-centered interstate network. In particular, the four-year expedition against Dayuan beginning in 104 BCE intimidated steppe powers and city-states into assisting the Han, in a response to the Han's demonstration that they could exert military influence west-ward, deep into the Tarim Basin, for a lengthy period. The change in attitude toward the Han presence was manifested in polities along the expeditionary routes that were forced first to provision Han troops and second to send royal children to the Han as hostages. A few city-states that refused to provision the troops either were destroyed or had their kings killed.[37] In this way the Tarim Basin and much of the steppe west of the Xiongnu state were drawn into the multiethnic Han order that had first emerged with the submission and resettlement of defectors from the control of the *chanyu*. This new Han-centered political network that integrated peer polities and lesser powers across multiple regions secured the status of the Han emperor as an unquestionable imperial authority in eastern Eurasia, whose power transcended all limits of geography and ethnicity and thus clearly extended beyond the authority asserted by the preceding Qin state.

The Han Empire as a Cosmopolitan Tianxia (80 BCE–100 CE)

At the same time that the Han state was externally establishing a network of states formally tied through submission to an emperor whose authority transcended the limits of a regionally limited Han culture, the internal structure of the state was steadily modified through the resettlement and incorporation of steppe peoples who were not drawn into the bureaucratic administration. This marked a third phase in the policies that elevated the emperor and turned a limited, territorial state into a cosmopolitan tianxia defined through the deliberate incorporation of multiple peoples with diverse cultures. In this case the emperor was elevated not merely through the delivery of hostages and tribute from kings of Central Asian states who recognized him as a supreme overlord but also through the service of steppe warriors who became part of the Han state through formal submission to the emperor but remained outside the administrative system that had previously defined the state.

As noted above, Emperor Wu's decision to wage war on the Xiongnu was accompanied by the policy of accepting the submission of lesser Xiongnu kings who chose to transfer their loyalty to the Han. These men and their followers were resettled inside the Han sphere as dependent states (*shu guo* 屬國) that remained under the authority of their own rulers and whose soldiers served as cavalry in Han armies. This policy was carried forward on a larger scale in the last decades of the Western Han, when the Xiongnu Empire had temporarily split into northern and southern coalitions, with the latter recognizing Han suzerainty and being resettled inside the bend of the Yellow River and farther south. The ruler of this surrendered southern coalition roughly followed the pattern established for the kings of the Central Asian states. On several occasions he visited the Han court, where he received lavish gifts and was granted the unique privilege of referring to himself by his full name rather than as "your servant [*chen* 臣] + personal name" and sent one son to act as a hostage and to be educated in Han elite culture.

Most of the southern Xiongnu who had surrendered moved back to the north after their link with the Han allowed them to defeat their northern rivals. However, in 49 CE the restored Xiongnu state again split apart in a succession struggle. The Han court resumed the policy of furthering this split by allying with one side and encouraging them to resettle inside the Han state, for whom they provided service as cavalrymen against their former fellows. This policy of resettling Xiongnu in the northwest was carried out on a much larger scale than in the Western Han, and it was supplemented by the practice of paying bounties for enemy heads to Xianbei and Wuhuan peoples. These had previously been part of the Xiongnu coalition but were now resettled in the north and the northeast of the Han state, where they continued to live under their own rulers as dependent states.

The policy of resettling steppe peoples inside the Han state was extended into a general reform of Han military forces. With the abolition of universal military service in 32 CE, the Eastern Han army was steadily restructured as a smaller military force consisting of professional soldiers and of convicts who were stationed in the vicinity of the capital, in small garrisons at the frontier, and in three major frontier military commands. Each of these commands was assigned the task of keeping an eye on the resettled barbarians, and two of them were named for the peoples whom they were intended to supervise. The commands were also intended to provide troops who would accompany the steppe cavalrymen mobilized to serve in the Han expeditionary forces that continued to war against the Xiongnu.[38]

Thus while the internally resettled steppe peoples continued to be guided by their own rulers, these in turn were loosely directed by military officers, but they remained quite separate from the standard administrative hierarchy. In this system the Han emperor became the sole point at which the two key constituents of the empire—the peasantry who paid the taxes and the steppe peoples who provided the army's key strike forces—converged. Through his role as sole suzerain over the surrendered steppe peoples, and following Ban Chao's re-conquest of the city-states of the Western Regions, the emperor was elevated to a position that completely transcended his status as lord of the Han population. In this way the increasingly multiethnic and multicultural aspects of the empire became the mechanism for simultaneously exalting the position of the ruler and extending the state across the steppes and the oasis cities. These developments assimilated the emperor ever more closely with the all-encompassing heaven envisioned by the philosophers.

The scale and importance of the use of non-Han soldiers in the Eastern Han has been demonstrated by Hsing I-tien. In an article on the Eastern Han's steppe soldiers, he lists fifty-one cases of the use of non-Han troops between 48 and 177 CE, making an average of once every two and a half years. In twenty-seven cases, more than half the sample, there is no mention of any other soldiers accompanying the steppe peoples, and in six of these the commander of the expedition was a steppe ruler. These steppe forces made up most of the expeditionary armies in 73, 89, and the early 90s that finally destroyed the Xiongnu coalition that for three centuries had been the greatest external threat to the Han. This evidence of reliance on non-Han cavalry is supported by the fact that the state-controlled grasslands and stables that had been used for the rearing of military horses since the reign of Emperor Jing were largely abandoned.[39]

This triumph of the Han through the incorporation of steppe peoples into an ever more cosmopolitan state was celebrated in a memorial written by Song Yi in 88 CE, one year before the Han's most decisive military victory against the Xiongnu:

> Since the rise of the Han there have been repeated offensive expeditions, but that which they gained never made up for what was lost. Emperor Guangwu [the Eastern Han founder], having personally experienced the trials of warfare, deeply penetrated the order of heaven and earth.

Following the steppe peoples coming to surrender, he nourished them under a loose rein. The people at the frontier were able to live and their military service was halted; up to today it has been more than forty years. Now the Xianbei are obedient and capture the heads of Xiongnu numbered in the tens of thousands. The Middle Kingdom enjoys this great achievement, and the peasants know nothing of its toil. In this achievement the Han has reached its apogee. The reason is that the steppe peoples attack one another, with no loss to the Han armies.[40]

This is an early formulation of what would become axiomatic as "using barbarians to control barbarians."[41] However, first, as Song Yi noted in his memorial, that technique depended on the initial practice of welcoming steppe peoples into the Han realm while not incorporating them under conventional bureaucratic administration. This policy of employing separate hierarchies of control to draw diverse peoples into a single political order that existed only in the figure of the emperor, in whom the two hierarchies converged, reappeared in diverse forms throughout the history of imperial China.[42] Thus this multi-ethnic, dual state that combined registered peasants who were bureaucratically administered with steppe soldiers who served the state under distinct forms of control became an enduring characteristic of the imperial order.

Second, the steppe soldiers not only fought other steppe peoples but also in some cases were employed by the Han ruler to suppress internal rebellions, much as foreign mercenaries were used by monarchs against their own people in early modern Europe.[43] Both these facts show that in the first century CE, steppe peoples had become a major constituent element of the Han political order without being placed under bureaucratic control. The first Chinese empire had been able to defeat its external foes and extend its power through remaking itself as a cosmopolitan tianxia, and all the subsequent states that ruled the northern half or the entirety of the old Han realm followed this pattern.

Cosmopolitan Polities after the Han

While the Eastern Han pattern of combining steppe peoples and peasants as two distinct elements in a single polity continued into later periods, the means by which they were brought together continued to evolve. First, at the end of the Han a new pattern emerged in which resettled steppe peoples no longer operated in their old communities but rather served as long-term soldiers in standing military commands. Although such men were no longer members of their traditional groups, they remained outside the conventional administrative order, participating in the state only through their enduring personal ties to their commanding officers. In such armies they were combined with former Han subjects who had gradually assimilated the martial customs of the steppe peoples, and the entire northwestern region increasingly became as much barbarian as Chinese. An army of this nature played the central role in the fall of the Han.[44]

Second, in the immediate wake of the collapse of the Eastern Han, only those who were able to marshal significant military forces could act at the imperial level, and internal steppe peoples were central to all such forces. This was particularly true of Cao, who relied on Wuhuan cavalry in his successful campaigns to reunite the drainage basin of the Yellow River and to push down into the middle Yangtze region. These and related forces remained central to the armies of the Cao-Wei state, as well as the Jin state that supplanted it. Most of the armies that fought in the Rebellions of the Eight Kings (*ba wang zhi luan*) that brought an end to the brief reunification under the Jin employed steppe cavalry as their chief striking forces.[45] Thus throughout the third and early fourth centuries CE the ability to command steppe soldiers remained essential to any claims to imperial power, just as it had been under the Eastern Han.

In the second decade of the fourth century CE, the Sino-nomadic fusion took on a crucial new aspect, as for the first time the steppe leaders abandoned their role as junior partners in the service of ambitious Chinese leaders and instead used their military forces to establish themselves as rulers over the peasant population. The first man to adopt this course was Liu Yuan, a highly Sinicized steppe leader who claimed kin links with the old Han imperial family and ruled over most of the southern Xiongnu, who had been resettled into the Yellow River region in the Eastern Han. These steppe peoples had largely become sedentary stock breeders, but their economic activities allowed them to continue to cultivate their skills as horsemen. Forming a coalition with the Xianbei, Di, and other steppe peoples, he declared himself "King of Han." His armies fought to the gates of Luoyang, and although he died before the Jin capital was taken, cavalry armies led by his younger brother Liu Cong and by Shi Le (another Xiongnu) sacked Luoyang in 311 CE and Chang'an in 317 CE. These victories led to the Jin court's flight to the lower Yangzi, and for the next century (the era of the so-called Sixteen Kingdoms) the entire drainage basin of the Yellow River was divided among multiple short-lived states formed by steppe rulers. When this region was finally reunited in the early fifth century CE, it was by the cavalry forces of the Tuoba rulers who established the Northern Wei state.[46]

In his study of the history of the relations of nomadic empires with China, Thomas Barfield has argued that the capacity of the Xianbei states, first under the Murong and subsequently under the Tuoba, to establish relatively stable polities and ultimately to reunify the Yellow River region was due to their ability to combine a Chinese administration of the peasantry with a nomadic soldiery. He treats this achievement as unprecedented and contrasts it with the earlier Xiongnu state that relied entirely on the forcible extraction of Chinese wealth. These achievements in turn, passing through the military reforms of the Northern Zhou in the old Guanzhong region, provided the ultimate foundation for the reunification of the former Han territories under the Sui that became enduring under the Tang.[47] This combination of the bureaucratic administration of a Chinese peasantry with the tribal control of steppe armies was indeed crucial to the Sui-Tang reunification, but it had in fact been anticipated by the Eastern Han in their triumph over the Xiongnu. The only difference was that in the case of the Wei, the steppe peoples provided not only the military forces but also the rulers. This evolution within the Sino-nomadic dual state from a predominantly steppe soldiery to steppe rulers was fundamental to the subsequent history of imperial polities in the area that has become China.

Conclusion

To summarize, from 200 BCE to around 100 CE, the Han evolved from a confined regional polity with multiple political centers into a cosmopolitan empire governed by a single supreme ruler who commanded the recognition and the services of the Han peasantry, the Indo-European oasis kingdoms of what is now Xinjiang, and large numbers of steppe peoples who lived in their traditional communities within the Han sphere. In the first stage of this transition the emperor asserted his superiority over his former peers through establishing direct relations of gift giving and kinship with the Xiongnu ruler. This relationship was articulated as the division of the world between two masters in a process that allowed each to strengthen his hitherto contested position within his own sphere. Once the possibility of feudal defection or rebellion had ended, the Han emperors reversed their established policy, which was now advocated only by those who sought to limit imperial power. The emperors instead now welcomed the submission of those who had previously belonged to the other master, and then launched a series of expeditions that encouraged further defections. The expertise and skills of these newly surrendered steppe peoples were in turn employed first to open communication with the more western steppe powers and with the city-states of the Tarim Basin, and in subsequent decades to extend Han power into those regions through a series of military campaigns. By the end of this process of suppressing challengers and promoting imperial authority, a whole range of peoples of varied cultures and regions were integrated into the radically expanded Han state structure, and a Han-centered interregional network was constructed that connected polities across the steppes and extended to the western edge of the Tarim Basin. This process of incorporation changed forever the nature of Han rule by making it explicitly transethnic and transregional, and this new form of state defined a vision of transcendent imperial authority that shaped the practices of all later state builders.

Han imperial power thus rose precisely by becoming multicultural and transregional, by decisively breaking with the established Qin political model, and by establishing a state that in many ways corresponded to the earlier philosophical vision of a single tianxia wherein all people, no matter how distant or alien, were brought together under the authority of a single ruler. The reciprocal interactions during this period between the inner workings of the Han state and its relations with foreign peoples and polities served to promote the Han emperor to the status of heavenlike authority across eastern Eurasia.

This account contrasts sharply with the received narrative of the Han, which deliberately ignores key internal differentiations and decisive external influences and declares the state to be based on the timeless existence of a homogeneous Chinese people that exists as an eternal, ahistorical category of explanation. To the contrary, the Han chronicles show that all parties that could promote the power and status of the ruling house were engaged either as allies or as part of the state structure. Differences in culture or regional origins were not a core concern in organizing the state, and nothing indicates that the peoples who participated in the state structure were thought to share a common history or culture. Indeed, imperial policies worked in the opposite direction. Even during the first century of Han history, both imperial rhetoric and action already demonstrated a pride in integrating peoples of varied cultural and regional backgrounds into the service of the emperor. In the process of becoming a multiethnic, transregional polity, the Han state changed forever the nature of imperial rule in East Asia and defined a cosmopolitan vision and reality of political authority that underpinned all later state builders in the region. The ultimate emergence of alien conquest dynasties following the collapse of the Han, and repeatedly throughout the later history of empires in East Asia, was in many ways simply the logical culmination of this process.

As a final point, in the above discussion we have treated the terms "tianxia" and "empire" as closely related, if not synonymous. To the extent that a Chinese category such as tianxia is to become part of a broader international discourse, it must be drawn into dialogue with related categories in other languages, of which "empire" is the prime example. This is particularly true in that many scholars have begun to discuss premodern or early modern empires as a political type defined by, among other characteristics, large size, cultural and ethnic diversity (espoused as a value), the pivotal role of local intermediaries, a supreme ruler as the meeting point of diverse communities, and so on.[48] Many of these features, as we have argued above, are precisely those that distinguish the Han and subsequent empires from earlier and later polities in the region. This is not to argue that the concept of tianxia should be folded into that of empire. To the contrary, it could prove a useful antidote to the sway of the Roman Empire as the exemplary case in the West of an empire.[49] Several features of the Roman state, etymologically reflected in the overwhelmingly military connotations of the terms "imperium and "imperator," may well skew our attempts to develop a model for polities of this type. However, studies of the concept of tianxia must by all means not be allowed to become another case of Chinese exceptionalism, remaining an eternally alien and exotic Other that by definition can speak only to and of itself.

NOTES

1. Levenson, "T'ien-hsia and Kuo." The same usage is espoused by Rossabi; see Rossabi, "Introduction." For Bol's argument, see Bol, "Government, Society and State," 140.

2. The discussion here is indebted to Yuri Pines.

3. For example, see Yang Bojun, *Mengzi yi zhu*, 30, 328; Jiang Lihong, *Shang Jun shu zhuizhi*, 57, 85; Wang Xianqian, *Xunzi jijie*, 114, 134, 172, 185, 326, 351.

4. Pines, "Changing Views of *Tianxia*," 106.

5. Lewis, *Writing and Authority*, 155–163.

6. On the decline of a recognized common culture in the Warring States and the increasing assertion of a distinct identity by Chu and Qin, see Pines, "Disputers of the Li," 20–21; Pines, "The Question of Interpretation." Also see Falkenhausen, "On the Typology of Chu Bronzes."

7. Wu Yujiang, *Mozi jiaozhu*, 160. The *Mozi*'s views on the universal range of tianxia are also discussed in Chen Guying, *Zhuangzi jinzhu*, 863.

8. For the *Mozi*'s ridicule of Zhou rites, see Wu Yujiang, *Mozi jiaozhu*, 267–268, 735. On the text's nascent cultural relativism, see also Pines, "Beasts or Humans."

9. The possible links of political imperialism with widening sympathies and ideas of a universal humanity are explored in Hayot, *The Hypothetical Mandarin*, esp. chs. 1–3.

10. *Chun qiu Gongyang zhuan zhushu*, Lord Cheng year 15, ch. 18, 7b–8a. On the *Gongyang Tradition*'s emphasis on the dichotomy of Xia and Yi, see Toshikuni, *Shunjū Kuyōden no kenkyū*, ch. 6.

11. The "Zhong yong" 中庸 chapter of *Li ji* describes how the fame and reputation of the "greatest sage under Heaven" would "overflow the middle states to reach the Man and Mo tribes." See *Li ji zhushu*, in *Shisan jing zhushu*, vol. 5, ch. 53, 13a–b. Chen Qiyou, *Lü shi chun qiu*, follows the *Mozi* in emphasizing the universal reach of the work of Yu; see 1514–1515. The *Mencius* on several occasions speaks of the eagerness of alien peoples to join the state of sages such as Tang. See Yang Bojun, *Mengzi yi zhu*, 45, 148. The *Xunzi* also reiterates that the lands of alien peoples should be incorporated into the unified empire of the sage. See Wang Xianqian, *Xunzi jijie*, 204–205, 300, 328–329.

12. Kern, *The Stele Inscriptions*, 12, 19, 23, 26, 27–28, 31, 32, 33, 35, 36, 39, 47. Explicit references to this universal state as tianxia appear on 13, 21, 37, 43.

13. The same vision is expressed in the supposed popularity among late Warring States rulers of Zou Yan's new, greatly expanded vision of the world. On this desire to surpass the Zhou by finding or creating a greater realm, see Lewis, *The Construction of Space*, 249–258, esp. 258.

14. Di Cosmo, *Ancient China and Its Enemies*, 186–188.

15. Sima Qian, *Shi ji*, 91.2063.

16. For a detailed discussion, see Meiyu Hsieh, "Viewing the Han Empire from the Edge," 26–34.

17. Sima Qian, *Shi ji*, 99.2718; 93.2633–2634.

18. Sima Qian, *Shi ji*, 93.2638–2639; 110.2895.

19. For an example, see Sima Qian, *Shi ji*, 106.2827.

20. For an analysis of the two masters model that took shape during the reign of Emperor Wen, see Hsieh, "Viewing the Han Empire from the Edge," 54–68.

21. Sima Qian, *Shi ji*, 110.2896–2897, 2902.

22. One typical method for the imperial court to accuse a subordinate king of treason was to argue that this king was in contact with the Xiongnu. For an example, see Sima Qian, *Shi ji*, 118.3076–3077.

23. Sima Qian, *Shi ji*, 99.2719; 110.2895, 2898; Ban Gu, *Han shu*, 2.89; 5.144.

24. Sima Qian, *Shi ji*, 110.2902.

25. Sima Qian, *Shi ji*, 110.2903–2904.

26. Ban Gu, *Han shu*, 5.140–141.

27. Sima Qian, *Shi ji*, 50.1990; 106.2827; 110.2904.

28. Sima Qian, *Shi ji*, 11.445; 19.1018–1021; 572078; 93.2639.

29. Sima Qian, *Shi ji*, 108.2861.

30. Ban Gu, *Han shu*, 6.162; 52.2399–2403.

31. Ban Gu, *Han shu*, 6.155–164.

32. Sima Qian, *Shi ji*, 20.1027–1029, 1031–1032, 1039–1047.

33. Sima Qian, *Shi ji*, 30.1425; 110.2909; 111.2934, 2945; 123.3167, 3170.

34. For some examples about the assistance provided by steppe informants, see Sima Qian, *Shi ji*, 123.3157 and 3159.

35. Sima Qian, *Shi ji*, 123.3168–3170.

36. Hsieh, "Viewing the Han Empire from the Edge," 116–123, 191–200, and ch. 4.

37. Sima Qian, *Shi ji*, 111.2915; 123.3175–3178.

38. Lewis, "The Han Abolition," 57–60.

39. Hsing I-tien, "Dong Han de Hu bing," 143–166; Fan Ye et al., *Hou Han shu*, monograph 25, "Bai guan er," 3582.

40. Fan Ye, *Hou Han shu*, 41.1415–1416.

41. Hsing I-tien, "Han dai de yi Yi zhi Yi lun," 9–53.

42. Thus under the Tang dynasty, the zones of fluctuating control over the registered Tang population and the steppe horsemen who served in the Tang armies were marked by the shifting geographic distribution of the "loose-rein prefectures" used to control the latter. In the same period, the dual nature of the state that included both conventional administration of the peasantry and military control of the steppe peoples was established by attributing the literary articulation of these two aspects to two different texts, the *Yu gong* and the *Han shu*. See Lewis, *China's Cosmopolitan Empire*, 27–29.

43. See, for example, Fan Ye, *Hou Han shu*, 38.1285.

44. On the military aspect of the fall of the Han and the central role of steppe standing military commands, see Lewis, "Conclusion," in *The Early Chinese Empires*; Barfield, *The Perilous Frontier*, 85–93.

45. Lewis, *China between Empires*, 33–37, 54–56, 58–62; Graff, *Medieval Chinese Warfare*, ch. 2; Barfield, *The Perilous Frontier*, 93–100.

46. Graff, *Medieval Chinese Warfare*, 48–73.

47. Barfield, *The Perilous Frontier*, 100–114; Lewis, *China between Empires*, 73–85; Graff, *Medieval Chinese Warfare*, chs. 5–6.

48. Notable examples are Burbank and Cooper, *Empires in World History*; and Barkey, *Empire of Difference*.

49. On the tendency in the West to use Rome as the ideal type against which all other cases are measured, see Duverger, *Le Concept d'empire*.

2

FROM EMPIRE TO STATE

Kang Youwei, Confucian Universalism, and Unity

Wang Hui / Translated by Ban Wang

*

A friend asked me why I use "empire" instead of "tianxia" in my analysis of China's imperial history, especially late Qing reforms and transformations. One reason is that tianxia tends to denote the uniqueness and continuity of Chinese culture in isolation from the world system. This essentialist use of tianxia falls victim to the false dichotomy of oriental empire and modern nation-state. Moreover, the concept of empire implies a dynastic genealogy of institutional forms, the formation of moral authority with religious significance, and a strategy for political legitimacy. All these elements could be described as political culture in modern parlance. Imbued with a vision broader than the concept of nation-state, "empire" may be a more productive term in highlighting the historical formation of political legitimacy. Based on culture and ritual, this political legitimacy hinges on the governing body's ability to incorporate different ethnic groups and populations from different regions, and different religions, into a flexible and pluralistic structure. In this chapter, by considering Kang Youwei's scholarship on Confucianism, I show that empire as a mode of political legitimacy and cultural politics resonates with the ideal of tianxia in its solutions to the problems of order and chaos. In Kang the idea of empire is derived from Confucian universalism, which presupposes a moral and quasi-religious framework anchored in a unitary, all-encompassing order. The concept of imperial authority is defined by a comprehensive framework of values and culture that evolved from imperial history and from Kang's rethinking and reinterpretation of the Confucian classics.

Feudalism and Unity in the Confucian Classics

In *A Study of Confucius as Reformist* (*Kongzi gaizhi kao* 孔子改製考) by Kang Youwei, the rise of rival feudal lords was the underlying historical context for the emergent philosophies and schools of thought during the Spring and Autumn and Warring States eras. The clashes and controversy among those schools of thought reflected the division and belligerence of feudal estates involved in constant warfare. In this situation, Confucius invoked the unitary agenda of King Wen of the Zhou (1152–1056 BCE). In the past, King Wen had sought to institute an overarching order based on rites and music to create a unified tianxia. Similarly, Confucius sought to create an authoritative order of morality and learning, and his strategies and reforms paralleled King Wen's political agenda. In this sense, Confucius was identical to King Wen in political aspiration. Confucius's attempt to set up an authoritative body of thought and morality went hand in hand with political and institutional reforms. It should be recalled that the Confucian school of thought was only one among many rival schools that competed for ascendency. This discursive conflict and diversity mirrored the quest for imperial, administrative unity, a projected political order that would override the rival feudal estates. There has been a perennial tension in Chinese history between unitary order and divisive feudalism. From books 2 to 6 of *Kongzi gaizhi kao*, Kang Youwei presents these telling titles: "Inquiry into Rising Schools of Thought Competing for Authority during the Late Zhou Dynasty," "Different Schools of Thought Emerged in Search of Authority and Political Reform," "The Thinkers Drew on the Past for Institutional Reform," "The Schools Attacked Each Other for Leadership," and "Inquiry into Mozi and His Disciples." Although books 7 to 13 specifically address and examine how Confucius engaged in institutional reform, books 14 to 20 revert to the discussion of Confucianism in controversy with various other schools of thought. They have suggestive titles such as "Attacks by Different Schools on Confucianism," "Growing Attacks by Moism and Daoism on Confucianism," "Confucianism and Moism Vying for Authority and Dominance," "Confucian Arguments against Various Schools," "Thriving Confucianism and Moism on

Equal Footing," "Inquiry into the State of Lu Adopting Confucianism as Official School," and "The Widespread Influence of Confucianism across Tianxia and the Warring States Era through Qin and Han." Kang Youwei's whole book ends with "Inquiry into the Founding of Confucianism as the Orthodox School of Thought after Emperor Wu of the Han Dynasty." The all-embracing unity achieved by Confucianism resulted from long-term clashes among different schools of thought. The grand unitary order of the Han dynasty established the leading status of Confucianism, which suggests that Confucianism was valorized as the heart of the new institutions in the dynasty. Kang writes,

> Of the ten schools of thought, the most interesting are only nine. They all arose in a time when the kingly way was on the wane and various feudal lords were trying to empower their regimes by force; when the lords' preferences and penchants varied widely and clashed. Thus nine schools arose, coexisted, and competed with each other. Each took a different view and upheld what it believed to be good. Scholars traveled and ran around to spread their doctrines and appealed to the needs of different feudal lords.... If a sage king accepted a scholar and was wise enough to discern a balanced, comprehensive doctrine, then a school of thought could empower and shore up a regime like legs and arms.... If a regime could cultivate the six arts, study and attend to all nine schools to draw from their strengths and discard their shortcomings, it could comprehend and embrace a myriad of discourses and doctrines.[1]

Thus, the rise of different schools was bound up with the needs of the feudal lords to shore up and consolidate their regimes, and their diverse, conflicted preferences drove various scholars to set up a preeminent school in the push for political reform. Confucius was not alone. Mozi, Guanzi, Yanzi, Jin Zicheng, Song Xing, Yin Wen, Yangzi, Huizi, Xuzi, Baigui, Gongsun Longzi, Deng Xi, Daoism, Legalism, the Logicians, the Yin-Yang School, the Experts in Diplomatic Affairs (Zongheng jia), and military strategists—all these camps strove for preeminence but also drew on resources from the past to reform the status quo. We witness a world torn apart by divisions in state territory and by rival feudal lords. In this context, the preeminence of the new sage king signaled a historic choice—a testament to the fact that Confucian learning had proved superior to other doctrines. While Kang Youwei vigorously defended the establishment of Confucianism as the orthodox order of teaching and learning, this does not mean he denied the insights and wisdoms of other schools and discourses. For Confucianism it was true that "the rites and rituals have been lost, only to be recovered on the margins of civilization" (li shi qiu zhu ye

禮失求諸野). The significance of Confucianism lies in its capacity to reconcile different doctrines, draw on strengths and shed weaknesses, and create a comprehensive school.

Kang's discussion of Confucianism as the authority among the diverse schools and of its institutional reforms belongs to the long-lasting debate in Chinese history around feudalism and unitary political order. His goal is to uphold Confucianism as the foundation for China's unity. In Kang's account, moral doctrine and learning merge with political order. Conversely, good political order is anchored in the canons of learning and moral doctrine. In this light, the severance of political order from moral teaching signals the corruption of authoritative discourse and the decay of political order. However, as the saying goes: "All rivers originate from different sources but converge to flow to the sea; all occupations pursue different businesses but apply themselves to a peaceful order."[2] This statement epitomizes the intimate ties between moral discourse and political order in Chinese antiquity and corresponds to Kang's later views concerning regional self-rule:

> In ancient times, feudalist estates prevailed in the realm, but the feudalist governance of the population could hardly work, for feudalism could very easily lead to loose and diffuse disconnections without the ability to cultivate a unified order. . . . Local self-rule came under the heading of feudalism [*fengjian* 封建] in ancient times. But the chaotic conditions in the past stemmed from feudalism centered on a feudal lord. The feudal hereditary lineage and private interest were breeding grounds for conflict and war. This is why feudalism could not work toward a unified political order. In the contemporary era of rising peace [*shengping* 昇平], people may return to a "feudal" situation where they are allowed to rule themselves and to have public deliberation; where each pursues private interest for the common good; natural resources are expanded and human capacity mobilized. Social virtue and morality become beautiful, and talent and intelligence come to fruition. This situation could resemble the states and counties in the United States. The localities have freedom of self-rule comparable to the order rooted in the linkages among major feudal lords, like the German states linked to each other in federation.[3]

Placing a premium on a united administrative order based on self-rule by prefectures and counties, Kang sought to reconcile separate governance in different regions. The creation of an authoritative Confucianism placed this political vision in the tradition of Confucian scholarship. In Kang's interpretation, setting up Confucianism as the authority would culminate in a "unified and peaceful order" (*zhi* 治). Thus, there is no sharp divide between the emergence of an authoritative school of thought from among diverse rival schools, on the one hand, and the unification of multiple rival feudal lords, on the other; there is no sharp distinction between moral discourse and political order. Seen in this way, the issue of unity and feudalism is not a matter of political tension; it also extends to the tension between doctrine and faith.

Moreover, these conflicts in the pre-Qin eras are also linked metaphorically to the world situation marked by rising and conflicting nation-states and civilizational clashes in the colonial era. Various schools of thought sought new authority, but they inherited knowledge and wisdom dating back to the Xia dynasty. The different schools stood apart, and each pursued its own path. They built theories and recruited disciples, with the goal of transforming the tianxia realm by reforming the institutions and consolidating authority. But due to diversity in personality and talent, each expounded one particular doctrine, which suffered from limitations and blindness. This inability to engage in dialogue and communication inevitably made for mutual attacks and divisive polemics. Kang Youwei extends this train of thought to the global context:

Diverse schools of thought in the West fared no better. During the time of antiquity, Buddhism and Brahmin came to preeminence in India, along with ninety-six other discourses of philosophy and doctrine. In Persia, Zoroastrianism set up schools and recruited disciples. In the West, Greek civilization reached its apex and boasted seven philosophers whose achievement culminated in Socrates. All around the world, different schools of thought and philosophy emerged and flourished—more dramatically and vibrantly than those in the era of the Spring and Autumn and Warring States! Gather the accomplishments of the diverse schools, and elevate a school to a sacred height, so that all people follow it and converge in a magnificent unity, and all will observe the norms that will regulate and guide countless generations. . . . [Thus] tianxia will follow and culminate in Confucianism, and the Grand Way [*dadao* 大道] will be integral and unified. This is why there were no diverse schools of philosophy after the Han dynasty.[4]

The relationship of unity to feudalism not only accounts for the rise and clash of different schools of thought but also describes diverse and conflicted schools and religions in foreign lands. The statement "Tianxia will follow and converge with Confucianism" describes "the sanctification of Confucianism as orthodoxy by ousting diverse rival schools" (bachu baijia, du zun rushu 罷黜百家獨尊儒術). However, around the world rival schools and religions had to converge in a unified order. Here, the forces pitted against each other create a focal point that relates the conflicts of the lords of Chinese antiquity to the clash of modern nation-states. This link ties together the "all-encompassing order" (*da yitong*), the sanctification of Confucianism at the expense of the rival schools, and the ideal of "great unity" (*datong*). The following quote from Kang's *Study of the Spring and Autumn Era and Dong Zhongshu* (*Chunqiu Dong shi xue* 春秋董氏學) could be read together with related passages in *Confucius as a Reformist* to see how the text articulates the movement from the clash of rival schools to the founding of orthodox Confucianism:

> Let's survey the beginning of the world from King Yu. The planet Earth originated from Mount Kunlun and emerged into an order. Confucius designed the hierarchy that divided the world into the Son of Heaven, feudal lords, and high-ranking officials. *The Spring and Autumn Annals* focuses on diminishing the power of the officials. So when the world is in disarray, it signals a time to clamp down on officials. In the world of rising peace, it is important to diminish the power of the feudal lords. In the world of universal peace, we can abolish the power of the emperor. . . . Since Confucius's reform there has been a tendency toward civilization. The Han dynasty looked much the same as the Roman Empire. . . . The more states arose and struggled for power, the more conflict and wars there were. This situation is ubiquitous in local areas like Guizhou and Yunnan—places divided and ruled by conflicting tribal chiefs. . . . Western civilization underwent three phases: from Babylon to Greek and Egyptian civilization. . . . The emperor took over popular power; the priests took over divine authority. Ethnicities and languages stem from Hindu civilization. Confucianism is a kind of fire religion and worships the sun.[5]

In discussing interstate clashes, Kang Youwei does not confine himself to China as a category or geographical entity. The diverse schools in the Spring and Autumn and Warring States eras, different religions around the world, and rival feudal lords have something in common. Trapped in their own tunnel vision and understanding of the world, all these particularistic views proved unable to "appreciate the beauties of heaven and earth, comprehend intricate intelligence of all things, and understand the whole meanings of the ancients. . . . They are unable to grasp the magnificence of heaven and earth and fail to recognize the genuine face of the gods and wisdom. . . . Scholars of generations afterward, unfortunately, proved blind to the purity of heaven and earth, to the grand body of thought by the ancients, and thus the integrity of discourses fell to pieces under heaven."[6] The grand order, all-encompassing Confucianism, and great unity stem from a pursuit of an integrative, unifying vision. This vision will be realized by overcoming clashes of philosophies, religions, and states and by bringing them into the fold.

Why did Kang Youwei try to demonstrate that Confucian reform was driven by a narrative of a unified, orthodox Confucianism dominating the other schools? Why did he render metaphorically the conflict of nation-states—a political matter—as a controversy among competing doctrines? One could point to the fact that Kang deployed his vast erudition and wide references in an attempt to counter the Old Text School at the technical level and used scholarly rhetoric to express a political will. But more important reasons are the following: First, Kang treats China as a civilization rather than a nation-state. He regards the conflict of nation-states in the nineteenth century as a clash of civilizations. In this sense, political conflict could be articulated as civilizational or religious conflict. Second, rather than regarding Confucian thought as one among multiple schools, Kang elevates Confucianism to a height that historically balanced and mediated diverse schools. These two points are manifest in his explanation of the power of Confucianism, which embodies a synthesizing, comprehensive structure of relations in history. Instead of a singular, narrowly conceived doctrine, it amounts to a form of civilization. The authoritative status of Confucianism was a product of historical relations and related discursive conflict. Kang Youwei never denied that Confucius was one of numerous thinkers who strove to build an authoritative school. On the one hand, only in its complex historical context can the sharp tensions between Confucianism and the rival schools (e.g., Yangzhu) and their subtle differences (Confucius and Mozi) be revealed. On the other hand, only in a state of diverse, opposing thoughts could a need arise to synthesize different schools, providing a space for divergence and recomposition. Ultimately, Kang regarded the establishment of Confucianism as a natural result of historical trends that culminated in the Mandate of Heaven.

From Empire to the Sovereign State: China's Self-Transformation

Kang Youwei's scholarship on the Confucian classics and related political practice represented not just an end of Qing New Text classical scholarship. It also projected the theories and orientations of the late Qing reform movement. Next I outline the historical importance of Kang's thought.

Within the tradition of commentary on Confucian classics, Kang Youwei delineates in a new way the main features of the modern world and China's place in it, to set new directions for political reform: "Today's world can be compared roughly to the rival states during the Spring and Autumn period, which is very different from the absolutist rule marking the Han, Tang, Song, and Ming dynasties. Thus we are witnessing unprecedented changes in several thousand years. . . . In this age we should rearrange the tianxia order of governance, not by keeping faith with the status quo, but through new innovations. To have the tianxia order, we should confront the world of mutually opposing states rather than preserve the classical unitary, noninterventionist order."[7] Kang links the essential meanings of the *Spring and Autumn Annals* to the modern system of nation-states, uncovering within Confucian scholarship the basic premises and logic for the late Qing reform programs centered on state building. This analysis, whether about competition or unity, does not merely refer specifically to China but also describes the modern world. The difference between these two conditions partly hinges on China's place in the world. The focus on competition rests on China's disadvantaged or marginalized position, whereas unity envisions China's superiority or centrality. The unitary image reflects an empire that knows no bounds, while competition relates to nation-states with clear divisions of inside and outside. In his petitions to the Qing emperor and his writings during the period of the reform, Kang set out to show the crisis besetting the tributary system under the Qing and the threat confronting the empire. He called for systematic reform by following Japan's example and Western models, which heralded the transformation of the empire into a modern state. Kang proposed a set of comprehensive reforms in the political system, the military, education, science and technology, the economy, domestic transportation, administrative and bureaucratic structures, the press, and foreign affairs. He made tremendous efforts to implement these reforms. In the later Qing era, Kang's program was the most comprehensive and had global significance.

In the project of building a modern Chinese state, Kang offered new interpretations of China by synthesizing and drawing on the New Text Confucianism of the Qing. While expunging ethnic elements, he rejected plans to divide China into decentralized provincial units or to establish a federation of provinces with shared yet decentralized powers. This allowed him to search for a source of identity for China at the cultural level and to find a theory of state formation at the political level that was antithetical to nationalism (national autonomy and ethnocentrism). Kang's theory is more intensely centralized than traditional political models would allow, but this theory is a natural continuation of the evolution of the empire. The key concerns of his political program were rejection of the hereditary aristocratic tradition and related regional self-rule; opposition to the division of the empire into a loose collection of multiple nation-states or federalized states modeled on Europe; and opposition to the nationalist tradition initiated by the French Revolution. He sought to implement an administrative reform centered on monarchical power and initiatives to directly transform the empire into a sovereign state, so that a united China would be able to attain a place in the world system of competing nation-states. If Dong Zhongshu's book *Luxuriant Dew of the Spring and Autumn Annals* (*Chunqiu fanlu* 春秋繁露) asserts the necessity of empire, Kang's *Study of the Spring and Autumn Era and Dong Zhongshu* and other Confucian commentaries argue for the imperative for China to transform directly from an empire to a sovereign state. Thus, a unified state and a corresponding cultural system to shore it up became the key to Kang's political program.

While he promoted the reform of the state system through a central monarchical authority, Kang validated Confucian doctrine and learning as the foundation of the new state. He thus strove to build a modern China and looked for its source of identity in its civilization rather than in political institutions, ethnicity, or kinship relations. The new monarchical order represented the spirit of state building of the new age. Monarchical centrism seeks to modernize by replacing the ancient aristocratic and feudal power and kinship relations with a new state system. By restructuring regional and social practices, the new state attempted to forge a more orderly, homogenous political form. Under such a statist system, the bureaucratic hierarchy and the legal system have universal implications, sharing affinities with the systems of other nation-states. This universal state should be seen, however, not as a duplicate of the European nation-state, but rather as a return to a Chinese political culture. Kang believed that Chinese identification transcends dynastic changes, ethnic relationships, and political orientation, based on Confucian universalism. In light of this perspective from within the history of the empire and an intellectual culture of Confucianism, Kang opposed revolution in favor of reform. Revolution involves dismantling old institutions by following the nationalist model of the French Revolution and transforming domestic ethnic relations within the empire in order to reform political relations under the state. Included under Kang's reform, however, is transforming the empire into a sovereign state by resorting to the cultural source of identification embedded within it. By maintaining the unifying power of a central authority, his reform encouraged the grassroots societies to govern themselves to reform the country's politics and economy. Revolution is an effective means of state building, whereas reform points the way to self-transformation.

To transform the empire into a state, Kang had to find solutions to its entrenched ethnic and tribal conflicts. He appealed to cultural symbols of China that transcend ethnic divides and relations. In modern political theory, the hallmark of the nation-state is its inner unity, with a highly unitary and homogeneous system presiding over heterogeneous ethnic groups, languages, cultures, and political entities. In contrast, the empire is fraught with more complicated relations and tensions among ethnic groups, regions, languages, and institutions. Loose social relations, multiple ethnicities, and heterogeneous cultures mark China as a multiethnic and multifaceted empire. In this loose aggregate,

> People do not concern themselves with affairs of the country. They only care about their family and kin and see the rest of the society as foreign to them. Even worse, different family names divide people; different regions, counties, and provinces are disconnected from each other. The Qing dynasty originated in the East, and came to possess the central realm of China, and went on to address the tensions from the Mongols, Muslims, and Tibetans and assimilate them into a unified realm. But the Qing empire maintained order by allowing each group to keep its old tradition and custom.[8]

Faced with the encroachment of the Western powers and on the cusp of transition from empire to state, the Qing Empire needed caution to handle the internal differences among ethnic groups, territorial boundaries, and different cultural traditions. The empire had to turn into a sovereign state in order to meet the challenges from inside and outside.

To address the threat of disunity from diverse ethnic groups and political arrangements, Kang Youwei sought to redefine the concept of being Chinese by negating the essentialist concepts of *yi* (barbarian 夷) and *xia* (the central realm of China 夏) as well as of the unity of the Han. A case in point is the changing of titles by Emperor Wen during the Northern Wei dynasty. The royal house changed the title of Tuoba to Yuan; the brother of Emperor Xian Qigu changed his title to Hu; the second brother Pu changed to Zhou; the third brother Tuoba changed his title to Zhangsun, and so on. There was a decree that ninety-nine honorable ministers and officials must change their names to Han names. As a result, "nine out of ten noble titles are from the Wei tribe," and the question of Han purity became pertinent. As Kang Youwei saw it, modern political institutions, such as constitution and parliament, the balance of power among three branches of government, legal autonomy, government accountability, and the election of representatives, were prevalent and widespread in many countries and not difficult to emulate. The far greater challenge was to achieve lasting unity. Based on these considerations, Kang not only distinguished Zhongguo (China) from dynasty titles (Qing) but also attempted to deploy China or Zhonghua as the basis for the inner unity of a sovereign state and for cultural identification.[9] At stake was not the negation of the orthodox order but a reinterpretation of it. In the late Qing discursive context, falling back on orthodoxy was necessary as the empire was transforming itself into a sovereign state. This epochal transformation did not, however, entail the total overhaul of the imperial system.

Kang opposed the federalist model that favors decentered and fragmented powers. However, he called for a constitutional monarchy and decentralization at the local level, grafting regional, grassroots powers onto central authority in order to make a unique political arrangement. He was searching for a way that a decentered centralism would allow the state administration to penetrate the fabric and all the corners of society in hopes of preventing the breakup of the empire. Confronting the volatile geopolitics of great power rivalry and China's besieged situation, this political concept also stemmed from a comparative analysis of different historical contexts in China and the Euro-American states, evoking certain elements of republicanism. Comparing these claims with his arguments against the state in his *Datong shu* (Book of the great community 大同書), we find that opposition to the structure of federated states is linked to his rejection of the Western nation-state. In *Datong shu*, he opposes the nation-state and calls for a united world community. But in *Kongzi gaizhi kao*, he argues against regional autonomy based on self-rule by each province (federation) and calls for deploying the empire's unitary power to insert China into the international relations marked by state rivalry. This is a case against national self-rule from the vantage point of the empire. Featuring a fundamental element of China's political reform, Kang's central challenge was: under the imperative of keeping intact the empire's territories, population, and cultural identification, how should China implement political reform? The major question, unique to China, was how to preserve the unity of the country in the process of reforming the state system.

Democratic transformations in the modern West are deeply connected with nationalism. As the nation-state broke away from the empire to assume self-rule, the nation became the carrier of the state, and the fundamental judicial and political constitution was premised on the equality of members of the national community. Harold Berman writes,

> The political and social philosophies that sprang from the Enlightenment were religions because they ascribed ultimate meaning and sanctity to the individual mind—and also, it must be added immediately, to the nation. The age of individualism and rationalism was also the age

of nationalism: the individual was a citizen, and public opinion turned out not to be the opinion of mankind but the opinion of Frenchmen, the opinion of Germans, the opinion of Americans. Individualism, rationalism, nationalism—the Triune Deity of Democracy—found legal expression in the exaltation of the role of the legislature and consequent reduction (except in the United States) of the law creating the role of the judiciary; in the freeing of the individual actions from public controls, especially in the economic sphere; in the demand for codification of criminal and civil law; in the effort to make predictable the legal consequences of individual actions, again especially in the economic sphere.[10]

However, state building in the late Qing era was fundamentally a process of self-transformation from an empire to a sovereign state. Thus, how to keep imperial sovereignty intact and the country united; how to free citizens from their particularistic, regional attachments to construct a sovereign subjectivity of the state; how to build a political order that guaranteed equality among diverse cultural identities across different regions while preserving their diversity—these concerns inevitably became the fundamental challenges confronting China's political and judicial system, interregional relations, and citizenship rights. Since an inner continuity persisted between the sovereign state and the empire, domestic political relations could not attain the tight national cohesion characteristic of the European nation-states. Centrifugal, separatist tendencies alternated with centripetal, uniting actions, depending on international and domestic circumstances. Despite all the criticism of Kang Youwei's political programs by statesmen and intellectuals of later times, the questions confronting and preoccupying Kang remain the major challenges facing Chinese society today. These are also key challenges confronting China's drive to reform its social system and to ensure that the source of cultural identification is under the state.

Combining Confucian universalism with a variety of Western discourses of science and politics, Kang Youwei constructed a grand utopian vision. Echoing and confirming this much-discussed universalism and Confucian worldview, the datong vision, with strong socialist overtones, transcends the state, ethnicity, class, gender, and other relations of hierarchy and domination. If we compare Kang's ideas of datong with his theory of the state manifested in his Confucian scholarship, datong shares a strong affinity with the da yitong (all-encompassing unity) model of the state. Both terms militate against the model of the nation-state. The purpose of *Datong shu* is to transcend the nation-state. In reconstructing monarchical authority, Kang Youwei became aware of the authoritarianism inevitably associated with the modern nation-state. The utopian vision of datong represents China's quest for capitalist modernity even as it tries to overcome modernity. It is a religious revolt against modernity in the midst of the drive to integrate China into capitalist secular development. Indebted to a linear evolutionary timeline and a forward-looking optimism, this vision follows nineteenth-century discourses concerning the nation-state, national territory, sovereignty, ethnicity, and division of labor. Yet on these bases, Kang builds a dialectical prospectus of datong. If his reconstruction of Confucian universalism to articulate an all-encompassing empire pursues modernity by reimagining the past, the construction of a unified world community of datong and its norms of governance pursues modernity by envisioning the future. Whether or not the world vision is articulated in a revised Confucian universalism, Kang's bold and far-reaching concept is deeply anchored in the evolving contexts and inner contradictions of modern history. The datong vision, therefore, has become a symptom of China's quest for modernity, an intellectual resource that has been revisited and rearticulated, fueling new intellectual vibrancy and new critiques. Whether or not Kang's vision is realistic and practical is not relevant. What matters is that he engaged the contradictions of the modern world. The key problems of modernity give rise to these ideas that inform and drive Chinese thought in a constant retrospection on the past and projection into the future. Although Kang's theory evinces tendencies similar to those found in the historical evolution of the European nation-states, his reform plans and datong vision contain socialist implications antithetical to the latter's secular totalitarianism. If we agree with Harold Berman that socialism shares "a common ancestry" with liberal democracy in Christianity, socialism is antithetical to the modern secularization process led by the nation-state.[11] Similarly, Kang's datong vision arises from within the Confucian tradition to challenge the interstate network of divided, belligerent nation-states. Paradoxically, his program is to transform China into a modern state. As Kang himself foresaw, this utopian vision was unable to address the problems facing China in his times. However, he revealed the deep contradictions plaguing the modern world system. For China as well as the world undergoing modernization, Kang's datong vision not only illuminates the inner contradictions of this process but also proffers a moral dimension beyond the modernization narrative, providing the possibility of social self-critique and political imagination.

The addition of Confucianism injects a quasi-religious dimension into Kang's political reform program. In 1856, Alexis de Tocqueville characterized the French Revolution as a political revolution in the guise of religious revolution. "The French Revolution, though political, assumed the guise and tactics of a religious revolution," for it was inspired by "preaching and propagandism."[12] According to Tocqueville, religions generally are concerned with humankind in the abstract, "without allowance for additions or changes effected by laws, customs, or national traditions."[13] Tocqueville's concept of religion derived from two distinct religious doctrines that seemed already apparent in the divergence between Christianity and paganism in the Greco-Roman empire: "The old forms of paganism, which were all more or less interwoven with political and social systems, and whose dogmas wore a national and sometimes a sort of municipal aspect, rarely traveled beyond the frontiers of a single country. They gave rise to occasional outbursts of intolerance and persecution, but never to proselytism. Hence, the first religious revolution felt in Western Europe was caused by the establishment of Christianity. That faith easily overstepped the boundaries which had checked the outgrowth of pagan systems, and rapidly conquered a large portion of the human race."[14] Given this distinction between Christian universalism and pagan particularism, Tocqueville viewed the secular French Revolution as a religious revolution. This was because the French Revolution "dealt with the citizen in the abstract, independent of particular social organizations, just as religions deal with mankind in general, independent of time and place. It inquired, not what were the particular rights of French citizens, but what were the general rights and duties of mankind in reference to political concerns."[15]

While Kang inquired into Chinese society and political arrangements, his visions for a new society had universal implications. Whether investigating Confucianism or scientific knowledge that classifies and orders the world, his quest for broad knowledge was universal. Alexis de Tocqueville regarded the French Revolution as marked by a tendency to transcend the nation-state, regional distinctions, and judicial, political differences. But unwittingly, Tocqueville hinted at how sharply paganism contrasts with Christianity, embodied by the framework of empire, thereby revealing Christianity as a religion of empire. Kang Youwei's datong vision represented the human condition but also stemmed from the universal dimension of the concept of China. China presupposes tianxia, premised on Confucian universalism, which aims to transcend place, the nation-state, and specific dynasties with its peculiar judicial institutions and political structures. Premised on universal tianxia or datong, Confucian universalism attempted to reconstruct and reform the imperial political system, judicial structure, and custom of a specific era. In this light, Kang's strong statist penchant also reflects an anarchistic position—a universalist impulse going beyond the state as well as any particularistic and provincial boundaries.

In the way Kang Youwei drew on natural science, political thought, education, and legal systems from the West in his attempt to remap the world, his work was new and innovative. But in the way these discourses and knowledge are implicated in a still-evolving history of the empire, his project, like his New Text Confucian scholarship, extends and modifies China's millennial history. Based on these observations, we may regard modern China's state-building project as the self-transformation of the empire. The Hundred Days reform movement masterminded and crafted by Kang and others ended in failure, but the basic visions of his political reform did not collapse. If centralized power is integral to the traditional imperial system, then Kang's thought and reform practice indicate that the new society would resort to a centralized authority much more than the ancient empire. The new society takes a much more hostile stance toward the multiple traditions, different seats of power, and diverse cultures and customs within a country. This accounts for the steady expansion of the traditional administrative structure of prefecture and county and for the progressive decline of other forms of self-rule on the local level. Centralized authority and its attendant administrative bureaucracy are not new constructs resulting from reform or revolution but lingering forms of the old system. These residual forms persist and continue to evolve in the new society, because they can meet the society's needs. The hostility of the modern state toward traditional forms and institutions should not be explained by locating its source within the inner tradition of an authoritarian state. Its root cause must be found in a broader context of the international system rooted in the political units of the nation-state. This is the lesson we may take away from Kang Youwei's works of Confucian scholarship and the *Datong shu*.

Regarding the three eras and datong, Kang wrote:

The Three Ages contain the essential meanings of Confucianism, which are articulated by the *Chunqiu*. The era that became legend was one of disorder; the age transmitted from hearsay was one of rising peace; the era that the world witnessed was one of grand peace and order. The era of disorder means that culture and learning were undeveloped and lay beyond the ken of the population. The era of rising peace saw a moderate growth and expansion of culture and learning, which was also an age of small prosperity and happiness [*xiaokang* 小康]. When it comes to the era of grand and universal peace, the distances between the great and small and the far and near are bridged and they are enfolded into one. Civilization, culture, and learning will attain a high level, encompassing all the realms and informing the entire society. The grand significance of

Confucianism tends to be associated with the era of xiaokang, and its subtle and hidden visions belong to the future era of universal peace. To inquire into Confucianism and to learn genuine lessons, one must make a distinction between these two bodies of meaning. That is the essential meaning of the *Chunqiu*.[16]

NOTES

1. Kang Youwei, *Kang Youwei quanji*, vol. 3, 38–39.
2. Kang Youwei, *Kang Youwei quanji*, vol. 3, 23.
3. Kang Youwei, "Gongmin zizhi pian," 28.
4. Kang Youwei, *Kang Youwei quanji* , vol. 3, 11–12.
5. Kang Youwei, *Kang Youwei quanji*, vol. 2, 561–563.
6. Kang Youwei, *Kang Youwei quanji*, vol. 3, 16.
7. Kang Youwei, *Kang Youwei zhenglun ji*, vol. 2, 151–152.
8. Kang Youwei, *Kang Youwei zhenglun ji*, vol. 1, 340–341.
9. Kang Youwei, *Kang Youwei zhenglun ji*, 341–342.
10. Berman, *Law and Revolution*, 31.
11. Berman, *Law and Revolution*, 31.
12. Tocqueville, *The Old Regime and the Revolution*, 25.
13. Tocqueville, *The Old Regime and the Revolution*, 25.
14. Tocqueville, *The Old Regime and the Revolution*, 26.
15. Tocqueville, *The Old Regime and the Revolution*, 26–27.
16. Kang Youwei, *Kang Youwei quanji*, 671.

3

THE CHINESE WORLD ORDER AND
PLANETARY SUSTAINABILITY
Prasenjit Duara

*

The rise of China has been accompanied by a palpable need among the Chinese to understand the significance of this ascendance and to project a vision of the world that does not reproduce the injustices of the earlier order. To do so, Chinese intellectuals and others have turned to resources within Chinese tradition. In this chapter, I consider the potential of historical universalism to embody such a vision. We need to take these universalisms seriously in part because modern universalisms that emerged from specific conditions in the West have not worked out satisfactorily. I also point to their limits and consider the possibility of a post-Western universalism that works with helpful traditions.[1]

First, why universalisms? In my understanding, a cosmopolitan world is now more necessary than ever before in history, as the nation and the world are increasingly mismatched. The nation-state system that culminated in the United Nations represented a prior globalization—a cognitive globalization—of norms and methods of institutionalizing power in nation-states to compete for global resources. I have argued that the globalism of the nation-state system was prereflexive or covert; the institutions of the nation-state sought to systematically misrecognize its global provenance and embeddedness in order to claim sovereignty and agency in global competition.

The competitive global order in which the nation-state had to survive and develop required not only a strong identity politics of self/other in relation to the outside (and the internal other) but also the promise of citizenship within. Arguably, the mobilization and sacrifice necessary for global competition were compensated for by the emancipatory rhetoric of citizenship. This relationship was particularly developed in the People's Republic of China (PRC) of the 1950s and 1960s, where the demands upon the populace to strengthen China economically and politically in relation to its enemies were premised on the promise of socialist utopia.

The powerful forces of economic globalization, particularly since the end of the Cold War, have altered this structural relationship between the nation-state and globalization. The rationale of the nation-state is no longer exclusively or overwhelmingly based on the protection of national sovereignty. Indeed, the state has aligned itself more closely with multi- and transnational interests, and the neoliberal economic order has spelled out an agenda of state withdrawal and privatization or corporatization of national public goods. Consequently, the globalism of the national order is no longer as covert as it was. Moreover, the ideology of nationalism has tended to transmute along with these changes. While national leaders can scarcely abandon nationalism, it is less dependent on state direction, inasmuch as it is an unreflexive reaction by the populace to the dangers and threats posed by overt globalization to stability, community, and the promise of citizenship.

The realignment in much of the world and China today presents in some ways a still greater mismatch between global influences and national institutions. Not only is there a deeper embeddedness and dependence of the nation on the world, many of the effects of globalization on society are no longer shielded by state institutions. National and local institutions of governance and delivery are ambiguously committed to projects of development, as they are also diverted by neoliberal goals of profit maximization. Most significantly, perhaps, the profit-maximizing drive of economic globalization has generated environmental degradation across the world that can no longer be addressed only by national policies. Ecological instabilities have effects on global resources such as water and agricultural goods that do not respect national boundaries. National wealth and national problems are generated on a global scale, whereas the institutions of remediation and justice function at national and local levels. In order to address this mismatch, nation-states will have to not only coordinate but also share sovereignty with regional and global entities.

Thus in my view, the Chinese conceptions of the new world order will need to respond to this fundamental mismatch and develop a cosmopolitan ideal, whether from Chinese historical traditions or from new conceptions of universalism. Let me offer a working definition of cosmopolitanism: it is the idea that all humans belong nonexclusively to a single community. Thus while this sense of belonging may be shared with other communities of identity, such as the locality, nation, or religion, the cosmopolitan community must be able to share sovereignty with any of these other communities. In other words, the institutions or representatives of the cosmopolitan community must be able to make sovereign decisions in some (mutually agreed upon) areas of political society.

Historically, most imperial cultures were justified by a universal ideal. The Chinese ideal of tianxia was perhaps the last, having survived institutionally until the end of the nineteenth century. Archaic universalisms tend to assume an unprovable Archimedean position located outside the world. Thus, from the perspective of situated knowledge they must reflect a particular origin and utility. Particular origins, however, cannot disprove the possibility of universal scope and acceptability, so their value remains. But so does the problem of historicizing their human and teleological values. Modern universalisms seek to justify their vision as nonparticularistic as well as nontranscendent. In the process, however, their effectiveness may have diminished.

Modern Universalism

Modern efforts to locate universalisms in secular ethical tenets—such as Kantian moral universalism, communism, or modernization theory—are in apparent retreat, precisely at a time when nationalism has succumbed to capitalist forms of universal commodification. Modern universalisms have not been able to link the goals they advocate successfully with the affective and symbolic force of the lived experience. Whether or not this has to do with the destabilizing effects of accelerating time or alternative ideologies like nationalism are historical questions that I will explore elsewhere. In this context, it is worth investigating how older universalisms sustained their ideals, even if the reality fell far short of the rhetoric.

Let me first turn to the reasoned cosmopolitanism or universalism of Immanuel Kant (1724–1804).[2] Kant's universalism is based on his moral concept of the categorical imperative, which holds that one must act through the maxims that one can at the same time will to be universal laws. A leading interpreter of Kant's moral philosophy, Onora O'Neill, has sought to demonstrate that the moral imperative furnishes the most elemental vindication for reason and human life (as social life). Reason is calculative and instrumental, but its fundamental character does not reside in these algorithmic functions. It lies rather in the moral authority that regulates reason and permits it to realize its designs. Only through its moral authority can reason overcome the disagreements among members in society or manage the paucity of resources. Moreover, reason cannot appeal to an external authority—outside of debate—such as a dictator, because then reason's power and abilities will break down.[3]

In this context, O'Neill emphasizes that the categorical imperative does not posit any substantive goals. Its regulatory function is negative.[4] It only prevents any person or group from claiming a special privilege or harming the interests of others. Thus, it undertakes the standpoint of everyone else—a universal point of view. Significantly, O'Neill seeks to demonstrate that this is not a transcendent position. She says, "The universal is not Archimedean. Rather the thinker constructs it by shifting his ground to the standpoint of others."[5] To be sure, she recognizes that this is Kant's greatest difficulty because it can produce inconsistency (and irrationality). But she nonetheless remains persuaded that Kant's categorical imperative does not deify reason; reason has to respond to the demands of justice in this world. The categorical imperative is thus quintessentially an Enlightenment product: it neither represents a particular point of view nor is transcendent.

Other interpreters of Kant see the categorical imperative in a distinctly religious light. Palmquist begins with the proposition that Kant regards Jesus Christ as the first person ever to view the coming kingdom of God as a radically moral kingdom. The kingdom of God in religion is closely related to the realm of ends, where humans work together through their mutual obedience to the moral law. That the world's political and religious kingdoms will become the universal kingdom of God is the kernel of rational truth. According to Palmquist, when the goal comes into full view, "the idea of immortality will no longer refer merely to a hope for everlasting life in another world—but to the realization of another way of life in the present world where the moral law is fully regulative in the heart of every human person."[6]

With my restricted reading of Kant and the Western philosophical tradition, I can scarcely intervene in this debate. Instead, I am interested in seeing to what extent Kant required or utilized such concepts as faith and transcendence to construct the modern universal. Interestingly, we may see this in his conception of history, particularly in the essay "Idea for a Universal History from a Cosmopolitan Point of View." Whereas transcendent religions equate the universal with God, Kant's starting point of inquiry into the history of humans is not God. Rather, it is, as he says, "this idiotic course of things human" from which the philosophical historian must seek the natural laws and end of history. He avers that history "is like the unstable weather, which we likewise cannot determine in advance, but which in large, maintains the growth of plants, the flow of rivers, and other natural events in an unbroken, uniform course."[7]

The "unsocial sociability of men" is the antagonism that produces creativity and culture but simultaneously threatens the fabric of society that humans are also bound to enter. The philosopher recognizes that the history of humankind is the realization of Nature's secret plan to bring forth a perfectly constituted state as the only condition in which the capacities of humankind can be fully developed and, further still, a cosmopolitan condition to secure the safety of each state and the civic union of the human race. Thus, "such a justification of Nature—or better, of Providence—is no unimportant reason for choosing a standpoint toward world history."[8]

Thus while God does not play a directly causal role in the world, the idea of history posits that its moral ends can be achieved if we act in the faith that they can be realized and in an exemplary way. This seems to be a transcendent or quasi-transcendent position that acknowledges the temporal and human condition of the world but locates the equivalent of the kingdom of God in what we might call a utopian end in this world, a position that would later be developed by Hegel and Marx. Moreover, Kant locates Nature or Providence as a placeholder for God that requires considerable faith and sacrifice. Kant says Nature has willed that man should aim at producing everything that goes beyond animal existence, and "that he should partake of no other happiness or perfection than that which he himself, independently of instinct, has created by his own reason." Nature aims more at man's "rational self-esteem than at his well-being."[9]

I want to identify a syndrome associated with modern universalism: there is no causal role for God or the transcendent in this system, but nonetheless larger moral forces work through history. These forces promise deliverance at the end of history, not by a transcendent salvation but through a deferred utopian salvation of humanity. However, this will not happen unless we will and act in the faith that it can be realized. This requires great sacrifice of our animal nature. Note the similarities and differences in this syndrome with the Axial Age conceptions of transcendence.[10]

The principal difference with Axial thought is that transcendence now no longer trumps history. Rather, transcendence in modern universalism is located at the end of history as a utopian moment that can be realized by willing and acting through history. A second point of comparison lies in the combination of reason and the sacred. Contemporary analysts of Axial Age philosophy have noted the tensions between the sacred and reason in Axial thought.[11] There were few ethical philosophies of the premodern age where the reasoned discussion of the good was not also bounded by the inviolable symbolism of the sacred. But historical sociology also reveals that the sacred bindings of the Truth, telos, or Dao can be more or less tight. The limited activism of the Confucian ideal of heaven or *tian* (beyond the correlative cosmology of the early period) in this regard makes this one of the more interesting cases for the modern period.

I believe the above analysis of Kantian universalism and its subsequent iterations through Marxism and modernization theory reveals that reasoned analysis also requires a sacralization of the telos—here the utopia at the end of history. Faith and sacrifice remain necessary for human salvation. But the ambivalence toward sacralization and the feeble cathexis of the transcendent or utopian telos renders modern universalism a weak force compared to its predecessors.

Tianxia and Tian

In contemporary China, one of the most noted advocates of tianxia for a new global order is Zhao Tingyang. He advocates a global philosophy "through the world" rather than "of the world," a perspective that would necessarily represent only the views of a certain part of the world. This work is well covered in this volume, so I will not spend much time elaborating it. In a recent essay, Zhao gives some insights into how the tianxia worldview emerged in the transition from the Shang to the Zhou dynasty at the beginning of the first millennium BCE. A limited power that succeeded a much larger empire, the Zhou devised a worldview that could control the larger entity by making global politics a priority over the local. This was a strategic act that eventuated in a long-lasting peace governed by a global worldview harmonizing differences in the world.[12]

In Zhao's view, the contemporary extension of the tianxia model would involve a world government controlling a larger territory and military force than that controlled by the autonomous substates. These substates would be independent in most respects, except in their legitimacy and obligations, for which they would depend on the recognition of world government. Rather than being based on force and self-interest, the cultural empire would use ritual as a means to limit the self and its interests. Tianxia is a hierarchical worldview that prioritizes order over freedom, elite governance over democracy, and the superior political institution over the lower level.[13]

William Callahan, who has launched a critique of Zhao's work, suggests that his conception of tianxia as a top-down project of bringing order to a chaotic or potentially chaotic world cannot be derived from the thinkers Zhao uses, such as Laozi and Zhuangzi. In their conception of utopia, *luan* represents a form of "decentered multiordering," not the kind of chaos that requires ordering from above.[14] Additionally, Wang Mingming tells us that the cosmology of tianxia cannot be grasped in a singular fashion. Rather, it has to be understood in its two different varieties, dateable to the periods before and after the Qin unification of 221 BCE.

In the classical pre-Qin period, tianxia represented a religious cosmology in which there was no strict demarcation of the human, natural, and divine order. There was no outside to this system that encompassed the different kingdoms or *guo*. Tianxia was organized according to a hierarchical theory of concentric circles around a cosmic-moral core of closeness to a transcendent heaven. Instead of a self-other relationship, a reciprocity of ritualized relationships existed within this concentric world. Wang argues that after the imperial unification, tianxia cosmology became subordinated to the imperial state (guo) and the earlier distinction between the Zhou imperial state and the realm of tianxia began to disappear. Imperial tianxia was also deployed to create a Sinocentric order of hierarchy in the empire and superiority in dealing with foreign tributaries and vassals.

Wang Mingming describes the means by which a ritual society was created in the Zhou by the *shi* class in order to build the ideal of tianxia or the great unity (*datong*). The rituals not only prescribed proper conduct and obligations for different classes of people but also subordinated the emperor himself, as the Son of Heaven, to heaven in the name of tianxia.[15] In this ritual order, the other was not strictly separated from the self and existed in a reciprocal relationship with it. In the period of the centralized imperial state, tianxia lost its character of unity in diversity and became equated with imperial rule. Access to the transcendent power of heaven became increasingly monopolized by the imperial center, especially through its elaborate and synchronized system of official sacrifices and rituals in authorized ceremonial centers throughout the world. Wang declares, "The concept of Heaven and all under Heaven now became manifested in the idealized perfect union between Heaven and Earth and the core role of the Son of Heaven in it."[16]

To be sure, in his later essays, Zhao acknowledges that the post-Qin ideal of tianxia became distorted, but his conception continues to offer a top-down method of political ordering as the essence of the tianxia system. This formulation of tianxia universalism has a number of problems. In the first place, unlike the Kantian principle, it is a substantive conception of order with a particular role for the state and a hierarchy of social groups that is unlikely to gain universal acceptability. Moreover, do we not presuppose a highly idealized conception of humanity and a literalist reading of rhetoric if we think that ritual order alone will restrain the politically superior to act benevolently? If ritual order did work well in the Zhou dynasty, we will need to consider a multiplicity of factors including kinship ties, differentiated control of resources, and a complex balance of power.

With regard to the contemporary utilization of tianxia, it seems rather odd to be applying an ancient system quite so mechanically to an entirely changed world. Moreover, since the political system is not based upon democratically elected leaders, we don't know who will represent world government and its vast resources. Such concerns are doubtless why Callahan suspects that this formulation of universalism may represent not a posthegemonic ideal but a new hegemony for a rising China.

A feature of the tianxia order worth dwelling upon is the method by which this order is secured. In his top-down system, Zhao believes that political leadership must emanate from the highest level—the tianxia political institution—to then be transposed to the lower levels (how the top controls the bottom is not clear) and not vice versa. This is thus a descending order from all under heaven to nation-states to families. At the same time as political order or control descends, an ethical order ascends from families to states to tianxia. This results in a relationship of mutual justification but would presumably also act as the system of mutual checks.[17]

The extent to which ethical order was able to check political power, needless to say, is a highly contested issue. My own view is that ethical remonstrance in late imperial society did not achieve a great deal politically. Nonetheless, the ethical life was undoubtedly a deeply meaningful and important ideal in Chinese society, and not merely for potential sage kings. The ritual system of imperial tianxia played a significant role not only in sustaining rituals in Chinese society but also in the ethical ideals embodied in tian—if not tianxia—that represented their foundation. It returns us to the ways the transcendent—in this case, tian—may develop a symbolic, affective, and motivating force in society.

Methodologies of Transcendence and Methodological Nationalism

Even if the imperial center appropriated access to the transcendent power of heaven, the imperial ritual system sustained the heaven-ordained cosmology as a transcendent frame of reference in the imperial Chinese world. Heaven as a source of transcendent power remained very powerful in projects of self-formation and self-cultivation, from such Confucian ideals as righteous service, remonstrance, and renunciation to syncretic ideals of spiritual and bodily empowerment and ethical duty. In these modes and methods of self-cultivation and their extension to wider levels of community and universe, we might find the historical sources of a new universalism.

Much has been written about Confucianism and the transcendent authority of heaven. The personal quest to become a sage (*junzi*) and the cultivation of the heavenly endowed nature (*tianming zhixing*) were the supreme goals of the committed Confucian, particularly in late imperial times, and best exemplified in the neo-Confucian school of Wang Yangming (heart-mind school or *xinxue*). One of the most radical thinkers of this school, Li Zhi, argued that the individual was endowed by heaven with the child's mind (*tongxin*) that was intrinsically capable of discerning good from evil and thus had no need to conform to external constraints in moral cultivation.[18]

The tradition of Confucian eremitism, where the true Confucian sage rejected political power or suffered from having opposed incorrect or immoral policies, certainly retained its rhetorical power through the late imperial period, especially when shrines to notable Confucians were created in local society.[19] Indeed, many adherents of Wang Yangming or the Taizhou school of neo-Confucianism subsequently played an important part in the popular syncretic movements (*sanjiao heyi*), which arguably became a dominant form of religiosity in Republican China. Not at all intrinsically oppositional or political, the syncretic movement was deeply redemptive and appealed to a notion of transcendence that combined the Buddhist and neo-Confucian doctrines of the mind.

Among the popular societies in the early twentieth century was a largely Confucian redemptive society called the Daodehui. I have written extensively about it elsewhere, so here will only point out that in the rigorous program of self-cultivation it propagated among its followers, it sought to work out important religio-moral tensions, indeed the tensions between reason and the sacred order.[20] Followers narrated their life stories, which typically involved grasping, through entirely rational procedures, the relation between the idea of heaven-endowed destiny—tianming (which may have included having to live with a concubine or a principal wife)—and the development of the equally heaven-suffused ethical will that they referred to as *lizhi*. The records of such societies in twentieth-century China are replete with exercises that represent what Michel Foucault has called "games of truth"—the practices by which experience is rendered as truth—which, from my perspective, is the truth of one's culture or one's time. The cultivation of the self links the transcendent reflexively with the experience of the ordinary to generate meaning and resolve for action in and through the world, perhaps especially the local world.

It seems to me that, at least as an initial step, we should be thinking about such modes of commitment through transcendence when we consider the possibilities of a universalism that may emanate from Chinese historical culture. Admittedly, this does not get at how a world political order may be generated, but it may be more useful to understand how a commitment to such an order may be generated. One may well ask why we need to turn to archaic forms when there have been other, modern modes of generating commitments. Revolutionary self-formation had of course a powerful impact in twentieth-century China. Apter and Saich have explored this process in some depth and also revealed its limits consequent upon its extreme politicization.[21] Nationalism is probably the most successful modern technique of creating commitment and resolve. But it too depends on the old religious values of sacrifice and suffering.

Indeed, nationalisms also posit a point of reference that transcends locality, family, and other particularisms for the sake of the imagined community. But the nation is a severely limited expression of transcendence precisely because it is based on a tribal self/other distinction. It is exactly what we need to transcend. Moreover, even for this limited form of transcendence, the nation has mobilized a panoply of sacred imagery through which it channels the loyalty and commitment of compatriots.

The problem with nationalism lies not only in that it limits transcendence and sympathy to the national community but also in that it subordinates or devalues the links between individuals and other expressions of community below and above the nation.[22] A program of shared sovereignty—a new universalism—can gain meaning only if it develops from the ground up, only if it can relate everyday experiences of the good to the universal. The local and the transcendent are mutually vindicating. In the remainder of this chapter, I want to propose sustainability as the transcendent goal of our time. I also want to see how the environmental program and movement in China may be able to incorporate such a long-term salvationist agenda by touching upon the discourses and practices that are shaping it.

Sustainability and Transcendence

The greatest obstacles facing the elevation of sustainability to a transcendent level are perhaps the imperative felt by the national populace and their leaders not to sacrifice national interests and the untrammeled power of capitalist consumption. The post–Cold War realignment mentioned above has been particularly conducive to these developments. The process of overcoming such resistance is, of course, multipronged, but it will require bodies of committed activists in civil society and state attuned to the urgency of planetary sustainability. Moreover, the methods used by such bodies are and will have to be both rational and symbolic. As we know, environmental organizations across the world, from the radical Earth First! to the Intergovernmental Panel on Climate Change, have been increasingly active. Intellectually and academically, the ground has been laid globally by the spread of the general field known as environmental ethics over the last thirty years. Movements following E. F. Schumacher's *Small Is Beautiful*, such as deep ecology, Buddhist economics, animal ethics, and ecofeminism, among others, have already established the possibility of sacralizing nature, or at least sacralizing wilderness.

Deep ecology is a philosophical and social movement that seeks to deprivilege humans as the center of the planet because this has led to untold destruction and mass extinction. The movement advocates a holistic philosophy that takes nonhuman life as an intrinsic value and seeks a better quality of life grounded by values rather than goods. This holism is particularly sympathetic to Asian and pantheistic wisdom traditions such as Daoism, Buddhism, and Native American religions. They also seek to affect policies and undertake activities that will achieve their goals. Roger Gottlieb, a deep ecology philosopher, has underscored the mystical and transcendent basis of "earth and all its life as an ultimate truth" in the movement against the collective violence toward the environment that is destroying the support systems of human life.[23]

He speaks of a "passionate, spiritually oriented, mystical communion with the earth and its many beings, a recognition of kinship with those beings that no more requires philosophical justification than does the connection we feel with our parents, pets, or lovers. As such, Deep Ecology is a spiritual philosophy; and the deepest experiences that animate its adherents are profoundly mystical." At the same time, Gottlieb wants to balance this mystical core with a less escapist and a more contemporary and rational view of social justice. He concludes, "And so, paradoxically, the wisdom of a mystical Deep Ecology can augment the powers and promises of the secular drive for just social transformation."[24]

Certainly, the natural world in imperial China was not perceived as something that needed to be subdued by willpower or force. Rather, according to Needham, nature represented perhaps the greatest of all living organisms, and its governing principles had to be well understood so that human life could live in harmony with it.[25] The process of self-formation was inseparable from nature. The indivisibility between inner self and outer nature in a neo-Confucianism highly influenced by Daoism and Buddhism is the condition for the quest of the true nature within that represents the elusive heavenly principles (*tianli*).[26] From the Daoists to the neo-Confucians (xinxue) right up to the adherents of the syncretic Morality Society, the practices of self-cultivation represented a turning back toward one's original nature that was simultaneously a move toward the quiet and pure nature of heaven and earth. Through this process, practitioners were able to fully develop their original nature while realizing the metaphysical character of the Dao.[27]

In modern Asia, however, since we have been obsessed with pursuing the modern goal of controlling and manipulating nature, our recent history has not provided many helpful examples. Elsewhere, I have tried to look at Rabindranath Tagore's efforts to invoke what we today call sustainability—but was called "pantheistic philosophy" in the 1920s—as a transcendent ideal for the world. In his critique of nationalism and instrumental modernity, Tagore sought to realize an alternative cosmopolitanism drawn from Asian traditions and embodied in Visva-Bharati (or the World in One Nest) University at Santiniketan. In the realm of Indian history, he was drawn to alternative popular traditions identified with medieval bhakti seers and sages such as Kabir, Nanak, and Dadu—the propulsive motor of transcendence—who broke through barriers of social and religious exclusiveness and brought together communities based on spiritual reform.[28]

What was unique and worthy of further inquiry in Tagore's effort was his approach to linking locality and local identity with the transcendent telos. It was a form of rooted cosmopolitanism that was expressed in the spirit of Santiniketan. While education had to be undertaken in a universal framework of understanding, the local represented the means of this understanding. The educational projects in Santiniketan celebrated different world traditions, but students also engaged with their environment and traditions. Tagore invented secular festivals for the celebration of the different seasons in the region and brought together the urban and the rural during harvest festivals. He started cooperative movements among the tribal and rural folk, seeking to educate them in health, agriculture, savings, and other modern ways of survival while encouraging the maximum preservation of their own local culture.[29]

I believe we can find similar efforts in the grassroots movements that were begun in Republican China by Liang Shuming, Tao Xingzhi, the Mass Education Movement of Jimmy Yen, the folklore movement of Zhou Zuoren and Gu Jiegang, and the early work of Fei Xiaotong and others. I have not yet had the opportunity to research their efforts in significant detail, but one area we need to explore is their connective methodology. How was the self to articulate the local, national, and the civilizational transcendent? How was the self to manage the inevitable tensions among these scales, but especially between the local and transcendent on the one hand and the national on the other? Moreover, in what ways were different civilizational traditions expected to interact to form the alternative global one?[30]

In today's China there have been some remarkable developments in the environmental movement. According to Guobin Yang, the recently mushrooming Chinese environmental nongovernmental organizations (NGOs) use web platforms for groups to self-organize and Twitter for flash mobilization. These civic forms are reaching a threshold where their voices are beginning to be heard by governments and even at a global level. Among all developing countries, the Chinese government's efforts in environmental education are probably the greatest. In 2007, President Hu Jintao coined the phrase "ecological civilization," through which he sought to replace economic construction as the core of development with sustainable development that must include a balanced relationship between man and nature. Together with many developed countries, in 2003, China mandated environmental education in the public schools. It has encouraged many local governments and groups to produce texts and programs for schoolchildren.

Yet there are many obstacles to the development of environmental education as a transformative force in society. The courses tend to be formalistic, and the seriousness of the enterprise may be undermined by the failure to include environmental education in the core official examinations. More generally, children as much as adults are relatively and increasingly alienated from the natural environment in their everyday activities. They cannot yet see how conserving the environment can contribute to their future careers. It is not producing a transformed self.

From an academic and research perspective, Zhang Yulin reveals the sorry neglect of environmental problems in the study of rural China. For instance, of the 747 articles carried by the flagship journal *Observations of Chinese Villages* (中国农村观察) between 1994 and 2007, only eleven dealt with environmental issues. Zhang also laments that the great leader of Chinese rural studies, Fei Xiaotong, who sounded the clarion call for rural recovery early in his 1930s studies of the intimate relations of the Chinese peasant and the soil (*xiangtu Zhongguo*), neglected or ignored the environmental effects of rural industrialization until very late in his life. Zhang believes that the drive to increase rural production at all costs and the nexus of interests pushing commercial technologies of intensive agriculture are responsible for much of the degradation of the environment as well as the rural self-governing and cooperative institutions. This drive may have also influenced the academic neglect of these issues.[31]

In more recent years, the new rural reconstruction movement (*xin xiangcun jianshe yundong*), led by figures like Wen Tiejun, Cao Jingqing, and Li Changping, has been more gradually successful in developing cooperative, protective, and integrated movements that do not focus only on economic or technical solutions for rural society. Moreover, while these leaders have clearly linked their movement to the wider global problems of sustainability, they also see themselves as inheritors of a century-long quest to revive the values of human relations and relations with nature that were hallmarks of Chinese rural society and culture.[32]

Over the last twenty years, environmental NGOs (ENGOs), as well as informal groups and movements, have mushroomed across the country. Indeed, Yang Guobin and Craig Calhoun have dubbed this activism the "green public sphere" in China.[33] According to the government-affiliated All China Environment Federation, in 2008, there were 2,768 ENGOs (employing 224,000 staff), which rose to almost 8,000 in 2013. Many thousands of others are not formally registered as ENGOs. Their role has been enhanced by recognition at higher levels of government of the environmental services they can render, such as enhancing environmental consciousness among the public and mobilizing for projects like reforestation. More importantly, they are able to serve as watchdogs to expose violations or nonimplementation of environmental laws. Of course, as civic organizations in the PRC, they occupy a vulnerable status; most are careful not to oppose state policies but serve rather in a vital supplementary role as pressure groups, guardians, and helpers for the victimized.[34]

The profile of activists and activities of the ENGOs suggests an orientation that transcends consumerist and materialist approaches to life, at least among the youth for the time being. Bao Maohong notes that 80 percent of the staff of the registered ENGOs is under thirty, and although over half of them have college degrees, they are motivated by their mission rather than their rather paltry, if any, salaries. Greenspeak tends to promote a new moral-spiritual/religious vision and practices and promotes volunteerism and civil participation in opposition to materialist and consumerist practices. The All China Environment Federation notes that 70 percent of the public it surveyed recognized and supported the activities of the ENGOs.[35]

The urgency to change environmental behavior has encouraged some important experiments in environmental education among grassroots environmental NGOs, especially in Yunnan, a province so rich in biodiversity that it is called the "cradle of NGOs." Robert Erfid's study of NGOs working in the Naxi region of Lijiang, and particularly Lashihai, shows how some of these small, shoestring-budget NGOs committed to environmental education have sought not merely to tailor environmental learning to local circumstances but also to engage children in a practical, hands-on education about the environment. For instance, the Yunnan Eco-Network and its director, Chen Yongsong, work with school-age youth to protect their local environment by having them visit forests, learn about and remove invasive plants, clear trash and create school gardens, and so on.[36]

Erfid emphasizes how environmental stewardship and sustainable behavior have to be learned practically, and that education must also cultivate the motivation to engage in sustainable behavior. The literature on this kind of motivation emphasizes personal understanding of nature—the process of self-formation—rooted in experiences of the nonhuman world. Historically the Naxi Dongba religion revered nature. Water and forests were sacred, and this permitted the people to manage these communal resources sustainably. Village regulations were set in stone stelae and backed by threats of divine and communal punishment for activities such as unnecessary deforestation and overharvesting wild game. Some of these NGOs have clearly learned the lesson of the importance of cultivating identification with the environment. They have turned to education about the locality—and not the environment in the abstract—through materials, *xiangtu jiaocai*, based on specific cultural and ecological characteristics of a place or region in order to foster a sense of roots and a "spiritual home" for youth.[37]

What we see happening in the corners of China is perhaps not very different from what is happening across many other parts of the world. It is a sign that sustainability is an emergent ideal, a new type of transcendence and sacrality with the capacity to motivate and mobilize individuals and groups. But even if it is a strong emergent ideal, it does not possess the institutional power or coherence to be able to share sovereign power in the near future. What it is capable of effecting at the moment is a more hidden or subterranean cultural process, referred to above as "the games of truth," whereby the individual is disposed to convert his or her personal experience into the truth and to read the truth into personal experience. This is a process that may well be indexed by such ordinary cultural events as the popularity of the film *Avatar*, which help to cathect the protection of nature with symbolic and aesthetic affect.

Conclusion

I have tried to suggest that historical universalisms may be useful for modern universalism in two ways. The wholesale adoption of archaic orders or their unmodified principles is unacceptably idealist and ahistorical. But some of their substantive goals, for instance, restoring the indivisibility of self and nature, could well serve as correctives to our condition. Also, we have much to learn from historical methodologies of reflexive linkages between the self and the transcendent in late imperial China. These lessons could make up for deficiencies in modern universalisms.

Proponents of modern universalisms have tended to lack confidence in investing the transcendent or utopian truths they propose with sacred authority. Their hesitation doubtless has good reasons, as we may see from the rampaging power of extreme nationalisms such as Nazism, built on sacralized emotions and aesthetics of hate triumphant over reason. Yet no movement of radical social change has succeeded without a compelling symbology and affective power. The principal question facing analysts of all forms of transcendent authority has to do with the interaction of the sacred and reason.

The question has been tackled by several modern thinkers, including Jürgen Habermas and Paul Ricoeur, but they of course deal almost entirely with the Abrahamic traditions and their legacies. Thus Ricoeur wants to restore God as a figure of hope, particularly in its preverbal manifestation before it belongs to the revealed word or Proclamation (e.g., in Genesis 1).[38] I see Ricoeur as arguing that the rational is itself dependent upon but also necessary for the symbolism of the sacred. The burden upon contemporary interpreters and philosophers of religion is to rationally explicate such figures of hope as a response to the avowal of radical evil. For Habermas, it is the persuasive force of communicative action that has to mediate the binding norms of ritual or sacred obligation (e.g., to the U.S. Constitution), which, of course, presupposes democracy.

In our own brief discussion of tian, we may find other ways and means of relating sacred authority to rational ends. Whether by the laywomen of the Morality Society or the Confucian sage, tian is viewed as the highest moral judge and the source of the moral mission for humans. Yet heaven is not anthropomorphic like God, and failure to follow its path does not result in punishment immediately or in the afterlife. Sor Hoon Tan suggests that the question of efficacy of tian in Confucian thought is ambiguous and has yielded several contradictory positions.[39] While staying with the insight of ambiguity and the nondeterministic nature of heaven's prescriptions, I believe we should also explore the role of the techniques and practices of self-cultivation in sustaining the ethical authority of heaven. As transcendence, heaven was tapped as a figureless figure of hope for a variety of ethical and empowering personal projects that validated this very transcendence.

Although to be sure, heaven's will was policed by the imperial state, the ambiguity of interpreting its personal message and the absence of an authoritative clergy also subjected this message to rational deliberation and empirical persuasion. By the Republican period, even the three sacred followings (*sangang*) for women could be interpreted with relative flexibility. Indeed, one might say that flexibility for self-empowerment undergirded tian's symbolic power. If tian could have such staying power for self-formation in the Republic, might it not again possess that power today? The dedicated ENGO activist may not be entirely different from a Confucian seeker of earlier times. If she or he could access the moral authority possessed by tian for personal empowerment and ethical commitment, China and the world might be the better for it. At any rate, contemporary universalist movements could well take a leaf from the methodology by which late imperial Chinese techniques of the self were empowered by the universal.

As for the tasks before us, not much mystery remains. The machineries of national governments need to be persuaded to devote as much time and importance to planetary sustainability in their educational and pedagogic projects as they do to national history and national identity building. This, in my view, is the challenge for the transcendence prophets of our time.

NOTES

1. A longer and expanded version (that includes India and other parts of Asia) of this paper can be found as chapter 1 of my book, Duara, *The Crisis of Global Modernity*.

2. Contemporary theorists have sought to distinguish cosmopolitanism from universalism because the latter is believed to presuppose a religious, particularly Christian, conception of common belonging of all as creations of God. Cosmopolitanism is regarded as less impositional (or universal from a particular perspective) because it is based on practices of common living and belonging in the world. Yet cosmopolitanism is also founded on a certain conception of universalism that denies other expressions. In a way, Kant's tendency not to differentiate the two sharply reflects the reality of their interpenetration. See Chernilo, "Cosmopolitanism and the Question of Universalism"; and Aguiar, "Cosmopolitanism."

3. O'Neill, *Constructions of Reason*, 13–23.

4. Note that this is the negative image of the positive Christian doctrine "Do unto others as you would have others do unto you"; that is, don't do anything that you would not want to happen to you or others.

5. O'Neill, *Constructions of Reason*, 26.

6. Palmquist, "'The Kingdom of God Is at Hand!,'" 434.

7. Kant, "Idea for a Universal History," 11.

8. Kant, "Idea for a Universal History," 25, emphasis added.

9. Kant, "Idea for a Universal History," 14.

10. Axial civilizations arose in Eurasia around the sixth century BCE, in which a split developed between transcendence and the mundane. The goals of these civilizations were embedded in a divine transcendent realm (tian in China) discontinuous with the human world. While no human—including the state—could fully realize its goals or will in this world, humans were expected to aspire toward their realization. Axial civilizations represented a new type of reflexivity that gave expression to a vision of the world that could be different from the here and now. As the vision became institutionalized, the transcendent realm became a new ontological basis for universal ethics in these religions. This included new ways of organizing society and demands for self-sacrifice.

11. According to Habermas, each Axial philosophy, including what Weber described as the "intellectual religions of the East," found its origins in both religion and philosophy. Each system of thought sought to take a synoptic view of the world as a whole from a transcendent point of view and to distinguish the flood of phenomena from the underlying essences. Moreover, reflection on the place of the individual gave rise to a new awareness of historical contingency and the responsibility of the acting subject. See Habermas, *Time of Transitions*, 18.

12. Zhao Tingyang, "A Political World Philosophy," 6–8. See also Zhao Tingyang, "Rethinking Empire."

13. Zhao Tingyang, "A Political World Philosophy," 11–18.

14. Callahan, "Chinese Visions of World Order." For the critique, see 753–756.

15. Wang Mingming, "'All under Heaven,'" 343–347. According to Sor Hoon Tan, with the Zhou revolution heaven or tian became more than the highest religious authority that it had been in the Shang dynasty; it developed a strong moral ideal and became the new basis of political legitimacy. See Tan, "Secular Religiosity in Chinese Politics," 116.

16. Wang Mingming, "'All under Heaven,'" 351–354.

17. Zhao Tingyang, "Rethinking Empire," 33.

18. Kim, "Political Unity in Neo-Confucianism," 246–263.

19. Dimberg, *The Sage and Society*.

20. See Duara, *Sovereignty and Authenticity*, ch. 4.

21. Apter and Saich, *Revolutionary Discourse in Mao's Republic*. See also Anagnost, *National Past-Times*.

22. Approaches that unconsciously adopt the nation-state's claims in history or in contemporary space adopt what has been dubbed methodological nationalism.

23. Gottlieb, "The Transcendence of Justice," 155.

24. Gottlieb, "The Transcendence of Justice," 165.

25. Needham, *Science and Civilization in China*, 242–244, 281. Needham also finds parallels with Indian thought on the "organism of the universe" (281 note c) and with the ideas of Whitehead (454); see also vol. 3 (1959), 152–153, 163–165, 196.

26. Zhu Renqiu, "The Formation, Development, and Evolution of Neo-Confucianism," 335.

27. Xiang Shiling, "A Study on the Theory of 'Returning to the Original,'" passim.

28. See Uma Das Gupta, *The Oxford India Tagore*, 172. For more extensive discussion of Tagore, see Gupta, ch. 7.

29. Sen, "Crisis in Civilization, and a Poet's Alternatives."

30. An Yanming, "Liang Shuming," 151–155.

31. Zhang Yulin, "'Tiandi yibian' yu Zhongguo nongcun yanjiu," 1–17. For his earlier views, see Fei Xiaotong, "Xiangtu bense," 1–7.

32. Day, "The End of the Peasant?," esp. 55–62.

33. Yang and Calhoun, "Media, Civil Society and the Rise of a Green Public Sphere in China," 211–234.

34. Bao Maohong, "Environmental NGOs," 1–16; "China's ENGOs Increase."

35. Bao Maohong, "Environmental NGOs," 3–8.

36. Erfid, "Learning by Heart."

37. Erfid, "Learning by Heart." See also Erfid, "Learning the Land beneath Our Feet."

38. Ricoeur reads Genesis 1 as a nonanthropocentric ordering of all life-forms into a cosmic biosphere that precedes and envelops the salvation history account. He argues that the Bible is a palimpsest of various modes of discourse. Ricoeur, *Figuring the Sacred*, 77; see also "Part III, The Bible and Genre: The Polyphony of Biblical Discourses," 129–180.

39. See Tan, "Secular Religiosity in Chinese Politics." The ambiguity of tian's efficacy is partly a result of its nonanthropomorphic character, being unable to love or punish, and is thus similar to religions with an empty transcendence.

PART II. TIANXIA,

CROSS-CULTURAL LEARNING,

AND COSMOPOLITANISM

*

4

THE MORAL VISION IN KANG YOUWEI'S
BOOK OF THE GREAT COMMUNITY
Ban Wang

*

Political Realism

In the world today, talk of global interdependence belies increasing divides between nation-states and people. Digital intimacy, standardized lifestyles and tastes, swift flows of information, massive immigration, and growing commercial ties between countries are fully matched by divisive nationalism, protectionism, identity politics, religious fundamentalism, and geopolitical rivalry. Torn between cooperation and self-interest, universal norms and particularistic attachment, how can an individual relate to a different culture? How can a group interact, communicate, and coexist productively with other groups? Since the advent of the Westphalian system, attempts to address these questions have articulated different visions of the world. Cosmopolitanism, a belief in humans' capacity to coexist and work together worldwide, is the most prominent of these attempts. In the aftermath of the Cold War, political life indulged in a cosmopolitan euphoria, as old and new economies intersected, markets expanded, goods circulated, and people immigrated across borders. But the euphoria quickly regressed to the particularistic principle of nationalism. The nationalistic turn claims that "a person's most fundamental political obligations are interconnected with the form of social life of which he is part, and which his political structures are obliged to protect."[1] In this situation, the cosmopolitan dream, by which a person can be both a citizen and a human person, has receded into the background.

Conventional political theory in the West has been skeptical of cosmopolitanism as a principle for international order. Although Immanuel Kant claimed that different societies might interact and communicate, the mainstream of political philosophy has centered on the sovereign nation-state as the fundamental unit in the international system. This prompted Martin Wight to pronounce that international theory has no place for the idea of world community and that "a tradition of speculation about the society of states, or the family of nations, or the international community . . . does not, at first sight, exist."[2] Instead of being construed in a language of law and morality and based on humans' rational capacity to coexist on the planet, the interstate space has been viewed as a field of struggle for rivalry and domination. The sovereign state as the principal power player in the Hobbesian struggle has preoccupied political thinkers and suppressed alternative world visions. In the wake of the events of September 11, 2001, John Mearsheimer has argued strongly about the great powers' tendency to act aggressively toward each other in the struggle for hegemony. Dismantling the "illusions" of a global trade network and peaceful social interaction, he insists on the perpetual power struggle between nations. The accelerated pace of economic globalization, he suggests, has misled many to believe that peace and communication among the great powers would be around the corner, and that the horizon of a family of nations was tantalizingly in sight. Citing expanded military bases and an arms buildup, analyzing how economic power translates into military might, and proclaiming the fiercely competitive nature of the powerful states, Mearsheimer asserts the perennial theme of political realism: "International politics has always been a ruthless and dangerous business." Great powers always fear each other and aggressively compete for hegemony. The top priority of each state is to maximize its share of world power at the expense of other states.[3] Confirming this perpetual struggle at the cultural level, Samuel Huntington, in his influential *Clash of Civilizations and the Remaking of the World Order*, depicts the conflict of civilizational and cultural identities. Relations among nations and peoples, in his view, always hinge on a rigid definition of who "we" are as opposed to "them": "People define themselves by reference to ancestry, religion, language, history, values, customs, and institutions. They identify with cultural groups: tribes, ethnic groups, religious communities, nations and at the broadest level, civilizations."[4]

The primacy accorded to particularistic loyalty to the state, nation, and cultural patrimony has reinforced the experience of political separateness, moral tension, racial divides, and geographical isolation. All these run counter to the cosmopolitan vision of an interconnected world.

Alternatives to political realism, however, have always been at work in the East and the West. Rather than aggressive power competition and paranoiac divides, thinkers have envisioned international relations based on rationality and moral improvement. Sensitive to the increasingly integrated world of the eighteenth century marked by accelerated interaction of people in travel and commerce, Immanuel Kant realized that human beings could not remain in their separate spheres of identification and value, but had to learn to live and work together with other cultures. This cosmopolitanism derived from a belief in humans as "self-developing and self-directing beings with the possibility of transforming existing relations of intersocial estrangement into relations of familiarity."[5] Now, this morally informed vision of relations between nations and individuals provides a comparative perspective for appreciating similar world visions of Chinese thinkers. Although the nineteenth-century encounter with the international system dealt a traumatic blow to the traditional Chinese worldview, modern Chinese reformers and thinkers have looked for a politically viable world by revitalizing the ancient tradition.

Inherent in the Confucian tradition, the notion of the whole world under heaven (tianxia) expresses an outlook beyond local community and ethnic lineage—a unified worldview inclusive of different cultural and ethnic groups. Unlike the menacing spectacle of national-cultural chauvinism attached to China today, Confucian universalism stems from a scheme of a ritualistic empire and does not accord with the modern empire marked by power alliances, strategic balance, and pursuits of hegemony. As Joseph Levenson noted, Confucian literati accepted cultural differences as the way of the world. Although they distinguished between the civilized and barbarians, they were aware that "the barbarians are always with us." It is inadequate to construe the Confucian world vision as cultural hegemony. For Levenson, it was "a criterion, a standpoint, not a point of departure." Chinese left home to travel and settle in other countries, but "not one had any Confucian pretensions to be bearing out a Word," as did Christian missionaries.[6] At the time when thinkers like Kang Youwei began writing about a different prospect of world order, however, Confucian universalism was challenged and threatened by Western powers.

This chapter considers how Kang Youwei revised the Confucian moral tradition in conjunction with Kant's notion of aesthetic humanity. In Kang's utopian imagination, we may discern a moral vision alternative to realpolitik in international relations.

Aesthetic Humanity and the Great World Community

Both Kant and Kang Youwei believed that morality and aesthetics could build bridges among peoples and nations. Kant's aesthetic notion of *sensus communis* resonates dramatically with Kang Youwei's vision of world community. While Kant is keen on generating a cosmopolitan ethic, Kang Youwei explores how cross-cultural sympathy and learning could be attained by way of the aesthetic.

The rise of aesthetic discourse in Europe was concomitant with the disintegration of the religious, unitary order. European civil societies emerged from the ruins of the theocratic regime, but modern society was constantly torn asunder by rival interests and agendas. Divided feelings and conflicted pursuits plagued individuals and states. Kant diagnosed this fragmentation and disharmony with a blanket term, "unsocial sociability."[7] The term refers to the individual's paradoxical tendency to associate with others socially while simultaneously competing with them in the pursuit of private interest. Social members are "bound together with mutual oppositions that threaten to break up the society," and each individual pursues private agendas detrimental to others.[8] Expounding this term in the famous essay, "Idea for a Universal History with a Cosmopolitan Purpose," Kant extends this domestic, interpersonal antagonism to that of mutually opposed, self-serving states in the international arena. Although in Kant's day increasing global commerce and transportation facilitated interaction among peoples and a sense of global connection was in the air, the world was a theater of war where each state was at another's throat. The aesthetic, which envisaged a shared plane of sense and sensibility over and above economic interest and geopolitical conflict, seems to offer an attractive solution to bridge the constant schism. Aesthetic experience in culture and the arts gestures toward a vision of rationally conceived society, where intersubjective feelings resonate and a genuinely human community seems tantalizingly close. Kant writes, "Beautiful arts and sciences, which by means of a universally communicable pleasure and an elegance and refinement make human beings, if not morally better, at least better mannered for society, very much reduce the tyranny of sensible tendencies, and prepare humans for a sovereignty in which reason alone shall have Power."[9] The aesthetic is a gateway of sense and sensibility, leading to reason and understanding. Sunk in their private sphere and sensuous needs ("the tyranny of sensible tendencies") and engrossed in survival, humans are bound to antagonize each other like barbarians. The aesthetic elevates humans to a higher level of culture and morality. Judgments of cultivated behavior and beautiful taste point to a common ground of social interactivity over conflict, a platform informed by the idea of sensus communis. Rather than crudely sensuous life governed by primal instincts, sensus communis claims a moral, rational capacity that transcends one's private, particular sphere by putting oneself "into the position of everyone else, merely by abstracting from the limitations that contingently attach to our judging." To extend empathy requires a cosmopolitan mind to set the individual "apart from the subjective private conditions of the judgment, within which so many others are as if bracketed" and to reflect on his own judgment "from a universal standpoint" by putting himself into others. The enlarged mind will suspend the individual's narrow-mindedness and rise above subjective conditions.[10]

Aesthetic experience contains pleasure common and sharable among all humans, forging affective and imaginary bonds conducive to reciprocity and sociality. By means of aesthetic communication, civil society is now reimagined as a public space for experiencing shared pleasure in arts and ritual activities rather than fraught with rivalry and conflict. A human being with aesthetic taste is sociable rather than self-indulgent, outgoing rather than inner directed.

Thus, the public sphere is pitted against the private sphere, the social against asocial behavior, broad-mindedness against the egotism of "unsocial sociability." Aesthetic experience delivers humans from this entrapment and enables us to "realize the ideal world of moral freedom in the given world of egoistic strife and unsociability through culture"; it minimizes "our natural bondage" by promoting humans' potential for moral improvement and purposeful action.[11]

Kant's idea of sensus communis, as Terry Eagleton says, proffers a comforting fiction of the universal embedded in humanity's aesthetic existence. Taste must be universal against private and self-interest: it "cannot spring from the object which is purely contingent, or from any particular desire or interest of the subject, which is similarly parochial." Since the rational is universal and cognition is supposed to be common to all individuals, the sharable pleasure we take in the aesthetic is "the knowledge that our very structural constitution as human subjects predisposes us to mutual harmony." To be human is to engage in the aesthetic activity of shared pleasure and to be ready to share with others the beautiful illusion of a consensus of feeling and understanding. Each of us partakes of this pleasurable communication, mesmerized by the prospect of "a universal solidarity beyond all vulgar utility." By means of sensus communis Kant offers a symbolic solution to the fragmentary, divisive jumble of prejudices, custom, and parochial habits of mind.[12]

Sankar Muthu elaborates on cosmopolitan implications of the aesthetic. Despite the troubling tendency toward unsocial sociability in market society, the impulse toward cultured interaction in Kant's time was becoming accepted by individuals raised above the level of survival and labor. The widespread communication practices in the eighteenth century—in salons, public places, and the arts—inspired Kant with a notion of aesthetic humanity. By engaging in arts and literature, by rising over and above the interests of self-preservation and pressures of survival, individuals are able to share pleasures and communicate judgment and taste, leading to a community of empathy and emotional resonance. From a broad humanistic perspective, Kant states, "Humanity [*Humanität*] means both the universal feelings of sympathy, and the ability to engage universally in very intimate communication. When these two qualities are combined, they constitute the sociality that befits [our] humanity [*Menschheit*] and distinguishes it from the limitations [characteristic] of animals."[13] The aesthetic of humanity hinges on a broader idea of human beings as cultural agents, figures who wield aesthetic power and remake the existing world in pursuit of political freedom. Endowed with the ability to inscribe the world with human values and to transform our natural drives, the cultural agent humanizes the world with aesthetic forms.[14] The world of humanity, rising above creaturely needs and material wants, also appeals to humans' aesthetic sensibility.

Rather than being a prisoner in a particular culture, the cultural agent connects the universal and the particular. The idea that all people are equally endowed with the ability to reflect on and improve their own inherited situation honors the commonality of humans. Although agents cannot choose where they are born and their trajectories bear particular footprints of circumstances, customs, and tradition, they can choose to reflect upon and transform the world they are born into—therein lies agential aesthetic humanity. By this logic, the cultural agent should grant equal respect to all historical traditions and achievements as ongoing products derived from rationality and creativity common to all. This respect for the particular as derived from the universal may lead to a mutual appreciation of a particular aesthetic taste bound up with a specific historical tradition.

If Kantian cosmopolitanism resorts to universal reason by way of the aesthetic, Kang Youwei retrieved a Confucian language of heaven to assert a universal logic for aesthetic communication. Kang Youwei's thinking responded to the collapse of tianxia's world order under the assaults of the international system. Literally meaning "all under heaven," tianxia refers to a moral and political order sustained not by the legal system and coercion but by ritual, music, moral norms, administrative hierarchy, and lack of differentiation among ethnic groups. The concept denotes a sphere of culture and value—a set of ideals and conduct to be internalized by all individuals and groups. In opposition to the Warring States in ancient China and the Westphalian system of nation-states, tianxia has resurfaced at the center of debate as a radically different vision. Rooted in Confucianism and the collective unconscious, tianxia, as Joseph Levenson has said, describes a world "whose values were Value, whose civilization was Civilization, a transnational antithesis to barbarism."[15] In the late nineteenth century, as colonialism and imperialism dragged China into the forest of nations, Kang realized that the ancient order was being cut down to size. In his *Book of the Great Community* (*Datong shu*), Kang notes that as "the globe is completely known, what was called the central empire [Zhongguo] and adjacent territories are but one corner of Asia and one-eightieth of the world."[16] Western encroachment broke up the moral fabric that maintained traditional communities, and the Central Kingdom was in tatters. Relations between China and other regions were no longer based on ritual, tributary networks, commerce, and family ties under the aegis of Confucianism, but were increasingly driven by ruthless competition, conflict, and domination. Aggressive realpolitik and the economic zero-sum game penetrated Chinese intellectuals' worldviews.

Kang Youwei's *Datong shu* assaults the reader with an excruciating list of miseries of the world: class oppression, national strife, civil conflict, natural disaster, diseases, bodies in pain, gender and race inequality, the lack of independence, and ignorance. Shortly after China's conflict with France in 1885, Kang fled Canton and returned to his native village to live a life of study and reflection in his ancestral house, Abiding Fragrance. Everyday when he stepped out of his quiet study, he was overwhelmed not only by the suffering and bickering of his neighbors but also the news of bloody interstate wars around the world and particularly in East Asia: "All the people of the whole world are but grieving and miserable people, and all the living beings of the whole world are but murdered beings. The azure heaven and the round Earth are nothing but a great slaughter yard, a great prison" (2–3; 63).

In response to the bloody conflict, Kang Youwei attempted to restore certain aspects of the Confucian worldview. As pragmatic reformers, Kang and his student, Liang Qichao, engaged with the Qing government and devised strategies to implement modern reforms in politics, education, economy, and social and gender relations. But Kang Youwei gave priority to moral and aesthetic problems in China's encounter with the world. He raised the question of how the sensibility of one person can and must connect and resonate with another in a world divided by boundaries and conflict, and how a far-reaching moral sensibility can be articulated. In a world of suffering and conflict, how can moral sensibility enable one individual to commiserate with another? What forms of aesthetic culture might foster this?

Like Kant, Kang Youwei thought of the world in terms of morality and the aesthetic. To him the aesthetic consists in learning from and immersing oneself in diverse cultures in a way that involves all senses and the soul. Learning allows us to have intimate access to others and fosters sympathy and shared appreciation of pluralistic cultural forms. The way to a united world is through aesthetic enjoyment and circulation of cultural traditions across national boundaries:

> I have drunk deeply of the intellectual heritage of ancient India, Greece, Persia, and Rome, and of modern England, France, Germany, and America. I have pillowed my head upon them, and my soul in dreams has fathomed them. With the wise old men, noted scholars, famous figures, and beautiful women of all countries I have likewise often joined hands, we have sat on mats side by side, sleeves touching, sharing our meal, and I have grown to love them. Each day I have been offered and have made use of the dwellings, clothing, food, boats, vehicles, utensils, government, education, arts, and music of a myriad of countries, and these have stimulated my mind and enriched my spirit. Do they progress? Then we all progress with them. Are they happy? Then we are happy with them. Do they suffer? Then we suffer with them. It is as if we were all parts of an electrical force, which interconnects all things, or partook of the pure essence that encompasses all things.[17]

This passage presents a vignette of long-distance learning and exchange by way of far-reaching sense and sensibility. The aesthetic subject, broad-minded and sensitive, embraces a spectrum of cultural heritages across the globe. Appealing to the senses as well as the intellect, the approach to foreign cultures involves the five senses, the imagination, and the soul. The lessons and wisdom are highly revered—the best that has been written and thought and preserved by "old men, noted scholars, famous figures, and beautiful women." "Beautiful women" serves as an erotic-aesthetic metaphor for cross-cultural experience. Rather than being dry and pedantic, learning is pleasurable through feminine charms and fleshed out in intimate experiences of touching, joining hands, sharing meals. Moving from body to soul, the aesthetic experience expands the spirit and enhances shared happiness. The parallel progress between "they" and "we" implies a common path of civilizational advancement, projecting a normative standard for assessing each particular culture. Cross-cultural learning is an educational as well as a maturing project, a process akin to the program of aesthetically inspired *Bildung* in German romanticism. While Bildung cultivates civic virtue purged of unsocial sociability, Kang's moral and aesthetic progress aims at the cultivation of noble virtue that may lead to intercultural understanding and sympathy.

Kang links cross-cultural reciprocity to the Confucian idea of *qi* (气), which can be translated as "electric energy or forces." Running through all boundaries of race, states, and regions, qi captures an embracing process and a cosmic substance, at once physical, biological, spiritual, and moral. Permeating heaven and earth, it flows through humans, animals, and plants. Akin to the concept of ether, qi drives and facilitates our perception and sympathy with everything and everybody else. Kang writes, "I have a body, then I share with coexisting bodies that which permeates the air of heaven, permeates the matter of earth, permeates the breath of man" (3–4; 64). Rather than a product of a particular tradition, the qi-filled body is heaven endowed under the rubric of *tianren* (天人) and is equivalent to another body, be it man or woman, high or low class. In the *Datong shu*, this heaven-endowed body functions as an equalizing principle and a source of critique of the arbitrary divisions of gender, class, ethnicity, and nation-state.

Rather than mere disembodied truth, qi is bodied forth by perception, sympathy, and benevolent social feelings under the sign of *ren* (benevolence, compassion, love). Ren describes an ethical sensibility and compassionate connectedness with others, regardless of their station and identity. In this sense, qi-based perception and compassion is as aesthetic as it is moral.

Datong shu opens with "Entering the World and Observing the Sufferings of Multitudes." Observing goes with empathy and compassion in the Bodhisattva of Compassion, invoking the mind's capacity to empathize with human suffering. Kang attributes the lack of sympathy to the absence of a far-reaching sensibility. In childhood Kang read about the well-known massacres in the Warring States period and the burning of France's city of Sedan by Bismarck. But he remained tone-deaf to those horrendous events. Treating this indifference as the lack of qi, he attributes it to the inadequacy of humanity, since all human beings under heaven are brothers of "the same womb" (5; 65). Humanity consists in sensitive awareness and outreaching compassion. "Hence, if men sever what constitutes their compassionate love, their human-ness will be annihilated, and return to barbarism" (5; 64).

The principle of benevolence is key to Confucian morality embodied by the Kingly Way (*wangdao* 王道). As a foundation for benevolent governance, the

Kingly Way denotes a capacious sensitivity to people's pain and suffering, well articulated by the Mencian motto "All men have a mind that cannot bear [to see the sufferings of] others" (人皆有不忍之心). *The Works of Mencius* illustrates this principle with an intriguing scenario. When King Xuan of the state of Qi saw an ox being led to sacrifice, he could not bear to see "its frightened appearance, as if it were an innocent person going to the place of death."[18] The king immediately ordered that a sheep should replace the ox. Mencius advised that this was a sign of the king's "unbearing mind," and if he could only apply this sensitivity to the state and the people, he would have the Kingly Way and attain orderly government. The king was not sure he could do that, because, like any other selfish man, he loved wealth and female charms. Mencius replied that all men had similar desires, but if the king understood that other people's desire was as valid as his own, he would take measures to satisfy popular desires and thus attain the Kingly Way, which is nothing but benevolence put into practice.

Rather than an administrative or legal entity, a political vision of the Kingly Way is primarily a moral one. If aesthetic experience in Kant facilitates social cohesion and sustains reciprocity of nations and peoples, Confucian benevolent government resorts to ritual, music, sensitivity, and compassion. Its object is the human body in all its creaturely, sensuous, and emotional attributes. As Terry Eagleton observes, the aesthetic concerns "nothing less than the whole of our sensate life together—the business of affections and aversions, of how the world strikes the body on its sensory surfaces, of that which takes root in the gaze and the guts and all that arises from our most banal, biological insertion into the world."[19] This aesthetic politics presumes a close fit between the well-being of a private body and that of the governing body, meaning that no political order could flourish that fails to take care of the lived experience of people.

Instead merely caring about the material well-being of the population, benevolent government promotes shared pleasure and forges emotional solidarity. Mencius offers another scenario that illustrates shared aesthetic experience as part of the Kingly Way. When the king of the state of Qi conveyed his worry about his indulgence in music, Mencius advised him reassuringly, "If the king's love of music were very great, the kingdom of Qi would be close to a state of good government." But it made a huge difference whether the king enjoyed music alone and with a select few or shared music with the majority of the people. In the former case, people would complain that the king, absorbed in pleasures enjoyed privately with a crony, ignored their distress and needs. The deprived people would frown on other aesthetic privileges, such as the beauty of the royal plumes, horses, and entourage. But if the king shared music with his people, and if the high and low all had equal access to music, the people would enjoy music as much as the king. The people would then rejoice in looking at the majestic beauty of the king's carriages and other pleasures.[20]

Shared joy in music is more than entertainment. It is both moral and political, because bodies and hearts are connected in emotional empathy, reciprocity, and conviviality. Mencius's moral precept illustrates this world: "Treat with reverence the elders in your own family, so that the elders in the families of others shall be similarly treated; treat with kindness due to the young in your own family, so that the young in the family of others shall be similarly treated— do this, and the empire may be made to go round in your palm."[21]

Extending these moral convictions to the conception of good government in modern times, Kang reconsiders politics in terms of the aesthetic principle of removing pain and seeking pleasure. In a way that resonates with the doctrine of natural right, he brings the notion of the pleasurable body to Confucian political culture. The standard for assessing the legitimacy of governance is not only political and moral but also aesthetic, emotional, and bodily. This standard derives from the aesthetic experience of shared pleasure and collective ritual. When it is fair and benevolent, a political order increases people's pleasure and reduces their distress.

This sensibility informs an unbroken chain of being extending from person to family to community and government, all the way to all humans under heaven. Kang depicts a rising scale of obligations from the lowest human unit to the broadest one:

> Master Kang says, being that I am a man, I would be uncompassionate to flee from men and not to share their grief and miseries. And being that I was born into a family, and [by virtue of] receiving the nurture of others was able to have this life, I then have the responsibilities of a family member. Should I flee from this [responsibility], my behavior would be false.... And why would it not be the same with the public debt we owe to one country and the world? Being that we are born into one country, have received the civilization of one country, and thereby have its knowledge, then we have the responsibilities of a citizen. If we flee from this [responsibility] and abandon this country, this country will perish and its people will be annihilated, and then civilization will be destroyed. (48; 65)

By this widening gyre of sympathy, imagination, and obligation, Kang Youwei suggests that a member of a local community could become a citizen of the world.

Addressing the possibility of perpetual peace and ending war, Kant argued that the republican state, based on the sanctity of right and representative government, offered the best hope for cosmopolitan world order. As citizens of a republic, the people would refuse to succumb to the arbitrary decision by a despotic ruler to go to war. They would judge a war by its potential damage to their own life and property and hence would be less likely to be coaxed into it by some extravagant national pride.[22] Aware of ideas of the people as citizens yet reared in a different moral tradition, Kang Youwei differs from Kant in his elaboration of the ethico-political doctrine of benevolent governance. By revitalizing Confucian notions of benevolent government, Kang extended the concept to the world in search of a vision of unified world community.

Terry Eagleton writes, "At the very root of social relations lies the aesthetic, source of all human bonding."[23] This insight illuminates the intimacy of morality and aesthetics at the center of politics and makes Kant comparable to Kang Youwei. Kantian aesthetic disinterestedness does not mean self-centeredness and lack of interest in morality and politics. Aesthetic detachment means indifference, it is true, yet not to others' interest but to one's own. The aesthetic subject is detached from one's own narrow sphere and self-absorption, from unsocial sociability. This reading of civic virtue resonates with Kang Youwei's ideas about sympathy, benevolence, and governance. Civic virtue is a "passionate affection for his fellow citizens and for shared conditions of their common life."[24] The aesthetic sensibility stems from the pity we feel for each other in the state of nature and is based on the empathetic imagination, which makes us capable of "transporting ourselves outside ourselves, and identifying ourselves with the suffering animal, leaving our being, so to speak, in order to take his. . . . Thus no one becomes sensitive except when his imagination is animated and begins to transport himself outside himself."[25] In Kang Youwei and Kant, the aesthetic raises the possibility of fostering a civic virtue of benevolence extendable to different peoples and communities in the world.

Revitalizing Confucian Morality

In the Confucian tradition, self-cultivation internalizes normative moral principles. But rather than being for personal perfection, spiritual practice must extend to social and political realms. Private learning needs to be upgraded to the scale of moral and social improvement. This underlies the ethico-political conception of social order. In actual dynastic changes, however, the moral core and sociopolitical practices diverged and split, frequently taking the form of a divorce between name and substance, an estrangement of morality from warped institutions. In the Spring and Autumn period, early Confucianism, exemplified by the *Spring and Autumn Annals*, arose as a form of moral, political critique against the collapse of ritual and music (禮崩樂壞). The *Chunqiu*-style critique sought to reinstitute a proper ethico-political order on the model of the golden age of the Three Dynasties. The scholar-officials over the centuries continued to exercise this ethico-political perspective and pass judgment on rulers and social ills. This sense of a split between the ethical principles inherent in ritual and music, on the one hand, and institutional corruption, on the other, ran through many schools of thought, but came to self-consciousness in the perennial project of commentaries on Confucianism.

Kang Youwei updated the Confucian critique of the separation of music from society, morality from politics. His accounts of the historical evolution of the three ages (三世) in his commentaries on the Confucian classics begins with the golden age of antiquity, when Great Peace (datong) prevailed. But the Three Dynasties in antiquity witnessed a devolution to the age of lesser tranquility, when people loved only their own kin and family and pursued private gains. This age declined further to the Age of Disorder in the times of Confucius. The process then gradually rose to the Age of Rising Peace and culminated in the Age of Great Peace. This narrative describes an ascending scale of moral principles, embodied by successive forms of social and political order. Before Kang made the first petition in 1895 to the Qing emperor, the idea arose in his short book *Renlei gongli* (Public principles of humanity) but was given fuller expression in *Shili gongfa quanshu* (Book of substantive public law). The failure of the petition forced Kang to move away from metaphysical arguments to a historical account of the evolution of government and society. Drawing on the New Text School of commentary of the Han dynasty, he built on the interpretations by Dong Zhongshu (董仲舒) and the *Gongyang* and *Guliang* commentaries. The New Text School regarded the *Spring and Autumn Annals* as an activist, reformist work of historiography and Confucius as a reformer. According to He Xiu, the earliest of the three forms of governance was one of decay and disorder. To rectify the political disorder, Confucius devoted all his energy to restructuring the state of Lu by recovering and transmitting the ritual and moral principles embodied by the Zhou order. This proactive agenda fuels a continuous narrative as the social order ascends to the stage of rising peace (*shengping* 昇平), in which Confucius extends the local principles to all other states and brings peace and order within the Middle Kingdom. The apex of moral triumph in the world is "universal peace," in which "the whole world, far and near, great and small, is like one."[26]

The reformist agenda of Confucius informs Kang's book *Confucius as Reformer*. Kang claims that while understanding a wide array of contradictory theories, Confucius did not simply transmit preexisting thoughts but rather revamped the ethico-political principles of the Zhou order, using an imagined past to transform the present.[27] As the uncrowned king (*suwang* 素王), Confucius rearticulated the Kingly Way through his study of institutional changes in the state of Lu. In the book *Li yun* (禮運), the three ages followed one another in a descending order. The sage rulers of the Three Dynasties had presided over an era of less tranquility or *xiaokang* (小康), marking a downward turn from the golden age to "a world marked by both military power and ritual morality." "The empire became a world of families where people love only their own parents and their own children [and] goods and labor are used only for private advantage."[28] Yet these forward and backward pointers along a historical timeline are not important. Kang envisaged instead an upwardly spiraling narrative that rises above historical reality according to a teleology. Due to the distortions coming from outside Confucianism and to institutional corruption, Chinese culture for thousands of years had remained at the xiaokang stage. The present modern period, however, was one of transition "away from a social system based on patriarchal clans and tribes and a corresponding political system based on the despotic authority of rulers over people or nobles over commoners." From this parochial and patriarchal xiaokang society, there would "emerge a world where the hierarchical distance between peoples and their rulers and between different individuals in their social relations would be markedly diminished." The political form embodying this new relationship would be the nation-state and constitutional monarchy.[29]

Some regard Kang's reading of the Confucian tradition as conservative, and others view his appropriation of Western democracy as a misguided cosmopolitanism. These two extreme views obscure the universal and moral aspirations in the *Datong shu*. Bogged down in a narrow view of morality, detractors miss the ethical orientation of Confucius as the uncrowned king and the politically comprehensive visions in Kang's reading of the *Spring and Autumn Annals*. The uncrowned king deserves honor and admiration from posterity, because he did not embody and defend the existing, established institutions, power, and moral values tied to a specific time or kingdom. Without title and position, the sage projected a new set of values. Though articulated in texts such as the *Analects*, these values are not manifest in a given institution or persona. Indeed, they are hardly traceable in empirical reality. In treating the vicissitudes of political order in the *Spring and Autumn Annals*, Confucius attempted to advance the normative, moral principles that, though derived from the specific circumstances—especially the state of Lu—were broad enough to transcend the actual conditions and applicable to other periods and states. As understood by Kang Youwei and the New Text school commentary, Confucius's moral project separates value from fact and extracts the genuine content from the institutionalized, ritualized forms. It separates the moral ideals of benevolent governance from the travesty of the institutions and from the corruption of legitimate status (*mingfen* 名份). Although as a commoner he was powerless to realize the new values within the established framework, Confucius tried to articulate what was impossible and impractical.

In his study of Confucianism, Kang Youwei admired the Duke of Zhou as the paragon of ideal morality and culture, but this is not to be read as the rear-guard preservation of the ancient order. Kang's elevated image presupposes that the Duke of Zhou occupied a position that seamlessly combined virtue, power, and authority (有德有位) and was capable of implementing universal public laws based on the Dao. The unity of morality and politics was precisely what Confucius looked forward to but failed to implement in his lifetime.[30]

Benjamin Schwartz emphasized this aspiration for ethical principles by contrasting the *Chunqiu* with the *Zuozhuan* (*Zuo* commentary). Just as Kang Youwei viewed the *Zuozhuan* as a distortion of the *Chunqiu* spirit, so Schwartz argues against the former as implying a might-makes-right, winner-takes-all history. For all its vivid accounts of alliances and counteralliances, power struggle and intrigue, and the rise and fall of states, the *Zuozhuan* reflects a "morality of pure political expediency and deplorable concern with 'success and failure' rather than with pure moral motivation." In today's parlance, the *Zuozhuan* narrative would be the language of realpolitik keyed to the cycle of war and peace—the currency of the Westphalian international system. Although *Chunqiu* also describes realpolitik in state making, military strategies, and diverse, brutal, and contradictory human behavior, this Confucian classic, Schwartz rightly cautions, can still be treated "ahistorically." Rather than plunging into the thick of melodramatic vicissitudes, the *Chunqiu* extracts moral precepts that "involved what might be called perennial and metahistorical principles of ethical and political judgment." This is the level to which the criteria of praise and blame (*baobian* 褒貶) pertain most judicially and effectively, holding up history not as a gripping, agonistic story but as a moral mirror of benevolence and justice.[31]

The *Chunqiu* is surely very much concerned with violations of social and political norms. Its anxiety over the breakdown of order is associated with an obsession with status obligation (*mingfen*). This concern became the target of the May Fourth iconoclastic critique and, by extension, Kang Youwei's intellectual innovation and monarchism. But if he agonized over the breakdown of order and violations committed by the warring states, Confucius cannot be equated with the defender of the aggressive regimes. Rather, he was critiquing and passing judgment on the status quo. Confucius acted more as a judicious innovator, a censorious judge, and a visionary thinker. In Schwartz's reading, the subjective and nonfactual aspect of ren (benevolence), not the reified social institutions, becomes the standard by which "the monstrous behavior and caprices of the authority and power holders are duly recorded." The moral principles shed light on the dire consequences of the decay of legitimate authority, whether it is due to subversion from below or to corruption of power holders or authority figures.[32]

Following Dong Zhongshu, an astute thinker on values and history, Kang derived from the historical periods a set of moral principles that transcend the mutations and corruptions associated with specific institutions. He strove to extend the moral principles derived from a particular society to interstate and cross-cultural relations. As Schwartz commented, just as the ethico-political truths of Shakespeare's plays or Aristotle are relevant to different centuries and cultures—a shared property of the aesthetic world community—so Kang Youwei's focus on the *Chunqiu* and three stages reveals an effort to apply universal ethico-political standards to the world community.

The three-stage narrative is not limited to China but heralds a global trend. After the age of chaos, there would arise xiaokang, a society of rising peace. By following the model of federated states in America and Germany, China would move forward to the great community of datong. A process of global democratization, based on the people's power and rule, is spreading modes of government compatible with the Confucian principle of benevolence.

Equality and Democratic Critique

Critics with nationalist sentiments have objected to Kang's attempt to follow the liberal model of social reform in the West. Liberals have charged Kang with promoting a conservative notion of constitutional monarchy. Just as Confucius attempted to extract moral principles from the actual events of the *Chunqiu*, so Kang Youwei sought to articulate a worldview based on his experiences in the West and to tease out ethical principles from Western democratic institutions. Although he frequently referred to the United States, Germany, or Belgium as the exemplary model, Kang was interested in genuine democratic aspirations not bounded by the institutional form of a particular nation-state. A notion of republicanism based on popular sovereignty and power sharing allowed him to envision a future society that would be united, democratic, and free. Consider his comments with regard to American democracy: "When states are autocracies, it is natural that they are self-centered" (86). American democracy broke aristocratic self-centeredness, and the constitutional movement established a legal framework. When states are democracies like the United States, they are well on their way to forging federated alliances, and social harmony may be on the horizon. Similarly, the people's empowerment in the drive for freedom and equality characterized the French Revolution as well as the national independence movements that challenged colonial rule.[33] This was possible because the republican principle of the people's sovereignty prevailed. "People only seek profit and benefit for themselves, and so when the benevolent men advocate the pleasure and profit of One World, it naturally accords with men's mind."[34] Since the democratic impulse is universal, it is not tied to a particular interest or identity.

If the pursuit of equality and benevolence is part of democracy—and Kang thought it is—then the notion is disengaged from the specific Euro-American context and held up as a universal principle. This transcendent move allows Kang to critique American institutions and practices for not living up to democratic principles. Although America is a democracy, it failed to measure up to its self-expressed standard, especially in matters of race, class, and capital-labor relations. In terms of equality, Kang appraised the Confucian vision of the ethical bond of social harmony and portrayed the sage as a democratic thinker *avant la lettre.* In the Spring and Autumn era dominated by the feudal, hereditary nobility, Confucius originated the idea of equality. "He made clear the unity [of the empire] so as to do away with feudalism, and derided the [institution of] hereditary nobility so as to do away with heredity of office. [He transmitted the ancient] assigned-field system [so as] to do away with slavery" (213; 135). In one breath Kang draws a parallel between George Washington and Confucius, between Confucian reform and the American constitutional revolution. Confucius "wrote the constitution of the *Chunqiu* so as to put a limit to the monarch's powers. He did not exalt himself to his followers and rejected the authority of great priests. Thereby caste was completely swept out from Chinese institutions. Everyone became a commoner; anyone could rise from common status to be ennobled, to be a minister of state, to be a teacher or scholar and be soaring in the sky, unburdened by the traits of selfishness" (213–214; 135).

Speaking of the Chinese translation of Alexis de Tocqueville's classic *Democracy in America,* Gan Yang notes that the Chinese title, *Meiguo de minzhu* (美國的民主), is misleading, because the adjective *meiguo* (American) limits democracy to one territory and community and thus obscures the French author's intention to discuss universal democratic principles. In his preface to the book, Tocqueville repeatedly expresses the intention to write about democracy as a "universal and permanent" question. Although the book delineates the transition from autocracies to the self-governance of the people, the French thinker claims that much of his book is about things "being American, but not democratic." The book's second volume, according to Gan Yang, makes a sharper distinction between "what is democratic" and "what is only American." By this distinction Tocqueville contends that democratization is a worldwide, irresistible trend.[35]

Gan Yang's separation of the ideas of America and democracy captures the way Kang Youwei approaches global democracy in the spirit of *Chunqiu* commentary. This spirit marks a critical vigilance that decouples value from history and runs through Kang Youwei's work. Kang elevates democracy as a set of values from its actual performance and lapses, and this influenced subsequent thinkers like Liang Qichao, Zhang Taiyan, and Lu Xun. In his response to Yan Fu, Liang Qichao asserted that Western democracy, understood as the people's equal rights, popular power, and self-determination, took off only in the nineteenth century. The democracy of Greek antiquity was a form of hereditary autocracy, not unlike the political structure in the *Chunqiu*. If one judges a democracy by how much power the people share in politics, many existing liberal democracies fall short. But democracy seems an inevitable world process that involves not only China but also those nations that deserve that honor. Certain Western nations may be ahead of China in building democracy, but this gap is not absolute. In a *Chunqiu* critical spirit, Liang claims that "actually existing" democracies are still trying to achieve inherent democratic goals, and they have yet not arrived. Frequently they regress from democracy.[36]

In this light, *Datong shu* does not simply draw on Confucian classics in an attempt to broaden certain normative, universal elements. The book is a bold attempt to lay out ethical principles that are universally applicable. These principles may carry the name of the Mandate of Heaven or democracy; they may be about benevolence, compassion, or aesthetic imagination, but they are not tied down to their original institutions and historical locus. Rather, they are deployed to hold governments accountable and to measure the distance between the expressed moral goal and institutional practice, between moral imperatives and political performance. Ethical principles, whether embodied by Confucianism or democracy, are not the exclusive, unique property of one particular nation-state and the product of a cultural group. This transcendent ethical imagination constitutes the key to Kang's vision of the great community.

1. Linklater, *Men and Citizens in the Theory of International Relations*, 4.

2. Martin Wight, quoted in Linklater, *Men and Citizens in the Theory of International Relations*.

3. Mearsheimer, *The Tragedy of Great Power Politics*, 2.

4. Huntington, *The Clash of Civilizations and the Remaking of World Order*, 21.

5. Linklater, *Men and Citizens in the Theory of International Relations*, 26.

6. Levenson, *Revolution and Cosmopolitanism*, 24.

7. Kant, *Political Writings*, 44.

8. Kant, *Political Writings*, 44.

9. Kant, *Critique of the Power of Judgment*, 301.

10. Kant, *Critique of the Power of Judgment*, 73–75.

11. Cheah, *Inhuman Conditions*, 96.

12. Eagleton, *The Ideology of the Aesthetic*, 96.

13. Kant, quoted in Muthu, *Enlightenment against Empire*, 148.

14. Muthu, *Enlightenment against Empire*, 144.

15. Levenson, *Revolution and Cosmopolitanism*, 20.

16. Kang Youwei, *Datong shu*, 69. For English translation, see Thompson, *Ta T'ung Shu*, 80. I use the English version with modifications. Further references to Kang's book are in parentheses with two page numbers in the text.

17. Kang Youwei, *Datong shu*, 5. I use Jonathan Spence's translation of this passage. See Spence, *The Gate of Heavenly Peace*, 66.

18. Legge, *The Works of Mencius*, book 1, ch. 1, part 7. I use Legge's translation with modification.

19. Eagleton, *The Ideology of the Aesthetic*, 13.

20. Legge, *The Works of Mencius*, book 1, part 2.

21. Legge, *The Works of Mencius*, book 1, part 2, ch. 1.

22. Kant, *Political Writings*, 100.

23. Eagleton, *The Ideology of the Aesthetic*, 24.

24. Eagleton, *The Ideology of the Aesthetic*.

25. Eagleton, *The Ideology of the Aesthetic*.

26. Feng Youlan, *A Short History of Chinese Philosophy*, 202.

27. Tang Zhijun, *Kang Youwei zhuan*, 75.

28. Furth, "Intellectual Change," 20.

29. Furth, "Intellectual Change."

30. Tang Zhijun, *Kang Youwei zhuan*, 24.

31. Schwartz, *The World of Thought in Ancient China*, 386–387.

32. Schwartz, *The World of Thought in Ancient China*, 387.

33. Kang Youwei, *Datong shu*, 148.

34. Kang Youwei, *Datong shu*, 149.

35. Gan Yang, *Jiangcuo jiucuo*, 259.

36. Liang Qichao, *Liang Qichao quanqi*, vol. 1, 72.

5

GREEK ANTIQUITY,
CHINESE MODERNITY, AND
THE CHANGING WORLD ORDER
Yiqun Zhou

*

It has been observed that modern Chinese intellectuals, even when they champion nationalism, have not for a moment abandoned the ideal of a universal utopia that transcends nationalistic boundaries, and that they are in fact also always expressing nationalistic concerns when they embrace cosmopolitanism or any other worldview with universal pretensions.[1] The inextricably intertwined relationship between the two apparently conflicting tendencies assumes a particularly intriguing form when these intellectuals contemplate China's present status in the world, not merely with reference to the recent history of the West but also going all the way back to the origins of Chinese and Western civilizations. While the fate of China in a modern world of nation-states is the underlying concern of the comparisons between ancient China and Greece, such comparisons are almost always expressed in civilizational terms, and the multifarious conclusions that emerge, which typically reflect imagination and prescription much more than disinterested historical inquiry, tend to be conceived as having universal significance for the past, present, and future of humanity. An examination of modern Chinese intellectuals' persistent engagement with ancient Greece reveals the tenacious appeal of the universal and civilizational claims inherent in the classical tianxia discourse, despite the fact that the nation-state is posited as both the starting point and the ultimate concern of generations of Chinese philhellenes.

Two Versions of Chinese Philhellenism

Widely regarded as the foundation of the Western tradition, ancient Greece has been treated with great admiration by Chinese intellectuals since the turn of the twentieth century, as they struggle with an unprecedented crisis in the history of Chinese civilization induced by the encounter with the West. In the complex and constantly evolving intellectual landscape of modern China, Chinese philhellenism has taken on many faces and spoken many languages. In accordance with the different ideological agendas and changing needs and self-perceptions of its Chinese advocates, Greek antiquity has been deployed for a range of discursive purposes.

For the sake of convenience, the two main Chinese approaches to the appropriation of Greek antiquity can be loosely labeled progressive and conservative. This division is adopted in the present study with the understanding that there is common ground between the two (the most basic being the shared belief that reexamination of the Chinese past and learning from the West are indispensable to the striving for a better future for China), that there is a spectrum of views within each camp, and that an individual may have mixed opinions at the same time or evolving positions over a lifetime.

Generally speaking, progressive philhellenism tends to hold up ancient Greece as a mirror against which Chinese antiquity is examined more for difference and deficiency than for similarity, and the comparison usually yields lessons that support calls for a thorough critique of Chinese culture, with the aim to change it so that it may survive and compete in the Western-dominated modern world. Under this broad rubric, we may further distinguish between those who justify a radical rejection of the Chinese tradition by pointing to the superiority that Western civilization enjoyed from the start, and those who attempt to salvage traditional Chinese culture by uncovering elements in it that are compatible with Western values. These differences notwithstanding, progressive philhellenism is united by a strong faith in historical progress culminating in the modern West and in the importance of international competition for national survival.

The conservative approach appears to have less coherence. Some thinkers emphasize affinities between ancient Greece and China and embrace the vision of a new Chinese culture that is part of a cosmopolitan order in which the finest elements of tradition and modernity and of East and West coexist and the wisdom of antiquity (Chinese as well as Greek) serves as antidote to the ills of the modern age. Others, while also focusing on the parallels between Greek and Chinese antiquities, do not develop a cosmopolitan enthusiasm but instead use the similarity to argue that the hope of Chinese modernization lies in the revival of China's own great ancient tradition. Still others, believing that there have been fundamental differences between Chinese and Western civilizations from the beginning and that each tradition has its own merits and shortcomings, envision a future in which a revitalized Chinese culture would save the world from the excesses of Western-dominated modernity. However, overall the conservative philhellenes tend to set greater value on the role of tradition (both tradition in general and Chinese tradition in particular) in the renovation of Chinese culture and to demonstrate nationalistic concerns in a milder and more accommodating manner than their progressive counterparts.

The homage paid to ancient Greece by Chinese intellectuals of diverse camps and persuasions, regardless of their attitudes toward their own ancient tradition, testifies to the undeniably hegemonic status of the West in the modern era. It also suggests that the vehement questioning of tradition in modern China is nevertheless qualified. The conservative and progressive Chinese receptions of ancient Greece bespeak both a strong consciousness of the authority of tradition and a yearning to claim a piece of antiquity in advancing competing conceptions of modernity. A comprehensive study of the divergent expressions of Chinese philhellenism in the last hundred years or so will shed much light on some hotly contested topics in China's tumultuous modern era: the relationships between tradition and modernity, between China and the West, and between cosmopolitanism and nationalism. This chapter offers a very preliminary sketch of the two main approaches, ending with the "Greek renaissance" brought about by the new economic and political standing that China has achieved in the world since the mid-1990s. An analysis of this contemporary phenomenon, the most recent development in the conservative Chinese reception of Greek antiquity, shows how far Chinese intellectuals have come since the turn of the twentieth century in their understandings of the relationship between tradition and modernity and in their perceptions of China's position in the world order. The latest Chinese philhellenic movement is also of special interest because it is informed by the powerful revival of the tianxia discourse in contemporary Chinese thought and exhibits by far the most salient combination of universalistic and nationalistic tendencies in the history of Chinese philhellenism.

Progressive Philhellenism

LIANG QICHAO (梁啟超, 1873–1929). To begin this survey of progressive Chinese philhellenism with Liang Qichao may raise many eyebrows. It is well known that Liang's attitude toward Western civilization underwent a significant change after World War I and that he sided with the defenders of traditional Chinese culture in the East-West cultural debate (*Dong Xi wenhua lunzhan* 東西文化論戰, 1915–1927).[2] However, in the history of Chinese philhellenism, it is unquestionable that Liang's early writings defined the basic model of the progressive approach to Greek antiquity, and his vision has influenced generations of thinkers who launch critiques of the Chinese tradition by comparing it with ancient Greece.[3]

Between 1898 and 1903, Liang Qichao wrote extensively on various aspects of ancient Greek civilization, from history and politics to philosophy, economics, and science. The following pieces have ancient Greece as their sole subject: "A Short History of Athens" (Yadian xiaoshi 雅典小史), "Short Notes on Sparta" (Sibada xiaozhi 斯巴達小志), "On Scholarship in Ancient Greece" (Lun Xila gudai xueshu 論希臘古代學術), and "Aristotle's Political Thought" (Yalishiduode zhi zhengzhi xueshuo 亞理士多德之政治學説). Important works in which ancient Greece occupies a prominent position include "Major Trends in the Evolution of Western Learning" (Taixi xueshu sixiang bianqian zhi dashi 泰西學術思想變遷之大勢), "A Short History of the Development of Economic Theories" (Shengjixue xueshuo yange xiaoshi 生計學學説沿革小史), "A Brief Examination of the Development of Science" (Gezhixue yange kaolue 格致學沿革攷略), and "Major Trends in the Evolution of Chinese Learning" (Zhongguo xueshu sixiang bianqian zhi dashi 中國學術思想變遷之大势). Briefer allusions to ancient Greece in Liang's prolific writings are too many to enumerate.

The reason for such lavish attention to ancient Greece, as Liang explains, is that it was the fountainhead of Western civilization, and without ancient Greece there would be no modern Europe. He also states that ancient Greece was a microcosm of contemporary Europe, and Athens was a microcosm of contemporary England.[4] Studying ancient Greece will, therefore, help the Chinese better understand the foundation of European superiority and Chinese deficiency.

For example, believing that a well-developed legislature is the key reason the political system of the Western countries is more advanced than that of China, Liang points out that from the beginning of the Western tradition, in the ancient Greek city-states, matters of the state were put to the citizens' assemblies for public deliberation and decision making. In his discussion of the focus on patriotism and martial spirit in Spartan education, he praises Spartan women for the valor and selflessness with which they exhorted their kinsmen to give their lives for their country, and compares them favorably with the images in classical Chinese poetry of tearful women who try to prevent their husbands and sons from going to battle. Lamenting that the lack of martial virtue has been the shame of the Chinese people for several thousand years, he urges his compatriots to emulate the Spartan spirit, vindicate their national honor on the battlefield, and fight for self-preservation in the face of rampant Western imperial encroachment. The same China-centered concern can be found in the comparison with ancient Greece that Liang draws in his long treatise on the patterns of Chinese intellectual history. According to Liang, the Chinese intellectual tradition fell short vis-à-vis its Greek counterpart in six areas: (1) the underdevelopment of logical reasoning, (2) the lack of science as a discipline of research, (3) the lack of an environment for debate and disagreement, (4) overly strong sectarian tendencies, (5) excessive reverence for tradition and established ways, and (6) overly strict adherence to the teachings of one's master.[5]

In two ways, these early writings of Liang set the model for the progressive use of Greek antiquity in modern China. First, the Greeks are invoked mainly for the purpose of identifying major deficiencies and deeply entrenched problems in the Chinese tradition, helping the Chinese people comprehend the proportions of the cultural crisis they are in, and urging them to make a concerted effort to save and renew their civilization. Second, Liang's analysis of the three major aspects in which ancient China lagged behind ancient Greece—patriotism and martial spirit, intellectual tradition, and political system—laid the groundwork for later philhellenic critique of Chinese culture.[6]

HU SHI (胡適, 1891–1962). For Hu Shi, the pre-Qin period (before 221 BCE) is the only time in Chinese history that can even be compared with that of the West, and China clearly comes out as inferior. Ancient Chinese culture pales in comparison with Greek achievements in literature, sculpture, science, and politics. Hu was particularly embarrassed by the yawning gap that already existed between Chinese and Greek mathematics in antiquity. Following such an inauspicious beginning, China lagged behind the West for the next two thousand years, during which many institutions and practices developed in Chinese culture that only added to its embarrassment.[7]

This view of Chinese and Greek antiquity is in keeping with Hu Shi's position on what should be done about China's past. He spearheaded the project of *zhengli guogu* (整理國故, reexamining and reorganizing the nation's tradition) to discover and promote elements in Chinese culture that bore affinities with Western culture and could serve as the indigenous basis for absorbing it and thereby thoroughly renewing the Chinese tradition.[8] In light of his opinion that the pre-Qin period represented the only time when the West's cultural achievements were still somehow within the reach of China and that a huge gap between Chinese and Greek science was already in place during that period, it is not surprising that his first major scholarly work, his doctoral dissertation at Columbia University, was devoted to the study of logic in pre-Qin philosophy. It is also not surprising that Mozi (墨子), whom Hu praised for being scientific and pragmatic, emerged as the hero in this study (taking up one-third of the space). A similar desire to reshuffle Chinese intellectual history and draw it closer to the Western tradition according to Western standards was to characterize Hu's later scholarly pursuits.

Although he is often classified as a champion of the radical rejection of tradition, Hu Shi's lifelong cause may be better understood in terms of an agonizing effort to deal with the tremendous burden of tradition, especially the ancient traditions of China and the West. The splendor of ancient Greece cast a long shadow over his perception of the entire premodern Chinese culture, and the resultant deep sense of cultural inferiority and a coexisting nationalistic sentiment led him to advocate a systematic reconstruction of the nation's past so that the Chinese people might have a new tradition to serve as their fresh starting point in the modern age.[9]

CHEN XUJING (陳序經, 1903–1967). The tension that Hu Shi felt between unreserved admiration for the Western tradition and a persistent desire to salvage China's own premodern heritage was not present in Chen Xujing, the staunchest advocate of "complete Westernization." In Chen's eyes, Hu Shi's otherwise accurate grasp of the relative merits of Chinese and Western cultures was unfortunately undermined by his illusion that similarity and compatibility could be found between the two by turning to China's classical antiquity and the non-Confucian traditions.[10] The difference between Chen's and Hu's attitudes toward China's own tradition is fully reflected in the former's rejection of the common perception that pre-Qin China was not inferior to ancient Greece in cultural achievements.[11]

Chen argues that the popular comparison of pre-Qin China and ancient Greece as equals is superficial, because it looks only at what each civilization had achieved at that stage, without considering their different potentials for development. The culture of ancient Greece had diverse origins and was open to foreign influences. The Greeks' strong consciousness of their cultural uniqueness and superiority did not prevent them from continuously and actively learning from others and modifying themselves, and as a result great dynamism and flexibility characterized every aspect of their society, from political and legal systems to ethics and material achievements. Chen especially commended the Greek philosophers for subscribing to the idea of progress and affirming humans' capacity to improve their environment. All these qualities endowed Greek society with vast potential for change and development.

In contrast, the culture of ancient China, from the time of the legendary kings (the Yellow Emperor, Yao, Shun, and Yu) onward, had long reached a state of homogeneity and stagnation. The much-celebrated cultural splendor of the Spring and Autumn and Warring States period (770–221 BCE) was largely limited to development in the field of philosophy, and the progress was quantitative rather than qualitative. Despite its apparent intellectual diversity and vitality, this period produced no school of thought that actively embraced a progressive understanding of history and culture (the Legalists being no exception). Nor did a more open and less chauvinistic attitude toward non-Chinese cultures come into being during these centuries of sociopolitical instability and chaos. Lacking creativity and resisting new and foreign things, the culture of China's classical antiquity possessed no potential for change and development whatsoever.

In short, even if the achievements of ancient China and ancient Greece might have been comparable,[12] in terms of potential the difference between the two is like that between the setting sun and the rising sun. The rest of the history of Chinese culture was just a simple continuation in time and expansion in scale of the patterns set in the pre-Qin period. It follows that there would be no point in attempting to rejuvenate Chinese culture by revisiting classical antiquity. Being old and closed off to change from the very beginning, China's classical antiquity had nothing to offer to its struggle for modernization. The only hope lay in resolutely abandoning the Chinese tradition and wholeheartedly learning from the West, a tradition that had always been dynamic and open beginning with the Greeks, in order to create a new Chinese culture on an equal footing with the West.

FROM GU ZHUN (顧准, 1915–1974) TO *RIVER ELEGY* (1988). To many of today's Chinese readers, Gu Zhun is a legendary name associated with the study of ancient Greece. In a series of notes written under adverse circumstances during the Cultural Revolution, Gu Zhun praises the far-reaching contributions of the Greeks to the world, namely, democracy, the rule of law, and political and intellectual freedom.[13] He points out that none of these existed in ancient China, where authoritarianism not only dominated political and social relationships but also impeded the development of any area of study that was not about ethics and ritual (hence the Chinese deficiency in mathematics and logic). Gu Zhun also makes much of the old idea that there was a fundamental difference between "maritime civilizations," of which ancient Greece was the first eminent example, and "nonmaritime civilizations," which included China, among many others.[14] Whereas the maritime civilizations tended to have a more open society and to develop political institutions that were conducive to greater public participation, the nonmaritime civilizations had an affinity for authoritarianism.[15]

The distinction between these two types of civilizations, made by Gu Zhun and others before him, provided the central motif in a TV series broadcast in 1988, *River Elegy* (*He shang* 河殤). Organized around a contrast between China's civilization of the yellow earth and the Western civilization of the blue sea, the series conducts a sweeping critique of the inward-looking, stagnant, and oppressive character of Chinese culture while eulogizing the openness, innovativeness, and freedom of Western culture. In this grand comparative narrative, ancient Chinese history was a process in which the yellow earth civilization steadily outpaced the influence of the blue sea civilization and eventually gained complete control with the elevation of Confucianism as a state ideology in the Han dynasty. As China was undergoing a tragic, continuous downturn during these centuries, the blue sea civilization was flourishing in the Mediterranean with the dominance of ancient Greece as a democratic, maritime power (episode 6). Once the separate tracks were set, history was basically a foregone conclusion, and the narrative takes a huge leap in time and picks up again from the fifteenth century, at the second rise of the blue sea civilization in Western Europe.[16]

The highly provocative rhetoric of *River Elegy* is commonly believed to have played a significant role in the intellectual fermentation leading up to the 1989 prodemocracy student movement in Beijing.[17] Through images and narration that evoke emotion, it throws into high relief all the major characteristics of progressive philhellenism. First, ancient Greece is used as a mirror and a yardstick; Chinese society not only was unlike it in the beginning but also became increasingly unlike it in the course of premodern history. Second, the stark contrast drawn between Chinese and Greek antiquity serves as a call for thorough critique and reform of Chinese culture and politics in the present.

Finally but most importantly, this approach subscribes to a progressive view of history, accepts Western modernity as the norm to which China must aspire to conform, and turns to Greek antiquity with the purpose of driving home for the Chinese the depth and scope of the problems with their own tradition.

Despite the high honors invariably paid to it by the progressive philhellenes, in this approach Greek antiquity is essentially basking in the reflected glories of Western modernity. Almost every author discussed in these pages, with the exception of Gu Zhun, paid much more attention to post-1700s Western ideas and institutions than to the adored Greeks. Practically speaking, their intention being to arouse their compatriots to take action to catch up with the West and embrace modernity, it may indeed have sufficed to use ancient Greece as a stereotyped symbol and to portray it in the image of the modern West and as the mirror image of ancient China. Consequently, ancient Greece in progressive use often seems like a phantom rather than a civilization grounded in real time and space and connected to the later Western tradition through provable lineage. Perhaps that can only be so. The progressive philhellenes hold a view of history and an understanding of China's position in the world that are not conducive to patient and disinterested inquiry. *River Elegy* has a memorable line: "The more ancient is a nation's tradition, the graver is the crisis [it experiences in modern times], and the graver is the crisis, the more fervent is the search for the nation's roots" (episode 1). In that quest marked by an unambiguously teleological view of history and a debilitating sense of crisis about being abandoned by history and the world community, the intellectual elite of an old and once-great civilization has created the phantom of ancient Greece as a mirror, a stimulant, and a model.[18]

Conservative Philhellenism

THE NATIONAL ESSENCE GROUP. The National Essence Group (Guocui Pai 國粹派), represented by Zhang Taiyan (章太炎, 1869–1936), Huang Jie (黃節, 1873–1935), Deng Shi (鄧實, 1877–1945?), and Liu Shipei (劉師培, 1884–1919), argued for full parallels between Chinese and Western history. Pre-Qin China was comparable to Greco-Roman antiquity in cultural splendor; the decline of Chinese culture following the establishment of the Qin Empire had its counterpart in the descent into the Middle Ages in Europe; and the twentieth century would see a revival of China's ancient tradition, just as the rebirth of the Greco-Roman tradition in the Renaissance marked the advent of modernity in Europe. In this version of comparative history, all modern Western ideas and institutions, from law and ethics to science and democracy, are attested in pre-Qin Chinese texts. Therefore, instead of being awestruck by the achievements of the modern West and ashamed of their own culture, the Chinese should reexamine the legacy of pre-Qin antiquity and seek therein the indigenous foundation for a strong and wealthy nation.[19]

This summary of the National Essence Group's use of Greek antiquity brings out an obvious paradox in their position on the relationship between China and the West. On the one hand, their enthusiastic embrace of pre-Qin antiquity as glorious and capable of generating new life for the Chinese tradition in modern times bears out their reputation as diehard defenders of traditional Chinese culture. On the other hand, the fact that they exalted pre-Qin China insofar as it was comparable to ancient Greece and allegedly contained seeds of modern Western ideas and institutions indicates that the value of Chinese antiquity had to be legitimated by Greek antiquity as well as Western modernity. The group's call to rediscover and revive China's national essence thus turns out to affirm the Western tradition, ancient and modern, as the ultimate measure of civilizational viability and greatness.[20]

DU YAQUAN (杜亞泉, 1873–1933) AND LIANG SHUMING (梁漱溟, 1893–1988). The thinkers Du Yaquan and Liang Shuming represent a very different conservative approach to Greek antiquity. Like the progressive philhellenes, they believed that there was an essential difference between Chinese and Western civilizations, that the divergence began in antiquity, and that the early parting of ways eventually led to the mighty clash between the two civilizations in the modern age.[21] Unlike the progressives, however, Du and Liang argued for the preservation of cultural difference in China's search for modernization, for two reasons. First, precisely because the difference between Chinese and Western civilizations was fundamental and deep-rooted, it would be difficult to erase it and attempt to make China conform to the Western model entirely. Second, Western civilization is not without serious flaws, and its cult of science, progress, individualism, and rationality (all with origins in ancient Greece) has resulted in massive, devastating wars and rampant anxiety due to the decline of spiritual life. Chinese civilization not only can provide the remedy for the ailments of the West but also has the potential, if its own problems could be corrected by selectively learning from the West, to become the beacon of hope for the world.[22]

The inference that Du and Liang drew from the fundamental divergence between Chinese and Greek antiquity struck a unique note in their time. The prospect that Chinese culture, improved and strengthened through judicious borrowing from the West, would provide the new paradigm for world civilization, however, appeared more like an illusion than a realistic idea. The radical difference that they saw between Chinese and Western civilizations and the crushing political and military reality that had for decades flaunted the success of the Western way made it questionable how their ideal—that traditional Chinese culture would emerge as the paradigm setter after receiving some supplement and enrichment from the West—could be realized. While logically as sound as the progressive use of Greek antiquity, Du and Liang's reasoning about the profound difference between ancient Chinese and Greek civilizations fell short in providing a clear and realistic goal or a pragmatic blueprint for achieving it.[23]

ZHOU ZUOREN (周作人, 1885–1967). Zhou Zuoren distinguished himself from all the other Chinese philhellenes discussed in this chapter in that he devoted decades to the study of Greek language and literature and had the most intimate, firsthand knowledge of the Greek tradition. Throughout his life, Zhou Zuoren had many occasions to explain why it was important to study ancient Greece. His major reasons can be summarized as follows.

First, Western civilization cannot be encapsulated by the experience of a few countries in postindustrial America and Western Europe. A close understanding of the "truth" (*zhenxiang* 真相) about Western civilization can only be obtained through a careful examination of its origin and basis in ancient Greece. Second, there are not only differences but also similarities between ancient China and Greece, and it would be instructive to examine both because the most desirable and viable way to reform Chinese culture would be to borrow elements of foreign culture that are compatible with the indigenous tradition. Third, Greek civilization has the most humanistic orientation in the world and can offer the most useful lesson for China, because Chinese civilization is also fundamentally humanistic; it would not be difficult for twentieth-century Chinese to understand and learn from the ancient Greeks.[24]

Zhou Zuoren's view of the value of Greek antiquity is consistent with his persistent promotion of a humanistic literature (*ren de wenxue* 人的文學). The Greeks were fascinating to him not because of their scientific and political achievements or their patriotic and martial spirit but because of the freedom, naturalness, and moderation with which they express their love of beauty and affirmation of life in their myths and literature. The strikingly humanistic character of Chinese culture, because it does not share the Greeks' passionate love of beauty and affirmation of life, can be marred by vulgarity and lack of warmth and vitality. Zhou Zuoren hoped that the Greek spirit would breathe fresh air into Chinese culture and help revive, enrich, and refine its humanistic tradition.[25]

Notably, whereas in his earlier career he had tended to look for resonances between Chinese and Greek cultures in formerly nonmainstream Chinese traditions such as popular literature, folktales, and informal works by literati, by the 1920s, Zhou Zuoren had come to believe that the creation of a new Chinese culture must be based on a recovery of the pre-Qin Confucian tradition. The revival of the original Confucian conceptions of *li* (禮, rites, ritual) and *zhongyong* (中庸, the doctrine of the mean)—not the distorted versions in Song-Ming neo-Confucianism—and a fusion with the Greek ideals of beauty and moderation would lead to the birth of a new moral order characterized by a perfect combination of freedom and discipline.[26]

What Zhou Zuoren admired in the Greeks and attempted to inject into a renewed Chinese culture were what he deemed to be universal values and ideals. He exalted the Greeks because, of all civilizations ancient and modern, East and West, they produced the most intense and yet most balanced expression of those values and ideals, and he believed that the natural affinities between the Greek and Chinese humanistic traditions yielded great potential for successful reception. Zhou Zuoren's endeavor to appropriate Greek antiquity was essentially guided by a vision of a universal human community that leveled national boundaries and disregarded nationalistic agendas.

Testifying to the powerful hold this vision exerted on Zhou Zuoren was his profound attraction to the culture of Japan, whose reputation as the "little Greece of the East" (*dongfang xiao Xila* 東方小希臘) he invoked with great fondness and appreciation.[27] The culture of the "little Greece" appealed to Zhou Zuoren because of what in his eyes it had in common with the literature and art of ancient Greece: a great sensitivity to beauty and the natural, ever-moderate and elegant articulation of such sensitivity. As an Eastern culture that had no historical connection with ancient Greece but gave such fine expression to the cultural ideals most fully exemplified by Greek antiquity, Japan demonstrated for Zhou Zuoren the complete compatibility of East and West and deserved admiration and careful study by Chinese in their painful struggle with their own shattered cultural identity. A utopian vision of a cosmopolitan culture was behind Zhou Zuoren's love of Greek and Japanese cultures as well as his conception of how Chinese culture could be renewed and what place it should occupy in the universal cultural community. The faith in universal values and the de-emphasis of nationalistic concerns in this vision may provide an important clue to Zhou Zuoren's eventual, tragic decision to collaborate with the Japanese during the Sino-Japanese War.

Zhou Zuoren was aware of the lack of support for his advocacy among his contemporaries. In a speech delivered at Peking University in 1930, he encouraged students to study ancient Greece. Assuring his audience that this was an undertaking "worth ten years of devoted effort," Zhou Zuoren told them that it befit the reputation of Peking University as a leader in higher education to look beyond the West in the past few centuries, which was but the subject of the "ordinary sort of learning" (*putong de xuewen* 普通的学问), and to seek the truth (zhenxiang) about Western civilization by going back to its origin.[28] He resorted to appealing to the audience's sense of elitism and unique social responsibility because he knew full well that he was pleading a cause at odds with the most pressing needs of his time. "Ten years of devoted effort" would not serve the purpose of those for whom it sufficed to invoke ancient Greece as the mirror image of ancient China and as the forerunner of the modern West, the truly great historical moment and the subject of learning that demanded the most serious study. Neither would the National Essence Group, Du Yaquan, and Liang Shuming care very much for any in-depth study of ancient Greece as long as the comparative work would enable them to conclude that China's hope lay in the regeneration of its indigenous tradition. Zhou Zuoren's cause, which sought in ancient Greece inspiration for the creation of a cosmopolitan order that transcended nationalistic aims, was doomed to be a lonely pursuit.

THE *CRITICAL REVIEW* GROUP. This group, best known for its polemic against the New Culture Movement and subjected to decades of opprobrium for its reactionary stance, gained its name from the journal that it published from 1922 to 1933, *Critical Review* (Xueheng 學衡). Its core members, such as Wu Mi (吴宓, 1894–1978), Mei Guangdi (梅光迪, 1890–1945), and Hu Xiansu (胡先驌, 1894–1968), were returned students from the United States, where they had studied with Irving Babbitt (1865–1933), professor of comparative literature at Harvard University and a proponent of New Humanism. Babbitt's New Humanism took aim at the tendency to privilege the material over the spiritual, emotion and instincts over reason, and liberty over self-discipline in modern Western culture. To combat these ills of modernity, as manifested in the ascendancy and celebration of science, democracy, and individualism since Bacon and Rousseau, Babbitt advocated returning to ancient Greece and also drawing on the wisdom of other ancient traditions such as Confucianism and Buddhism. Babbitt's intellectual legacy fundamentally shaped the cause of the *Critical Review* Group.[29]

The group launched its challenge to the agenda of the New Culture Movement by pointing out that it was wrong and misleading to focus on select ideas from the modern West and promote them as if they represented the whole of Western civilization.[30] At their most polemical, Wu Mi and Mei Guangdi asserted that the ideas imported by the activists of the New Culture Movement were just "dregs" (*zaopo* 糟粕) and "poisons" (*duzhen* 毒鸩) of Western culture.[31] These teachings became popular in China both because they were newfangled and appealed to the materialistic and democratic taste of the masses and because no better alternatives were offered by scholars who had a thorough understanding of Western culture.[32]

Such alternatives, of course, were to be found in Irving Babbitt and his New Humanism. Babbitt had truly grasped the essence of Western tradition, and his program could solve the problems of Western modernity, save China from the crisis caused by a mania for modernizing and catching up with the West, and usher in a new world culture that transcended national boundaries and honored the universal and eternal values in Eastern and Western traditions. In this new cultural order, the ancient sages of Greece (Plato and Aristotle), China (Confucius and Mencius), and India (the Buddha) constituted the fountain of wisdom, and they were shown to speak a common language concerning the most fundamental issues of humanity. Although Babbitt encouraged Chinese students to study Buddhism with the aim of exploring its spiritual and moral relevance to contemporary China, he understood Confucianism as an essentially humanistic tradition and believed that the Chinese renaissance should consist in reviving Confucianism and borrowing from the Western humanistic tradition that began with the Greeks. The joint efforts of all humanists East and West, Babbitt hoped, would create a cosmopolitan world without the intervention of an ecumenical religion.[33]

Babbitt's vision, which was cosmopolitan and humanistic and made antiquity a guiding and correcting force in modern life, fully informed the *Critical Review* Group's major positions on how Chinese culture should be reconstructed. First, culture should be defined as the best and most lasting of the ideas, institutions, and practices produced in a society, and classical antiquity should enjoy privileged status in a cultural tradition because of its foundational role and because it has stood the test of time.[34] Those who are willing to devote themselves to the study of Plato and Aristotle will also revere Confucius and Mencius, whereas those who fail to understand the truth about Western culture and only pick up its dregs will necessarily attack the mainstream tradition of premodern China and elevate previously marginalized thinkers, texts, and ideas.[35] Second, the reconstruction of Chinese culture must begin from a serious study of Confucianism and Greco-Roman antiquity, with a goal of creating a new culture that fuses the finest elements of Eastern and Western traditions.[36] Although Buddhism and Christianity have played crucial historical roles in China and the West and could provide resources for the making of a new Chinese culture, the radical decline of religion in modern times and the fact that Confucian humanism provided the foundation of premodern Chinese culture make it compelling to focus on the common ground between Confucianism and Greek philosophy as the starting point in the reconstruction project.[37]

Instead of taking an interest in ancient Greece almost entirely for the light it sheds on the triumph of the West in the modern period, the conservative philhellenes tended to have great reservations about the progressive assumption that the modern West represented the height of Western civilization. Therefore, they were more likely to promote the study of Greek antiquity because it might provide something better than the modern West. In the same connection, the conservatives were more likely than the progressives to regard ancient China and ancient Greece as equals in terms of civilizational status, regardless of whether they saw fundamental affinities or differences between the two. It follows that they were also more likely to insist that the mainstream premodern Chinese tradition (namely, Confucianism) must play a positive, even central role in the new Chinese culture, though some of them advocated reviving classical Confucianism and some favored neo-Confucianism. Finally, all philhellenes shared a strong sense of mission to save Chinese civilization by learning from the West, but some conservatives were simultaneously attracted to the search for universal values in Chinese and Western cultures, a drive that toned down the nationalistic character of their appropriation of Greek antiquity.

It is not difficult to see that conservative philhellenism would lose out to its progressive counterpart. The goals of learning that emerged from the progressives' comparison of Greek and Chinese antiquities were clear, tangible, and of immediate relevance to the nation's struggle for basic survival and minimum respect in the presence of numerous foreign powers. By contrast, the conservatives' preference for the wisdom of antiquity over that of recent times, their declaration of faith in a bright future for an indigenous tradition that was in ruins, and their yearning for a cosmopolitan order that recognized no national boundaries could only appear irrelevant, impractical, and illusory. The phantom of Greece created by the progressives was powerful and persuasive because it offered a mirror into which the disoriented Chinese looked and saw what they had never been and must strive to become, and they had a real-life example, the modern West, close at hand to give them a keen understanding of what was extraordinary about that alien ancient tradition. All that conservative philhellenism had to offer, in contrast, was vague, pale, and lacking in credibility. What was the new culture that perfectly combined the best of Chinese and Western civilizations going to be like? Under what circumstances would a revived Confucianism be given a chance to provide the core cultural values, not only just for China but also for the entire world? How likely were imperial exploitation and international competition to give way to the reign of a humanistic cosmopolitan order? With conviction and advocacy as the only answer to these hard questions, a fantastic utopia would remain the major contribution of conservative philhellenism.

From the Mid-1990s to the Present

The progressive approach to Greek antiquity has continued to dominate scholarly literature in the two decades or so since *River Elegy*. Many scholars, when making comparisons between ancient China and Greece, do not seem any less enthusiastic than the producers of the 1988 TV series and tend to express their admiration for the Mediterranean civilization in the strongest possible language. For example, one calls Athenian democracy "the most splendid and wondrous flowering in human history." Another marvels at how democracy was able to shine again in all its vitality and splendor in the modern West two thousand years after Athens. Two scholars mean it as the highest praise for the ancient culture of Chu (楚) in southern China when they say it rivaled Greece as a peak of ancient civilization. And, as a last example, one scholar, quoting Edith Hamilton's (1867–1963) famous statement that ancient Greece was ancient only in chronology and modern in spirit, pronounces that the entire world is now embracing Greek civilization and believes that China's future lies in active participation in that irresistible trend.[38]

The continuing popularity of the progressive approach to Greek antiquity notwithstanding, the important changes that have taken place in China's status in the world since the mid-1990s and the corresponding transformation of the Chinese people's perceptions of the West and their own ancient tradition are fully reflected in the emergence of a new philhellenic movement. Under the stewardship of Liu Xiaofeng (劉小楓) and Gan Yang (甘陽), both of whom have had extensive experiences in the West, a phenomenal campaign has been launched to promote the teaching and study of Greek classics in Chinese higher education. While in broad outlines these advocates' orientation may be classified as conservative, it also displays some important deviations from their conservative predecessors and simultaneously some interesting similarities with the progressive philhellenes.

Liu and Gan have exerted their efforts on two major fronts: the publication of a large series called Canons and Interpretations (Jingdian yu jieshi 經典與 解釋), among which translations of Greek classics and modern interpretations have the pride of place; and the push for the establishment in universities of general education programs centered on the reading of the "great books" that began with the Greek tradition.[39] This effort culminated in the founding of experimental programs at Zhongshan University and Renmin University in 2009 and 2010 in which students devote most of their four years in college to studying the languages and cultures of ancient Greece, Rome, and China.

Underlying Liu and Gan's ambitious enterprise is the belief that the modern West's distance and alienation from its roots in ancient Greece is comparable to the gap between modern China and Chinese antiquity and that a return to Greece is necessary for a critical examination of Western modernity and a revival of the Chinese tradition. The envisioned revival will reject the paradigms—from values to ways of thinking—set by the modern West and ground itself in a creative reception of the wisdoms of both ancient Greece and ancient China. This being their goal, it is understandable that Liu and Gan have chosen Leo Strauss (1899–1973), the political philosopher who conducted sustained critiques of modernity by invoking the Greeks, as their major source of inspiration in the interpretation of Greek texts.[40]

The Liu-Gan project bears numerous similarities to the cause of the *Critical Review* Group. Both take as their starting point a critical attitude toward the modern West; both turn to Greek antiquity for the vantage point it may provide in critiquing Western modernity; both lionize modern Western thinkers who question the materialistic, individualistic, and democratic orientations of modern Western culture (Babbitt and his colleague P. E. More in one case and Nietzsche, Heidegger, and Leo Strauss in the other); both place Chinese and Greek antiquity on the same footing in their attempts to reclaim the Chinese tradition; both find it necessary to give Confucianism an important place in the remaking of the Chinese tradition; and both adopt a stridently elitist attitude in their advocacy.[41]

Despite all these parallels, there are crucial differences between the aims and stances of the activists in the two movements, which are ultimately due to tremendous differences in their historical circumstances. With a desperate need to legitimate their conservative cause, the *Critical Review* Group eagerly embraced Babbitt's teachings, and they were contented with the belief that the resonances between the texts of ancient China and Greece sufficiently validated the wisdom of the Chinese sages. Liu and Gan demonstrate much greater self-confidence and are much more assertive. Both declare that the age in which the Chinese devoutly and simplistically looked up to the West is over.[42] They present the introduction of Strauss's teachings to the like-minded intellectuals of contemporary China as a "*meeting* of classical minds" (*gudian xinxing de xiangfeng*), that is, as an event and a contact characterized by mutual recognition and equal exchange. Indeed, Liu's statement that China has arrived for this historic rendezvous after a century of disorientation, whereas the West has lost touch with the classical mind for three hundred years, suggests that, contrary to the familiar refrain that China is behind and needs to catch up with the West, he is claiming a position of priority and advantage for China in the construction of a new world order.[43] This is certainly a bold and unprecedented stance among all Chinese intellectuals of the past century or so who have preoccupied themselves with the vexing relationships between China and the West and between tradition and modernity.

The *Critical Review* Group and the Liu-Gan project also differ in their universalistic versus nationalistic concerns. The *Critical Review* Group, who fought their major battle against the progressive intellectuals of the New Culture Movement and were only grateful to have on their side the authority of Babbitt in the struggle for the survival of the Chinese tradition, also faithfully subscribed to their mentor's vision of a cosmopolitan community united by universal, humanistic values and hoped for China to become an integral part of that world order. Liu and Gan, by contrast, have cast their eyes on the achievement of a new world status for Chinese culture that is in keeping with the rise in its economic power, and accordingly adopt a strongly nationalistic posture.

For Gan, the purpose of studying Greece and Rome is to enable Chinese to reexamine Western modernity and China's own antiquity and thereby regain the cultural confidence that they lost for too long and have just begun to recover in the midst of China's remarkable economic takeoff. As Gan puts it, concern with the rise of China should be the driving force behind Chinese interest in Western antiquity, and the study of the Greco-Roman tradition carried out in China is part of Chinese, not Western, scholarship.[44] Liu's manifesto, "Strauss and China," opens with and repeatedly returns to the question, "Why, unlike the introduction of any other Western ideas into China in the past century, has the entrance of Strauss caused so much surprise and anxiety among China watchers in the West?"[45] His answer is this: because all previous Western ideas that influenced China presumed the triumph of the West in the world and the inevitable assimilation of China into an ostensibly universal but actually Western-centered system of politics and culture, whereas Strauss's teachings have the potential to lead the Chinese to reject such an assumption and to embrace their own ancient tradition with confidence and conviction. Liu seems to take pleasure in noting the concern and unease thus aroused among Western observers, and he no doubt understands his own mission as seizing the historic moment to cause a dramatic reconfiguration of the world system of values and beliefs that displaces the centrality of the modern West in favor of the authority of antiquity, both Chinese and Greek.

In Liu's historical vision, this reconfigured world system succeeds the universal order created under the auspices of Enlightenment ideology, which swept away China's *tianxia diguo* (天下帝國, empire of all under heaven) and dominated the Chinese quest for modernity for a century.[46] The new world order, to be constructed through a meeting of classical minds, so far remains an ambition. Will it be a continuation of the Enlightenment vision, except that Chinese and Greek antiquity will now replace the modern West as the new yardsticks of universality? Or, in view of Liu and Gan's insistence that the study of Western classics should serve the cause of China's rise, will it be in essence a universalization of tianxia, in which the values and ideals of a revived Chinese civilization will effortlessly radiate to the rest of the world?[47]

If all Chinese philhellenes prior to the mid-1990s, like other modern Chinese intellectuals, to various degrees shared both universalistic and nationalistic aspirations, never before have the two coexisting interests been manifested with greater confidence and assertiveness than in the two architects of the latest philhellenic movement. Will Chinese and Greek antiquity come out of the meeting of classical minds as full equals in terms of the guidance they can offer for the future of humanity? Or is it true that in reality any universal order will be achieved through the domination of one culture or of a fusion of compatible aspects of multiple cultures?[48] In the final instance, will the meeting of classical minds play out as a reengagement between the Enlightenment concept of world order and revived and revamped visions of tianxia and *wangdao* (王道, the kingly way)?[49] These questions remain to be answered, contingent upon political and economic developments in China and in the world and also upon the ongoing formation of the self-images and self-expectations of Chinese intellectuals. In this process the philhellenes, progressive or conservative, will continue contributing to the larger intellectual discourse that has been driven by the double forces of nationalism and cosmopolitanism for over a century and is entering an exciting new stage, now that the nation has moved far beyond the struggle for basic survival and is poised to claim a new cultural presence in the world.

NOTES

1. Luo, *Minzu zhuyi*, 199.

2. On the complexity and evolution of Liang's intellectual sympathies over his lifetime, see Huang Kewu, *Yige bei fangqi*.

3. For example, both Chen Duxiu (陳獨秀, 1879–1942) and Hu Shi testified that reading Liang Qichao's writings on Western civilization disabused them of the ignorant notion that the West was just an upstart, having had some good fortune in recent times. See Hu Shi, *Hu Shi zizhuan*, 47, 89; Chen Duxiu, "Bo Kang Youwei zhi zongtong zongli shu," 68.

4. Liang Qichao, "Lun Xila gudai xueshu," in *Yinbing shi heji* (Wenji 12), 61; Liang Qichao, "Yadian xiaoshi," in *Yinbing shi heji* (Zhuanji 16), 1–2.

5. All by Liang Qichao, "Lun lifa quan" (論立法權,), in *Yinbing shi heji* (Wenji 9), 102; "Sibada xiaozhi," in *Yinbing shi heji* (Zhuanji 15), 11–12; "Zhongguo xueshu bianqian zhi dashi," in *Yinbing shi heji* (Wenji 7), 33–38.

6. Due to space constraints, in the following pages I shall focus on the latter two aspects. Lu Xun's (魯迅, 1881–1936) "The Spartan Soul" (*Sibada zhi hun* 斯巴達之魂), written in 1903, is an example of the attempt to use the Greeks to arouse the Chinese people's patriotic and martial spirit. It is possible that Lu Xun had been directly inspired by Liang Qichao's *Short Notes on Sparta*. See Chen Shuyu, "Sibada zhi hun," 62.

7. Hu Shi, "Xinxin yu fanxing."

8. On the zhengli guogu undertaking, see Hon, "National Essence," 269–278.

9. For discussions of Hu Shi's mission for a Chinese renaissance, see Grieder, *Hu Shih and the Chinese Renaissance*; Ouyang Zhesheng, "Zhongguo de wenyi fuxing."

10. Chen Xujing, "Quanpan Xihua de liyou" 全盤西化的理由, in *Chen Xujing xueshu lunzhu*, 77–80. All citations of Chen's works are from this anthology.

11. All by Chen Xujing, "Quanpan Xihua de liyou," 84; "Jindai wenhua de zhuli" 近代文化的主力, 90; "Dong Xi wenhua fazhan de bijiao" 東西文化發展的比較, 274–277.

12. Chen did not think this was the case. He believed that no match could be found in ancient China for Euclid's geometry, Thales's astronomy, Plato's political dialogues, and Aristotle's systematic study of a whole array of disciplines and subjects such as biology, politics, and ethics. See Chen Xujing, "Dong Xi wenhua fazhan de bijiao," 278.

13. Gu Zhun, *Xila chengbang zhidu*, was first published in 1982. More writings were included and published as *Gu Zhun wenji* in 1994.

14. The idea of geographical determinism was often invoked by modern Chinese intellectuals in conducting cultural comparisons. For example, Du Yaquan, who is discussed later, would also trace the differences between ancient Chinese and Greek civilizations to their distinct geographical conditions, though he would arrive at a different conclusion as to how to evaluate such differences.

15. The "Gu Zhun fever" that arose in the mid-1990s following the publication of *Gu Zhun wenji* exalted Gu Zhun as a champion of political and economic freedom and identified him as a key figure, alongside such greats as Liang Qichao and Hu Shi, in the lineage of liberalism in modern China. The evaluation of Gu Zhun's historical significance, which to an important degree revolves around the validity of his views on ancient Greece and its legacy in the West, became a contentious topic in the debates between liberal and New Left intellectuals at the turn of the twenty-first century. For a glimpse of the ideologically charged controversy over the writings of Gu Zhun, see Jiang Xianbin, "Ba Gu Zhun huangei lishi."

16. Su Xiaokang and Wang Luxiang, *He shang*.

17. Zhang, *Mighty Opposites*, 196–201; Zhao, *The Power of Tiananmen*, 72–74.

18. It is a theme in *River Elegy* that China failed to take up the invitation of history in premodern times and that the Chinese people are finally again in a position to do so and should not let that opportunity pass by. It also warns that China is in danger of "being stripped of membership in the global community" (*kaichu qiuji* 開除球籍) if its people do not realize the growing gap between China and the Western countries (episode 4).

19. Deng Shi, "Guxue fuxing lun"; Huang Jie, "Huangshi lisu shu."

20. On the National Essence Group, see Hon, "National Essence," 246–255; Zheng Shiqu, *Wan Qing guocuipai*.

21. For instance, reminiscent of the central motif in *River Elegy*, Du Yaquan argues that the different geographical conditions in the Yellow River valley and the Mediterranean gave rise to the different civilizations of ancient China and Greece, one characterized by its emphasis on moral discipline and harmony with nature as well as in society, and the other characterized by its emphasis on competition and human effort. See Du Yaquan, "Jing de wenming yu dong de wenming" 靜的文明與動的文明, in *Du Yaquan wenxuan*, 243–244.

22. Du Yaquan, "Zhanhou Dong Xi wenming zhi tiaohe" 戰後東西文明之調和, in *Du Yaquan wenxuan*, 266–271; Liang Shuming, *Dong Xi wenhua ji qi zhexue*.

23. Du Yaquan and Liang Shuming were both major participants in the East-West cultural debate against such New Culture representatives as Hu Shi and Chen Duxiu. See Hu Fengxiang, *Shehui bianqe*, chs. 4–5.

24. Zhou Zuoren, "Zhongguo de guomin sixiang" 中國的國民思想, in *Zhou Zuoren wen leibian*, 1:805–806; Zhou Zuoren, "Xila xianhua" 希臘閒話, in *Zhou Zuoren wen leibian*, 8:64–65.

25. On the central concern with humanistic values in Zhou Zuoren's writings on ancient Greece, see Wang Yougui, *Fanyijia Zhou Zuoren*, ch. 5.

26. Zhou Zuoren, "Li de wenti" 禮的問題, in *Zhou Zuoren wen leibian*, 9:28–29.

27. For example, in Zhou Zuoren, "Xila zhi yuguang" 希臘之餘光 and "Beida de zhilu" 北大的支路, in *Zhou Zuoren wen leibian*, 8:109, 4:728.

28. Zhou Zuoren, "Beida de zhilu," in *Zhou Zuoren wen leibian*, 4:728. Fourteen years later, he quoted from this speech in an essay titled "Xila zhi yuguang" (8:109).

29. *Critical Review* frequently published introductions to Babbitt's ideas and translations of his works. For Babbitt's influence on the group, see Duan Huaiqing, *Bai Bide*.

30. Tang Yongtong, "Ping jinren zhi wenhua yanjiu"; Mei Guangdi, "Ping tichang xinwenhua zhe"; Wu Mi, "Lun xinwenhua yundong."

31. Mei Guangdi, "Ping tichang xinwenhua zhe," 73–74; Wu Mi, "Lun xinwenhua yundong," 78, 82.

32. Mei Guangdi, "Ping tichang xinwenhua zhe," 74–75; Wu Mi, "Lun xinwenhua yundong," 78–79. For a recent reevaluation of the polemic between the *Critical Review* Group and the New Culture champions, see Feuerwerker, "Reconsidering *Xueheng*."

33. Bai Bide, "Bai Bide zhongxi renwen jiaoyu shuo," 47–48; Mei Guangdi, "Xianjin xiyang renwen zhuyi," 36.

34. A bold expression of the group's elitist view of culture and learning can be found in Mei Guangdi, "Lun jinri wuguo xueshujie zhi xuyao." He states that a true democracy should aim at raising the level of the masses and enabling them to participate in elite

culture and enjoy the "scarce and precious products" of philosophy, arts and letters, and science rather than forcing the intellectual elite to lower themselves in order to cater to the masses (140).

35. Wu Mi, "Lun xinwenhua yundong," 83. Without naming names, Wu Mi criticizes Hu Shi by stating, "If someone is a believer of Dewey's pragmatism, then he will necessarily exalt Mozi above the rest of the philosophers."

36. Examples of statements on the group's cosmopolitan ambitions: Mei Guangdi, "Xianjin xiyang renwen zhuyi," 36; Wu Mi, "Lun xinwenhua yundong," 96. For a general discussion of the role that Greco-Roman classics played in the group's cultural project, see Saussy, "Contestatory Classics."

37. Wu Mi, "Lun xinwenhua yundong," 96.

38. Li Yujie, *Zhongguo zaoqi guojia*, 529; Yang Shiqun, *Dong Zhou Qin Han*, 145; Cai Jingquan, *Chu wenhua*, 1, 2; Liu Chenglin, *Jitan yu jingjichang*, 304–305.

39. As of January 2015, over 350 titles have been published in Canons and Interpretations. In the reading list that Liu recommended for the general education programs he designed, six out of the fifteen basic Western classics were Greek texts (covering epic poetry, tragedy, history, and philosophy). One Roman epic and four texts in the Judeo-Christian tradition, and Bacon, Shakespeare, Lessing, and Nietzsche complete the list. See Liu Xiaofeng, *Chongqi gudian shixue*, 314–319.

40. The 1980s essays collected in Gan's *Gujin zhongxi zhi zheng* foreshadow some of his current positions regarding the relationships between China and the West and between tradition and modernity. Gan's latest important statement on Greco-Roman learning, made at a forum on Western classics in 2009, has been published under the title "Zhongguo jiandanhua xuexi xifang de shidai yijing jieshu le." Liu's representative views may be found in the following works: "Shitelaosi de lubiao," "Shitelaosi yu Zhongguo," *Chongqi*.

41. Liu and Gan's positions in this respect are expressed in their general education curriculum and also in such works as Liu Xiaofeng, *Rujiao yu minzu guojia*; Gan Yang, *Tong santong*; and Gan Yang, "Zhongguo daolu." In making a case for their general education programs, Gan and Liu are explicit about their aim to train an intellectual and moral elite who rise above the pragmatic and materialistic pursuits that define the pedagogical goals of most Chinese universities. The elitism pervading Liu's works on Greek learning finds a peculiar expression in his attraction to Strauss's distinction between two forms of philosophical teachings: esoteric and exoteric. In order to protect themselves from misunderstanding and persecution, philosophers often have to hide their real teachings in secret writing, which can only be decoded through careful reading by the initiated, whereas what they openly profess is only intended for the uninitiated and does not contain the truth. Liu's fascination with this idea can be glimpsed in the anthology *Ciwei de wenshun*.

42. Liu Xiaofeng, "Shitelaosi yu Zhongguo"; Gan Yang, "Zhongguo jiandanhua."

43. Liu Xiaofeng, "Shitelaosi yu Zhongguo."

44. Gan Yang, "Zhongguo jiandanhua."

45. Liu Xiaofeng, "Shitelaosi yu Zhongguo." For testimony to the attention that Western scholars are paying to China's engagement with Strauss, see Lilla, "Reading Strauss in Beijing."

46. Liu Xiaofeng, "Shitelaosi yu Zhongguo."

47. Lilla's reference to the Roman Empire in his essay on the Strauss phenomenon in China may reflect this idea. Remarking on the time and energy that young Chinese admirers of Strauss are devoting to the study of ancient languages and texts, Lilla concludes his essay with the statement, "They are not in a hurry. Rome wasn't built in a day."

48. Gan Yang suggested as much at the symposium on his book *Wenming guojia daxue*, held in Beijing on December 30, 2011. He called Samuel Huntington, author of *The Clash of Civilizations and the Remaking of World Order*, the only American intellectual who could more or less be considered a thinker. The full transcript of Gan Yang's remarks at the symposium can be found at http://chinadigitaltimes.net/chinese/2012/01/甘阳:《文明 · 国家 · 大学》新书发布会上的讲话/, accessed January 14, 2017.

49. In Chinese-language scholarship, there has been a remarkable resurgence of interest in these two related, venerable concepts in Confucian political thought. See Gan Chunsong, *Chonghui wangdao.*

6

REALIZING TIANXIA

Traditional Values and China's Foreign Policy

Daniel A. Bell

★

Tianxia—usually translated as "all under heaven" or "the world"—has been central to Chinese political thinking and has shaped the way that China has dealt with the rest of the world for over two millennia. According to Li Yangfan, tianxia is the key idea that differentiates Chinese from European political culture.[1] Whereas the idea of a state with fixed territorial boundaries has been central to Western political culture, Chinese political culture has been shaped by a more global perspective.[2] Instead of viewing itself as one state in a competitive international environment of other states, China has viewed itself as the center of a world that should be unified and peaceful.

Ironically, China has more recently become known as a country that seems obsessed with sovereignty. Although the concept of sovereignty had European origins (the term came to China via a process of transplantation that includes a Japanese interlude) and ran counter to core aspects of indigenous Chinese approaches to territory, it became the mainstream way of thinking about territory among political and intellectual Chinese elites in the twentieth century.[3] The roots of China's political Westernization date from China's military defeats at the hands of Western powers in the mid- to late nineteenth century. Chinese elites could no longer see themselves as occupying a symbolic world in which their polity possessed a superior normative value; instead, they became preoccupied with the painful reality that their country was peripheral within the expanding Westphalian international order. If China was to survive, it had to adjust to this new system.[4]

In the early twentieth century, the influential Chinese intellectual Liang Qichao criticized the Chinese for excessive idealism: "The Chinese people have never taken the state as the highest entity; they believed there must be an entity higher than the state and exercising control over all states. That was tianxia." Traditional politics "did not take the tranquility and happiness of a single state as its ultimate purpose, but had the tranquility and happiness of all mankind as its final aim." In a dangerous and Darwinian world system of competing states, Liang thought that this was a shortcoming that must be corrected immediately, and he repeatedly called on his countrymen to give importance to "the state."[5]

The establishment of a relatively strong and secure Chinese state in 1949 meant that China had less reason to worry about survival as a political community. However, the Korean War, instability in minority regions, and the break with the Soviet Union (not to mention a degree of paranoia among ruling elites) led China to adopt a rigid posture regarding territorial boundaries.[6] In the early 1990s, global condemnation of the Tiananmen Square crackdown and the collapse of the Soviet empire made the regime even more sensitive about outside interference, and the Western idea of respect for state sovereignty and territorial boundaries became an entrenched mode of political discourse. The key was to ensure survival of the political community. Chinese Communist Party rulers claimed that opening up China to interference by foreigners would open a Pandora's box, with the country plunging into civil war, poverty, and chaos.

Such sentiments are receding with time. Clearly China is stronger than before and does not have to worry as much about foreign incursions. The realities and responsibilities of being a great power are gradually rendering preoccupation with state sovereignty less central. "To each his own" in international affairs no longer makes any sense. With China's economic integration into the global market, it has the power to influence economic actors around the globe (and vice versa). The environmental consequences of China's economic growth (it has become the largest emitter of greenhouse gases) threaten the rest of the world. It has been blamed for supporting repressive regimes in Ethiopia and Zimbabwe. If China affects the rest of the world, how can it ask the rest of the world not to interfere with its own internal affairs?

Faced with such concerns, China has begun to play a more responsible and cooperative role in international affairs. It has shown willingness to settle long-standing territorial disputes with its neighbors.[7] It has sent four thousand soldiers and police to participate in fourteen UN peacekeeping missions: more than any of the other five members of the UN Security Council.[8] China has participated in antipiracy operations off the coast of Somalia and has helped with an increasing number of humanitarian missions abroad: soon after Japan's devastating earthquake and tsunami in March 2011, Chinese rescue teams were mobilized to help with the recovery process, and Chinese defense minister Liang Guangjie publicly offered military aid. China's response to the Libya crisis in spring 2011 is an even more striking example: China's representative to the United Nations quickly voted for the UN sanctions against the Qaddafi government, and for the first time China dispatched a warship and four military aircraft that evacuated 35,860 Chinese nationals and 2,100 foreigners from Libya.[9]

Of course, such efforts often fall short of what the Chinese government ought to do. But what exactly is the government supposed to do? What moral principles should inform China's foreign policy, the way China deals with the rest of the world? Not surprisingly, perhaps, traditional values help Chinese leaders make sense of the new emphasis on international responsibility and also help to provide moral resources for social critics to expose the inevitable gap between the ideal and the reality. In the context of the broader revival of Confucianism, the ideal of tianxia has been revived for the purpose of rethinking China's role in Asia and beyond.[10] But what exactly is tianxia? And how can it help us to think about China's role in the world? The rest of this chapter focuses on these questions.

The Concept of Tianxia

The first point to make about tianxia is that it is a vague concept that has been used differently in different times (and differently in the same times).[11] To further complicate matters, the term has sometimes been used in a descriptive sense meaning the whole world and other times in a normative sense as an ideal that contrasts with reality. Tianxia predates Confucianism, but Confucian thinkers—along with other thinkers in the late Warring States period—emphasized its political, normative dimension.[12] In the *Mencius*, for example, the term is used eighty-six times and often refers to an ideal of a unified world without any territorial boundaries governed by one benevolent ruler, meant to contrast with the ugly reality of small states competing ruthlessly for territorial advantage.[13] Once the warring states had been unified by Qin Shihuang and the new centralized state he created (and later emperors re-created) viewed itself as the empire at the center of the world, the term often took on more descriptive meanings. In the Tang dynasty, for example, tianxia referred either to the area actually governed by Tang rulers or to the whole world with Zhongguo (China) at its core, surrounded by other countries.[14] In the seventeenth century—toward the end of the Ming and in the early stages of the Manchu-governed Qing Empire— Confucian thinkers explicitly drew on the normative implications of tianxia for critical purposes. Huang Zongxi criticized the rulers of his day for treating tianxia as something meant to serve their own interests rather than the people's interests.[15] His contemporary Gu Yanwu explicitly distinguished between the fall of the state (国家) and the fall of tianxia, arguing that the common people's obligation is to the latter but that securing the state or dynastic polity is the concern of rulers or officials.[16] His point is that political dynasties will collapse when they fail to provide for the people's needs and gain the people's trust.[17]

In contemporary times, tianxia was famously revived by the philosopher Zhao Tingyang, who gave it a normative definition. According to Zhao's influential formulation, tianxia has three meanings: a geographical meaning referring to the whole world; a psychological meaning that the hearts of all the world's peoples are unified, like a big family; and an institutional meaning of a world government with the power to ensure universal order.[18] Zhao's ideal echoes the early twentieth-century Confucian-inspired thinker Kang Youwei's political ideal of *taiping shi* (global peace), in which people are freed from particular attachments and all goals are shared in common, but it's worth asking if these ideals are really consistent with Confucian values.[19]

Zhao claims that his ideal derives inspiration from the values and practices promoted by the founding fathers of the Zhou dynasty approximately three thousand years ago—the same sage-kings who inspired Confucius—but it is radically inconsistent with the key Confucian value of graded love. Zhao's global government is supposed to be supported by the world's people psychologically bound like an intimate family (the second feature), but this ideal owes more to imported traditions like Christianity, Buddhism, and Marxism that aim to break down particularistic attachments.[20] Consider the reference to tianxia in the *Great Learning*. This Han dynasty work—subsequently canonized by the Song dynasty scholar Zhu Xi (1130–1200) as one of the four Confucian classics—opens with the famous passage, "The extension of knowledge consists in the investigation of things. When things are investigated, knowledge is extended; when knowledge is extended, the will is sincere; when the will is sincere, the mind is rectified; when the mind is rectified, the personal life is cultivated; when the personal life is cultivated, the family will be regulated; when the family is regulated, the state will be in order; and when the state is in order, there is peace throughout the world [tianxia]." Starting from the moral ordering of the individual person and the family, an important goal of Confucianism is to bring order to the state and thereby to spread peace throughout the world. The ideal is a harmonious political order of global peace. But nowhere does the *Great Learning* state that ties to people outside the state should be as strong as ties to people within the state. The reason is simple: ties should be extended from intimates to others, but with diminishing intensity as distance increases. We owe more to intimates (starting with the family) than to strangers, both because they are the main sources of happiness and because we need to reciprocate for what they have done for us. Hence, the web of obligations that binds citizens is more intense than the one binding foreigners. As Joseph Chan puts it, "The Confucian view that it is natural and right for a person to show more concern for people close to him or her than to strangers would lead one to accept at least some kind of territorial boundary that distributes more resources to citizens of a community than to outsiders."[21]

But the *Great Learning* reminds us that it shouldn't end there. Just as we should extend ties beyond the family, so we should extend ties beyond the nation. It is also natural and right to extend concern to outsiders, though less and less as ties extend further and further from the political community. Hence, Confucianism should not view special concern for fellow citizens as a politically necessary compromise, a second-best deviation from an ideal world. Nor is it just a necessary mechanism on the way to the politics of global love and government. At least some sort of special commitment to a particular political community is required by the logic of graded love, and it should be extended (in diminishing degrees) to outsiders.[22]

In short, a Confucian-inspired defense of the ideal of tianxia would not involve a world government that has ethical and political priority over national states (not to mention an anarchist or communist ideal of abolishing the state). It would involve thinking about the sorts of obligations that we owe to people living outside the territorial boundaries of our states, even though they are not as great as the obligations we owe to fellow citizens. Of course, the ideal of tianxia would have to be modified from its understanding in imperial times. Nobody believes that China is the center of the world (or the universe), so the question is not what Chinese rulers owe to "barbarians" living outside the country but rather what they owe to people living in other countries. Given that the Chinese state finds itself at a time of transition from an age of survival to an age of expansion and global influence, it seems a particularly topical question to think about. But the value of tianxia by itself can't do all the work. We need to look to other values for a fuller picture of a morally informed approach to Chinese foreign policy. For this purpose, I draw on contemporary Chinese thinkers who work within a Confucian political framework to develop ideas for China's foreign policy.[23] Along the way, I make comparisons with liberal and Marxist approaches. Let me then turn to key Confucian political values—hierarchy, harmony, and meritocracy—and say a bit about how they might inform China's foreign policy in ways that are both humane and realistic.[24]

A Hierarchical World Order

Contemporary Chinese thinkers have explicitly called into question the liberal ideal of equality between sovereign states, arguing instead for more hierarchical arrangements between states in the international arena. As one might expect, critics in the West have raised doubts about this Chinese project. William Callahan, for example, has charged that Zhao Tingyang's ideal of tianxia masks an effort to replace Western hegemony with Chinese hegemony.[25] But Zhao's latest work responds to such concerns. He explicitly argues for a world organization that would have more territory and resources than any one state (including the Chinese state): "The world government directly rules a land called King-land, about twice the size of a large sub-state, and four times that of a medium sized sub-state and so on. The military force controlled by the world government is greater than those of large, medium and small sub-states with a ratio of 6 to 3, 6 to 2 and 6 to 1 divisions. This proportional design limits the King-land of the world government in its advantages over the sub-states either in resources or military power."[26] Zhao's proposal may help alleviate concerns about Chinese hegemony, but it's unclear how it could be realized in the actual political world: as Zhang Feng puts it, "The critical flaw of Zhao's thesis is his failure to outline any clear pathway that might lead to the creation of the world institution of the *tianxia* system.... He insists on the priority of the world institution, yet surprisingly fails to provide any description of how it might come about ... and [be] maintained."[27]

Yan Xuetong's defense of a hierarchical world system, with China as a major power, is more realistic. Yan draws on the thoughts of the pre-Qin thinker Xunzi to question the ideal of equality between states: "After the Treaty of Westphalia of 1648, equality of state sovereignty developed to become a universal moral international norm. Xunzi's thought is the exact opposite of equality of sovereignty.... According to Xunzi's interpretation of Five Services, distinctions in international norms should be decided according to a state's status in international society."[28] Given China's decisive influence on the global economy and its increasing ability to project military power, Yan argues that China should play a more major role on the world stage and should come clean in doing so: "China should not adopt the United States' current way of acting, saying that all states are equal while in practice always seeking to have a dominant international status." Moreover, such hierarchical arrangements can actually benefit weaker states because this sense of dominance means that states have extra responsibilities, including the provision of assistance to poor countries. Rather than insisting on reciprocity with weaker states, China should try to gain their support by allowing for differential international norms to work in their favor. In the cooperation of the 10 + 1 (Association of Southeast Asian Nations [ASEAN] and China), for example, "China is required to implement the norm of zero tariffs in agricultural trade before the ASEAN states do. This unequal norm enabled the economic cooperation of the 10 + 1 to develop more rapidly than that between Japan and ASEAN. Japan's demand for equal tariffs with ASEAN slowed the progress of its economic cooperation with the ASEAN states, which lags far behind that of China and ASEAN."[29] Yan adds that hierarchical norms also contribute to international peace: "If we examine recent international history, we can see that in those areas that implemented international norms, international peace was better maintained than it was in areas that had norms for equality. During the Cold War, the equal status of the United States and the Soviet Union was such that they undertook many proxy wars in order to compete for hegemony, while their special status in NATO and the Warsaw Pact, respectively, enabled them to prevent the members of those alliances from engaging in military conflict with one another." Here too, the extra responsibilities for the major powers in hierarchical systems may actually benefit the weaker ones: "China should propose that large states and small states have different responsibilities, and that different states should respect different security norms.... If nuclear weapons do not proliferate, then nuclear states must strictly adhere to nonproliferation while providing security guarantees to nonnuclear states."[30]

Allen Carlson suggests that a hierarchical system may also contribute to solving territorial disputes with China's neighbors because China's leaders might place less emphasis on the sanctity of boundaries than is currently the case: "In a reconstituted *tianxia* system, the territorial and jurisdictional concerns which have so preoccupied China's leaders over the course of the last century could be re-imagined as issues involving peripheral regions, not zero-sum disputes over sovereign recognition. In this sense, a *tianxia* order might pave the way for the novel solution of such controversies, and as such lead to greater stability within the region." The problem, as Carlson goes on to note, is that the large states along China's periphery are likely to construe an attempt to impose (or even articulate) a new normative hierarchical order in the East Asian region as a threat: "Within such a system it is clear that it is China that is to occupy the paramount position, while those along its margins are expected to accept such dominance and show fealty to the center. Obviously, within such an order there is no rhetorical space for any external arbitrator of normative principles, such as the United States."[31]

To be fair, Yan himself explicitly argues that the tribute system is outdated for the modern world—"In fact, any effort to restore the tribute system will weaken China's capability for international political mobilization."[32] He recognizes that neighboring states in East Asia would be likely to welcome a system that enshrines second-class status. It could also be argued that the tribute system itself is a largely an invention of Western Sinologists and cannot usefully explain China's interaction with its neighbors over long periods of time.[33] In historical practice, Chinese imperial courts did not usually use the idea of tributary relations to interfere in the internal affairs of neighboring states, and the states on China's periphery often had complete independence.[34] So the charge that neighboring states would be expected to show fealty or pay tribute to China may not stick. But there is the issue of the United States' military dominance in the region, and it's hard to imagine that any reconstituted hierarchical order with a greater role for China based on its growing economic and military power would not involve any substantial change in that respect. So how could China gain the trust of its neighbors such as South Korea and Japan, who seem distinctly worried by China's growing military might? China's bellicose approach to regional territorial disputes in 2010 only reinforced these concerns, and any talk of ending military alliances with the United States seems further removed than ever.

Yan does not explicitly address this issue, but his theory of political leadership may be helpful in alleviating concerns. To make itself a rising power that is welcomed by the rest of the world, Yan says that China should act as a humane authority that does good in the rest of the world. Yan's theory of political leadership is directly inspired by pre-Qin thinkers. In contrast to Marxists, who believe that economic might is the key to national power, and to neoconservatives, who believe that countries should rely on military might to get their way, Yan argues that political leadership is the key to national power and that morality is an essential part of political leadership. Economic and military power might matter as components of national power, but they are secondary to political leaders who act in accordance with moral norms.

Of course, China must show more evidence that it is acting according to humane norms before it can persuade its neighbors that it should take on more responsibilities in the East Asian region (and that the United States should close its military bases). And it must begin at home. As Yan puts it, "For China to become a superpower modeled on humane authority, it must first become a model from which other states are willing to learn."[35] Yan argues that the modern equivalent of humane authority is democracy—"I think that in their respect for norms, the modern concept of democracy and the ancient Chinese concept of humane authority are alike"—but he doesn't spell out in detail the implications for domestic political reform.[36] What is clear, perhaps, is that other countries are not likely to be inspired by a thin-skinned regime that imprisons leading artists, peaceful political reformers, and public-interest lawyers.

Political Meritocracy

Whatever their rhetorical support for the idea of democracy, Confucian-inspired reformers made political meritocracy one of their key ideals. Whereas Marxists aim for an ideal world without any government—in "higher communism," the state would have withered away because there is no need for instruments of violence in a classless society, and liberal cosmopolitans tend to be inspired by Immanuel Kant's ideal of a federation of republican (or democratic) governments that can converge on the value of global peace—Confucians are explicit that any government concerned with the world would have to be composed of above-average moral and political talent.[37] There should be equality of opportunity in education (有教无类, as Confucius put it in the *Analects*, 15.39) and government, but not everybody will emerge from the educational process with equal capacity to make competent and morally justifiable political judgments. Hence, an important task of the political system is to identify and select those with above-average capacity.

Perhaps the most influential statement of Confucius's own highest political ideal is the account of the Great Way (大道) in the *Record of Rites* (*Liji* 礼记), a work compiled during the Han dynasty on the basis of older materials. This ideal is described as an age when the world worked for the interests of all people (*tianxia wei gong* 天下为公), and these characters are immediately followed by an ideal of political meritocracy: "the worthy and the able were promoted to office 选贤与能." In an article on tianxia, Liu Junping, a philosopher at Wuhan University, draws on this passage to defend a political ideal where the most talented members of the community occupy political posts.[38] Zhao Tingyang is even more explicit: "The unspoken theory [within the concept of tianxia] is that people do not really know what is best for them, but that the elite do, so the elite ought genuinely to decide for the people."[39] Of course, Zhao has a powerful world government in mind—not realistic today—so it's worth asking what the ideal of political meritocracy would mean for a Chinese government inspired by the ideals of tianxia.

Yan Xuetong proposes that China should learn from Xunzi's recommendation of strategy for a rising power, which "stresses human talent, that is, focuses on competition for talent." Again, he critiques the status quo: "At present, China's strategy of seeking talent is still mainly used for developing enterprises and has not yet been applied to raising the nation as a whole. Talent is still understood as having to do with technicians rather than politicians or high-ranking officials." Talented people are available, but they are not always chosen: "Xunzi thinks that there are many talented people with both morality and ability, and the key is whether the ruler would choose them."

Drawing on historical examples, Yan puts forward some strategies for finding talent. First,

> the degree of openness is high: choosing officials from the whole world who meet the requisite standards of morality and ability, so as to improve the capability of the government to formulate correct policies. For example, in ancient times, the Tang Dynasty in China and the Empire in North Africa, Spain, and the Middle East, in the course of their rise, employed a great number of foreigners as officials. It is said that at the peak of the Umayyad Empire, more than 70 percent of its officials were foreigners. The United States has attained its present hegemonic status also by its policy of attracting talented and outstanding foreigners.

In other words, the main competition with the United States should be for human talent rather than for economic or military superiority.[40]

Second, Yan argues that officials should be held responsible for their mistakes. He opposes lifetime job security, which increases the risk of officials becoming corrupt, lazy, and prone to repeating mistakes. In the more meritocratic societies, "unsuitable government officials could be speedily removed, reducing the probability of erroneous decisions. This applied to all politicians and officials, if they lost their ability to make correct decisions for any reason, such as being corrupted by power, being out-of-date in knowledge, decaying in thought, suffering a decline in their ability to reflect, or experiencing deterioration in health. Establishing a system by which officials can be removed in a timely fashion provides opportunities for talented people and can reduce errors of policy and ultimately increase political power."

Yan also argues for the establishment of independent think tanks that would provide professional advice on policy. At the moment, "the research institutions attached to our government agencies are not think tanks in the strict sense. Their main task is to carry out policies, not to furnish ideas. To undertake the work of a think tank is to exercise social responsibility." Institutions similar to think tanks existed in the past (e.g., Confucian academies in the Song dynasty), but "since the founding of the new China in 1949, the state has not allowed high officials to have their own personal advisors or to rely on nongovernmental advisory organizations."[41]

In short, China can increase its political power by adopting a more meritocratic system of selecting political officials and advisers. But this leads to the question of what exactly these talented and public-spirited politicians and advisers should aim for. I leave aside domestic policy; here the question is how to aim for the good of people living outside China's boundaries who are affected by China's policies. To repeat, China does not have the same obligations to foreigners as to its own citizens, but tianxia means that it does have some obligations. So how can one increase the likelihood that it would aim for the good of noncitizens? In addition to Yan's suggestions—more employment of foreigners, more job accountability, and more independent think tanks—there are other possibilities.

Most important, perhaps, there is a need to recognize that China's own policies—keeping its currency low to help with Chinese exports, greenhouse gas emissions, and so on—may have negative consequences for other countries. Hence, there may be a need for a separate political institution composed of deputies who have the explicit task of deliberating about and serving the interests of noncitizens. The deputies could be selected at least partly by modernized competitive examinations that test for knowledge of international affairs, basic economics, and the Confucian political classics, and their power can be checked by such means as term limits and stiff penalties for corruption.[42] Of course, such proposals are far removed from the current reality, not just in China, but also in democratic states, where rulers selected by the people have obligations to the community of voters and nobody represents the community of nonvoters (including foreigners) who are affected by government policies. But they are less utopian than Zhao's proposal for a world institution that has ethical and political priority over actually existing states. And if China really is moving toward a form of government inspired by tianxia and related Confucian political values, it is not impossible to imagine an institution explicitly designed to serve the interests of noncitizens.

More realistic (in the short term) is that China can assist other countries that are seeking to build up meritocratic rule. Just as the United States promotes democracy abroad via government-funded foundations like the National Endowment for Democracy, so the Chinese government can fund an institution—let's call it the National Endowment for Meritocracy—that would fund experiments in political meritocracy designed to improve governance in other countries. Western powers may not be interested, but there will be takers in Africa and elsewhere.[43]

Social Harmony

The value of harmony is central to Confucian political ethics, and the famous line from the *Analects* that exemplary persons should pursue harmony (和) but not sameness/uniformity/conformity (同) is well known to most Chinese intellectuals. The contrast between harmony and sameness originated in the *Zuo Zhuan*—a text of narrative history of the Spring and Autumn period compiled no later than 389 BCE that was canonized as one of the thirteen Confucian classics—where it clearly referred to the idea that the ruler should be open to different political views among his advisers. As Li Chenyang explains, the value of harmony also affirms the value of mutual accommodation between cultures: "The Confucian maintains that the harmony model should be used in solving conflicts between cultures in today's world. In the harmony model, when cultures conflict, the best way to handle conflict is not to protect one's own ground and try to eliminate the opponent; it is to find a way to work out an arrangement that allows oneself as well as one's opponent to adjust. . . . Through mutual adjustment and mutual accommodation we reshape the situation into a harmonious one."[44] Hence, contemporary defenders of the ideal of tianxia repeatedly draw on the ideal of harmony to argue for respect for different cultures and value systems.[45]

But respect for different cultures does not mean equal respect for all cultures. Just as Christians think that Christian values are superior to other religions' values and liberals believe that liberal values are superior to other political values, so Confucians believe that Confucian values are superior to non-Confucian values. Societies that value meritocracy, harmony, and other Confucian values such as ritual are superior to those that don't. The early Confucians recognized that there were different kinds of states in the Spring and Autumn and Warring States periods, but they differentiated between peoples on the basis of level of cultural development, meaning commitment to Confucian culture, rather than ethnicity or territory. The term "China" referred to a cultural entity bound by Confucian culture, and in principle it was open to anybody who partook of those norms, regardless of race or ethnicity. Those who did not were considered to be "barbarians," but everyone in principle could be "civilized."[46]

What are the implications for China? On the one hand, Confucianism can serve as the moral basis for a critique of ethnic-based notions of nationalism and citizenship. It is true that the reality has often deviated from the ideal. Han Chinese racism was far from uncommon in imperial Chinese history.[47] In the early twentieth century, the Confucian reformer Kang Youwei (1858–1927) selectively appropriated Western racial categories and created a taxonomy of hierarchical races according to white, yellow, red, and black skin colors, with the former two superior to the latter two.[48] Today, Confucian intellectuals in China no longer use such racial or ethnic categories. John Makeham argues that "cultural nationalism"—the conviction that the unique culture associated with the nation constitutes the basis of national identity—is shared by a wide spectrum of participants in contemporary Chinese discourse on Confucianism.[49] But (re)Confucianizing China—meaning the building of a national identity centered on commitment to Confucian values—does not rule out the possibility that non-Chinese (people who are not ethnically Han and/or do not have Chinese citizenship) can be Confucians. Tu Weiming, the most prominent Confucian in the English-speaking world, goes so far as to argue that Confucianism must take root outside of China before it can be promoted successfully within China: "Whether Confucianism [will have] vitality in the [rest of the] twentieth century will principally be determined by whether it is able to make its way fully back to China via New York, Paris, Tokyo. . . . It must confront the challenges of American culture, European culture, and East Asian culture (that is, industrial East Asia), and furthermore sow seeds and take root in these cultures."[50] Jiang Qing, the most prominent political Confucian in mainland China, argues that Confucian values cannot accommodate central Western values, but he also rejects racialist and ethnic forms of nationalism. The only relevant criterion for admittance to the Confucian nation is commitment to Confucian values.[51]

Still, there may be a worry that Confucianism's confidence in its values could translate into "civilizing missions" outside the Confucian nation, similar to John Stuart Mill's justification for British imperialism in India on the grounds that the "barbarians" were insufficiently rational to govern themselves.[52] But Confucians argue for the use of soft power—moral example, ritual, and persuasion—to bring the non-Confucians into the fold. It is true that the practice has often deviated from the ideal. The Ming dynasty's strategy against the Mongols, for example, "placed a high degree of value on the use of pure violence to solve conflicts."[53] But Jiang Shidong, who teaches law at Beijing University, argues that Confucian political values have also underpinned relatively humane ways of dealing with cultural conflict. He argues that the "one country, two systems" formula for Hong Kong is rooted in Confucian values such as tianxia that justify a hands-off approach for the rule of outlying territories. The model was implemented in Tibet during the Qing dynasty and in the early days of Mao's rule, and Jiang suggests that the same model can be used to govern Tibet in the future.[54]

The ideal of tianxia, however, suggests that China should concern itself not just with cultural groups within the country and neighboring jurisdictions but also with the question of how to promote its political values to the rest of the world. If Confucians rule out force (except in cases of just war; see note 24), then other mechanisms are available. Nongovernmental organizations (NGOs) based in the United States, such as Freedom House, rank countries according to their support for political freedoms, the implication being that other countries should conform to the ideals espoused in the U.S. Constitution. China, in contrast, can promote the ideal of harmony. This is perhaps best done via NGOs, because official support is likely to arouse political suspicion. Hence, one might imagine an NGO—let's call it Harmony House—that relies on rigorous empirical methods to determine the extent of harmony in the world. Countries could be ranked according to a Social Harmony Index that measures rates of crime and incarceration, gaps between rich and poor, and success at dealing with cultural conflict in a peaceful way. Countries that do well on the index could set a model for other countries.[55]

Conclusion

In sum, I have drawn on the works of contemporary Chinese political thinkers for the purpose of spelling out some of the practical and institutional implications of a Chinese foreign policy inspired by tianxia and related Confucian political values. I do not mean to imply that we need to stick to a Confucian framework when thinking about a morally justified approach to Chinese foreign policy. Nor do I mean to deny that freedom, democracy, and human rights have a place in China's future. But a Confucian moral framework might be most psychologically compelling in a Chinese context and hence might have more causal power than other frameworks. From a normative standpoint, my own view is that a Confucian-inspired foreign policy is both realistic and humane and can improve upon some of the drawbacks of liberal and Marxist approaches. But the reader will no doubt disagree, and I look forward to the criticisms.

This chapter is reprinted from *Confucianism for the Contemporary World: Global Order, Political Plurality, and Social Action*, edited by Kristin Stapleton and Tze-ki Hon (Albany and New York: SUNY Press, 2017). The editor thanks SUNY Press for permission to reprint. The author is grateful for comments from Tze-ki Hon, Kristin Stapleton, and Ban Wang; comments by conference participants at the State University of New York, Buffalo, conference on New Confucianism, April 27–28, 2012, and the Tianxia Workshop at Stanford University, May 6–11, 2011; and helpful e-mails and articles sent by Yuri Pines and Justin Tiwald.

1. Li Yangfan, "'天下' 观念" [On the concept of "tianxia"], 113–114.

2. To be more precise, the idea of a state with fixed territorial boundaries was central to Western political culture in ancient Greece and has been since the peace of Westphalia in 1648. It could be argued that the Roman sense of territory was no stricter than in Han or Tang China. I thank Qian Jiang for this point.

3. This may oversimplify imperial Chinese history. As early as the Song dynasty, there were values and practices that anticipated modern-day concerns with sovereignty. The Chinese empire was subject to repeated invasions from outside, and boundaries became more rigid and fortified; outsiders were portrayed in a more negative light; wars were justified in terms of the protection of territory; and Confucian intellectuals penned novels and historical works and defended rituals that justified patriotic attachment to China (as opposed to tianxia). See Ge Zhaozhao, 宋代《中国》意识的凸显 [The prominence of "China" consciousness], 5–12.

4. Carlson, "Reimagining the Frontier," 3–4.

5. Liang Qichao, quoted in Luo, "From 'Tianxia' (All under Heaven) to 'the World,'" 96. Liang gradually came to a more positive view of the world thinking implied in tianxia. After World War I, he argued that political rulers should not simply be concerned with making their own nation strong and prosperous; they should also be concerned with the fate of the world. Liang explicitly criticized Western nationalism for being too narrow and argued that the West should learn from the traditional Chinese idea of tianxia to expand concern beyond the nation (Chen Zehuan, "Individuals, Nation States, and the World").

6. China's participation in the Bandung conference in 1955 and Zhou Enlai's efforts to establish friendly ties with newly independent states in Asia and Africa that were strongly interested in a strict view of sovereignty are other factors (I thank Kristin Stapleton for this point).

7. Travel, "Regime Insecurity and International Cooperation," 46.

8. Gill and Huang, "Sources and Limits of China's Soft Power," 22.

9. Yan Xuetong, "How Assertive Should a Power Be?"

10. Carlson, "Moving beyond Sovereignty?," 96.

11. Li Yangfan, "'天下' 观念" [On the concept of "tianxia"], 107, 111.

12. Pines, "Changing Views of *Tianxia* in Pre-imperial Discourse," 105–106.

13. Pines, "Changing Views of *Tianxia* in Pre-imperial Discourse," 108.

14. Li Fang, "An Analysis of 'China' and 'Tianxia.'"

15. Liu Junping, "'天下'宇宙观的演变及其哲学意蕴" [The development and philosophical meaning of tianxia cosmology].

16. The phrase "天下兴亡，匹夫有责" (adapted from Gu Yanwu's original formulation: 保天下者，匹夫之贱与有责焉耳) is known to most high school students in China but is used almost interchangeably beginning with "heaven" or "state." The critical import of Yan's phrase is lost because either way it is taken to mean that ordinary citizens should serve and care about the well-being of the state.

17. Gan Chunsong, 儒学概论 [An introduction to Confucian studies], 250.

18. For Zhao's latest formulation, see Zhao Tingyang, "All-under-Heaven and Methodological Relationism."

19. This ideal also influenced Sun Yat-sen and a youthful Mao Zedong (see Bell, *China's New Confucianism*, 23–24).

20. Zhao Tingyang, "All-under-Heaven and Methodological Relationism," 79.

21. Chan, "Territorial Boundaries and Confucianism," 81.

22. In principle, that community need not be the nation. The nation has emerged as the main source of political identity in the modern world, but things can always change in the future; for example, cities can become a more important source of political identity (see Bell and de-Shalit, *The Spirit of Cities*).

23. I use the term "Confucian political framework" loosely. For example, Yan Xuetong draws on a wide range of pre-Qin thinkers, including non-Confucians (see *Ancient Chinese Thought*), but in this chapter I draw upon his interpretation of Xunzi, who can (controversially) be labeled a Confucian.

24. Another key Confucian political value is the idea that tyrants should be punished. I have drawn implications for debates about just and unjust war in Bell, *Beyond Liberal Democracy* (ch. 2) and *China's New Confucianism* (ch. 2) and won't repeat myself here. See also Glanville, "Retaining the Mandate of Heaven," 323–343.

25. Callahan, "Chinese Visions of World Order," 749–761.

26. See Zhao Tingyang, "All-under-Heaven and Methodological Relationism," 73–74.

27. Zhang Feng, "The Tianxia System."

28. Yan Xuetong, *Ancient Chinese Thought*, 104, 105. Xunzi was not typically viewed as a Confucian thinker in imperial Chinese history because he began with the assumption that human nature is bad, in contrast to the official Mencian view (from the Song dynasty onward) that human nature is good. In my view, however, the starting point doesn't make much difference because Xunzi allowed for the possibility of moral transformation via the use of ritual, and his core moral concerns fit in the Confucian tradition (see Bell, *China's New Confucianism*, ch. 3).

29. Yan Xuetong, *Ancient Chinese Thought*, 16, 17.

30. Yan Xuetong, *Ancient Chinese Thought*, 106.

31. Carlson, "Moving beyond Sovereignty?," 101, 102.

32. Yan Xuetong, *Ancient Chinese Thought*, 104.

33. Zhang Feng, "Rethinking the 'Tribute System,'" 545–574.

34. Zhuang Guotu, "略论朝贡制度的虚幻" [An account of the illusion of the tributary system], 1–8.

35. Yan Xuetong, *Ancient Chinese Thought*, 99.

36. Yan Xuetong, *Ancient Chinese Thought*, 17. For a detailed account of what humane authority (王道) means for domestic constitutional reform, see Jiang Qing, *A Confucian*

Constitutional Order. Jiang argues that democracy is only one of three sources of political legitimacy (the others being heaven 天 and earth 地) and on that basis defends a tricameral legislature, with each part expressing a different source of legitimacy.

37. Karl Marx did not spell out what he meant by higher communism in any detail, but the outlines of his vision are discussed in his last major work, *Critique of the Gotha Program*. On liberal cosmopolitans, see, e.g., Doyle, "Kant, Liberal Legacies and Foreign Affairs," 205–235, 323–353.

38. Liu Junping, " '天下'宇宙观的演变及其哲学意蕴" [The development and philosophical meaning of tianxia cosmology], 102.

39. Zhao Tingyang, "Rethinking Empire from a Chinese Concept," 32.

40. In a similar vein, Zhao Tingyang advocates freedom of migration on (at least partly) meritocratic grounds, noting that "most of the famous ministers, generals and think tankers in states, for instance in the later period of the Zhou dynasty, were foreigners from other states, never accused as traitors. Traveling far and wide, Confucius was one of those who tried their fortune in other states" ("All-under-Heaven and Methodological Relationism," 74).

41. The discussion of Yan Xuetong's work in this section draws on my introduction to Yan's book *Ancient Chinese Thought*, 13–15.

42. For similar ideas, see Jiang Qing, 生命信仰与王道政治 [A faith in life and the Kingly Way]; Bai Tongdong, "A Mencian Version of Limited Democracy," 19–34; Chan, "Democracy and Meritocracy," 179–193; Li, "Where Does Virtuous Leadership Stand?," 531–536; and Bell, *Beyond Liberal Democracy* (ch. 6) and *China's New Confucianism* (ch. 1). Chapter 4 of my book *The China Model: Political Meritocracy and the Limits of Democracy*, however, points to an alternative model of vertical democratic meritocracy that may be more realistic.

43. Such efforts are already taking place on an ad hoc basis: for example, several government officials from Africa, Latin America, and South Asia are undergoing training at the China National School of Administration (国家行政学院) in Beijing. South Africa's president, Jacob Zuma, has praised China's relatively meritocratic system of selecting and training cadres. As the African National Congress transforms itself from a revolutionary movement to a modern party responsible for running a state, it can learn from the experience of the Chinese Communist Party, which has gone from rewarding "red" (commitment to the revolution) to rewarding expertise and talent (again, I do not mean to imply that the Chinese political system is as meritocratic as it should be; the reality is that factors such as *guanxi* and loyalty to leaders influence political promotion more than they should). In Ukraine, the Meritocratic Party stands for "meritocracy as a basic principle for effective functioning of society, politics, and government" (LinkedIn, http://www.linkedin .com/company/meritocratic-party-of-ukraine) and here too the Chinese experience of economic development under the guidance of meritocratically selected cadres may be helpful.

44. Li Chenyang, "The Confucian Ideal of Harmony," 583–603. See also Li Chenyang, *The Confucian Philosophy of Harmony*.

45. See, e.g., Wang Dasan, "儒家天下觀念與世界秩序重建" [The Confucian concept of tianxia], 12–13; Liu Junping，" '天下'宇宙观的演变及其哲学意蕴" [The development and

philosophical meaning of tianxia cosmology], 102; Mou Zhongjian, "Shi tianxia yi jia haishi ruorouqiangshi" [Is it tianxia or the strong prey on the weak?], 2.

46. Gan Chunsong, "王者无外"与"夷夏之防" [The Kingly Way without outsiders], 9.

47. Dikotter, *The Discourse of Race in Modern China*.

48. "Race and Racism in Asia: Race and Racism in China," JRank, http://science.jrank.org/pages/10955/Race-Racism-in-Asia-Race-Racism-in-China.html.

49. Makeham, *Lost Soul*, 9.

50. Tu Weiming, quoted in Makeham, *Lost Soul*, 36.

51. Let me support this point with an anecdote. A couple years ago, I visited the Confucian temple in Beijing with Jiang Qing and about fifteen young Confucian scholars. We made our way to the main hall to bow to the statue of Confucius, and Jiang was asked to lead the ritual. One of the young scholars questioned whether I was supposed to join the ceremony. Jiang forcefully objected to the ethnic nationalism underpinning the question. Confucianism, he said, is for tianxia. I joined the ritual.

52. See, e.g., John Stuart Mill, "Considerations on Representative Government," ch. 4, http://socserv.mcmaster.ca/econ/ugcm/3ll3/mill/repgovt.pdf.

53. Johnston, *Cultural Realism*, xi. Zhang Feng, however, argues that the Chinese state during the same period relied more on moral power vis-à-vis the Japanese and (especially) the Koreans ("Regionalization in the *Tianxia*").

54. Jiang Shigong, *Zhongguo Xianggang* 中國香港, 112–121, 149–158. But for a critique of Jiang's view, see Chen Guanzhong, "中國天朝主義與香港" [China's tributary system and Hong Kong].

55. For a preliminary effort to construct such an index, see Bell and Mo, "Harmony in the World 2013."

PART III. TIANXIA

AND SOCIALIST

INTERNATIONALISM

*

7

TIANXIA AND POSTWAR
JAPANESE SINOLOGISTS' VISION
OF THE CHINESE REVOLUTION

The Cases of Nishi Junzō and Mizoguchi Yūzō

Viren Murthy

*

We usually understand tianxia, or "all under heaven," as a concept related to the political and philosophical imagination of premodern dynastic China. With the collapse of the dynastic system after the 1911 revolution, China moved from "all under heaven" to the world of global capitalism. After this, and especially in revolutionary China after 1949, those who would attempt to recover the concept would risk appearing anachronistic. This is of course the point made by Joseph Levenson and others since: that in the late Qing dynasty, Chinese intellectuals began to see tianxia as incongruous with the real world. Consequently tianxia and the whole Confucian worldview became a mere symbol of identity. While there have been huge debates about the extent to which we should follow Levenson's idea for understanding late Qing or Republican thought, there has been less questioning of the existence of Confucian remnants in Maoist self-understanding. However, in postwar Japan, Sinologists constantly returned to the concept of tianxia and to premodern Chinese thought more generally to find the origins of modern China, and especially the Chinese Revolution of 1949. To some extent, this gesture mirrored American Sinologists who wanted to explain China's path to communism in relation to the Chinese past. While many American Sinologists wanted to explain why Chinese history took a wrong turn, Japanese historians attempted to uncover in Mao's China the possibilities for a different future related to a dialectical interpretation of the Chinese past.

Although some attention has been paid to early Japanese Sinology (Fogel, Tanaka), scholars have generally neglected the study of Japanese works on China after World War II. This period is significant because Japanese Sinologists' writings from this time dovetail with the quest for alternative modernities that prevails today. In the wake of defeat at the hands of the United States, many Japanese Sinologists looked to China as an alternative modernity rooted in more traditional forms of thought and political organization. They often connected this alternative to a particular response to China being forced to join the global capitalist system of nation-states and its resistance.

Below I examine the work of two postwar Japanese Sinologists, Nishi Junzō (1914–1984) and Mizoguchi Yūzō (1932–2010), focusing on their respective attempts to understand revolutionary China in relation to the world of tianxia. Although their work aligns with that of alternative modernity theorists in form, Nishi and Mizoguchi each have different conceptions of "alternative." Nishi, writing in the 1950s and 1960s, conceives of the alternative as a socialist future based on the Maoist experience, while in the conjuncture of neoliberal capitalism, the demise of third worldism, and the decline of the socialist states during the 1980s and 1990s, Mizoguchi thinks of China as expressing a type of identity. Through examining their works, we gain a better understanding of twentieth-century Japanese Sinology, and a critical analysis of their writings helps us to grasp the larger issues of whether revolutionary China represents a rupture or a continuity with the past and the question of Chinese modernity in relation to the larger global capitalist world. Each of the above Sinologists asks to what extent the Chinese past could play a role in enabling us to imagine a radically different global future. Nishi and Mizoguchi express a hope for a future beyond capitalism without completely grasping the conditions for the possibility of such a future.

Writing immediately after the war in the 1950s and 1960s, Nishi argued that Chinese thinkers from Zhang Taiyan to Mao Zedong were able to imagine global emancipation by turning the world of tianxia on its head. Moreover, this was only possible, according to Nishi, because of the combination of tianxia spatiality and the temporal lag of Chinese modernity. In short, the multiple temporalities of global capitalism and the unevenness of China made it possible to turn the Chinese worldview inside out and turn the people into *tian*.

In other words, the people become the ultimate standard in politics. In the late 1980s, a younger Sinologist, Mizoguchi Yūzō, published his famous book *China as Method*, which criticized the claims of previous Japanese Sinologists, saying that their vision of China was actually a mirror of Japan rather than an understanding of China's own indigenous logic of modernity. Mizoguchi and Nishi never openly discussed their differences, but by bringing their ideas about tianxia, China, and modernity together, one can get a sense of the stakes in mobilizing narratives of temporal and spatial unevenness or inequality to imagine a different future. Nishi stresses resistance to global capitalist imperialism and a temporal lag connected to global uneven development. Mizoguchi criticizes Nishi, but proposes his own narrative of alternative Chinese modernity by emphasizing a different social logic derived from the premodern Chinese world. Mizoguchi contends that earlier Sinologists made a mistake by taking "the world as method and China as goal." This is his way of saying that they began with fixed assumptions about the world and then used this worldview to analyze China. Against this Mizuguchi posits a world that emerges from its constituent elements. In other words, although we could call Mizoguchi's work another version of a China-centered history, his aim is clearly to construct a new world through his scholarship. Mizoguchi's world picture stresses the continuity of the past and present against Nishi's more radical vision of rupture and resistance to imperialism.

Nishi and Mizoguchi each attempt to posit a new world of difference by rereading tianxia. In place of Nishi's Hegelian reading of tianxia and a revolutionary rupture that turns it on its head, Mizoguchi attempts to follow the remnants of the past in the present. In contemporary Japan and perhaps elsewhere, the debate between Nishi and Mizoguchi appears to be resolved in favor of the latter's approach. However, toward the end of the chapter, I suggest that Nishi's discourse of tianxia as the alienated potential of political power, while seemingly a far-fetched Hegelian interpretation of the Chinese past, partially grasps the alienating structure of capitalism. In other words, although Nishi understands capitalism primarily in terms of class, his larger analysis gestures at a more fundamental characteristic of capitalism, namely the alienation of humanity. In particular, Nishi's emphasis on the people as the alienated potential of history remains relevant in an age of imperialist and capitalist crisis. Moreover, if Mizoguchi is correct in suggesting that Nishi puts the world before China, the problem lies in how to think China's relation to the world. This involves asking how to understand the destabilizing power of the remnant in relation to the constitutive powers of capitalism.

Foundations: The Legacy of Takeuchi Yoshimi

Nishi Junzō and Mizoguchi Yūzō each draws on the legacy of perhaps the most influential postwar Sinologist and literary critic, Takeuchi Yoshimi (1910–1977); hence, a brief discussion of Takeuchi's work will help us grasp their respective views on Chinese modernity. Themes in Takeuchi's work recur in Nishi and Mizoguchi, such as the critique of the positivism of Japanese Sinology and the emergence of an alternative Chinese modernity out of creative use of its being incorporated into the global capitalist system later than Western nations.

Takeuchi was born in 1910, on the eve of the transformation from the Meiji to the Taisho periods, and began to study Chinese literature in 1931 at Tokyo Imperial University. This is precisely the period in which Japan began to escalate its involvement in China and invaded Manchuria. Japanese imperialism in China had as its counterpart efforts at mobilizing popular sentiment in Japan.[1] In popular culture and more widely, there was a sense that winning over China was part of a larger regional project of Asia. In this context, like many Japanese Sinologists, Takeuchi was torn between his admiration for China, with a critical stance toward the West, and the actual policies of the Japanese government in China, which became increasingly apparent as the war progressed.[2]

Despite or because of Japanese involvement, modern and contemporary China was a rather unpopular field of study in Japan in the early 1930s; among the thirty-odd members in his cohort, Takeuchi was the only one who focused on the modern period, or post–May Fourth literature. In the summer of 1932, Takeuchi went to Manchuria on a grant from the Japanese foreign ministry. He had a genuine fascination with China. He wrote, "The moment I went, I felt that this was home. What mattered now was not whether doing Chinese literature would be interesting or not; I simply felt I could do nothing else."[3] Apart from this specific feeling, which would influence his views on China and Asia, the concept of feeling would form a crucial part of Takeuchi's work in years to come. In particular, he would resist rationality and science in the name of subjectivity and literature. Throughout the prewar and interwar periods, Takeuchi constantly debated with his fellow Sinologists, especially scholars who were proponents of *shinagaku* (China studies). Against their stress on objectivity, Takeuchi would stress the open space of the subjective, which would eventually come to signify China.

Shinagaku, also called Kyoto shinagaku, represents an important shift in both politics and epistemology in Chinese studies beginning during the late Meiji, a period of intensive capitalist development in urban areas and of restructuring of academic institutions in the service of the nation-state. As China and Japan were conceived as nation-states, Japanese Sinologists during this period had something of a Levensonian moment with a Japanese twist. Prior to *shinagaku* and modern *kangaku*, which were established respectively in Kyoto University and Tokyo Imperial University, Japanese Sinologists studied China from a perspective modeled on Confucian studies. China was not considered separate from Japan, and Confucianism served as the foundation of value. For these scholars, the world of tianxia stayed at the center, but at times, such as during the Tokugawa period, Japanese Confucians believed that this center had moved to Japan. This shows that the decentering of China had a different effect in Japan, since it was connected to their own identity. For Japanese Sinologists, the negation of China was to some extent a self-negation combined with a reconstitution of both Japan and China in the space of social science and the world of nation-states, both of which were inextricably connected to the development of capitalism in Japan. This new space of social science expressed the homogenizing logic of capitalism, and was constantly perceived as placing both individual and national subjectivity at risk.

In this way, Japanese Sinology constantly faced the antinomies between the politics of the nation-state and the universality entailed by social science. This in turn was connected to two different modes of power contradicting each other: the modern imperial power of the emperor in Tokyo and global structures of capitalism and the interstate system, which entail the abstraction associated with social science. The methods of social science imported from the West were perhaps common to Sinologists both at Tokyo Imperial University and at Kyoto University, but while the Tokyo school underscored the politics of the nation, the Kyoto school emphasized universal objectivity. Two central figures around Chinese and Oriental philosophy (*toyō tetsugaku*) in Tokyo, Inoue Tetsujirō (1855–1944) and Hattori Unokichi (1867–1939), are famous for their reinterpretations of the significance of Confucianism as a philosophy stressing loyalty, especially to the emperor. Against the Chinese studies of Tokyo Imperial University, Kyoto shinagaku advocated scholarship independent from imperial politics. At the same time, shinagaku scholars argued that one should understand China as one nation-state among many. Rather than as a universal root of value, they advocated thinking of China as particular rather than universal. In other words, shinagaku scholars negated China as tianxia and replaced it with an idea of China as part of a world system of nation-states.

Takeuchi Yoshimi aligned himself with the scholars of shinagaku against the previous model of China as tianxia and also against the Tokyo school's emphasis on the emperor. But one could argue that Takeuchi's aim was to repoliticize

Sinology in a new way through appealing to literature and subjectivity. This subjectivity emerges in response to the reifying forces of the state, science, and domestic and international capital. It is important to distinguish between these different mediations of the modern capitalist world, since it allows us to grasp the spaces of politics and hope that emerge between them. At the same time, reification encompasses various practices, such as the capitalist market, the global system of nation-states, and science. In this context, people might perceive something like a general pattern of reification, which they abstract from the above distinct but interrelated practices in a global capitalist world. We will get a better sense of representations of such patterns of reification when we deal with Nishi's work, but Takeuchi saw reification exemplified in the China scholarship of his times.

In the early 1930s, he made two criticisms of shinagaku, both of which would be related to a new politics. First, he claimed that these scholars remained focused on ancient China rather than contemporary China; second, he attacked their simple reliance on the methodology of social science that sought to objectify China and claimed that with such an approach, they would be incapable of understanding literature. Although the first question attempts to restore China's contemporaneity, the second attempts to negate the abstract time of social science. In this latter context, Takeuchi emphasized the creative power of the subject. Moreover, neither kangaku nor shinagaku were up to the task. Kangaku's methods were outmoded and shinagaku ended up being mere positivism.[4] One way of overcoming the positivism of Japanese Sinology, which he would later associate with the West, was to shift the emphasis to literature.

This is not the place to go into Takeuchi's ideas about literature, Sinology, and politics, but a few points are worth mentioning because they influenced the direction of future Japanese Sinology, and Nishi and Mizoguchi in particular. Takeuchi believed that the spirit of literature was intimately connected with a form of self-negation that created a new subjectivity and that Lu Xun, the father of modern Chinese literature, embodied this spirit. With this gesture, not only did Takeuchi attack the scholars of shinagaku, but he also confronted scholars who attempted to understand Lu Xun as a nationalist. Against this reading, Takeuchi developed a complex interpretation of Lu Xun as a writer as opposed to a thinker. In Takeuchi's view, Lu Xun was a wanderer whose literature emerged from a fundamental awareness that he compared to religious awakening and often used amorphous terms such as "nothingness" to describe. By constantly using language in a way that plunged him into an abyss, Lu Xun incessantly re-created himself. According to Takeuchi, these aspects of Lu

Xun's literature were extremely meaningful in terms of Chinese history and as an ideal for Japanese literature.

By the end of the war, Takeuchi emphasized more clearly the universal significance of Lu Xun's literature and his idea of incessant self-renewal for a new politics. Takeuchi attempted to think the universality of the Chinese experience of revolution in the twentieth century and contended that China's resistance to imperialist expansion from the periphery of the global capitalist system could serve to create an alternative world.[5] At this point, China would form a new type of universal, different from tianxia.

Immediately after the war, Japanese intellectuals had a new interest in China. Throughout the modern era, China has played an important role in shaping Japanese self-identity, but early postwar Japan represents something of a rupture in the way Japanese Sinologists invoked temporality in relation to China. During this time, many Japanese intellectuals looked to China as a model, not because of its past, but because of its present and its possible future. Even before the 1949 revolution, Japanese intellectuals were introduced to positive appraisals of communist struggles in China through translations of books by Western journalists, such as Edgar Snow's *Red Star over China*, which appeared in 1946, and also through Japanese Communist Party members who were in Yan'an during the war, such as Nosaka Sanzō.[6]

After the war, China and Japan did not have any diplomatic relations, which encouraged the vision of China as an outsider and as an imaginary standpoint from which to look critically at the Japanese government and its relationship with the United States. China's victory against Japanese and American imperialism entailed the possibility of a society that overcame capitalism and the Cold War binary opposition between the United States and the Soviet Union. Moreover, China represented subjective creativity against the reified objectivity of the West. Takeuchi's 1948 essay, "What Is Modernity? The Case of China and Japan" (first published as "Chinese Modernity and Japanese Modernity: Taking Lu Xun as a Clue"), was an attempt to explain why and how China was an alternative, and in it he further analyzed some of the themes dealt with in his pre- and interwar writings.

Takeuchi pointedly contrasted Chinese and Japanese responses to modernity and tried to explain the creative potential of China. His argument about the connection between Chinese modernity and potentialities of the revolution of failure are particularly important for understanding Nishi Junzō's analysis of tianxia. Takeuchi juxtaposes the Meiji Restoration and the 1911 revolution to explain why China could resist Western imperialism while Japan ended up mimicking the West and itself became imperialist. He contends that both China and Japan were late-developing countries and that initially both tried to catch up with the West. The Chinese and Japanese governments accepted the West as a universal standard and a temporal understanding of themselves as behind. Under these circumstances, they attempted to reform. The Japanese were successful and ended up becoming similar to the West, but in China, because conservative forces were too strong, the government and reformers' plans to approach the West were repeatedly thwarted. Out of this failure, out of being reduced to nothing, emerged the possibility of a new universality that would not imply imperialism. Repeated failure thus plunges a nation into the abyss and becomes symbolic of self-negation and subjective potential at a national level.

In Takeuchi's view, this results in the government giving way to the force of the people, who can replace the simulation of reforms from above with a real revolution from below. Takeuchi seeks a universality that is not imposed upon the people from outside but emerges through the people as subject. This subject cannot be objectified or represented through the objectifying methodology of social science, and hence previous Japanese Sinologists had overlooked it. Consequently, they misunderstood Chinese modernity and the Chinese Revolution of 1911.

Takeuchi was ambivalent about the connections between the Chinese Revolution and the past. On the one hand, in "What Is Modernity?," he emphasized that even though in the twentieth century, scholars attempted to find the roots of Chinese modernity in the past, such as in the Song and Ming dynasties, such projects were all made possible through modernity and colonialism.[7] However, in another essay, he claims that Lu Xun's awareness of life might be connected to the "spirit of primitive Confucian religion" (*genshi kōshi kyō*).[8] This latter gesture is relatively rare in Takeuchi's work and never developed as a historical narrative. Nishi Junzō and Mizoguchi Yūzō, however, partly affirm Takeuchi's above narrative, while attempting to explain how some of the structures of the world of tianxia remain in Mao's China. In other words, they each supplement aspects of Takeuchi's narrative with a discussion of how China's past enabled it to develop an alternative modernity and an alternative future.

Nishi Junzō and the Negative Dialectics of Tianxia

Nishi Junzō was born in 1914, about four years after Takeuchi Yoshimi, and he graduated from Tokyo Imperial University in 1937 with a degree in Chinese philosophy. By this time, he was already proficient in German idealism and specifically Hegelian thought, which pervades his work. Although he is known as a supporter of Mao, in his early years he worked for a conservative think tank associated with the Ministry of Education's Division of National Spirit and Culture. Much of Nishi's writings about tianxia stem from the work of his father, Nishi Shinichirō, a conservative scholar of ethics and one of the first students of Inoue Tetsujirō. Given the above background, it is not surprising that Nishi grafted conservative and radical impulses onto China. The convergence of radicalism and conservatism is possible because both have as their target some form of capitalist modernity and Western imperialism. Nishi's own shift from conservatism to radicalism is expressed in his representation of China, where radicalism emerges out of a determinate negation of a certain conservative structure, namely tianxia.

In 1937, Nishi Shinichirō and his student Koito Natsujirō published a book, *Ri no igi to kōzō* (The meaning and structure of rituals), which claimed to grasp the essential structure of Chinese culture through studying ritual. In other words, although China did not have unity as a state, it had a cultural unity that emerged from its rational moral worldview.[9] Nishi and Koito explained the metaphysical foundations of this worldview, including the relationships among heaven, things, and people. They read heaven (tian) as an absolute, which transcends people and things. Because heaven transcends things, they argued that in China there is no national unity but a cultural unity, which has vague boundaries. This is why in China, a number of ideals, such as the Great Community, go beyond national divisions.

Nishi Junzō reinterprets the above ideals in postwar Japan while continuing his father's critique of the West from both political and epistemological perspectives. Indeed, in his view, Chinese ideals can be comprehended only by creating a new epistemology and subjectivity. Like those of Takeuchi, Nishi's early essays were directed against Japanese Sinologists and their scientific framework, which eclipsed subjectivity because it fragmented and objectified reality. He claimed that the modern Western gaze had made China into an object and their detailed analyses were devoid of significance. In his essay on Japanese studies of Chinese thought, which was first presented at a symposium organized by Tsuda Sōkichi (1873–1961), a famous shinagaku scholar, then published in 1940 in a journal called *Kokumin seishin bunka* (The spiritual culture of the nation), Nishi argued that making China into an object created a gap between subject and object, which had to be overcome: "The China within the framework of *shinagaku* is not China, but the framework of knowledge in *shinagaku* itself. Rather, those who treat China as a thing are themselves things. Because there is an abstract framework of things and knowledge, there is a separation between subject and object. Moreover, subject and object each further cause knowledge and things to become abstract."[10] This was a type of double attack on one of his teachers, Tsuda Sōkichi, who not only emphasized objectivity but also constantly pointed out the inferiority of China in relation to Japan, using the modern West as the standard. Nishi claimed that shinagaku degenerated into a formalism in which the mediation of the framework of science produced an object that did not exist. Moreover, when shinagaku scholars took things, especially China, out of organic context to study them as objects, they automatically abstracted themselves from holistic goals and contexts and consequently became abstract subjects standing against objects.

Nishi's critique of the split between the subject and object reflects a general theme in Japanese thought at the time, especially among philosophers of the Kyoto school, such as Nishida Kitarō. These philosophers attempted to combine Buddhism and German idealism to revive Japanese culture against the fragmenting forces of modernity. Christian Uhl has argued that Takeuchi's reading of Lu Xun was an attempt to fuse Kyoto school philosophy with Lu Xun to rethink Chinese modernity and its significance for Japan. Nishi's case is somewhat similar, but, being a student of Chinese philosophy and in particular Song and Ming Confucianism, Nishi sought to revive the Chinese Confucian worldview against Western modernity. In general, we can see that in postwar Japanese Sinology, Mao and revolutionary China play a role somewhat similar to Japan and even the emperor, in the prewar period, as a fulcrum of resistance.

In prewar Japan, and for Nishi in particular, the revival of Confucianism was often an integral part of the revival of the Japanese spirit. He asserts that overcoming the China of shinagaku and returning China to itself in its vitality would be essential training (*tanren*) for Japan as well. Japanese wartime ideology claimed that Chinese culture had itself been lost and had to be rescued by Japan, and Nishi early on propounded a philosophical version of the same thesis when he contended that Lin Yutang's work showed that the Chinese themselves had contributed to making themselves objects.[11]

In 1942, Nishi was sent to Seoul University to become what he would later describe as a "colonial official."[12] From 1943 to 1951 he did not publish anything, so these eight years were, borrowing Takeuchi's words, a period of "conversion" (*kaishin*). In Takeuchi's discussion of Lu Xun, he claimed that Lu's period of conversion occurred from before the 1911 revolution up to around the May Fourth Movement, when Lu Xun began to write literature. Conversion is different from *tenkō*, which can also be translated as "conversion," because in tenkō, one loses the self and merely moves from one position to the other. For example, Takeuchi claims that the Japanese turn toward the West is a tenkō representing a loss of self. Put differently, the object changes, but there is no internal change of the subject. Conversion, on the other hand, resembles what happened to Lu Xun and, in Takeuchi's view, what happened to China itself. That is, as one attempts to grasp the self, the self changes from the inside rather than the outside.

This description is apt for Nishi because after the war, he probably experienced a tension between his Confucian critique of reification and Western imperialism and his discontent with Japanese imperialism, which also drew on Confucianism. He would not publish anything about the Japanese invasion of Korea until late in his life, in the 1980s, but from 1951, he would reinterpret Confucianism in light of Maoism, which became a symbol of a double resistance against both Japanese imperialism and Western imperialism. Nishi attempted to push Confucianism to its logical conclusion, which would imply revolution. Moreover, Mao encompassed an epistemological resistance that Japanese Marxism and the Japanese Communist Party could not provide. In Nishi's view, Mao's resistance was possible because of a Hegelian sublation (*Aufhebung*) of the Chinese Confucian past and the world of tianxia.

In 1953, he published a well-known essay titled "Tenka, kokka ie no shisō" (The thought of tianxia, the state, and the family), which begins to outline his ideas about how the concept of tianxia could be potentially revolutionary because it was grounded in morality. Nishi contends that although the family and the state imply certain hierarchies, the power of the ruler is based on the moral authority of heaven (tian) and tianxia. For this reason the relationship between the ruler and the minister is different from other relations: it is not determined a priori by kinship or blood, such as the relationship between father and son. Rather, tian entails an a posteriori category of morality, which serves as a condition for the purely formal relationship between the ruler and the minister. In other words, although Confucian morality places great emphasis on loyalty, classical Chinese texts predicated this loyalty on morality.[13] To some extent, by reinterpreting Confucian morality in this way, Nishi also responds to Inoue Tetsujirō and Meiji scholars at Tokyo Imperial University, who were concerned about the revolutionary potential of Confucianism and consequently stressed the concept of loyalty. Nishi here invokes the difference between the Chinese worldview of tianxia and *tianming*, which is different from the idea of *tenno* (emperor) and so on. He believes that a space for politics opens up in this idea of tian, which goes beyond lineage. In so doing, he echoes earlier liberal thinkers such as Fukuzawa Yukichi, who famously claimed, "The Japanese people suffered for many years the yoke of despotism. Lineage was the basis of power. Even intelligent men were entirely dependent on the houses of high lineage. Throughout the land there was no room for human initiative; everything was in a condition of stagnation."[14]

Of course, where for Fukuzawa, China was even more ensconced in the problems of custom and lineage, Nishi's view of Chinese Confucianism seemed to offer another path. In Nishi's view, the above moral principle of Confucianism potentially leads to utopian structures such as Xiao Kang and the Great Unity. He describes these political ideals in a manner that suggests that they anticipate socialism, but at the same time represent people without subjectivity:

> The Great Community, tianxia, is common property [*kō*]. Each human being lives publicly.... Labor and family members are all not private property. The whole community is ordered and hence there is no need for the use of force. So it appears that in the Great Community, there is no need for power. It appears to be a world in which there is a need neither for a system of ruler and ruled nor for familial morality. One does not see any power coercing or oppressing the people. However, is there something that can oppress or coerce the people? There is no case where the people have awareness and seek rights and then resist power. It appears as if there is no power, but this is not because they negated power. This is a world in which the idea of power does not exist. The root of the principle of the Great Community is the people who lack awareness and power, a people who are devoid of subjectivity; people are merely things.[15]

This reading of Confucianism as lacking subjectivity is of course reminiscent of Maruyama Masao and others, who saw the resistance of Confucianism as one of the reasons for the emergence of fascism in Japan. In other words, the lack of democracy in Japan was supposedly caused by the remnants of Confucian thought. Nishi continues aspects of Maruyama's work, but he stresses reification, applying his critique to premodern China and even its highest ideals, such as the Great Community. According to Nishi, there are glimmers of subjectivity in Song Confucianism and outside the Confucian tradition, but Chinese subjectivity really emerged during the twentieth century with Zhang Taiyan and Mao. In the 1960s, Nishi published two essays that showed how twentieth-century thinkers from Zhang Taiyan to Mao Zedong turned tianxia on its head to create the conditions for a new world. Here we see the difference between Nishi and Maruyama; unlike Maruyama, postwar Sinologists such as Nishi saw potential for change in Chinese culture itself.

Nishi lays out this context in "Chūgoku shisō no naka no jinmin gainen" (The concept of the people in Chinese thought), published in 1960, and in

"Mu kara no keisei: 'Ware no jinmin' no seiritsu ni tsuite" (Constructions from nothing: On the establishment of "we the people"), published in 1964. These were of course written after the turmoil surrounding the Security Treaty in 1960, when anti-American sentiment was clearly increasing along with an interest in popular movements. The critique of Western imperialism is more prominent in "Constructions from Nothing," but "The Concept of the People" also begins with a discussion of the difference between Chinese and Western modernity in a manner that echoes Takeuchi.

Like Takeuchi, Nishi contends that Chinese modernity is constituted by resistance to modernity, which was imposed on it from the outside. From the beginning, Chinese modernity, like Japanese modernity, emerged in the context of uneven global development. The result was the emergence of people with a different perspective from the liberal one, and Nishi connects this revolutionary people to the structure of tianxia. He constructs a scene at the end of the Qing dynasty in which an imperial dynasty confronts imperialist nation-states. The imperial frame is a hierarchical structure that hinders the spontaneous action of the people of tianxia. Tianxia has a dual structure, with hierarchical power on the one hand and a principle of moral obligation to the people on the other. In the face of imperialism, the imperial hierarchy experienced a crisis, leaving an opening for the people to emerge. In short, the reified structures that made people into things broke down and consequently unleashed popular potential.

Nishi understands Chinese history as a discourse about alienation and domination. By the early twentieth century, the Chinese people simultaneously confronted two adversaries, dynastic hierarchy and imperialism. The emergence of Marxism as a tool to attack both feudalism and imperialism was a common theme in modern Chinese historiography, but Nishi contends that an element more fundamental than Marxism is required to grasp Chinese resistance. In "Constructions from Nothing," he cites Mao Zedong to explain his point:

> In this movement of resistance, from the Opium War in 1840 until the eve of the May Fourth Movement in 1919, in a total of more than seventy years, the Chinese never had an ideological weapon capable of fighting imperialism. The worn-out and rigid ideological weapons of feudalism were broken during the war, and they declared defeat. With their backs against the wall, during their bourgeois revolutionary period, the Chinese were forced to use ideological weapons or political policies such as evolution, natural rights, and bourgeois republics from the imperialist

countries' weapons arsenal. They created political parties and created revolution, hoping to defend against foreign powers on the outside and create a republic of China inside with precisely these weapons. However, these were also like the ideological weapons of feudalism—they were extremely weak, and these were also defeated.[16]

Nishi admits that the usual conclusion drawn from the above passage is that China had to wait for the ideological weapons of Marxism-Leninism in order to develop resistance. However, Mao asserted that resistance began in the nineteenth century. Moreover, and perhaps more importantly, Mao called the 1911 revolution a revolution against imperialism, thus stressing not only resistance to capitalism but also resistance from a structurally uneven standpoint.

Nishi suggests that Japanese scholars have not been able to understand this element of Mao because they have focused too much on Western influence. Since the war, he laments that Japan's identity has been constructed around a Japan-U.S. axis that has overlooked Japan's relationship to its former colonies and in particular China. So the question of the 1911 revolution brings us back specifically to the conditions for the possibility for China's resistance to Japan, but also for the possibility of a New China and a New World.

In Nishi's view, we can grasp this something else at the base of the 1911 revolution by studying late Qing thinkers, such as Tan Sitong, Kang Youwei, and especially Zhang Taiyan. Nishi believes that Zhang Taiyan, especially his writings from the years 1906–1911, expresses this anti-imperialistic resistance in the 1911 revolution, because his political theory during this time constantly turned around the problem of nothing. Nishi sees a dialectic of at least three different "nothings" coming together to make resistance possible. First, there is nothing as an ideological vacuum: as Mao noted, ideologically China was reduced to nothing; feudal weapons and imperialist bourgeois weapons were reduced to nothing. By the time of the 1911 revolution, Chinese tradition and polity were reduced to pure negativity. Here we already have a second nothingness— the late Qing political structure reduced to nothing. Usually, being reduced to nothing is not considered a positive characteristic, but Nishi draws on Buddhism and Hegel to reveal another aspect of nothingness: it is a fundamental characteristic of subjectivity, which resists reification, which is a third nothing. By mediating this last vision of nothingness with tianxia and the subjectivity of the people, he creates a new political perspective from which the people are a collective subject that can potentially overturn any structure that is imposed on them, such as nation-states, contracts, and so on.

In Nishi's view, Zhang Taiyan used this negativity for the purposes of resistance. It is not surprising that Nishi's analysis revolves around Zhang's famous essay in the journal *Minbao*, "On the Five Negations," first published in 1907. Unlike Takeuchi, Nishi ties Zhang Taiyan's nothingness to Marxist categories, such as capitalism and class. In particular, through reading a number of Zhang's texts, Nishi concludes that Zhang Taiyan's nothingness refers to the people and that they are the subjects who enact the various negations (of the state, imperialism, capitalism, and eventually themselves). Each of these political structures, such as the state, limits the pure negativity of the people, and thus Zhang's people resist them.

From Nishi's perspective, Zhang inverted the basic structure of tianxia. He describes the Chinese conception of heaven and its inversion in a uniquely Hegelian manner:

> According to the thought of the dynastic system of China, on the level of existence, heaven is nothing=no limits=all-encompassing [無＝無限定＝全有], hence the things under heaven are existing=relative=themselves empty [有＝相対性＝自体空無]. . . . Zhang twists this around and turns it into a world that goes from being to nothing and buries itself. In other words, the people, who are nothing in front of the Son of Heaven, realize this nothingness and together . . . take revenge.[17]

Nishi's narrative follows Takeuchi's, but he takes his cue from Zhang's famous statement "rely on the self, not on others."[18] In Nishi's view, Zhang's idea of the self does not rely on others, but this does not mean that it is purely independent. It emerges only in the face of others and only as a provisional (仮現的) subject.[19] Nishi has chosen a term that is used in Buddhism to express the incarnation of spirit provisionally for a specific task and is related to another term, *keshin* (化身, *nirmāna-kāya*), which specifically refers to the "provisional manifestation of the Buddha." Nishi uses this term to signify the transcendent nature of Zhang's subject, which implies that because this subject is nothing equals limitlessness, after negating all antagonistic others, the provisional self must itself dissolve.

As Nishi explains, Zhang's subject, which is nothing, which is the people, resists not only imperialism but also internal enemies such as landlords, capitalists, and the dynastic system. With this interpretation, Nishi could connect Zhang Taiyan to Mao. He claims that Zhang's thought is a "pure nihilism" without any positive or active content.[20] However, in an essay, "Tetsugaku no unmei ni tsuite" (On the fate of philosophy), written three years later, in 1967, he contended that Zhang's philosophy aimed for a utopia of singularity: "What does real nothingness mean? Here there are probably individuals and groups with identity, but there is no relationship of ruler and ruled between them. From the point of view of totality and also from the point of view of individual cells, each cell or totality has singularity [*dokujisei*], and while it advocates its singularity, there is no conflict between cells. They expand into infinity. This world of nothingness can be called either an agglomeration of 'scattered sand' or one totality."[21] Nishi attempts to go beyond the opposition between an alienated collective such as the nation-state and the individual, which is implied in the reference to Sun Zhongshan's metaphor of scattered sand that Sun hoped to unite into a nation. Nishi suggests that Zhang points to the possibility of a world in which scattered sand no longer stands opposed to community. In other words, in this world, community no longer stands opposed to the members who make it up. Moreover, given that this community is based not on a particular group of citizens but on the people as nothing, it goes beyond the politics of the nation or identity.

Nishi describes the people as precisely those who realize this philosophy beyond the opposition between community and individual, and eventually beyond boundaries: "In China, the rulers gave form, but this is because of the existence of the people who are 'things' without form. Can 'things' without form be exhaustively contained by form? The rulers who give form are essentially in despair. . . . In this way, through facing nothingness, the awareness of a subject that negates itself emerges and then philosophy is born. The people, who are ruled over, are precisely those who realize this philosophy."[22] Notice that this quote begins with China and ends with the people as nothing and therefore without a nation. Nishi believes that Mao continues the legacy of the people when he asserts that the people are blank, but uses Marxism-Leninism to give Zhang's initial resistance a positive form and make it part of a larger transformative and transnational project. Mao's state was precisely the provisional subject that was supposed to help China and the world to realize the potential embodied in the concept of tianxia, so that the old universality of tianxia becomes a new type of universality beyond the antinomies of individual and community or nation and world. This is precisely the world of true nothingness, which we saw above.

Nishi's vision came under strong attacks from Japanese Sinologists in the postwar period, and the whole vision of Maoism began to crumble in Japan during the 1970s and 1980s. It was in this later context that Mizoguchi Yūzō developed his theories about tianxia and Chinese modernity through critically engaging Nishi and Takeuchi.

Mizoguchi Yūzō and an Alternative Chinese Early Modernity

Mizoguchi Yūzō was born in 1933 and so, unlike Takeuchi and Nishi, he did not have the experience of partly collaborating in the war and then having to atone for prewar activities after 1945. Moreover, he was educated primarily during the postwar period and wrote most of his influential works in the 1980s and 1990s. He would have been intellectually active from the mid-1970s, which could be characterized by a shift from a Fordist to a post-Fordist mode of capital accumulation, accompanying a move away from state-centered models of capitalism globally. Although there has been some debate about the extent to which this model applies to Japan, Yoshimi Shunya has argued that the period from the 1970s should be called a post-postwar society (*posuto-sengo shakai*).[23]

Yoshimi describes the economic and political changes during this period in the following standard manner: "After the 1970s, there were continuously phenomena such as world finance moving through a fluctuating market system, oil money rising, the socialist systems collapsing, repeated financial crisis and disturbances to nation-states."[24] In Japan this was expressed in the different policies of Ikeda Hayato–Tanaka Kakue and Nakasone Yasuhiro–Koizumi Junichirō. The conservative party of Tanaka invested money obtained through development in local areas to support industries and build dams. The Nakasone-Koizumi regimes, which could be characterized as neoliberal, rolled back big government and privatized various public services, including railways. From this perspective, Japanese neoliberalism was contemporaneous with the better-known neoliberal policies of Reagan and Thatcher.

Given that political agency and imagination were largely related to state power, the shrinking of state-funded projects accompanied a weakening of hope in the possibility of a radically different future. In other words, the existence of state-socialist regimes and a welfare state facilitated the imagination of utopias beyond the nation-state and capitalism. In the absence of these, people felt less tension between the realities of everyday life in the market and a dream of a more just world. Such changes caused people to retreat from the ideals of emancipation found in Marx and Mao.

At the same time, this weakening of the welfare state and the ideal of socialism did not imply the receding of Japanese nationalism. On the contrary, the 1980s saw an increase in Japanese discourses, such as *nihonjinron*, connected to the prominence of Japan as a global capitalist power and related to looking back to the origins of Japanese culture and thought. For example, in the 1980s, Nakasone promoted think tanks focused on traditional Japanese culture, such as the Nichibunken in Kyoto.[25] Such projects were associated with what was called internationalism, which entailed representing the nation to the world. Mizoguchi was clearly responding to this context, but as a Sinologist going back to the past in the 1980s, could not avoid the question of Mao and the revolution.

The case of Mao involves another dimension: the nature of changes in China after the 1970s. Although the political and economic changes from Mao's China to Deng's and beyond resemble the shift from Ikeda to Nakasone in that market reforms were implemented in both periods, the more important point is that the image of Mao in Japan began to change radically. Because diplomatic relations between China and Japan resumed in the 1970s, there was an increasing flow of information from China, and the Japanese public and Sinologists were more aware of Chinese condemnation of aspects of the Mao regime, such as the Cultural Revolution.

In this context, in the 1980s, Mizoguchi aimed to rethink the significance of China by critically reflecting upon Takeuchi and Nishi. Takeuchi died shortly after Mao in 1977, which coincided with shifting trends in Japanese Sinology. Mizoguchi was one of the first to assess the significance of Takeuchi's work after his death, and the complete works of Takeuchi Yoshimi were compiled by the publisher Chikuma shobō in December 1980. In the same month that the complete works were published, Mizoguchi began to publish a series of essays rethinking Chinese modernity. He asserted that Sinologists of his generation, brought up during and after the war, did not criticize China but attacked intellectuals such as Tsuda Sōkichi, who adhered to modernization theory, criticized China, and often supported the invasion of China. Mizoguchi singles out Takeuchi Yoshimi's *Lu Xun* and his essay "What Is Modernity?" as exemplary of the postwar vision of China, which "was a self-criticism of a modernization theory that aimed to leave Asia. He turned to the opposite position, which was pushed aside, namely China, and longed for an Asian future. To put it plainly, the starting point of our Chinese studies was first longing [*dōkei*]."[26]

When writing these words, Mizoguchi is of course also engaging in self-criticism, since he admits in a number of places that he chose to study China because he was enamored with Mao Zedong and the Chinese Revolution.[27] He claims that the Chinese modernity of Nishi and Takeuchi emerged from their own desire and their critique of Japanese colonialism rather than from Chinese history itself. One could say that Mizoguchi gestures back toward the epistemology of shinagaku, since he wants to reveal a China-in-itself. He claims that the Chinas of Takeuchi and Nishi are not adequate to their object. However, the China-in-itself that Mizoguchi ends up discovering overlaps with theirs, since Mizugochi also affirms a different Chinese modernity. In this sense, it is

China not just as object, but as a history with meaning for understanding the Chinese and global present.

Similar to Nishi, Mizoguchi returns to Chinese intellectual history to understand the special characteristics of the revolution and to find the possibility of another modernity. However, by the 1980s and 1990s, because the grand narratives of Marxism, Maoism, and imperialism had become unpopular, scholars had to search elsewhere in Chinese history for contemporary significance. Unlike Nishi and Takeuchi, who connected Chinese modernity to imperialism and global capitalism, Mizoguchi returned to a narrative expounded by Naitō Konan and others, seeking the indigenous origins of Chinese modernity in developments in the Song dynasty. Building creatively on that legacy, Mizoguchi especially stressed transformations occurring in the Ming and Qing dynasties. In addition to a situation in which global capitalism and imperialism impose standards that have to be resisted by anti-imperialist and socialist forces and where modernity is imposed on China from the outside, Mizoguchi sees a world in which there are many paths to modernity and the Chinese path represents a type of socialism.[28] Indeed, this is the key to his famous phrase cited earlier, that one should take "China as method," as opposed to the exclusive focus on imperialism.

Mizoguchi's most famous work is perhaps his 1981 book, *Chūgoku zenkindai shisō no kussetsu to tenkai* (The development and refraction of premodern Chinese thought), which examines the emergence of certain concepts related to late Ming and early Qing intellectual history. Mizoguchi wrote this book in response to various debates about Ming-Qing intellectual history and the problem of modernity; it is a landmark in the study of Chinese thought. He responds to Shimada Kenji's *The Setback of Modern Chinese Thought* (*Chūgoku kindai shii ni okeru zassetsu*), published in the 1950s, in which Shimada had already claimed that there were elements of modern Chinese thought in the Ming dynasty. In Shimada's view, however, such elements never came to fruition because of the setback that occurred in the Qing dynasty. Mizoguchi opposes Shimada's setback (*zassetsu*) with refraction (*kussetsu*). This refraction is not just a question of the continuity of modernity and various debates about the philosophy of the Ming dynasty philosopher Li Zhi (1527–1602), but includes a larger question about the nature of Chinese modernity in relation to its Western counterparts. In Mizoguchi's view, the influence of the legacy of Chinese thought allowed China to develop a different path toward modernity, which most Japanese Sinologists, including those in favor of the revolution, have overlooked.

Mizoguchi brings out the theoretical dimension of his work in *Hōhō to shite no chūgoku* (China as method), which echoes Takeuchi's essay of the 1960s,

"Asia as Method," and was published in 1989. In this book he reflects more clearly on his theoretical contribution to the concept of tianxia. The book opens with a reprint of his piece criticizing postwar Japanese Sinology, mentioned above, but Mizoguchi includes a number of essays in which he shows the influence of the Chinese past on Chinese modernity. In the fourth chapter, echoing Nishi, he contrasts tianxia with the concept of the state (*guojia*) and asserts that tianxia is broader, without boundaries, and has a direct link to the people. In Mizoguchi's view, tianxia does not emerge in modern China through negative mediation, as it does in Nishi's work, but for Mizoguchi as well, tianxia goes against a kind of abstraction. He not only argues that Sun Zhongshan's ideals of tianxia and *wangdao* are an attempt at thinking a different type of equality, he also relates these concepts to Asia and Africa. He notes that in Africa and Asia, boundaries and the idea of the state are a result of colonialism. This logic leads him to separate nation from state. In so doing he cites Sun Zhongshan, who asserts that "if the Kingly Way made from natural force forms the nation, the way of the hegemon, which is made from human power, makes the state."[29] In making this statement, Mizoguchi anticipates a great number of Sinologists and social theorists who would make a similar point in the early 2000s. For example, Rebecca Karl, in *Staging the World*, separates *minzuzhuyi* nationalism from *guojiazhuyi* nationalism, where the former is considered genuine resistance to power. Michael Hardt and Antonio Negri also credit the third world nationalisms with unleashing the power of the multitude against imperialism.[30] However, they lament that once these countries form a nation-state, they lose their progressive origins. Similarly, Mizoguchi laments that the idea of the Kingly Way / nationalism is truncated in Sun's thought because he forces it into a framework of the nation-state.

In the 1980s, when Mao's China was often criticized for being statist totalitarianism, Mizoguchi attempted to bring back aspects of the Chinese tradition and Maoism that resisted the nation-state. He thus looked to late Qing thinkers who attempted to develop this concept of tianxia outside the boundaries of the state by engaging with Kang Youwei and Liu Shipei. He focuses on how Liu develops the idea of people's livelihood outside of the state as he posits an ideal of a world without classes and without government. Moreover, Mizoguchi emphasizes that this vision of tianxia has an antimodern element, since Liu was against industrialization because it would destroy agriculture and handicrafts. Hence Liu posited an agricultural ideal against civilization. More than Nishi, Mizoguchi is concerned about the remnant of Chinese history and of tianxia, which lies behind his argument.

For example, Gu Yanwu distinguishes between the loss of the state (*wang guo*) and the loss of tianxia (wang tianxia). The state is lost when a new dynasty emerges, but tianxia refers to a moral imperative connected to the ideals of humanity and righteousness (*ren* and *yi*). Moreover, Gu contends that even if the state perishes, the people remain, but when tianxia is gone, so are the people. Tianxia, unlike the state, represents the everyday, which is why the people have responsibility. This shows the connection between the virtue of humanity and the people, which again echoes Nishi in showing how the people are the foundation of moral imperatives and that rulers lose tianxia when they go against the people. Moreover, tianxia can turn into a revolutionary force that goes against the state.

Mizoguchi is especially interested in the historical conjuncture of tianxia, imperialism, and the nation-state. In this case, the multitude, represented by terms such as *shengmin* (生民), turns into the people or citizens and thus is subsumed into a different system of control. There is a sense in which such conceptions continue to work within the new Chinese state and make it somewhat different from most European states. For example, Mizoguchi notes that Sun Zhongshan's concept of *seimin/shengmin* refers to an egalitarianism beyond formal equality. However, in the modern world of nation-states, tianxia becomes subordinate to the nation-state and loses its potential.

Mizoguchi finds traces of attempts to bring tianxia into the modern world and focuses specifically on Liu Shipei. He notes how Liu, perhaps anticipating Mao, draws on tianxia to combat industrial, technological civilization and affirm agricultural life. This move responds to a loss caused by capitalist development associated with the West. Capitalism implies a separation of politics from daily life and therefore a system of democracy and human rights that allows capitalist exploitation. As Ellen Wood writes, "Only capitalism, with its distinctive relation between political and economic spheres, has permitted this new concept of democracy, in which democratic rights are confined to a 'formal' political sphere, while class exploitation remains intact in other domains."[31] Liu counters this modern tendency toward fragmentation and argues for a world where "the multitudes' happiness is like that of a family."[32]

Mizoguchi compares Liu's above remarks to the conservative scholar-official Liu Yanghong, who opposed the self-strengthening movement in the late 1880s. Although their politics might be seen as opposed, Liu Yanghong also based his thinking on the universal values of benevolence and authoritativeness and used such concepts to distinguish China from the West. He wrote, "Western countries use wealth to create wealth; China uses not being greedy to create wealth. Western countries use strength to create strength; China uses not coveting victory to emerge victorious."[33] In this passage, Mizoguchi shows how Liu Yanghong draws on Confucianism to change the terms of the debate. In other words, "wealth" and "victory" in the "China" clauses refer to a different type of society. However, both of the above Lius are now criticized for being conservative. Although Liu Yanghong attacked capitalism, he is criticized for supporting the landlord class and feudal economics. Liu Shipei's critique of Western representative government led him to support Yuan Shikai's despotism. Mizoguchi ends his essay by saying that although the scholars criticize the Confucian ideals of tianxia as backward in relation to modernity, such concepts might contain another modernity that could reveal what is problematic about the nation-state model, which was forced upon Asia by the West.[34] Mizoguchi's emphasis on agriculture and critique of industrialization could be read as a more cautious gesture toward Maoism as the other modernity that China pursued. In short, Mizoguchi has attempted to provide a narrative based on the indigenous development of Chinese history to show that Maoist/Confucian resistance to capitalist modernity was possible and could still be meaningful today.

Note how Confucianism and Maoism have come together again, but differently than in Nishi's work. In Nishi's case, Maoism and Zhang Taiyan's thought emerge dialectically out of Confucianism, as a type of sublation (Aufhebung) after the Confucian worldview is negated. Mizoguchi sees this as a mistake and finds remnants of the Chinese tradition coming back to haunt capitalist modernity. Moreover, he contends that the ideologies of capitalism tend to make the Confucian remnant invisible.

Unlike Nishi, Mizoguchi does not discuss capitalism in most of his writings, possibly downplaying the effects of imperialism. However, about ten years after Nishi Junzō passed away, Mizoguchi contributed an essay to a volume devoted to Nishi's work, *Nishi Junzō: Hito to gakumon* (Nishi Junzō: The person and his scholarship), and made some observations about capitalism in China and Japan. Toward the end of this essay, Mizoguchi contextualized Nishi's position in terms of the development of capitalism in China and Japan and asserted his hopes for an alternative:

If we take the example of cars in 1950, Japan produced 300,000, in 1960 produced 480,000, in 1970 produced 5,300,000, and in 1980 produced 11,000,000. So we see that the 1970s were especially a period of high-paced "modernization." . . . On the one hand, in 1993, China produced 1,000,000 cars, which was about the same as what Japan produced in

1962 and 1963. However, in 1983, China produced 2,500,000 televisions and in 1989, it produced 2,700,000, the highest in the world. . . . Since the 1980s, China has also "modernized" at a feverish pitch.[35]

Mizoguchi's comment about China economically overtaking Japan and posing a threat to the United States could be seen now as prescient, at least, since this is the current portrayal of China in the mainstream media. In Mizoguchi's view, for Japan and other Asian countries, the increase in production enabled them to overcome their inferiority complex with respect to Europe and the United States. Asian countries' increasing productivity was paradoxically part of a project of leaving Asia and entering Europe and also of gaining self-respect for themselves as nations. But this whole process has as its background the homogenization of life under capitalism, which had constantly haunted Japanese Sinology in the form of social science and modernization theory.

Mizoguchi explains that his aim in writing Chinese intellectual history is precisely to combat this homogenization: "I believe that in the next century, which faces a world homogenized based on the principle of a capitalist market and a world where the blind pursuit of profit penetrates . . . individual values, one must find a different principle that will counteract the above tendency in the cultural worlds of Asia, Europe, and Islam. . . . The 'power' of philosophy is probably to counter this principle, criticize it, and to construct a principle that is capable of sublating it [shiyō]."[36]

In this context, Mizoguchi makes another gesture in the direction of tianxia and the people and underscores that the above task is not only for the Chinese people but for humanity in general. The work of philosophy is to find a principle that resists the basic principle of capitalism. This may appear abstract, but it echoes Hardt and Negri's reflections about language in empire, when they write, "All the elements of corruption and exploitation are imposed on us by the linguistic and communicative regimes of production: destroying them in words is as urgent as doing so in deeds."[37] Philosophy, in Mizoguchi's view, could precisely enable this destruction of capitalist regimes of exploitation by pointing to alternatives that existed in the past. The concepts of tian and tianxia are significant because they go beyond the boundaries of nation-states and point to a type of collective responsibility, along with collective practices based on an alternative ethical system. In this way, he provides a more positive understanding of tianxia than did Nishi and claims that there is no distinction between ruler and ruled in the Chinese concept of heaven. Rather, heaven is "natural and synthetic and through these characteristics, it is essentially the people."[38] While Mizoguchi uses the term "jinmin" for "the people," his meaning is better understood in terms of Hardt and Negri's multitude to the extent that we are dealing here with a noninstitutionalized force, rather than the modern concept of citizenship.

By rereading the concepts of tianxia, people or multitude, and Chinese modernity, Mizoguchi reconstitutes the resistance that pervaded the works of Nishi and Takeuchi. Following from this, his reading of Mao's work is mediated by his examination of the Chinese tradition. However, his comments about global capitalism and the possibility of its sublation pose again Nishi's questions of revolution and the reconstitution of community. Even if critique and sublation at the level of language are part of the process of real sublation, at some point one would have to connect philosophy with practice in a world where the two are often institutionally separate. The question that Mizoguchi and other critics of the capitalist present must face is how to translate philosophy into practice.

Conclusion: Global Capitalist Domination
and the Principles of the Past

Nishi and Mizoguchi each read China to find an alternative universality that goes beyond the homogeneity of capitalist modernity. Moreover, despite the differences in their respective positions, they both try to break free from modernization discourse and argue that unevenness and so-called backwardness could lead to different historical paths. Mizoguchi would even reject terms such as "backwardness" and argue that the residues of the Chinese past point to a different modernity, and could continue to point to a different future.

This is a gesture that various scholars on the left, even Marxists, who are usually hostile to the concept of alternative modernity, have attempted. For example, the Marxist-humanist Kevin Anderson's book *Marx at the Margins: On Nationalism, Ethnicity, and Non-Western Societies* focuses on Marx's writings on the non-Western world in order to show that there could be multiple paths to socialism.[39] A more ardent critic of alternative modernity, Harry Harootunian, argues that Marx did not adhere to a unilinear model of development and believed that the Russian experience showed that countries on the periphery of the global capitalist system could "utilize residues of prior modes of production to create either a new register of formal subsumption or bypass capitalism altogether."[40] Although Mizoguchi does not use the term "modes of production," the question of residues is crucial to his work.

Interestingly, Mizoguchi stresses a type of national multiculturalism precisely when countries previously on the periphery of the global capitalist system are fighting for a place in the center and making cultural claims; because they began producing a larger percentage of the world's gross domestic product, they can overcome their feelings of inferiority. Mizoguchi himself points out that there could be a new type of uniformity behind the mask of national particularity. After all, such claims to national particularity are inextricably connected to the principle of capitalism. So the question that Mizoguchi poses but is not able to answer is how philosophy can live up to its task of producing a principle that could transform and even sublate capitalism. At this point the concept of philosophy in relation to the people as multitude or even the people as tianxia could serve as a regulating principle, but more would need to be said about the relationships among the logic of capitalism, the logic of multicultural nationalism, and the domination or resistance of the people.

Here Nishi's notion of the formless people or multitude who could constantly re-create themselves through denaturalization is helpful, but it would have to be integrated with Mizoguchi's description of a blind productivity that has eclipsed East and West alike. Without theorizing it, Mizoguchi's description of rapid increases in productivity in China points to the production of relative surplus value. Unlike absolute surplus value, relative surplus value implies the production of surplus without extending the length of the working day. In other words, to produce relative surplus value, capitalists use machines and technology to reduce the amount of time that workers must work to produce the value of their own labor power and thus increase the time that they produce surplus value for capitalists. Moreover, capitalists who are the first to employ new technology are able to sell products priced below their value, because they are producing commodities using less than the average socially necessary labor time required to make them. However, such increases in surplus value are only short-lived, because once other factories begin using the same improved technology, the average socially necessary labor time to produce a given commodity decreases. The result is the redefinition of the labor hour at a faster pace, requiring people to produce more in one hour, which causes an increase in the general pace of life and an imperative to produce still more in a given time.[41] This logic of course continues with future technological breakthroughs. This explains the statistics that Mizoguchi lists above, which reveal of course a tendency that continues even today, when the number of cars in China greatly exceeds the figures that Mizoguchi quoted.

Mizoguchi's multicultural worldview overlooks the role of class in the global capitalist world. People participate in the reproduction of capitalism, but for huge parts of the population, the increase in the number of cars does not mean much. Indeed, many of these people might work in sweatshops and continue to produce absolute surplus value or some form of hybrid surplus value. These people are especially not subjects of the above process and are probably excluded from Mizoguchi's multicultural utopia. From this perspective, we need perhaps to combine Mizoguchi's view, which stresses the manner in which remnants of the multitude come back to haunt the present, with Nishi's conception of the people as alienated. Nishi's heaven and Takeuchi's Europe were both totalizing visions constituted by what they oppressed and excluded, namely the subjectivity and agency of the people. Moreover, their praise for Mao was based on the idea that he understood the power of the people as nothingness, as having the power to constantly destroy forms that were placed on them.

Mizoguchi's remarks, along with a look at China today, show that Nishi and Takeuchi's hope of a Chinese alternative inspiring the world to overcome capitalism dialectically has not been realized; their dream has become the subject of jokes. Indeed, a popular parody of a socialist song runs, "the reactionaries have not been beaten and imperialism returned holding leather briefcases."[42] This suggests that in addition to looking at the reconstitution of the outside of capitalism, one must infuse critical discourse about China with the more traditional Marxist insight that the overcoming of capitalism, as a cultural and economic totality, must emerge from the contradictions of that system itself. Indeed, Nishi's description of tianxia as embodying the alienated power of the people perhaps better describes the logic of capital than something peculiar to China. The formless people as a potential subject of history can emerge on the world stage only through making use of the contradictions of capitalism, such as between the increasingly superfluous nature of proletarian labor combined with its necessity for the production of value. The project of overcoming the homogeneity of capitalism, not to mention social domination, requires that one ask about the kinds of politics that would be required to replace the runaway productivity of capitalism with production organized under collective control.

NOTES

1. Young, *Japan's Total Empire*.

2. Guex, *Entre Nonchalance et Désespoir*.

3. Olsen, *Ambivalent Moderns*, 48.

4. Takeuchi, "Watashi to shūyi to chugoku bungaku" [Myself, surroundings and Chinese literature], 71.

5. I have explored his work in another essay; see Murthy, "The 1911 Revolution and the Politics of Failure."

6. Baba, *Sengo nihon no chūgoku zō*.

7. Takeuchi, "Chūgoku no kindai to nihon no kindai," 12.

8. Takeuchi, *Rojin*, 205.

9. Nishi and Koito, *Ri no igi to kōzō*, 449.

10. Nishi, *Nishi Junzō chosaku shū*, 1:5.

11. Nishi, *Nishi Junzō chosaku shū*, 1:4.

12. Sakamoto, "Nishi Junzō," 72.

13. Nishi, *Nishi Junzō chosaku shū*, 1:254.

14. Fukuzawa, *An Outline of the Theory of Civilization*, 84.

15. Nishi, *Nishi Junzō chosaku shū*, 263.

16. Quoting from "Weixin lishiguan de pochan," 4:1402–1403. Cf. Nishi Junzō, "Mu kara no keisei," 20.

17. Nishi Junzō, "Mu kara no keisei," 26.

18. The phrase is from Zhang Taiyan's 1908 "Da Tie Zheng," 369.

19. Nishi Junzō, "Chūgoku shisō no naka no jinmin gainen," 209.

20. Nishi Junzō, "Chūgoku shisō no naka no jinmin gainen."

21. Nishi, *Nishi Junzō chosaku shū*, 3:131.

22. Nishi, *Nishi Junzō chosaku shū*, 3:132.

23. Yoshimi, "Rekishi ha doko he iku no ka."

24. Yoshimi, "Rekishi ha doko he iku no ka," 208.

25. Ivy, *Discourses of the Vanishing*.

26. Mizoguchi, *Hōhō to shite no chūgoku*, 32.

27. Mizoguchi, "'Ten' to 'jinmin' ni tsuite," 161.

28. Mizuguchi's work could be understood as part of a global trend, since he was questioning the narratives of imperialism with respect to Chinese modernity around the same time that Paul Cohen was urging for a China-centered history. The irony of this comparison is that in the late 1980s, when Paul Cohen's book was translated into Japanese, the publishers thought that the title, *Discovering History in China*, would not sell, perhaps since Japanese scholars had been doing that for quite some time. Hence they changed the title to *Chi no teikokushugi: Orientalizumu to chūgoku zō* [Cognitive imperialism: Orientalism and the image of China], trans. Satō Shinichi (Tokyo: Heibonsha, 1988). This title makes it appear that the book is about imperialism. See Cohen, *Discovering History in China*.

29. Quoted in Mizoguchi, *Hōhō to shite no chūgoku*, 123.

30. Hardt and Negri, *Empire*.

31. Wood, "A Manifesto for Global Capitalism?," 80.

32. Mizoguchi, *Hōhō to shite no chūgoku*, 127.

33. Mizoguchi, *Hōhō to shite no chūgoku*, 127–128.

34. Mizoguchi, *Hōhō to shite no chūgoku*, 123.

35. Mizoguchi, "'Ten' to 'jinmin' ni tsuite," 170.

36. Mizoguchi, "'Ten' to 'jinmin' ni tsuite," 171. "Shiyō" is the Japanese translation for Hegel's Aufhebung.

37. Hardt and Negri, *Empire*, 404.

38. Mizoguchi, "'Ten' to 'jinmin' ni tsuite," 171.

39. Anderson, *Marx at the Margins*. See my review in *Journal of World History* 23, no. 1 (2012): 209–214.

40. Harootunian, "Who Needs Postcoloniality?," 43.

41. Marx, *Capital*; Postone, *Time, Labor and Social Domination.*

42. 反动派没打到，帝国主义夹着皮包回来了。The original lines were 反动派被打倒 帝国主义夹着尾巴逃跑了 (The reactionaries were beaten, and the imperialists grabbed their tails and fled), from the song "Socialism Is Good" (社会主义好). Original song written and composed in 1957, lyrics by Xi Yang and Li Huanzhi.

8

CHINA'S LOST WORLD
OF INTERNATIONALISM
Lin Chun

★

Postrevolutionary China aspired to proletarian internationalist principles. By a symbiotic logic, socialism and internationalism were interwoven ideologically, practically, and geopolitically. Any erosion of the former would cause and indicate the corrosion of the latter, and vice versa. This chapter traces the domestic ethnic and foreign policy trajectories of the People's Republic of China (PRC) as the two interconnected wings of internationalism against a changing background of Chinese socialist formation and transformation. Initially a main player in the historical movement of international communism and later a willing participant in capitalist globalization, China remains unsettled and ambiguous in a world increasingly integrated as much as torn apart.

This chapter begins by discussing the emergence of modern China as an exploited and oppressed class nation, signified by the rise of revolutionary Chinese nationalism following imperialist encroachment in the mid-nineteenth century. The next section looks into new China's internal and external relations after 1949, in terms of its socialist commitment and policy frameworks within many imposed economic and geopolitical constraints. The third section focuses on the negative impacts of the Sino-Soviet split on both the communist and nonaligned third worlds; China's rapprochement with the United States is also evaluated in that context. The last section briefly examines globalist and traditionalist responses to the present crises in the country and argues for a socialist alternative. Only by resuming and developing socialism can the lost world of internationalism be reclaimed in China as the answer to its national and global challenges.

The Making of China and the Emergence of a Class Nation

The growth of historical China, which originated in the Yellow River basin, drew on a rich array of sources over the *longue durée*, from East and inner Asia as well as the West via Eurasia and the south into Oceania. Many ties have formed over millennia among the interacting cultures and peoples in the regional "spaces of flows."[1] Turning a traditional empire or civilization into a nation in modern times did not require or involve a negation of the inherent multiplicity of the Chinese identity, which encompasses diverse demographic, geographic, cultural, and socioeconomic constituents. With its vast and fluid inner and outer frontiers often bypassing formal regional, ethnic, territorial, and other institutional boundaries, China cannot be and has never been a singular monolith but always one country comprising many worlds.

A ramification of this formative and interactive history is the general pattern of gradual amalgamation, more than rapid conquest, between and among the natives of Central Plain descendants and other communities near and far. The synchronous agencies of this integrative course toward "great unification" in China proper on all sides should be properly appreciated without any European preoccupation with the disintegrative process toward the national markets and states. In China, different groups, at least the larger ones, intermingled with one another, rather than assimilating in either direction. The prevailing conception of Sinicization is likely a myth.[2] Domination and subordination inevitably divided rulers and subjects, but the former were not always of Han origin and the latter always included a significant non-Han population. This population was diversely identifiable and mostly self-ruled in various local forms to various extents. By and large, a resourceful society, loosely identified as Chinese and aided by a politically minded central state, managed multiple ethnicities and different religions within and/or without the Han majority. Moreover, the Han was just as plural in its own historically amalgamated constitution and regionally differentiated by local customs and dialects. The gradual formation of a Chinese nation or *zhonghua minzu* did see countless conflicts, but the process still distinctively differed from that of the nation-states emerging from ethnic cleansing and interstate warfare in the West. The "pacified empire," as Max Weber calls it, rarely engaged in military aggression partly due to its time-honored, inward-looking, and racially inclusive worldview.[3] The revolutionary reconceptualization of Chinese commitment to national unity and autonomy and its postsocialist transmutation are discussed in the following sections.

Economically, China had some sophisticated productive and commercial advances centuries prior to European capitalism. When China led the way in output and short- and long-distance trade in a disparate world economy, Europe was peripheral. As acknowledged by comparative economic historians, from the collapse of the Roman Empire up until around 1800, China was ahead of most countries in material production, technology, commercialization, urbanization, and monetary wealth and was a driver of the regional economy.[4] If the Weberian question of why the Chinese nevertheless did not launch their own industrial revolution can be raised again, it is not because of any conceptual acceptance of biased Western universality or anybody's failure in the European shadow. Rather, Weber's question is still interesting in that the presence or absence of the necessary dynamics for the genesis of industrial capitalism can be better elucidated. Steep silver drain or languishing of cottage industries in the Yangtse delta traceable to the early Qing period, for example, was part of the same process of the rising global dominance of capitalism and its imperialist imposition and colonization.

China's economic fate was profoundly political, not only because it tested an ailing Chinese state but also because that state was symptomatic of an utterly contradictory global transformation. A traditional advantage had been translated into a sheer disadvantage in an era of intensified globalization of capital. In particular, imperialism is endemic to the global system of capitalism as the vehicle of primitive accumulation where trade and looting or conquest were interchangeable. The Europeans extracted resources and wealth on a far-reaching and colossal scale, which allowed them to afford various degrees of "ecological substitution" or relief, as in the case of appropriating and owning the New World as both a population outlet and a source of land-intensive primary products.[5] The colonies became a vital means of production, buttressing a division of labor in which the imperial powers relied on slave plantations and mines as well as trade and drug wars abroad. Through forced unequal exchanges, this relentless hegemonic agenda eventually shaped a world divided by rich and poor countries. Countries became rich by subjugating the poor ones, which then sank into poverty through deprivation. The two Opium Wars of the 1840s triggered a physical "slicing of China" by competing imperialist powers—hence the country's "semicolonial and semifeudal" nature, as depicted in the Communist Party analysis. China's subsequent social and governing crises were then directly attributable to foreign invasions and destruction, including astronomical figures of war reparations from the imposed unequal treaties. An ancient political economy of continental scope and almost unparalleled wealth and confidence had fallen prey to the capitalist jungles.

Weber was especially astute on the contrast between a China (post–Warring States) without "armed peace where several competing autonomous states constantly prepared for war" and a Europe full of intraimperialist wars where the "pacification of a unified empire was lacking." Capitalism was actually "conditioned through war loans and commissions for war purposes." The lack of colonial relations handicapped the East as compared with occidental types of economy or "the varieties of booty capitalism, represented by colonial capitalism and by Mediterranean overseas capitalism connected with piracy." In his account, Chinese geography presented barriers to similar expansionist impulses and actions in China, but the more important roadblock stemmed from "the general political and economic character of Chinese society" and state. "Just as competition for markets compelled the rationalization of private enterprise, so competition for political power compelled the rationalization of state economy and economic policy."[6] Compared with Western imperialism, Chinese virtue had now been condemned and beaten.[7] This important emphasis on the crucial role of war and war financing in the making of modern Europe as an exception, not the norm, has been developed extensively by influential contemporary scholars, and anticipated the massive financialization of the entire capitalist operation today.[8]

To follow China's torturous passage in the modern world is to comparatively situate its evolving position in the global system of capital accumulation and expansion since the "long sixteenth century" (1350–1650). In such an era, China, like any other individual society, might be properly understood only within its epochal parameters of capitalism, or what came to be known in the Marxist analysis as uneven and combined development. Due to the system's structural unevenness, a potential privilege of backwardness could enable the margins to overtake the center through learning and leaping.[9] However, unlike the rise of the West, this optimism about the ascendance or resurgence of the rest is conditioned on the subjugated peoples breaking free from the imperialist chains. A logical implication is that capitalism cum imperialism entails extraction, domination, and sabotage, and ultimately hampers development. As shown in the Chinese experience, modernization through imitating the West to achieve a homegrown, robust national capitalism was an illusion violently dismantled by foreign aggressors in collusion with a domestic comprador class as a by-product of semicoloniality. Not until after 1949 did China begin to recover and develop, only because the revolution changed the country's international position and fashioned a socialist developmental state. The argument that incipient capitalism appeared as early as the Song-Ming period (around the twelfth and thirteenth centuries) is a politically charged counterfactual conjecture to implicate imperialist intervention for having fatally blocked China's natural course. Whether or not this is the case, and regardless of the virtues and vices of capitalism, this view unmistakably clarifies the causal sequence that national revolutions took place not where capitalism succeeded but where it failed.[10] Plenty of historical and empirical evidence shows also that capitalism was far from a model or panacea ready for every nation to acquire; its growth actually relies on underdevelopment outside its core zones. By definition imperialism is therefore intrinsically constitutive of capitalist development.[11]

As the totalizing capitalist mode of production and extraction has a complex and differential temporality that divided the modern world into so-called earlier and later developers or advanced and backward nations, most obviously "at the level of the class order generated by it," the modernizing Chinese story is in essence locked on a course of catching up. It is, so to speak, one of the struggle and triumph, as well as dilemmas and retrogressions, of a class nation.[12] Foreign disruptions not only deepened China's imperial decline and politico-social crises but also awakened the Chinese people, as Marx and Lenin famously viewed it. The Chinese responses since the upheavals of Taiping Rebellion to the country's exploited and oppressed class status in the world culminated in the twentieth-century Chinese revolutions. The Marxist origin of conceptualizing class nation in the political and intellectual context of proletarian internationalism might have been forgotten, but its contemporary relevance has never been more pressing. Ernest Gellner wrote that "only when a nation became a class . . . did it become politically conscious and activist . . . [as] a nation-for-itself."[13] This image helps explain how China, a culture or civilization hard to define within the European nation-state perspective, could have emerged as a truly coherent and proud modern nation and achieved formidable national development.

The prominent new Qing historians are stimulating not because they have correctly discredited Han-centrism in regionalist interpretations of the making of China and its unprecedented territorial reach but by rendering it impossible to evade the critical question about revolutionary Chinese nationalism. Perhaps against their intention, such interpretations turn out to concur with the communist argument in the background: nationalism of oppressed peoples was a legitimating and popular aspiration that was politically constructed into an integrative force. In revolutionary China, national liberation was cultivated into a cohesive, rallying ideology influencing a substantively shared national self-consciousness of an all-inclusive population. Internal class relations had to be readjusted in accordance with China's external class status in the global political economy, in which domestic bureaucratic capital served as the local pillar of imperialist international capital. These intertwining relationships explained the dual social-national character of the communist revolution.

The multicultural Chinese configuration, however, is an anomaly in the nation-state model based on unified national markets and governments for capitalist development achieved mostly via financial-military means in Europe. Absent an imperial breakdown into smaller states, the image of modern China violates the European conception of nation antithetical to empire. The Chinese temporal-spatial duality of both state forms of nation and empire, deemed utterly anachronistic, baffles and disturbs the standard modern sensitivity.[14] However, holding a benchmark Europe against a deficient China, these binaries are not only parochial and hypocritical (forgetting a guilty record of racism, colonialism, and imperialism) but also blind to China's incontestable accomplishment in its status as a major secular and independent political community. The centrality of a sovereign people as the new national subject is a definitive marker of any modern nation. Also missing is the spread of multinational states, hence a negation of the established nationalist logic.[15] This is precisely why the ethnically defined breakup of communist federations was reactionary and obsolete. In the same vein, the fundamental difference between oppressor/aggressor and oppressed/defensive nations must be observed, hence between the two kinds of nationalisms. Although such categorizations can change, and within oppressed nations there could be more progressive or conservative variants, any undifferentiated notion of nationalism would be conceptually flawed and politically complacent. In this context, the concept of class nation is shorthand for oppressed nations in the capitalist epoch of world history.

The identity of a class nation is rooted in both class and nation. Apparently such a nation cannot pretend class peace at home while engaging in antiimperialist struggles. The communist revolution in China simultaneously pursued national and social liberation. The united front of the Communist Party epitomized a partial suppression of class interests and conflict at the time of national crisis. The party's ethnic policy also had a united front aspect, especially when it came to the task of winning over minority elites. But the policy had to be fundamentally class oriented because of the effectively class status of ethnic minorities, hence class ethnicities in prerevolutionary Chinese social and regional structures, similar to the whole country being a class nation in the global system. In logical consistency, this dual recognition also provides theoretical justification for communist international relations. A conscious nation-for-itself, China in revolution sought international alliances for support and security. That class nations of the world should unite is determined by the global power of a transnational bourgeoisie and world capitalism, and is perfectly in line with classical proletarian internationalism.

Revolutionary Nationalism and Third World Internationalism

The political revolution of 1911 overthrew the last dynastic court and set up the first Chinese republic. The Qing territories had been by and large preserved under the banner of unified "republicanism of five nations" (Han, Hui, Mongol, Tibet, and Manchu) along with the smaller minority groups. Subsequently the communists went to great lengths to transform social relations in a land revolution against "imperialism, feudalism, and bureaucratic capitalism." Their most innovative strategy was to seize power by encircling the cities. The cities as counterrevolutionary strongholds were besieged by means of building grassroots red regimes in rural peripheries. A unique "people's war" involving peasant mobilization, this state building from below politically trained a people in an optimal institutional expression in the party's "mass line" politics. Reversing its oppressed class position in stark contrast with crippled colonial modernity, new China was able to be largely self-reliant in its socioeconomic modernization. The Chinese Revolution was thus a world historical event that created a powerful socialist state, halting capital's global scramble in a land containing one-fifth of humanity.

The Chinese Marxists defined their revolution as *new* democratic for the socialist outlook in its maximum program beyond national independence and the policy of land to the tiller specified in its minimum program. This anticapitalist ambition was what categorically distinguished the communist revolution in China from the *old* bourgeois revolutions, which only paved the way for capitalist development. China's industrial working class, however small in the early twentieth century, was indispensable in sustaining this crucial distinction.[16] Growing from the worker-peasant alliance, the revolution's united front was one of its "three magic weapons" (as Mao put it), along with party construction and armed struggle. Its inclusion of the national bourgeoisie, along with the intellectual and professional progressives and patriotic intermediate social groups, was premised on the double class nature of the revolution, socially and nationally. Again, it was due to the nation's proletarian status and the revolutionary leadership of the Communist Party as an ingenious working-class organization that the Chinese Revolution became part of the world socialist revolution initiated in October 1917.[17] "Class," after all, cannot be a positivist sociological category but is meaningful and denotable only within its concrete political-economic context. Likewise, the formation of a class nation had to be itself a matter of political struggle, and China as a class nation emerged only through revolutionary mobilization within its liberation movement.

The year 1949 signifies not the end but the beginning of this new democratic embracing socialist revolution, as China went on to nationalize industries and collectivize agriculture in the 1950s. Internationalism in this period had two organically interconnected policy dimensions: domestic ethnicity and foreign relations. The former was concerned with ethnic equality against majority chauvinism and the latter national sovereignty and peaceful coexistence against imperialist hegemony. That is, socialist nationalism and internationalism, possessing a globally proletarian quality, were tied together to the extent that any retreat from one would undermine the other. Ultimately, it was revolutionary nationalism and by extension internationalist solidarity among the oppressed peoples—class nations of the world and class nationalities within China—that conferred on the modern Chinese identity a cohesive self-consciousness. Indeed, the communist revolution was itself a historical process of forging the multiethnic Chinese nation.[18]

Consider first internal ethnic relations and minority rights. As mentioned, imperial rulers, of Han or non-Han origins, used a sophisticated mix of mutuality and repression to manage diversity within a broad tributary fold of protection, subordination, and coexistence. In contrast to early modern Europe, such relations pursued regional stability through tributes from peripheral entities and bestowing gifts in return from the center. Other methods ranged from tribal autonomy and political marriages to forced expulsion or integration. The late Qing crises included distrust not only between the Han population and the Manchu aristocracy but also among different ethnic groups. Foreign invasions as well as local despots and warlords only invoked more conflicts. The Republican revolution quickly overcame its initial anti-Manchu racial perception and proclaimed universal republicanism. Sun Zhongshan's notions of Asianism or "eastism" emphasized the revolutionary obligation of supporting the "bullied peoples" (*shouqu renmin*). Following Marx, who claimed that "no nation can be free if it oppresses other nations," the communist revolution engaged in emancipation and extended sympathy for the "weak and small nations."[19] It aimed at liberating China from not only foreign powers but also ruling-class racism at home. This twofold commitment to national liberation was the political basis of a cohesive Chinese nation and people, and hence the constitutional foundation of the PRC. Amalgamating the majority and minorities into a supreme sovereign subject was "we the people" in action. Their newly constructed identity became a primary marker of class power.

The moral commitment to equality and common prosperity of all nationalities was prerequisite to socialist ethnic policies and minority regional autonomy.[20] To address historical injustice, one of the first tasks the PRC government tackled was to dispatch hundreds of work teams to carry out a painstaking identification program for individual and communal ethnic/religious identities to be formally claimed and classified. The difference between this work and the notorious colonial techniques of divide and rule was obvious and categorical, as the former was done only to protect and promote the minorities. It indeed ended up rescuing disappearing languages, cultures, certain medical and other beneficial traditions, and quite a few vanishing groups themselves. However artificial or excessive the project might have been in hindsight, it was necessary groundwork for implementing preferential treatment and other egalitarian reforms. Remarkably, even major constitutional amendments have never touched Article 4 on ethnic equality, solidarity, minority rights, and mutual assistance. But then the other side of the same point is that if this article had been ideologically and legally upheld by the socialist mandate, the weakening or loss of that mandate would lead to neglect or abuse of minority interests and rights. For Mao and colleagues, combating and curbing "great Han chauvinism" as more dangerous than ethnic nationalism was a constant task. This is regrettably no longer the case in the official agenda in the last two decades or so.

Under the guidelines of inventive quasi-federalism of multileveled autonomous governments, five provincial administrations of regional autonomy were established in the 1950s and 1960s, supplemented by dozens of autonomous municipalities and prefectures and over a hundred autonomous counties. This institutionalization was designed with great care and an understanding of regional autonomy as more significant than ethnic differences, given the fact of mixed nationalities in most minority areas and needed economic cooperation for the underdeveloped regions.[21] In such multilayered jurisdictions, local governments via local people's congresses "have the power to enact regulations on the exercise of autonomy and other separate regulations in accordance with the political, economic, and cultural characteristics" of their localities (Articles 115 and 116). Clearly, this configuration of socialist semifederalism was intended to optimize coordination so as to allow unity in diversity and every group to flourish. Socialist China thus for the most part avoided the familiar consequences of imposed communal and ethnic borders and other arbitrary ethnic partition or cleansing in lost homelands, broken lives, split loyalties, and personal tragedies. Also put in place were affirmative action policies in education, health care, production subsidies, and welfare provisions to redress past hindrances and victimization of minorities under the old regimes.[22] To reduce regional disparities, the central government consistently made huge investments in infrastructural upgrading in the poorer minority heartlands while sustaining large-scale transfers of funds, technologies, public service facilities, and experts from coastal provinces. A paternalistic overtone notwithstanding, on balance, internal peripheralization did not happen. Substantial social gains, vindicated by human development measurements and overall intergroup peace, were largely sustained until the negative turns of the 1990s.

Concerning the limits of minority rights, the Chinese communists retreated from their earlier position on national self-determination by prohibiting secession in the constitution.[23] The 1954 constitution endorsed autonomy only within a unitary state: the "national autonomous areas are inalienable parts of the PRC." This change, however, came for a sound reason. Apart from the hostility of the capitalist world toward the new regime and thus the danger of disunity, China did not follow the USSR due to the two countries' different histories and revolutionary experiences. As Zhou Enlai explained, unlike the Soviet Union, where the right to self-determination was a key policy for the socialist state to distinguish itself from the Tsarist empire, China became itself an oppressed nation in the mid-nineteenth century. Moreover, the Chinese Revolution rallied its forces from the multiple ethnicities on the rural margins. People of various ethnic origins joined the Red Army, as in southwest China during the Long March, and communist organizations and bases were set up not only in the northwest Hui region but also in Inner Mongolia and Xinjiang. Zhou also argued for locally congenial institutional mechanisms to counter imperialist attempts at manipulating ethnic divisions.[24] In other words, the revolutionary project of national liberation predetermined its unwavering insistence on national independence and integrity; the former was conditioned on the latter. In a most unfortunate twist, Zhou's warning anticipated a central Asian geopolitical nuisance, which later developed between China and the Soviet Union, eventually destroying not only the movements for international communism and third worldism but also the socialist assets of the two countries.

This leads us to the other dimension of internationalism. China's revolutionary path differed significantly from mobilization for independence and postcolonial nation building in much of the third world, though many affinities and important ties existed. The victorious revolution in the world's largest poor country was itself a major contribution to the postwar reordering of the world. The Chinese Revolution, with its far-reaching global impacts, was never merely a Chinese event. That is, socialist nationalism is a nationalism defined by socialism, not the other way round, and an antithesis of bourgeois nationalism (and, for that matter, anticommunist sorts of national socialism). Moreover, socialism has to be international because its enemy, capitalism, is a global system, and because the continuation of socialism depends on its development beyond national borders. Socialism in one country is by definition unsustainable. New China thus went out of its way, in spite of its own acute economic difficulties, to aid socialist revolutions and progressive regimes and forces in other countries. These dimensions of internal and external solidarity were necessitated by the success and consolidation of the Chinese Revolution.[25] They were interpenetrated and mutually reinforcing on the same agenda of defeating capitalism and replacing it with a socialist alternative.

The first daring act of the newly founded PRC was to enter the Korean War (1950–1953). However debatable certain details of relevant decisions may remain, the main historical narrative is unequivocal regarding such factors as the Seventh Fleet deployed to the waters around Taiwan and American contemplation of crossing the Yalu River, even using nuclear weapons, and, above all, the Chinese and Koreans forcing the Americans to sign an armistice in Panmunjom. Having just "lost China," the United States saw Korea as a battlefield for trying to regain its Far East frontier of the Cold War via devastating hot wars, later also in Vietnam. Likewise, the wars in Korea and Vietnam (where the Vietnamese communists were first to win at Dien Bien Phu and later to take over the U.S. puppet regime in the south for unification) intimately mattered to China. China's involvement, from field troops to free weapons (as in Vietnam) and other assistance to its socialist neighbors, was predicated on proletarian internationalist principles as much as its own security. It also supported revolutionary nationalist movements elsewhere, morally or materially—from the communist guerrillas in Southeast Asia and Arab socialism and nationalism to the Palestinian cause and black liberation. As typified in Korea, "that Chinese generation shed blood for the construction not only of a new China but also of a new world."[26]

Meanwhile, Cold War geopolitics was harshly imposed on the young communist regime as a tough test. Soviet aid in the first decade of the PRC through the bilateral friendship treaty between the world's two largest socialist states was crucial, substantive, and appreciated.[27] The wide-ranging aid projects helped lay the foundation for China's industrialization. That fraternity, however, didn't last. Mounting disagreements starting in 1956 led to China's rejection of the camp analysis of communism versus capitalism in the early 1960s. Instead of two camps, the globe was now seen as divided into three worlds; instead of the initial theory of a French origin, on Mao's map the United States and USSR belonged to the hegemonic first world; Japan, Europe, and Canada the second; and China along with Asia (except Japan), Africa, and Latin America the third.[28] This view highlighted a broad area for popular politics that challenged the spheres of two competing superpowers. Identifying itself with the third world rather than the Soviet bloc, China nevertheless firmly defended its own version of socialism in opposition to what it considered bureaucratic and statist under Stalin and capitulationist and social imperialist under Khrushchev. As such, "China was entirely encircled by hostile powers—the USSR to the north and west, and the US initiated military pacts on either end. In addition, there was no one to argue China's case at the UN" until 1971, when Beijing finally replaced Taipei to represent China.[29] Still, proud and self-reliant, China managed to gain some precious space for itself to attain genuine autonomy and remarkable development in an extremely treacherous and complicated geopolitical milieu.

The socialist and third worlds were natural allies. To a definitive extent, socialism, third worldism, and internationalism were inseparable.[30] The socialist self-identity of both the Soviet and the Chinese state implied in one way or another anticapitalist foreign policies. There was also the attraction of socialist egalitarianism. Since equality "held an important place in the imagination of the anticolonial movements," the third world emerged as a regional project that aspired to global transformation.[31] Without exporting revolution, the socialist commitment to the world's class nations sustained a selective strategy of foreign interventionism. Attacking the "revisionist" worldview of the Soviet leadership, the Maoist three-world theory, along with a continuing revolution in China from 1949 to the radicalism of the Cultural Revolution, exerted wide appeal to proponents of decolonization, the global 1968, and the antiwar movement over Vietnam. China's antihegemonic stance had strength against the narrow and closed Cold War logic. "That the Chinese communists resisted the idea that the darker nations should be divided into the sphere of influence of the two powers made it a principled ally of the third world."[32] Eventually, however, the rigidity of opposing the Soviet Union bore seriously negative consequences.

Often dismissed by those who mistake the third world position of antiimperialism for political neutrality, the first Afro-Asian conference in Bandung, in 1955, enjoyed the backing of both Moscow and Beijing, with China being a major player. The Soviet Union requested an invitation from the organizers to its Central Asian republics and published a joint declaration with Yugoslavia a few weeks later to affirm the concept and project of the third world as a significant advance in world peace. Based on the "five principles of peaceful coexistence" earlier codified between China and India (1954) concerning trade and communication in the Tibetan region, the participants agreed on ten principles of national sovereignty and integrity, equality of all races and nations, and nonintervention in international affairs. Zhou Enlai, the PRC premier, skillfully secured a popular front–style platform despite some antisocialist voices, gaining "a diplomatic victory for China."[33] President Sukarno, the host and a personal friend of Zhou's, made a most powerful speech on third world unity. Apparently, China had to pursue a balancing act among its contradictory goals of supporting the communist parties in the region, achieving a united front with third world regimes, and minimally protecting ethnic Chinese, mostly as business elites in Southeast Asia. It managed for the time being with no small difficulties, ranging from communist organizations being illegal and brutally suppressed (e.g., in Egypt under Nasser) to anti-Chinese sentiments and riots in Indonesia and Malaya.[34]

With Bandung as the precursor, Yugoslavia, India, and Egypt initiated the nonaligned movement (NAM), which became an autonomous force in a superficially bipolar world. The founding event in Belgrade in 1961 was followed by meetings hosted in Cairo, Lusaka, Algiers, Colombo, and Havana in the 1960s and 1970s. The more radical phase of the movement followed the 1959 Cuban revolution, which also marked the participation of Latin America. Che Guevara's conference speech in Algeria in 1965 identified Cuba as "an underdeveloped country as well as one that is building socialism."[35] The Tricontinental was founded in Havana in 1966, marking a third worldism almost identical with third world socialism. While left-wing popular movements spread throughout the three continents, by the late 1970s neocolonialism and neoliberalism began to incorporate many developing countries, deepening their economic dependency in a changing global political economy in the aftermath of the oil crisis and relinquishing of the gold standard. The gradual transmutation of the third world from a politically transformative agent to an economic project of growth pitted the poorer nations against each other in the Cold War divide for financial assistance. The formation of G77 was again confined to a narrow development agenda under the monopoly power of the U.S.-led G7.[36] The seventh NAM conference, held in 1983 in India, probably signaled the end of an era, although the labels "third world" and "nonaligned nations" both stayed alive (the latest, seventeenth NAM summit in Venezuela, in September 2016, centered on the theme "peace, sovereignty and solidarity for development"). "New Delhi allows us to write the obituary of the Third World," as leaders of diverse ideological persuasions and regime types in the Global South had largely abandoned the ambition of equality and justice for a different world.[37] It is now from below, third world socialism began to find new voices and forums (see the last section).

China supported the Second Economic Seminar of Afro-Asian Solidarity held in Ben Bella's Algeria before the country's 1965 coup. However, due to its growing enmity toward the Soviet Union, and for that matter the Warsaw pact and Tito's "betrayal" of communism, and an unexpected border conflict with India, China increasingly saw NAM as a rival. This further alienated some of its earlier socialist as well as bourgeois nationalist allies. The Cubans were now allied with the Soviets after a few failed attempts at mediating between the world's two largest communist parties after Khrushchev stepped down. China had otherwise stood fast throughout for Congolese independence, the Algerian revolution, and anti-imperialist struggles in many other countries. This stance continued and was especially high-flying during the Cultural Revolution, even though it was also seriously distorted by the Maoist strategy and rhetoric of antihegemony. Not exactly replacing traditional Marxist class analysis, antihegemony nevertheless highlighted nationalist causes with a strong ideological and cultural dimension. China thus kept its development aid and friendship diplomacy especially to Africa in the forms of donations, interest-free loans, and direct construction projects as well as technological transfers and training programs, mostly in agriculture. The TAZARA, designed and built in the late 1960s and early 1970s to connect two cities in Tanzania and Zambia respectively, was the single longest railway in sub-Saharan Africa at the time. It exemplified an alternative to the prevailing first world / third world relationship poisoned by condescension and unequal exchange.[38]

Retreat from Communism and Third Worldism

In 1964, when China's ruptures with the Soviet bloc and certain third world countries worsened, Mao still called, over the anti-American popular protests in Panama, for a "broadest united front" of "the peoples of the socialist camp, of Asia, Africa, and Latin America, of every continent of the world, of all the countries in love of peace and all the countries suffering from aggression, control, intervention, and bullying from the United States" to "counter American imperialist aggression and war policies and defend world peace."[39] However, the retreat had already begun, with the 1962 Sino-Indian War as a tragic signpost. Mao's sense a few years earlier had been that the quarrel was a family affair—"family and friends quarrel; tensions will pass." Yet Nehru's "forward defense" did not help. A pragmatic issue of borders (fueled by the Tibetan exiles) was allowed to escalate into a matter of nationalist principle; and "such high-minded ideas on internationalism and mutual respect for sovereignty... could not withstand older ideological and cultural pressures." Secular internationalism collapsed on both sides, damaging the hard-won dynamic of the third world as a promising political platform. India, which led the nonaligned group at the UN on disarmament and peace, resorted to its own arms buildup. China's foreign policy, dictated by its opposition to the USSR, "wound its way from Bandung to a rapprochement with the US and its impossible alliances with dictatorial regimes."[40]

Historical tensions between the Soviet (and the Comintern) and Chinese communist parties since the 1920s were first over the revolutionary strategies in China and later about certain territorial issues that China viewed as legacies of imperialist Tsarism. Mao recalled in his conversation with the Soviet ambassador Pavel Yudin, and on other occasions, that Stalin had advised against the communist force fighting the civil war after 1945 and then the People's Liberation Army crossing the Yangtse to defeat the Guomindang in 1949, because he "never had faith in the Chinese people."[41] Yet the twentieth congress of the Communist Party of the Soviet Union (CPSU) in 1956 was the turning point in the Sino-Soviet relationship. The Chinese were angered by Khrushchev's secret speech, which shocked the Chinese and other communist parties. Despite their grievances toward Stalin, the Chinese were principled and saw de-Stalinization as a serious mistake, and published two *People's Daily* editorials in response to the event, followed by open letters and nine major commentaries in 1963–1964 criticizing Soviet revisionism and "social imperialism."[42] China refused the military cooperation proposed by Khrushchev in the late 1950s, conceiving it as "big country" and "big party" chauvinism. China also shelled Jinmen in August 1958 without forewarning the Soviets, in support of the Iraqi revolution and opposing the U.S. intervention in the Middle East during the Lebanon crisis. In 1960, the Soviet Union unilaterally withdrew aid and experts from China, breaking the contracts and abandoning many of their unfinished industrial and defense aid projects at a huge economic cost to China.

Without looking into the Sino-Soviet debate, which had a real ideological and theoretical significance, suffice it to note here that the division revolved around Khrushchev's new doctrine of peaceful transition to socialism and peaceful competition between the East and West, as well as the party (and state) immersed in the whole people. The Chinese regarded the doctrine as irresponsible and a betrayal of the Marxist positions on class struggle and world revolution; hence they saw the Sino-Soviet split as a line struggle of the international communist movement. The argument involved three main questions about the nature of imperialism, peace and war, and relationships among the communist parties. On this China represented the more militant wing of international socialism, in line with radical third worldism and armed national liberation. Revolutionary violence, for instance, was necessary in Frantz Fanon's analysis of the need to launch a colonized people on the path of freedom by lifting their subjectivity from subservience, which corresponded to Mao's emphasis on the ideological function of revolutionary mobilization and socialization. Ironically, the USSR was still the world's first-ever workers' state founded on genuinely communist and internationalist premises, despite its political and bureaucratic degeneration since the 1930s.[43] For these reasons, it would be mistaken to take the Sino-Soviet disputes as mainly of a nationalistic nature. They were rather genuinely concerned with certain fundamental differences in the two parties' interpretations of socialism and capitalism. In the Chinese critiques, the charge of revisionism referred directly to capitalist restoration and other forms of departure from the socialist cause.

Soviet practice therefore did not really live up to its belief in the possibility of peaceful paths to international harmony. Improvements, accompanied by a degree of caution in intervention, also became visible in the 1960s.[44] There was a real internationalist aspect to the Soviet Union's foreign commitment and policy as, after all, "the USSR [was] not subject to the logic of imperialism." In fact, the new wave of third world revolutionary movements "occasioned a substantial and visible exercise of Soviet military power in support of them." The USSR supplied the heavy military armor and expertise needed for victory in Vietnam and later also for the Sandinistas in Nicaragua, and provided airlifts and strategic equipment for Cuban forces in Angola and Ethiopia when South Africa invaded (backed by the United States, China, and Zaire). The Soviet leaders "degraded the concept of proletarian internationalism," but still furnished indispensable economic and military aid to national liberation.[45] Soviet troops were directly deployed in Afghanistan (however disastrous it was) and military advisers dispatched elsewhere to oppressed and destitute fighters in third world jungles. "Even where there was no Soviet military involvement as such, states allied to the USSR or revolutionary movements in conflict with the West were in some measure protected," as in Iran.[46] Even if such Soviet involvement was motivated less by any ideology than by its own security considerations or its need to balance Chinese influence, the USSR was a brake on imperialist war and money machines. This can be better appreciated only after the fact: the disappearance of the Soviet Union was by all good measures "an unmitigated catastrophe," especially in global politics.[47]

China's preoccupation with counterhegemony led to its categorical misjudgment on the Soviet Union. Whatever its many faults, the Soviet Union could not be an enemy of socialism and national liberation. Soviet support was indispensable for the world's class nations and could indeed have been a far stronger force in promoting socialist and third worldist causes if intracommunist divisions did not arise. The same can certainly be said about China. The Soviet power also protected many progressive governments and movements the world over. Its nuclear umbrella covered China as well, even at the peak of the Sino-Soviet dispute.[48] Against such a backdrop, it appeared that the Chinese committed a series of errors in handling internal disagreements among the communist parties as well as the complicated relationship—congruities or incongruities—between internationalism (class based) and third worldism (nation based). Similar to its domestic policy error of confusing the two kinds of contradictions, the Chinese party mistook contradictions between China and the Soviet Union, contradictions among the people, for those between the enemies.[49] In its adventurist assertion on world revolution, disregarding its superior united-front strategies, China suffered from a kind of left infantilism. Eventually, to relieve itself from an impossible isolation caused by targeting both the United States and the USSR, China took a drastic turn toward the United States in order to counterbalance the Soviet threat.

The defense of the Soviet Union here does not mean that the CPSU was on the right side of the dispute. Rather, each party must take its due responsibility for the irreversible, fatal damages they inflicted on the international communist and prosocialist movements. Khrushchev was also personally responsible for many of the disputes that originated from his "secret speech" in 1956 and developed in his opportunistic foreign policies (e.g., adventurism followed by surrenderism during the Cuban missile crisis) and chauvinistic attitude toward the Chinese and a few other smaller communist parties. He even used the language of "yellow peril." Mao, on the other hand, eventually abandoned his effort at "considering the overall interests" and allowed nationalistic feelings to dictate Chinese responses to events after the mid-1960s. By changing the struggle against global capitalism to a struggle against hegemonic powers, much of the class content was overtaken by nationalist sentiment.

With China seeing the Soviet Union as its main enemy, its foreign policy and relations involuntarily became either blurred or outright detrimental to socialist internationalism. As China started to court the United States, it sided with Pakistan against Bangladeshi independence and sent emergency aid to Sri Lanka to put down the left-wing Lanka Sama Samaja Party's insurgency in 1971. It praised the Greek military junta in 1972 and welcomed Gaafar Nimeiri of Sudan to Beijing after the dictatorship's massacre of its communists in the same year. It quickly recognized the 1973 coup in Chile and expelled the Chilean ambassador to China when he refused to comply with Pinochet. It also joined a counterrevolutionary coalition against the popular Angolan government that had just emerged from a long war against Portuguese colonialism. Later it opposed the Afghan communists as well, again along with the United States, Iran, and Pakistan.[50] To be fair, new China's international environment had been extremely complex and difficult, and Beijing was genuinely threatened by Soviet military attacks. Suspicious of U.S. interest in such an attack, Mao confronted Henry Kissinger in one of their meetings in 1973 and proposed a "horizontal line" of the United States, Japan, China, Pakistan, Iran, Turkey, and Europe to counter the Soviet Union.[51]

Meanwhile, communist infighting spread from the Sino-Soviet split to factional struggles in many communist parties between and among the Maoist and other Marxist variants. "The result was an ever more accelerated disintegration of the internationalism of the classical communist movement, as communist states multiplied." Earlier fractures between Yugoslavia and the USSR or Albania and Yugoslavia notwithstanding, the Sino-Soviet conflict escalated into an armed border clash in 1969, "permanently destroying any chance of unity in the communist world." Then, in a further twist of the spiral, wars broke out between successive communist states, from Vietnam in Cambodia to China in Vietnam, with the signal exception of Cuba standing firmly internationalist. China's 1979 war against Vietnam was worst of all, as a display of loyalty at assuming its diplomatic relationship with the United States.[52] Given Zhou Enlai's earnest commitment on behalf of the Chinese leadership in the 1960s to supporting the peoples of Southeast Asia, had he lived to see the war, he would have died of anger. Eventually, the event arguably of the greatest global and geopolitical significance in the postwar era came in 1991, but "the slow collapse of the Soviet Union began with the 1956 Congress of the CPSU, and the split with China in 1960."[53]

If bureaucratic nationalism functioned as the culprit in intracommunist relationships, a Marxist explanation is that it "was materially rooted in forces of production that were objectively less internationalized than those of the capitalist world. This nationalism in turn blocked any chance of overcoming the lag."[54] Aside from the controversial issue of a new class of communist rulers, this nationalist pattern was a response to capitalist crusades against communist regimes ever since 1917. It can be seen in such striking contrasts in Asia as between the blockaded and the fostered—the U.S. anticommunist allies enjoyed enormous aid and open markets in the West and Japan. The related problem of statism and bureaucratization was debated in Ho Chi Minh's Vietnam, redressed in policy experiments in Mao's China, and fairly kept at bay in Cuba. Yet in addition to centralized and often also personal powers and cadre privileges that nurtured corruption and degeneration, internal conflicts demoralized and exhausted both the socialist and third worlds. Decolonization did not live up to its promise of egalitarian democracy and popular control; in many postcolonial countries the domestic bourgeoisie, or rather feudalistic local regimes, were vulnerable to regression, from military coups and even civil wars to ethnic and religious strife. Divisive identity politics betrayed the ambition and energy of earlier liberation struggles.

Beginning with the Sino-Indian War, which injured the credibility of both countries, the third world became increasingly divided while competing for favor and aid between China and the Soviet Union. A telling story of the 1965 Jakarta preparatory conference (before Suharto's coup) for the second Asian-African conference scheduled to convene in Algiers shows the extent of this sad turn. As what India called the troika of China, Indonesia, and Pakistan initiated the meeting, antagonism among the Bandung nations played out in the Sino-Soviet discord as a major irritant. A controversy over India's proposal to invite the Soviet Union, deemed to be geographically Asian, and the Chinese delegation's rejection alone was bitter enough to stir disunity among the participants.[55] The second Bandung was in the end aborted—because of China's insistence (on technical grounds that the Soviet Union was more European), no consensus could be reached, so the conference had to be cancelled. This hurt China's reputation and its relations with a number of its third world friends.[56] The Sino-Soviet split compromised principles, obstructed progress, and weakened both sides while undermining the common anticapitalist project across the continents. Departing from socialist internationalism, socialism and third worldism went down together.

Again, both the PRC and the USSR must bear the responsibility for the third world's diversion from its original agenda of national liberation and development, as well as the popular drive for a new global order. As the communist ruling parties failed to either present a coherent model of socialism or consistently support the newly independent nations, the nonaligned movement exhausted itself with toxic wrangling and lost its appeal even before the end of the Cold War. Most nonaligned countries were aware of how impossible it was for them to gain anything from the former metropolitan masters for their own socioeconomic benefits. The communists in these countries, however split as well, were often the backbone of social change. The irony is that while selectively shoring up certain progressive or even revolutionary enterprises, the socialist states were bound by the capitalist hegemony and had to make allowances for various regimes in the underdeveloped world. The USSR often watched with folded arms when dictators cracked down on labor activists or the military's counterinsurgency campaigns wiped out leftist rebels. Even China, widely accused of being too extreme, steered clear of exporting revolution. It stood idly by, for example, when hundreds of thousands of communists and perceived sympathizers were massacred in Indonesia in 1965.

While the USSR and PRC each had once played a critically positive role in world affairs by constraining the Atlantic powers, they had also compromised ideological and moral commitments and missed many opportunities to advance the internationalist cause. Beneath the surface of relative Soviet passivity in the guise of peaceful transition and China's passage from radical independence to leaning toward the United States was the same Cold War logic of détente. Originating in the Yalta deal of a balance of terror, détente was designed to avoid a third world war, which could be a nuclear holocaust.[57] If the Chinese position was more regrettable, it is because unlike the Soviet Union, China was itself a third world country and had been baptized in a revolution of national liberation. Moreover, as the Soviet state grew into a status quo managerial gatekeeper, China's Cultural Revolution not only touched the soul of its own people but also altered the orbit of communist movements incarcerated by the statist impulse. These differences made China's steady alienation from so many fellow socialist and third world countries all the more painful and costly. An era of raging and promising popular participation for global equality and justice was over.

However, the following clarification remains especially important. If revolutionary China's tacitly positive response to the U.S. olive branch in 1971 (after it rebuffed U.S. initiatives in 1968–1969 as China was engaged in aiding Vietnam) was still a geopolitical strategic move and conditional on behalf of its national interest and bilateral equality, reformist China was ready to make weightier concessions. The Maoist endeavor was to weaken global hegemonic powers by playing with their mutual contradictions to reduce the pressure on China from what was perceived as an imminent war threat while gaining the country needed space for autonomy. In contrast, the post-Mao regime largely abandoned the anti-imperialist stance as such, participating in a wishfully collaborative yet unipolar world. The reformers hastily reversed initially shallow, selective, and self-protective relinking and tried to appease the rule makers of globalization. Obvious continuities notwithstanding, discontinuities between these two moves are vital. Mao's era and the post-Mao reform represented two different Chinas on the world stage: between socialism and socialism with

Chinese characteristics (which in reality is capitalism with Chinese characteristics); between internationalism marked by solidarity among class nations and a globalism of *jiegui*, getting on the track of globalization; between independence and subordination; and indeed between revolution and counterrevolution. If Mao had occasionally deviated from the socialist and internationalist principles due to nationalistic impulses, he and his colleagues nevertheless retained them as long-term goals. His successors conversely became cynical about socialism altogether, or even lacked any serious sense of national and popular interests.[58] The essential difference then is both ideological and strategic, concerning China's national orientation and international relations. In retrospect, China's eventual shift toward an alliance with the United States is of spectacular significance: by fueling global capitalism with its outstanding labor force and vast market for capital's "spatial fix" and further financialization, as well as certain political collaborations, China in a way rescued a global system, at the cost of its own distinguished identity and independence since 1949.[59]

Meanwhile, the decay of socialism also gravely impaired ethnic relations inside China, most acutely in Xinjiang and Tibet. Socialism is intrinsically internationalist on the common ground of universal emancipation, and the internal and external are two sides of the same coin. A socialist state is thus expected to respect, protect, and support its own national minorities and help the world's oppressed nations, which is integral to socialist internationalism. Regressions from communist solidarity and from anticapitalism in China caused both twisted foreign policy stances and intensified ethnic strains at home.

China's current spatial politics regarding regional and ethnic relations is a blending of old socialist paternalism, new capitalist developmentalism, and iron-fisted campaigns against separatists and terrorists, echoing the U.S. war on terror. This has resulted in a vicious cycle of resistance and oppression, attack and revenge, involving mounting fear and alienation. Without any formal change in the ideology of equality or institutions of autonomy, ethnic and religious tensions seem a by-product of a general crisis of legitimacy. The state-sponsored relentless accumulation of capital has wounded minority pride, cultures, and peace, and undermined the entire edifice of socialist fundamentals geared toward popular power and welfare across communities. In particular, the return of unchecked Han prejudice began to be institutionalized, which breeds social polarization as much as national disintegration.[60] Inequalities are not specific to ethnic groups during economic reforms, but market pathologies can be amplified in minority regions. This impasse amounted to an identity or legitimacy crisis of the People's Republic itself. The socialist aspiration is not only to manage multiple ethnicities but also to celebrate it within a common citizenship. In its absence a contentious ethnic politics ethnicizes social issues or essentializes ethnicity in interpreting social relations. However, it is class that is at the root of a wrong world of class nations, nationally and globally;[61] and changing the world requires a long war of position, beginning with reclaiming socialist internationalism.

Globalism, Traditionalism, or Universal Emancipation

The post-Mao economic reform, pursued in parallel with capitalist neoliberal mutations, has since the 1990s (save the first reform decade) turned China into an open, willing, and rule-obeying participant in globalization, and hence the largest new market and growth center of the global system. Along the way, China's political class, nominally still communist, has allowed what in effect must be recognized as a bureaucratic-capitalist transition. In China as elsewhere, capitalism keeps inflicting calamities upon societies and nature, producing commercial homogeneity as much as social disparities by its polarizing tendency. In these circumstances, China may still grow bigger economically, but only at the price of being exploited, subordinated, unstable, even in some visible way colonized (concerning, for example, how penetrating foreign capital has already become in Chinese industries and finance), and probably explosive and reactionary—recall Marx's fear of counterrevolution in newly converted capitalist regimes.[62] Without a decisive political reorientation, China will lose its original substance and distinction as a people's republic established at the immense cost of the lives of its devoted and heroic sons and daughters. Such a reorientation is realistic not only because the existing model of development is socially and ecologically unsustainable and continues to generate resistance, but also because innovations increasingly emerge to catalyze changes. Where to next, then, if past missteps can still be turned around for a new beginning?

A most self-deceptive option, officially promoted, overtly or tacitly, is deepening the reform or *shengai*, involving fuller global integration through further economic opening, privatization, financial liberalization, and market deregulation. The antisocialist liberals endorse this economic agenda while advocating specific political reforms. Such reforms would aim at a degree of formal democracy while opposing state control over dissent, but would also seek designated political and legal institutions to match, facilitate, and protect elite wealth and power. Without understanding the damage of departing from socialism and internationalism, the globalist project is both illusory and dangerous. On the one hand, unprecedented inroads by casino capital and multinational corporations have created extremely high rates of profit for themselves and exploitation for Chinese workers, pushing China toward wider and deeper economic dependency, financial volatility, and political incapacity. On the other hand, China's position in the global division of labor is such that, paradoxically, the country must also handle its own overcapacity and underconsumption—due to a large low-income population as a result of inequalities—to move further up from the low end of the global production chain. As its outbound investment and acquisition attempts surge, China has joined the global scramble for resources from minerals to land, driven by its growing demand for both energy supply and space for surplus capital.

Whereas new China had once categorically distinguished itself from the old colonial powers in its third world aid programs, today it is not obvious whether Chinese capital and business overseas, via state and private companies alike, are not purely motivated by profits or resources and energy quest, or even a diversion of attention from internal discontent. It would be too early to liken the Chinese overseas pursuits to the familiar patterns of capitalist imperialism because of their very different historical records. And depending on political struggle, China is still open to adjustment and may stand guarded against exploitative international relations and expansionism. However, as the world's largest importer of certain essential commodities, China is already in the game of global accumulation and competition.[63] The alarming concept of subimperialism in the shadow of an overblown discourse of China rising, debated in China (and Taiwan, concerning cross-strait economic relations), is a sensible warning against a looming peril.

China's "one belt, one road" strategy, promoted to define the country's future development, has to be viewed in the context of these factors in the background. Focusing on huge investments in exploration and grand infrastructure construction, the new silk roads by land and sea are intended to reach mines, ports, techno-industrial zones, and markets in Central Asia, Southeast Asia, and Africa, connecting South America as well and Europe through western and southern Chinese provinces. The optimists are hopeful that such a strategy, if free of the dictation of capital and territorial ambitions, will counter the U.S.-Japan maritime dominance in the region and even alter the entire capitalist system. As such, even cosmopolitanism is far from internationalism, the project could be a "world historical" initiative in negating the supposed end of history.[64] The skeptics point out many obstacles, from global capitalist domination to China's structural and ideological integration into that world system. For example, disregarding the stated intention of Chinese government, such a project may well follow its own market logic to rouse varieties of actors in "an unbridled commercial frenzy," as private enterprises in particular can venture out and strike deals without any public plan or state direction.[65] More seriously, it would be hard to imagine anything like a transnational commercial network operating by socialist means within the overriding order of global capitalism. In the shadow of its collective memory, China knows only too well about colonial and imperialist practices, and how the richer and stronger countries could endure surplus retention unrealizable in the poorer and weaker ones. To change the situation, the socialist states had previously followed their moral duties to aid the third world, including a noble tradition of China in Africa.[66] But that mandate hardly exists anymore, as the socialist states themselves have receded if not vanished. The new silk road ambition and certain negative practices concerning resource depletion and labor relations would have little chance to appeal or succeed politically if Chinese leaders are unwilling or unable to reverse the recent course while tapping into the resource of socialist and internationalist legacies.

China's pledge of nonexpansionism is grounded in its historical record but cannot be a guarantee for the future. Moreover, this strategy has to be scrutinized in terms of its economic and geopolitical viability in the first place. If the Chinese economy still lacks a self-reliant foundation for security, if it is open to financial vulnerability and turmoil in the global markets, if its domestic needs for food sovereignty, integrated welfare, technological upgrading, and much else are unfulfilled, and if its business models overseas are just as exploitative and environmentally degrading, then aren't there less wasteful and less risky ways to develop than investing massively abroad? Operating globally provides no assurance of local benefits; a potential drain of reserves or pileup of debts could also instantly wipe out short-term gains. Further still, it is realpolitik that will determine to what extent China can continue its overseas adventures. Unlimited expansion of Chinese capital is hardly rational without the backing of minimal parity between China and its competitors in terms of military capacity and geopolitical spheres of control and influence. Despite its market integration and collaborative gestures, China remains a quasi-enemy in the perpetual Cold War mentality, and the United States has reaffirmed its pivot to Asia, aiming at containing China. The world's hegemonic power and its obedient international community are left with little space for any illusion. Ultimately, the logic of global rivalry over power and resources could lead to conflicts and war with unimaginable devastation.

At home, state-led and market-centered developmentalism aggravates already dire ecological and demographic conditions. And related problems multiply for minorities. Neglected or misconceived in the strategy of going west are ethnic relations, which are socially and politically sensitive. The blind belief that economic growth can redress local grievances and solve pressing problems, ethnic or social, has long proven deadly wrong. Muslim societies in the vast and resource-filled region of Xinjiang, for instance, resent their ever more marginalized and disadvantaged position in language education and cultural heritage, in the job market, government posts and professional circles, and regular points of service such as travel arrangement and hotel registration. Similar situations and attitudes are visible in Tibetan areas as well, in response to both the ever-greater scale of commercial standardization and Han and Hui migration and types of repression. To be sure, China's ethnic minorities should and can succeed socioeconomically, culturally, and politically in a context of beneficial and positive linkages with overall national development. They have both constitutionally enshrined moral rights and institutional means at hand to modernize in their own terms and rhythms, as a matter of self-determination. But that would require a full set of policies faithfully implemented according to constitutional minority rights, ethnic autonomy, and religious freedom under the principle of the solidarity of all nationalities and equal citizenship. Presently no democratic agenda is on the table for sincere consultation and conversation with ethnic minorities for policy reform. Yet popular trust has to be restored before any grand plan, however favorable to local peoples and regions it may be, can be carried out.

Now if the globalist option is either reckless or illusory, would traditionalism be an alternative? Leaving aside the literature of cultural conservatism from the left (in terms of Confucian socialism, etc.) and from the right (that reverses the communist negation of traditional values), old-fashioned or radical in advocacy, the concern here is limited to the most promising interpretations of tianxia. This Sinological idea signifies a spatial cosmology of grand unification, claiming diverse races and cultures all under heaven to be embraced in constant amalgamation and universal harmony. One of its self-contradictions is the theoretical difficulty of identifying the "barbarians" (*yi*) versus the civilized (*xia*). The modern application of tianxia is confronted above all with the formidable obstacle of the entities of nation-states and international relations, conceptually and practically. Without firm, stably definable outer boundaries, tianxia is an imaginary of moral rule by the Mandate of Heaven: from equal sharing of land and wealth to the Confucian belief in people as the foundation of state and government (*minben*, as elaborated in *Mencius*). Among the most idealist readings of the ancient wisdoms is that the Chinese word for "politics" (*zhengzhi*) means "justified order," which defines a polity not opposite but alternative to politics as public life. "[The Greek] polis developed state politics, while all-under-heaven invented world politics."[67] Hailed as a superior theory for global governance and world peace, tianxia is centered in harmony and based on "an ontology of coexistence," seeking "reasonable resolutions of conflicts and stable security by building truly reliable correlations of mutual benefit in the long run, as well as reciprocal acceptance of the other's values." Ideally, then, it represents a framework of relational universalism or compatible universalism, transcending the Kantian uniform universalism of perpetual peace.[68]

Undoubtedly, against a culturally nihilist attitude, useful elements in China's indigenous traditions comprising a rich array of thoughts can be dialectically reappropriated.[69] But like it or not, the revolutionary and postrevolutionary modern traditions are overwhelmingly more powerful, precisely because traditional China was proven incapable of preserving itself, let alone changing or participating in making the rules of the global order. After all, it was the epic communist revolution that has remade China and lifted its multiethnic people. It is this "revolutionary break with the past" required by modern transformations that defines the nation after 1949, completely recasting its internal and external relations. The transformation also has a potent cultural dimension. As Mao put it, a great revolution has rejuvenated a great culture of the Chinese people, and the process will continue. "This culture, concerning its spirituality, has exceeded that of the entire capitalist world." Using Lu Xun as an example, Mao depicted the literary giant's unyielding integrity without bowing and cringing as representing "the most precious quality" of an oppressed nation.[70] Some affinities might be found here with both individual uprightness and moral justice of a rebellious populace ending tyranny in ancient teachings. But today's Confucian revivalism signals a politics of defeat and escapism, and as such it certainly does not intend to invoke that particular radicalism. However bizarre (e.g., communist secretaries kneeling in an ancestral temple in Qufu, Shandong, the birthplace of the saint), it bespeaks acute social crises and ideological bankruptcy that official China should appeal to Confucius.

Confucianism, however decorated or modernized, is no soft power to match the capitalist ideology of liberal democracy and market efficiency. Its conservative doctrines, from belittling women to endorsing elitism and submission, make it hopelessly obsolete. It is, after all, an ideology of the premodern ruling class. Even if tianxia in particular offers some positive imaginations, it has an imperial stigma and is entirely toothless facing the capitalist industrial-financial-military complex, which also extends a long arm of cultural and media power. A uniformly benevolent and ascendant Chinese tradition and its potential globalization are a fantasy and no valid alternative to either Eurocentric or capitalist vices anyway. Yet often as part of the rise of China discourse, traditionalism can be politically inflected for a postsocialist function. It is projected that with the rising influence of China, a peaceful Chinese state would enhance the chance of greater equality in the world and for a noncapitalist, East Asian model of development to be globally emulated.[71] Similarly, a universalist geopolitical narrative blends the two ideas of tianxia, in which frontiers are intentionally unfixed and nonhegemonic, and the new silk roads are distinguishable from the old colonial order of trade and conquest. Such a blending would be a cure for global fragmentation and conflicts as the Westphalia system becomes ever more anachronistic.[72]

Yet neither globalist uniformity constituted of multilayered domination as opposed to internationalism nor cultural particularism antithetical to socialism can be the future for universal emancipation. The only plausible position will still find recourse to the communist original. In the end, socialism is not a national variant that makes globality or modernity plural. The global nature of capital and capitalist unilateral integration necessitates the universality of its opposition; nothing less, and nothing of an ethnocentric disposition, can possibly be up to the role.[73] Meanwhile, as socialism cannot have a foothold and grow only in one country, socialist nationalism has to be simultaneously internationalist. In other words, socialism is also the only insurance against chauvinism and imperialism. This indivisibility and mutuality of socialism and internationalism, or incompatibility between socialist internationalism and exploitative expansionism, is again a matter of not only morality but also realpolitik. Any credible political argument on China's direction today would require its domestic and foreign relations to be articulated in the same vein.[74] Without attending to relevant critical theories of nationalism and international relations, the point here is simply that nationalism needs to be checked by socialism and internationalism. In other words, nationalism could be reactionary or oppressive without the constitutive role of a democratically organized people proudly multicultural and equal. Such peoples must also form alliances globally with one another in changing the world.

Instead of neo-Confucianism that tends to be Han-centered, or capitalist globalism that promotes market values and profits over needs, socialism remains the only global prospect capable of protecting and developing a social contract of universal rights and welfare. The PRC state presupposes cultural and institutional multiethnicity and carries a sacred duty of securing sovereignty, integrity, unity, and harmony. This duty is socialist in the sense that it is taken as a matter of defending and completing the revolution, ultimately measured by its victory over capitalism and imperialism. In the socialist past the

Chinese treated struggles of other class nations as their own. In contrast, China's current foreign policy and general attitude toward the world are rightly criticized for their indifference or even hostility toward certain progressive causes and global social movements. Its unprincipled pro-U.S. stance, in particular, needs to be rectified. If socialism is still valid for China, the country should join the global reconstruction of a southern front or Bandung 2, with a long view of restricting capital, socializing monopolies, and definancializing economic management the world over—the opposite of what is going on under present policies.[75] China is yet to be an active participant in the World Social Forum, along with the Third World Forum, created in Dakar in 1975, and the World Forum for Alternatives, launched in Cairo in 1997. And it has yet to honestly scrutinize official socialism in both its rhetoric full of theoretical inconsistencies and its distance from recognizably socialist policies. By the internationalist logic, only such a move would improve China's own image and conditions in the global environment.

To recover lost internationalism in China is to regain and develop Chinese socialism. The two projects merge and are embedded in each other's ambition of overcoming capitalism. The retreat of the People's Republic from a challenger to a collaborator in the global system marks a world-historical defeat, no less than that of the collapse of the Soviet Union. But neither of these two cases has to be stuck where it is. The class nature of the state is key; and depending on politics or, more concretely, transformative popular struggle from direct producers of all walks of life, the now powerful bureaucratic-comprador-financial capitalist interests are not undefeatable. As the fundamental contradictions and social-environmental unsustainability under capitalism keep fueling resistance and reconstruction, politics will be back in command. Ultimately, socialism and internationalism remain the only contour for Chinese as much as universal renewal.

NOTES

The author is grateful for Ban Wang's editorial help and his invitation to the tianxia conference held at Stanford University in May 2011. Discussions at the conference stimulated the writing of this chapter.

1. Lattimore, *Inner Asian Frontiers of China*; Fletcher, "Integrative History"; Perdue, "History without Borders."

2. A typical example is given by Lattimore in *Inner Asian Frontiers* about changing functions of the Great Wall in a long history of interactions between an agricultural Chinese society and its nomadic neighbors through the ebb and flow of not only wars but

also, and more often, peacemaking and integration. For an influential debate over assimilationist interpretations in historiography, see Rawski, "Reenvisioning the Qing"; and Ho, "In Defense of Sinicization."

3. Weber, *The Religion of China.* The notion of "the barbarians" in traditional Chinese perception was not a racial but a cultural concept.

4. Nolan, "The Silk Road by Land and Sea": "China's traditional international trade was tiny in comparison with the vast volume of internal trade. However, it was highly significant in terms of the deep interconnections between China and the regions immediately around it to the West and the South." Trade relations "stimulated nautical technical progress" as well as "a deep long-term symbiotic, two-way flow of culture."

5. Pomeranz, *The Great Divergence*, 22, 239, 287–288; Frank, *ReOrient*, 30, 172–173, 334–339.

6. Weber, *The Religion of China*, 26, 103–104, 61–62. "The original accumulation of capital during late medieval times in Europe entailed violence, predation, thievery, fraud and robbery. Through these extra-legal means, pirates, priests and merchants, supplemented by the usurers, assembled enough initial 'money power' to begin to circulate money systematically as capital" (Harvey, *The Enigma of Capital*, 47).

7. China, "unlike the major European states, has not tried to colonize areas of the world poorer or weaker than itself." Comparatively, "unlike pre–World War II Japan, it has not waged ruthless warfare against its neighbors.... Unlike the United States, it has not set up military bases all over the world.... Unlike the Soviet Union, it has not engaged in a massive arms race with the world's other 'superpower,' nor has it installed client governments in nations on its border" (Schweickart, *After Capitalism*, 174). "In sharp contrast to the European powers and their colonial-settler descendents, China did not seek to construct an overseas empire" (Nolan, "Imperial Archipelagos," 80).

8. For example, see Tilly, *Coercion, Capital, and European States*; and Ertman, *Birth of the Leviathan*. See especially Arrighi, *The Long Twentieth Century*, ch. 1 and 96ff.

9. This thesis has an origin in Russian revolutionaries and the dilemma of "socialism and backwardness." For its contemporary revival see, for example, David Harvey: "Uneven geographical development is not a mere sidebar to how capitalism works, but fundamental to its reproduction" (*The Enigma of Capital*, 58–60, 213).

10. As Immanuel Wallerstein put it, nothing is regrettable in "China, India, the Arab world and other regions" not proceeding to capitalism, thus being "better immunized against the toxin" (*The End of the World as We Know It*, 179–181).

11. Pockets of successful late development, such as the Asian tigers, heavily depended on the aid and markets the United States offered to its Cold War allies in the region. Insofar as such pockets cannot alter the basic pattern of a world polarized between rich and poor countries, the main proposition of dependency theory holds.

12. For class order, referring to Marx's conception of the historical time, see Anderson, "Modernity and Revolution," 101. Duara noted "class-nation" or class/nationalism as a trope in communist and anticolonial revolutions (*Rescuing History from the Nation*, 12–13).

13. Against what he saw as Marxist "wrong address theory" by which "the awakening message was intended for *classes* but by some terrible postal error was delivered to *nations*,"

he reconciled the two identities in the sense of collective consciousness (Gellner, *Nations and Nationalism*, ch. 9). But Marx and Engels were clear in their position of defending proletarian nationalism preconditioned on class power: theoretically, even if "working men have no country," "the proletariat must first of all acquire political supremacy, must rise to be the leading class of the nation, must constitute itself as the nation . . . though not in the bourgeois sense of the word" (*The Communist Manifesto*).

14. The conflation, both descriptively (of an awkward and backward political entity) and conceptually (concerning disparities between the Sino-zone and Europe), indicates impeded development: "empire" signifies premodernity and despotism in contrast to the sovereign modern nation capable of progress and democracy. See Wang, "The Politics of Imagining Asia," 16–18.

15. "The political and the *national unit* should be *congruent*." Gellner, *Nations and Nationalism*, 1.

16. In the first half of the twentieth century, China's relatively small industrial working class was still significantly larger in size and stronger in political capacity than the national bourgeoisie, due to substantial foreign presence in the Chinese economy. Workers in foreign-controlled factories were a growing class, while domestic industrialists and merchants were a shrinking one, squeezed between landed interests and foreign capital.

17. Against orthodox Marxism and developed from Lenin's insight on the awakening of Asia and the Bolshevik revolution and its peasant-soldier soviets, these ideas, best articulated in Mao Zedong's *The Chinese Revolution and the Chinese Communist Party* (1939) and *On New Democracy* (1940), are among the theoretically most significant Chinese contributions to Marxism.

18. See Lv, "The Narrative of the Images of Ethnic Minorities."

19. Addressing the Irish question, Marx warned that "the English working class will *never accomplish anything* before it has got rid of Ireland" (to Engels, December 12, 1869, in *Marx and Engels Correspondence* [London: International Publishers, 1968]. Lenin restated this position in "The Right of Nations to Self-Determination" (1914), in *Collected Works of Lenin*, vol. 20. See also Chauhan, *Nationalities Question*, 101–112.

20. Despite old and new criticisms of the notion of nationality for its Soviet origin or allegedly negative function of impairing unity, I consider it to remain necessary from a socialist internationalist perspective. The same can be said about self-determination in the Chinese context of regional autonomy as well (Lin, "Modernity and the Violence of Global Accumulation").

21. Again, Zhou Enlai explains these considerations with superb clarity; see "Ethnic-Regional Autonomy Enhances Solidarity of Nationalities and Common Progress" and "On a Few Questions concerning Our Nationality Policy," in *Selected Writings of Zhou Enlai on the United Front*. The Xinjiang Autonomous Region, for example, is home to forty-seven mostly Muslim communities with an Uyghur majority alongside the Han.

22. For example, the programs were so effective that they had "encouraged Han people to marry into or otherwise seek to join these nationalities." Between 1982 and 1990 alone, the Hui population grew by 19 percent (Goossaert and Palmer, *The Religious Question*

in Modern China, 375). Heberer notes that the proportion of China's minority population grew from 6.1 percent in 1953 to 9 percent in 1995: a few groups doubled, tripled, or more in size ("Some Considerations on China's Minorities," 3). By 2005, the population of the Tibetan Autonomous Region had grown 15.6 percent, of which the Tibetans accounted for 11.3 percent, as compared with the national average of 5.9 percent (Ma, *Social Development and Ethnic Relations*, 68).

23. One of the "ten great demands" published by the Communist Party in 1928 was to "unify China and recognize . . . [minority] national self-determination." The Jiangxi Soviet emulated the USSR in 1931 in pledging that the non-Han toiling masses would "have the right to determine for themselves" whether they wished to establish their own state, join the socialist Chinese union, or form a self-governing unit inside the union. Mao told Edgar Snow in 1939 that after revolutionary victory, Tibet, Mongolia, Burma, Indochina, and Korea could become autonomous republics voluntarily attached to a Chinese confederation. The party then formally envisioned a democratic "federal republic based on the free union of all nationalities" in 1945. See Connor, *The National Question in Marxist-Leninist Theory*, 68, 74, 82–83. Relevant original documents are collected in Brandt, Schwartz, and Fairbank, *A Documentary History of Chinese Communism*.

24. Zhou, *Selected Writings of Zhou Enlai on the United Front*.

25. Mao: "The people who have gained revolutionary victory must aid the liberation struggle of other peoples. This is our internationalist duty" ("Meeting with Friends from Africa," August 8, 1963, in *Quotations from Mao*, 178).

26. Wang, "The Korean War."

27. Yet the Soviet aid was not gratis and loans were not interest free. They were repaid by Chinese exports and international currency. Of China's debt to the Soviet Union of 15.2 billion rubles, only about a third was economic and the rest was half-priced weaponry used in the Korean War (see Wu, *Ten Years of Debate*, 216–217, 232, 443).

28. The three-world theory was first coined by Alfred Sauvy in France and popularized mainly as an alternative perspective to the basic premise of the Cold War. See Berger and Weber, *Rethinking the Third World*.

29. Prashad, *The Darker Nations*, 37. Mao said that "it was our third world brothers who have brought us in." Indeed, without radical enlargement of the UN membership, the PRC seat would not have been possible.

30. However, in Ahmad's critique, the third world was merely anticolonial nationalist in orientation and the three-world theory "had neither a central doctrine nor a fundamental core which constituted it theoretically." As an ideological formation, it "redefined anti-imperialism not as a socialist project to be realized by the mass movements of the popular classes but as a developmentalist project to be realized by the weaker states of the national" (*In Theory*, 292–293).

31. Ahmad, *In Theory*, 9. See also Hoselitz, *The Progress of Underdeveloped Areas*. Westad concluded that "the most important aspects of the Cold War were neither military nor strategic, nor Europe-centered, but connected to political and social development in the Third World" (*The Global Cold War*, 396).

32. Prashad, *The Darker Nations*, 37. As the Soviet and Chinese versions of the theory were head-on conflictive, it was the Chinese version which "seized most radical imaginations

in subsequent years" and "had the widest global currency," albeit "with all kinds of anti-communism assuming an anti-Soviet form" (Ahmad, *In Theory*, 306).

33. The left (China), center (India and Burma), and right (Turkey and the Philippines) spoke at the conference, with praise as well as attacks on the Soviet Union and China. Even the "neutral" states like India had supported U.S. invasion in Korea and only moved closer to the Soviets after Bandung. Premier Zhou took a conciliatory tone and had tea with Nehru and U Nu as well as the rightists. "The pacific approach by the Chinese delegation reflected the general Chinese communist orientation toward foreign and domestic policy" (Prashad, *The Darker Nations*, 34–37).

34. The case of China's ambivalence toward Indonesia exemplifies such difficulties, where Beijing concurrently maintained its comradeship with the PKI, a united front with the government, and its expected help to Indonesian Chinese. See, for example, Zhou, "Ambivalent Alliance." Yet the Chinese maneuver devastatingly failed ten years later when Suharto's coup eliminated the PKI altogether.

35. Guevara, "At the Afro-Asian Conference in Algeria."

36. It must be clarified that the struggles for development are both rightful and important. Development is apparently also politically charged. Examples worth mentioning are the New International Economic Order and New World Information and Communications Order, among others. They were adopted in the 1970s; the latter was incorporated by the UN, leading to many more antipoverty and development projects in the next three decades, including the UN Millennium Development Goals, 2000.

37. In New Delhi, Castro turned over the chair of the NAM conference to Indira Gandhi as new leader of the movement. It nominally still represented two-thirds of the UN members and contained more than half of the world population (Prashad, *The Darker Nations*, 210).

38. The Chinese practice was probably also a contrast, though in a very different context, with trade relations between the Soviet Union and its satellite states within the Warsaw Pact.

39. "The Chinese People Firmly Support Patriotic Struggles for Justice by the Panama People," *People's Daily*, January 12, 1964.

40. Prashad, *The Darker Nations*, 174. Wu's account portrays a reactive Chinese position to Indian provocations in *Ten Years of Debate*, 319–324.

41. Lynch, *Mao*, 142–143; Heinzig, *The Soviet Union and Communist China*, ch. 3. Also notable is the intention of the Chinese communists on the eve of their victory that they would like to have diplomatic ties and good trade relations with the United States rather than leaning on one side of the Soviet Union. See also Brandt, *Stalin's Failure in China*.

42. See relevant documents in The "Great Debate": Documents of the Sino-Soviet Split, Marxists.org, https://www.marxists.org/history/international/comintern/sino-soviet-split/; and Gittings, *Survey of the Sino-Soviet Dispute*.

43. The regime that emerged from the Bolshevik revolution "was the first and only state in history to include no national or territorial reference in its name—it would simply be the Union of Soviet Socialist Republics." That is, "the intention of its founders was unconditionally internationalist" (Anderson, "Internationalism").

44. Anderson: "Such developments persuaded many communists shaken in 1956 that the legacy of the October Revolution was, if with zigzags, being gradually redeemed rather than irretrievably abandoned" (*Spectrum*, 285).

45. See Halliday, "Marxist Analysis and Post-revolutionary China," 2; Gleijeses, *Conflicting Missions*.

46. Miliband, *Class War Conservatism*, 255, and Fred Halliday quoted on 266.

47. Hobsbawm, *Age of Extremes*, quoted in Anderson, *Spectrum*, 313. According to Wallerstein, for the United States too, the Soviet collapse was "an absolute geopolitical catastrophe" because it eliminated on the one hand the U.S. argument that the noncommunist world should follow its leadership, and on the other the Soviet role in restraining actions that might lead to military confrontations among major states ("What Cold War in Asia?," 23–24).

48. An earlier example is Khrushchev's letter to Eisenhower in September 1958 after the Taiwan Strait crisis over Jinmen, in which he declared that any aggression in China would be taken as aggression against the USSR and the Soviets would defend China (Wu, *Ten Years of Debate*, 117).

49. In "On the Historical Experience of the Proletarian Dictatorship II," published in the *People's Daily*, December 29, 1956, it was stated that the basic contradiction of the era was between imperialism and socialism, and against this general background contradictions among socialist countries and communist parties must be considered "contradictions among the people" so as to pursue unity in the anti-imperialist struggle. Mao did continue to stress, as in December 1959 and early 1960, that the Chinese must prioritize solidarity, which was seen as "in the fundamental interest of the Chinese people as well as the peoples throughout the world. The two big socialist countries should unite" (Wu, *Ten Years of Debate*, 54, 151, 157).

50. Miliband, *Class War Conservatism*, 232; Prashad, *The Darker Nations*, 174. Halliday commented at the time that as China encouraged "the most belligerent and reactionary imperialist politicians," it was hard to see what the Chinese could do "to take their betrayal of foreign revolutionary movements further in their attempt to win friends" ("Marxist Analysis," 2).

51. Mao's two conversations with Kissinger in 1973 are recorded in *The Chronology of Mao*, vol. 7.

52. According to Brzezinski, Deng Xiaoping told Cater on January 28, 1979, during his visit to the United States that "he's going to shortly undertake a punitive expedition against Vietnam." http://2001-2009.state.gov/r/pa/ho/88112.htm.

53. Wallerstein, "What Cold War in Asia?," 24.

54. Anderson, "Internationalism."

55. Weinstein, "The 2nd Asian-African Conference," 370.

56. In the case of Africa, this was primarily attributable to "the basic incompatibility between Chinese foreign policy objectives and the goals of the African states," as between the outlook of a world revolution with the third world as the global countryside and African desire for peace and development after decades of conflict and destruction (Yu, "China's Failure in Africa," 468).

57. At the first Afro-Asian-Latin American people's solidarity conference in Havana, January 1966, where "the Sino-Soviet dispute was aired fully," Wu Xueqian, leader of the

Chinese delegation, challenged the Soviets by posing to them such questions as why the Soviet Union discouraged national liberation wars, saying that "a little spark may cause another world war." Why did it collaborate with the United States in the UN by voting to send troops to suppress the Congolese people's struggle, support the Dominican cease-fire resolution, and back Southern Rhodesian racism? Why did the Soviet Union sit with the representatives of Taiwan, South Korea, and South Vietnam to discuss the founding of the Asian Development Bank? Why did it demand Soviet-Chinese joint action while also attacking China for aiding communist Vietnam? And why did the Soviet Union also guarantee in its communication with the United States that there should be no war in the West, thereby enabling the United States to transfer troops to South Vietnam? (Yu, "China's Failure in Africa," 464). These were serious charges, though not all necessarily fair.

58. For example, see Deng Xiaoping on why socialism is not what Africa should be hurrying to pursue in his conversations with African guests in Beijing, 1980–1989, in *Selected Writings of Deng*, vols. 2 and 3.

59. The double denotation of "spatial fix" in Harvey's analysis refers to borderless capital flows as well as the function of such expansion in mitigating capitalist crises. The resilience of capitalism is nowhere better demonstrated than in its transformation of China—"neoliberalism with Chinese characteristics" (Harvey, *A Brief History of Neoliberalism*, ch. 5). Cf. Lin, *China and Global Capitalism*, ch. 4.

60. By the PRC's constitution and relevant laws regarding regional autonomy, 70 percent of regional and lower-level administrators are required to come from local ethnic groups. However, in reality the Han now regularly outnumber non-Han cadres, especially in more responsible positions such as party secretary. Moreover, minority communities are seriously underrepresented in the national legislature and government bodies, and their members take far fewer leading posts than in the socialist past. The army and police are also grossly disproportional in their ethnic compositions. See, for example, Ma Rong, *Social Development and Ethnic Relations*. In particular, lack of democratic consultation and conversation between the center (along with its regional appointees) and local leaders and intellectuals increases the dwindling of mutual trust. The latter's allegedly diminishing civic loyalty to the Chinese nation in turn rationalizes an overestimation of, and excesses in handling, separatist tendencies (Tohti, "Why Have the Uyghurs Felt Defeated?").

61. Lin, "Modernity and the Violence of Global Accumulation."

62. Marx, "To Engels," 1858, in Marx and Engels, *Collected Works of Marx and Engels*, vol. 40, 345–346.

63. Sivji, "Preface," 3; Moyo, Yeros, and Jha, "Imperialism and Primitive Accumulation."

64. Cf. Wang, "The Taiwan Question." He is, however, not blind to purely materialist motives as an expression of "political philistinism." One of the positive considerations here is China's unique path of nation-state creation through anti-imperialist revolutions.

65. For a sketch of the plan by a skeptical observer, see Levine, "China Is Building." Among critical analyses of the debate inside China, see Zhang, "One Belt One Road," and Lu, "Has China's 'Going Out' Squeezed World Development?"

66. The duty to aid the third world has been best and most consistently exemplified by Cuba. As Che Guevara explained, it is "our profound conviction" that the socialist

countries must help pay for the development of countries now starting out on the road to liberation: "There should be no more talk about developing mutually beneficial trade based on prices forced on the backward countries by the law of value and the international relations of unequal exchange that result from the law of value" (March 25, 1964, UN World Conference on Economics and Development in the Third World). Insisting on unconditional support for the third world, he considered such support to be necessitated by the collective fight against imperialism (Afro-Asian Conference, Algiers, February 24, 1965). *Che Guevara Reader.* Similarly, Mao told President Nyerere of Tanzania that the Chinese and Africans were friends and China's relationship with Africa could not be exploitative or imperialist (in *Selected Writings of Mao,* vol. 8, February 19, 1965).

67. Zhao, "All-under-Heaven and Methodological Relationism," 46.

68. Philosophically speaking, methodological relationism is superior to methodological individualism in the actual world, and hence, in a "worldview constituted by and defined in terms of relations, other people stand out as paramount." Consequently, human obligations and human rights are treated as parallel values (Zhao, "All-under-Heaven and Methodological Relationism," 48–51, 62–65).

69. It is often argued that ancient Chinese teaching is nature friendly and can be revived to help address ecological and environmental problems today. For an empirically based critical evaluation, see Elvin, *The Retreat of the Elephants.*

70. Mao, "The Bankruptcy of the Idealist Conception of History," in *Selected Writings of Mao,* vol. 4.

71. Arrighi in *Adam Smith in Beijing* (2007), summarized in Zhao, "All-under-Heaven and Methodological Relationism."

72. For example, Yin, "De-frontiers," 7–9, 18.

73. On the capitalist international, exemplified by the supranationalist European Union, note the structural change from the mid-1960s of the primacy of democratic over national values: "A key consequence of this change was a shift, within the reigning ideology of the advanced capitalist state, from the nation state to liberal democracy as the dominant means of discursive integration of the laboring classes of the west." That is, the decline of nationalism in the West corresponded to the rise of liberal representative democracy as the modal type of the capitalist state and a superior legitimating tool of social integration and control (Anderson, "Internationalism").

74. Lin, *China and Global Capitalism,* ch. 8.

75. Amin, "China 2013," 24–27.

9

CHINA'S TIANXIA WORLDINGS
Socialist and Postsocialist Cosmopolitanisms
Lisa Rofel

*

A prevalent myth endlessly recycled in the West since the mid-nineteenth century is that China has a long history as a closed culture, inward looking and inward bound. This echoes another myth from colonial evolutionary theory that Chinese culture was overly developed to the point of stultification. Though nothing could be further from the truth, Western media, popular culture, political pundits, conventional historiography, television programs that purport to introduce China to a Western audience, international film festivals, and art exhibits all cite one another on these myths in a repetitive chain of colonial-inspired significations. Edward Said alerted us to this recursive Orientalism some time ago.[1] Even Chinese authors have repeated this myth. Perhaps the best-known example, written by Chinese intellectuals, is the 1988 television documentary *He Shang* (River elegy). *He Shang* is a six-part documentary that aired on CCTV one year before the Tiananmen demonstrations. The series argued that China's supposed historical decision in the fourteenth century to give up maritime exploration hindered its growth and development, resulting in a conservative, stagnant, land-based civilization. China was then easily defeated by countries with maritime strength. Today, *He Shang* argued, China needs to open itself to influences from over the seas. Though *He Shang's* embrace of economic reform initially led to support for the series by top government leaders, after the Tiananmen demonstrations they denounced the writers and producers as anticommunist. Yet *He Shang* ironically mirrored some of the assumptions embedded in the government's program of economic reform, namely that during the Maoist period China had been closed off from the world and now, in official language, China was opening itself to the outside world.

This chapter is an attempt to challenge these myths. I begin by revisiting the socialist period and China's role in creating a world of socialist internationalism. I then consider the current period of economic reform. The prevalent idea that China was closed during the socialist period and is now open is in effect a statement about moving from one kind of world, focused on alliances with what we used to call the third world, to another kind of world, focused on interactions with a capitalist West. Rather than reproducing the closed/open metaphor, we should instead attend to different kinds of "worlding" projects. We can then appreciate how these projects are both similar to and different from China's classic normative concept of tianxia.

The concept of worlding allows us to move beyond notions of static, ahistorical, evolutionary, singular, or transcendent worlds. To appreciate the import of the worlds of socialist internationalism and postsocialist economic reform, and their relationship to tianxia, we would do well to avoid assumptions of historical teleologies, evolutionary developmentalism, or a kind of globalization that assumes discrete geographical locales are added onto an already formed universal world. Rather, we should follow the lead of such scholars as Pheng Cheah and Mei Zhan to understand the processes of worlding, and by extension the worlds of socialist internationalism and postsocialist capitalism, as imaginative and contingent projects.[2] For Cheah, in a discussion on the role of world literature, world-making activity "enables us to imagine a world." Indeed, following Goethe, Cheah argues that there are two concepts of a world: as a physical extension and as a normative phenomenon. Worlding does not result in uniformity, according to Cheah's reading of Goethe, but rather a revelation of universal humanity across particular differences. The point is not to think alike or share exactly the same values but to understand one another. Indeed, making a world is an ongoing process of negotiation across differences. Worlding is thus found in the "intervals, mediations, passages and crossings between national borders."[3]

Zhan's discussion complements Cheah's, analyzing the contemporary worlding of traditional Chinese medicine. For Zhan, worlding is a translocal, always emergent project of knowledge production that entails "transformative relations . . . enmeshed in sociohistorically contingent productions of difference."[4] Zhan emphasizes the distinction of this concept of worlding, with its ruptures and displacements, from an emphasis on globalism, with its assumptions of totality. Instead, Zhan examines the multiple, entangled ways of being human in the world. Both Cheah and Zhan, following Heidegger, consider a world as an ongoing process of becoming, of being-in-the-world. Heidegger also reminds us of the open-ended nature of worlds, including our social inquiries into them.[5]

These concepts of worlding echo the notion of tianxia, which means "all under heaven." From early dynastic times, tianxia was a Confucian precept for uniting various tribes and peoples under central imperial rule. It had a connotation of morally correct governance. Tianxia indicated those places that had come under the civilizational complex of the Middle Kingdom (what today we call China), and it was a universalizing concept: it had no borders, unlike the nation-state. While differences among peoples were recognized, if they embraced the central kingdom's civilizational complex, then they could become part of tianxia. Peter Perdue has called it an "intercultural language" that served multiple purposes for its participants.[6] Like worlding, tianxia recognizes difference within universality and also implicitly highlights the tensions between the production of difference and the embrace of a universal set of beliefs and values. While the concept of worlding does not center on one country, civilizational complex, or nation, it too recognizes hierarchies of belonging. Finally, while the Middle Kingdom imperium may have believed in its civilizational superiority, it nonetheless incorporated ideas and cultural practices from elsewhere—witness Buddhism, not to mention more mundane items like food. These aspects of worlding enable us to reexamine the worlds that China has imagined itself as belonging to. We will see strong resonances of tianxia in the world of socialist internationalism and both a significant departure from and echoes of tianxia in the postsocialist period.

The Worlding of Socialist Internationalism

Although the dissolution of the Soviet Union was not that long ago, it seems as if it could have occurred in a distant, misty past. The conflicts that led to the suspension of relationships between China and the Soviet Union lie even further in the past, perhaps where most hope no one will think about them ever again. Post–Cold War ideologies have made socialist internationalism appear to be a ridiculous, impractical, and dangerous fantasy that never had much real traction. Global capitalism has produced historical amnesia.

If we allow these post–Cold War ideologies to rewrite history, we will have embraced a teleological notion of progress, forgetting Walter Benjamin's warnings that this notion actually stultifies real historical transformation.[7] We should heed his call to wrest the past away from a conformism that supports the powerful, for he warned that even the dead will not be safe if we fail to do so. To move beyond these ideologies, we might begin by recognizing that socialist internationalism was a work of political imagination, to imagine a world outside of the capitalist West. It was a world built on the politically utopian idea that the international proletariat, with their unified interests, would bring about a global revolution to end exploitation and social injustice wrought by capitalism. This socialist dream was universal; the immanence of proletarian revolution would transcend local, regional, and national boundaries.[8] Somewhat in contrast to the worlding of cosmopolitanism that Cheah discusses, the countries that were part of the socialist international were assumed to share a unified political vision. However, it was also assumed that they each had their historical, cultural, and national differences. The universality of this worlding project was thus never meant to erase those specificities. Rather, it was meant to bring into being a world wholly different from the world of capitalism; indeed, to overcome capitalism and make that system a thing of the past. The point, then, was not to erase difference but to learn how to translate it, to paraphrase Cheah, into socialist universalism.

In this sense, this socialist world resonates with the imagined world of tianxia. It was based on a universalist set of precepts that all were supposed to share across their various cultural and historical differences. It presumed not to erase those differences but to work across and through them, the people sharing them with one another. It imagined itself as crossing conventional geopolitical boundaries, as did tianxia. As Dai Jinhua has argued, during the Cultural Revolution the term "tianxia" was often invoked in Red Guard slogans to indicate an imagined alternative world.[9] And, as I argue below, this socialist international tianxia was also built on hierarchies that were ultimately its undoing.

Although a work of the imagination, socialist internationalism was also fully institutionalized. In that sense it further echoed tianxia. At its height, its broad geographical reach stretched from Berlin to Havana to Beijing, and to sympathetic allies in most Western countries as well. Socialist cosmopolitanism was centered in Russia, though it also included Eastern Europe and other Asian nations. China and other young socialist states initially followed the Soviet model in their political, economic, and cultural infrastructures. Politically, the Soviet Union built the communist bloc first through the Comintern, or Communist International (also known as the Third International), and then, after World War II, by installing communist parties in Eastern Europe. The Chinese Communist Party (CCP) was established during the 1920s with the support of the Comintern. The Comintern was dissolved during the war, to be replaced after the war by the Cominform, or Communist Information Bureau, which was dissolved in the 1950s. But communist parties maintained international political alliances through periodic international conferences and bilateral treaties.

Given the Cold War, most bloc members viewed close bloc alignment as important for national survival.[10] Mao and the CCP, for example, viewed the world in terms of a united front ideology. That is, they saw the Western imperialist powers as temporary allies who would take advantage of China and intervene to prevent revolution and the socialist bloc as the most reliable source of support.[11] As Steven Goldstein argues, "In contrast to the Western imperialist states whose interests were only momentarily and intermittently congruent with those of China and who pursued a foreign policy based on gain and advantage, the Soviet Union was presented as China's 'revolutionary comrade' with whom a relationship could be maintained based not on mutual advantage but rather on 'principle.'"[12] While the Soviet Union maintained clear dominance over this bloc, Stalin began to accord China a special relationship, given its size. The Warsaw Pact, or Warsaw Treaty Organization of Friendship, Cooperation and Mutual Assistance, formed in 1955 and formally dissolved only in 1991, was a military pact in response to NATO. Complementing the Warsaw Pact was the Council for Mutual Economic Assistance. China signed bilateral treaties with the Soviet Union and other members of the Soviet bloc. This bloc was always subtended by its ideological commitment to socialism. Indeed, conflicts over how to interpret that commitment, not the triumph of capitalism, ultimately subverted the bloc.

Politically, then, one can see both resonances with and differences from tianxia—resonances in its imaginative reach, and differences in its political implementation. Unlike the classic tianxia, this new tianxia did not place China at the center of this universal world. Indeed, that was one reason it split with the Soviet Union, for Chinese leaders were unwilling to accept the latter's positioning of itself at the apex of a socialist hierarchy. Moreover, there were explicit and overt conflicts over how to interpret socialist internationalism. Conflicts occurred in China over dynastic rule and, as Perdue has pointed out, ultimately over which peoples and practices could be brought into the tianxia fold, but they were not explicit debates about how tianxia as a concept should be understood.[13]

Economically, the socialist world built an alternative economy that tried to replace the capitalist world system. This alternative economy had an obvious and profound impact on the economic development of China and other socialist nations.[14] Both domestic development and foreign trade occurred within it. Following the model of the Soviet Union, China and other socialist states instituted central state control of their national economies and drew up national economic plans, with an emphasis on heavy industries. The socialist world economy had a council for mutual economic assistance, initiated by the Soviet Union, which pressured participant countries "to limit trade with the capitalist states and to strengthen the economic integration of the socialist camp."[15] While this integration was clearly strategic, it was also always based on a worlding project of political imagination about overcoming the depredations of capitalism. The new socialist government in China actively developed a feeling among its own citizens of socialist cohesiveness and shared goals with this socialist world. This cosmopolitanism was based in a socialist world economy that helped China recover from a century of instability and war.

Culturally, when the CCP formed the People's Republic of China (PRC) in 1949, they conceived of China from the beginning as a state within the emerging "socialist camp."[16] Many Chinese cadres and intellectuals went to the Soviet Union to study Russian, which was the main foreign language taught in Chinese universities. They also went to study art and music, as well as engineering and the natural sciences. In the Soviet Union these students mingled with foreign students from throughout the socialist world. China fostered this socialist cosmopolitanism through the promotion of cultural exchanges, including "mutual visits of orchestras, writers, and drama troupes, the participation of Chinese delegations in international competitions and festivals, and the exchange of students in fields such as arts, drama and music."[17] Volland points out that an especially important cultural exchange was the translation of literature throughout the socialist world. Those literatures that reflected the socialist spirit were translated into the multiple languages of that world and became a shared literary canon from Poland to North Korea and the PRC. Russian novels predominated, but Chinese proletarian fiction also circulated.[18] Well-known authors were translated, but so were socialist juvenile and young adult literature and heroic stories of revolutionary martyrs.[19] In addition, Soviet films circulated widely throughout China and the rest of the socialist bloc. The Society for Chinese-Soviet Friendship had branches in twenty-three Chinese provinces and cities; it offered numerous lectures, speeches, and photo exhibits.

China signed cultural cooperation agreements with not only the Soviet Union but also Poland, Hungary, East Germany, Bulgaria, and Romania. In Asia, it had such agreements with North Korea and North Vietnam. Visiting delegations enabled personal ties to develop between writers and artists. At the congresses of the Soviet Writers' Union, held in Moscow, and the conferences on world peace, well-known Chinese writers attended. The World Youth Festival gathered younger writers; those from China, in addition to writing, offered musical and acrobatic performances as well as participating in sports competitions.[20]

China was part of this worlding of socialist internationalism even before the CCP established the PRC in 1949. From its beginning, the CCP saw itself as oriented simultaneously toward nationalist and internationalist goals. As Kirby argues, it was never China's aim to build socialism in one country. The Soviet revolution offered a model for other revolutions in the name of communism. More significantly, the Soviet Union was intimately involved in Chinese domestic politics from the 1920s, giving aid and political advice. As Kirby notes, long before 1949, China was being incorporated into this system through formal tutelage in everything from policy toward nationalities to its tax system to the role of party cells in factories and ministries.[21] The later tensions between China and the Soviet Union have obscured the fact that they also had a history of cooperation. China and the Soviet Union signed a treaty of friendship in 1950 in which the Soviet Union agreed to provide massive loans and aid for construction projects, as well as outright free technology transfers. Bilateral trade increased exponentially; "between 1950 and 1961 the Soviet Union provided forty-five percent of China's imports."[22] Between 1950 and 1966, according to Dittmer, the Soviet Union helped China to construct virtually all of its heavy industries, from iron and steel to electrical equipment to chemical production to China's first atomic reactor.[23] Soviet technical advisers spent time in China, and thousands of Chinese scientists, technicians, and workers trained in the Soviet Union, while students completed their undergraduate studies there. As a result of this Soviet assistance, China witnessed impressive economic growth during its first Five-Year Plan (1953–1957).[24]

As we are now so well aware, this world of socialist internationalism was fraught with relations of power and inequality, contradictions and paradoxes. Politically, the Soviet Union sought to maintain its dominance through material dependency and negative sanctions. The socialist world economy was challenged by the fact that almost all the countries emphasized similar domestic economic plans, thus creating bounded economies that made it more difficult to trade with one another. The economic vision of the bloc as a whole was not, for better or worse, built on geographic specialization or an international division of labor.

China's relationship with the Soviet Union was always fraught with ambivalence. The Soviet Union maintained a historical legacy of prerevolutionary expansionism toward China when it claimed Outer Mongolia. Despite the Soviet Union's public renunciation of imperial Russia's actions, Stalin continued to intervene in northern Manchuria and hold sway over Xinjiang.[25] After Stalin, the Soviet Union did forfeit their claims in northeastern China, yet continued to maintain as much control as possible over trade and joint ventures. Socialist internationalism in this sense also echoed tianxia, for the latter was built on hierarchies of power and inequality among different geopolitical kingdoms, tribes, and peoples. Of course, for most of tianxia's dynastic history, the idea of egalitarianism among peoples did not exist. Socialist internationalism, by contrast, emerged in a post-Enlightenment world.

Despite these problems, Kirby concludes that the socialist world economy was crucial for China's economic development in the PRC's first decade.[26] Indeed, it helped China to build its military and industrial power. In its first decade of existence, the PRC relied heavily on trading with the Soviet bloc and on massive Soviet aid, on terms that were meant to help China and other socialist countries to develop, rather than at their expense. Moreover, the socialist world economy did not emphasize intellectual property rights. Technological knowledge was freely transferred. China and other countries in the socialist bloc paid very low interest rates for credit and very low fees for Soviet advisers. Barter of goods among the socialist states was seen as quite fair. As multilateral transactions grew, the one-price rule for goods within the socialist bloc was maintained. In other words, countries did not try to take advantage of one another's needs to manipulate the price of goods sold or bartered. As Kirby concludes, these negotiations were marked by a sense of solidarity: "The concept of 'brother countries' was taken seriously, and the broader cause of building socialism appears to have been a factor facilitating compromise."[27]

Immanuel Wallerstein has argued that the socialist bloc never operated as an autonomous, alternative historical system.[28] He has consistently maintained that there has existed only one world economy, the capitalist world economy, and that the socialist bloc was constrained to operate in relation to it and ultimately within it. Although post–Cold War history has certainly proved him correct, it is essential to emphasize the political imagination that sought an alternative to capitalism, which initially inspired socialist internationalism and whose glimmerings as an alternative were in fact discernable through much of the twentieth century.

China split with the Soviet Union over several causes: Mao disagreed with the Soviet decision to work toward peaceful coexistence with the capitalist world, and especially with the United States, since Mao believed in the inevitability of international class war; he disagreed with the Soviet approach to the third world, which favored national alliances between communist parties and the national bourgeoisie, while Mao favored wars of national liberation; and he disliked the hierarchical relationship China and other socialist countries had with the Soviet Union. Further, China broke with the Soviet model of development and adopted its own path, which was linked to Mao's hope to surpass the Soviet Union as the ideological leader of the socialist world.[29] Mao and other leaders were also offended by the manner in which some Soviet advisers and leaders treated China.[30] Given China's recent semicolonial history, it is not surprising that they did not want the Soviet Union to become their next semicolonial brother.

Goldstein has argued that Mao's approach to relationships with the Soviet Union must be viewed in light of his concerns about the appropriate course for socialism within China and that the change in his thinking about the Soviet Union was driven as much by his change in domestic vision as by the global impact of Soviet policies.[31] That is, the dialectical relationship in Mao's thinking between nationalism and internationalism shifted in the late 1950s. He became concerned with the increased institutionalization of the relationship and therefore too much dependence on foreign aid, to the detriment of China's own need for self-reliance (*zili gengsheng*) and self-esteem. He worried about the continuation of a dependence mentality, a blind faith in foreign technology, and what he viewed as regressive ideological developments coming from the Soviet Union. Nationalism, for Mao, was not merely about national sovereignty but more importantly about a national spiritual transformation. One could say, then, that the contradictions between nationalism and internationalism were never resolved. As Shen has argued, communist party leaders in the countries of the socialist bloc believed they shared the goal of proletariat internationalism, but they had not developed any actual means for negotiating different needs between countries and regions.[32]

Here we can see some differentiations from tianxia, for the tensions between nationalism and internationalism would have been unfamiliar to the classical world. However, one could argue that the various wars in China over dynastic succession, while not based in nation-states, showed glimmers of the concern with having one's own kingdom, country, or cultural group predominate over tianxia. Indeed, China's subsequent pursuit of a different path to socialist internationalism also echoes tianxia's concern about who carries the proper Mandate of Heaven.

After the deterioration and then break in relations between China and the Soviet Union in 1962, China developed cultural and diplomatic ties with the decolonized nations of Africa and Asia, trying to rebuild itself as the cultural center of the third world. It was a different version of socialist internationalism than that prescribed by the Soviet Union, one that focused on third world revolutionary struggles against Western imperialism. As Chen Zhimin has argued, "Mao's decision to reject the Soviet version of socialist internationalism did not lead to a rejection of socialist internationalism *per se*. On the contrary, Mao proposed an alternative version, a Chinese version of socialist internationalism, which was more radical, revolutionary and militant as well as being in line with Mao's view of Chinese nationalism."[33]

Chinese leaders saw their nation as a role model for other third world developing nations who had also experienced colonial exploitation. They viewed China as united with other colonized nations by a shared history of colonial oppression and "a common antagonism to both the colonial powers of Europe and the rich world in general."[34] On the other hand, they viewed the third world as a neutral zone rather than part of either the socialist or the capitalist world.[35] On this basis, China participated in the Bandung conference of nonaligned countries held in Indonesia in 1955. But then Mao began to espouse national liberation struggles, with international class war as the goal. Chinese leaders also thought the West would attack not the powerful socialist countries but countries in the third world, which were more vulnerable. They thought it was imperative to support anti-imperialist struggles. Thus, during the 1960s, China supported communist movements throughout Southeast Asia and Africa, as well as the Palestine Liberation Organization in the Middle East. In Africa, China established diplomatic relations with various new nations, and provided economic assistance and established cultural and trade agreements. These relations were strained by China's Cultural Revolution but then reaffirmed in the early 1970s.[36]

China did not merely engage in rhetoric but also provided material and medical support to third world nations. In Africa, the PRC provided arms and money, food and medicine, as well as development aid. China built the celebrated Tanzania-Zambia railway, loaned goods to formerly colonized African nations in order to weaken the residual grip of the European powers, and through the Eight Principles of Chinese Aid offered low-interest and interest-free loans, generous repayment periods, and a directive that China's technical support workers should receive the same salary as their African counterparts.[37] China made clear sacrifices for this aid, including sending thousands of tons of grain to African states during the Great Leap Forward famine, depriving China of skilled engineers and doctors by dispatching them to Africa, and letting go of potential trade profit by teaching Africans how to grow tea.[38] Mei Zhan argues that throughout the 1960s and 1970s, China exported traditional Chinese medicine (TCM) as a preventive medicine for the rural poor, which "helped envision and produce a 'proletarian world' that China strove to champion."[39] The worlding of TCM was oriented toward serving the peoples of the third world. Unlike today, TCM was therefore mainly oriented toward Africa, Asia, and Latin America. "As the Soviet Union and the United States were also sending medical teams to the third world, the encounters between 'Chinese medicine' and 'biomedicine' were not about local-meets-universal but about competing universals."[40]

Students from these third world countries were also sent to China to learn medicine as well as other skills, funded originally by the World Health Organization and the Chinese government. Zhan concludes that China's subaltern status in a world of nation-states was produced by the worlding of the figure of the international proletariat.[41] In return, the African states were critical in voting China into the United Nations in 1971. China then continued to champion third world countries' rights to a fair share of the international economy. However, it also attempted to play out its own international struggles with the United States, the Soviet Union, and Taiwan through African politics, and its aid was often strategic in this regard.[42] It was unsuccessful, however, as most African governments disliked China's political interference.

This later history of socialist internationalism departs quite markedly from tianxia in the sense that there are obviously competing visions of how the world should be organized. China's vision of socialist internationalism competed not only with a Western capitalist world but also with the Soviet Union's version of socialist internationalism. While dynastic rule in China obviously entailed both military and political conflict, it was over who should rule the one world that was then envisioned to exist.

World revolution was the task of this new version of socialist internationalism. It departed from the milder version of Soviet internationalism and committed to supporting revolutionary forces around the world. Yet even after the Sino-Soviet split, China continued to sign bilateral agreements with other socialist nations in the 1960s and beyond. China's split with the Soviet Union and its commitment to international class struggle, including ideological and material support for revolutionary movements, made it fall between the two blocs, an ultimately untenable position.

It is so easy now to dismiss this era as one long mistake. And of course, given the conflicts over power and autonomy within the socialist bloc, not to mention power struggles within China, one could easily dismiss this imagined world as filled only with repression. What leads me away from that conclusion is the structures of feeling engendered during this period among Chinese citizens. I was alerted to these structures of feeling by the memories shared by friends in China who described in great detail the Soviet films they used to watch and the Soviet books they used to read. Many intellectuals had learned Russian, and though in the 1980s they sometimes shook their heads at the uselessness of it, they nonetheless talked about it as a sign of their cosmopolitan worldliness. They thus separated their dislike of the Soviet government from their affective attachments to Soviet cultural productions developed during their youth. Indeed, the Soviet novels that were most popular in China in the 1950s have been successfully reissued in the current era of postsocialist economic reform.

Postsocialist Cosmopolitanism

The economic reform era, beginning in the early 1980s, has witnessed a dramatic transformation in the worlding of China. Stated another way, the world in which China imagines itself is dramatically distinct from that which it imagined in the socialist era or certainly in the classical world of tianxia. This world is centered on the capitalist West, even as China reaches out to invest in Africa, Asia, and Latin America. China has entered into a post–Cold War world economy dominated by the United States. Following Zhan, one can argue that ruptures and displacements lie at the heart of this postsocialist worlding project.[43] First and foremost, China has produced a displacement from within by distancing itself from a socialist past that it now all but repudiates. Displacement of this past allows for an affective, imaginative, and ideological conversion from one worlding project to another. Under Maoist socialism, China saw itself as a leader of the world, a leader in making a world. With economic reform, China has seen itself as behind the (capitalist) world, needing to catch up. Though recently this temporal anxiety has seemed to abate, the motivating force behind economic cosmopolitanism continues to be the desire for equality with or even to surpass the West. In this sense, one finds traces of the socialist past, though now enacted from within an imagined world of capitalist advancement.

This worlding project entails novel forms of entanglements and productions of different others, even as it contains echoes of not only the socialist past but also the semicolonial history that continues to animate this postsocialist world for China. Yet I would argue that this postsocialist world is much further away from any concept of tianxia than the socialist past. The postsocialist world is explicitly imagined as full of divisions and competitions, of irreconcilable differences. There is no vision of a world that unites all, pace Hardt and Negri, though one could perversely argue that the World Trade Organization (WTO) implicitly contains the seeds of such a view.[44] War is considered the norm, whether through actual violence, ideological rhetoric, or political maneuvering. This condition of perpetual war is based on the confluence of the end of the Cold War; the desire for absolute dominance on the part of the United States, expressed through military power; the rearrangement of the global economy; and the resistances expressed to these forms of dominance. There were certainly military conflicts within a world imagined as tianxia, but they were at least imagined as leading to a reunified world.

Politically, this postsocialist world has no unifying vision, nor any unifying organization. Hence its dangerous instability. There are, however, regional organizing efforts, such as the European Union, MercoSur, UnaSur, NATO, and the Shanghai Cooperation Organization (bringing together China and Russia, along with Central Asian countries). These organizations involve not only political cooperation but also economic and military alliances. Yet as events have shown in Europe and countries bordering Russia to the south, these organizations are experiencing upheavals from within. Economically, there exists nothing like the world of socialist internationalism that tied countries to aid from the Soviet Union. Since the end of the Cold War, the United States has similarly dropped its advocacy of modernization, which was its version of encouraging dependence on U.S. aid. Neoliberalism is the U.S.-dominated vision of a free-for-all in the world economy.

The one institution that purports to be universally inclusive is the WTO. But the WTO focuses exclusively on economic trade, although trade agreements have implicit political implications. The WTO is an extension of the General Agreement on Tariffs and Trade (GATT) signed after World War II as part of the Bretton Woods agreements to stabilize the world economy.[45] After numerous rounds of negotiations on tariffs in the intervening years, the WTO was formed in 1995, at the end of what is known as the Uruguay Round and after the first member countries signed the Marrakesh agreement. Dedicated to the idea that trade between countries should be freed from government intervention (i.e., free trade liberalization), the WTO extends GATT's coverage of trade

in goods to trade in services, intellectual property rights, and financial investments. Contrary to the popular assumption that it presents a unified package
of neoliberal agreements to each of its members, the WTO actually attempts
to hold together a welter of special cases and specific exemptions, quotas, and
tariff levels for hundreds of different goods, industries, and services. The details
of the separate agreements for each country are based on whether a country
can get itself labeled underdeveloped or developing. Most importantly, these
details implicitly reveal the central role of culture and history in deciding how a
country should enter the WTO, even as the organization presents its neoliberal
principles as universal and timeless. For example, the goal of the negotiations
over China's entry into the WTO was to produce a "desiring China" that would
not only create an internal machine yielding endlessly proliferating desires for
foreign goods and services, but also make China into that object which others
could desire freely, without obstruction.[46]

The WTO, in its role of facilitating the ceaseless global search for profit,
adjudicates between licit and illicit capitalist desires and among accusations
that blur the line between legitimate and illegitimate capitalism. Indeed, tracing the accusations and counteraccusations the WTO adjudicates, one might
define the heart of capitalism as resting in unfair competition. The WTO makes
weighty claims for economic purification but must engage with the messy cultural practices of specific geopolitical histories. The seemingly pure economic
forms and actions that its rules and regulations specify—efficiency, transpar-
ency, liberalization, predictability, national treatment (i.e., no discrimination
against foreigners in favor of domestic industries and companies), avoidance of
unnecessary barriers to trade—cannot contain some of the unruliness of historically and geopolitically informed economic action.[47]

One could argue that the essence of the WTO lies in market romanticism,
an ideology of complete market freedom, a theory that the market itself can
create the greatest good for society.[48] Market romanticism is thus the belief that
so-called free competition will automatically lead to progress. This is the way
that countries with strong economies demolish countries with weak economies, not allowing them any self-protection. Indeed, the rules and regulations
of the WTO have overtaken democratic processes within nation-states. The
WTO's worlding project thus rests on the dialectics of competition and monopoly, market freedom and ongoing insecurity, regulatory action and clever rapa-
ciousness. This is the world within which China now negotiates its place.

The WTO, as I said, could be viewed as echoing tianxia, but only in the sense
that it purports to have a universal reach. Yet it departs from tianxia in the application of its precepts. Although ideologically it presents itself as applying

the same precepts to all nations, in fact the details of WTO agreements belie that claim. Its claim that its ideology of market fundamentalism should be universally embraced echoes tianxia, not in the specific content of tianxia beliefs but in the idea that one set of precepts applies to all. Yet, unlike the classical world of tianxia, the WTO world includes winners and losers. Of course, the hierarchies of the WTO also echo those of tianxia. Tianxia was never a world of egalitarianism. But the WTO opens the way for destruction of other countries and other worlds, a goal that was not at the heart of tianxia.

After China's entry into the WTO in 2001, direct foreign investment increased, tying it more tightly to a capitalist global economy, but one that is far from unified. By 2002, China had surpassed the United States as the most favored destination for foreign direct investment.[49] However, in the modern era, unlike the colonial era, the Chinese government has been determined to maintain its sovereignty. The dominant investments continue to come from overseas Chinese in Hong Kong and Taiwan, but Japan and the United States are not far behind. In turn, Chinese investors, mostly from state-owned corporations, have invested heavily in Latin America, Africa, the Middle East, and Asia in their search for energy and other resources.[50] The Chinese government has also acquired a good portion of U.S. government debt. It has thus far conducted these international investments without any accompanying military interventions. These measures, along with the promotion of transnational capitalism, have contributed to the emergence of a bourgeoisie and substantially increased social and economic inequality in China.[51] China's transnational economic pursuits are intimately defined through its domestic economic policies. The Chinese government has promoted a market economy, the redistribution of wealth, privatization, and the end of social welfare. Indeed, as Ching Kwan Lee has argued, China has exported its problems with environmental pollution and economic growth and inequality to countries of the Global South.[52]

Transnational capitalism within China has meant that foreign entrepreneurs now reside in the major metropolises of China, from places including Hong Kong, Taiwan, Japan, and the United States, but also Korea (both North and South), Southeast Asia, and all the European countries as well as various African nations, Latin American countries, and countries of the former Soviet Union. In Shanghai, for example, foreign entrepreneurs live in the same areas that colonial settlers had inhabited before. Chinese entrepreneurs as well as workers have also moved in large numbers to the countries in which mainland Chinese companies have invested.[53]

In this postsocialist context, China's culture has emphasized a new kind of cosmopolitanism, resulting from multicultural metropolises, which has fostered specific expressions among Chinese residents that are largely though not exclusively influenced by U.S. culture.[54] American consumer culture predominates, manifested in sports clothing, fast-food restaurants, gyms, bourgeois pet culture, Hollywood films, and music such as rock and hip-hop. There are also cultural influences from Japan, South Korea, Taiwan, and Hong Kong, and to a lesser degree from Europe.[55] The latter is most evident in the realm of fashion, though even there, influences from East Asia are strong. Shanghai today is a metropolis of foreign investment dollars, driving up the cost of real estate. It is a city of "upscale Japanese restaurants, German luxury cars, Korean movies, and Parisian clothing fashions."[56] As in the prewar era, Shanghai is also a city of what Chris Connery has called "image-generation."[57] The cosmopolitan commingling of these cultural influences makes China's metropolises, especially Beijing and Shanghai, into global, cosmopolitan cities par excellence. Still, the language everyone is supposed to learn is English.

Cosmopolitanism has been constructed in relation to what the government calls "socialism with Chinese characteristics." Socialism with Chinese characteristics is how the Chinese state has brought capitalism to China. It also means new ways to value human activity and new ways of worlding China. Cosmopolitanism is a site for the production of knowledge about what it means to be human in a postsocialist, post–Cold War world, and is intimately tied to the emergence of a middle class in China. Unlike the socialist cosmopolitan, who was supposed to focus on revolutionary sacrifices and heroism, this postsocialist citizen is supposed to cultivate a wide range of different desires, from consumption to work to sex.[58] There has been a strong emphasis in China on consumption and mass culture. While this kind of cosmopolitan self is most successfully embodied by middle-class youths, workers and rural migrants also embrace these desires. For the latter, cosmopolitanism means transcending the divisions within China, especially between rural and urban areas, which has made rural residents into second-class citizens. It means learning how to live in China's metropolises as opposed to the countryside, learning new consumption habits, new ways to carry the body, and new ways of living.[59]

Consumption has been positioned not merely as that which will satisfy a hunger for a nonascetic life distilled from the Maoist era, but as that which will provide answers to all longings and aspirations. For that reason, I call this conviction "consumer fundamentalism." Consumer fundamentalism incorporates the pleasures of consumption into a belief that this is where the deep answers to life's dilemmas lie. More like religion than economics, it is founded on eschatological anxieties about hopes and dreams for the future. Like religious fundamentalisms, it offers a literalist interpretation of consumer practices and, most importantly, renders dangerous any desires to turn elsewhere or raise other questions subsumed under consumption, such as questions of social inequality, social justice, or the appropriate role of the state. My concept of consumer fundamentalism is not meant to belittle the true pleasure of citizens in China in the increased comforts of everyday life. Rather, it is meant to highlight the beliefs that surround these pursuits. Consumer fundamentalism might be a universalizing precept, but unlike tianxia, it does not carry with it a set of explicit moral precepts or a conceptualization of how these practices might lead to a world that is orderly and stabilized. To the contrary, built into consumerism is a constant deferral of desires that are never quite fulfilled.

Postsocialist cosmopolitanism rests on important structured dichotomies and forgettings that reinvent the recent socialist past as something to be left behind: the politics of the past versus current consumerism and the search for wealth; kinship obligations versus the search for happiness; and communalism versus the search for freedom. Each of these dichotomies lauds consumerism, wealth, happiness, and freedom as the way to a Chinese cosmopolitanism of the future by positing them against a past reinterpreted as full of constraints, hardships, and kinship oppression. This past is a forgetting of the political passions and freedom from parents under socialism that also satisfied intense desires, at least for a time. It is also a forgetting of an internationalist dream, one that was full of contradictions and yet also built cross-cultural interactions that were aimed at overthrowing capitalism.

This postsocialist cosmopolitanism with its revisionist history is far from tianxia in that the latter assumed a universalist reenactment of the past, rather than a post-Enlightenment notion of linear progress through time. Overall, politically, economically, and culturally, the era of economic reform has much fainter resonances with tianxia than the socialist period. There is no unifying political vision; economic activity is seen as inherently competitive, leading to inevitable division, destruction, and war; and culturally there is not the kind of belief that existed under tianxia, echoed by socialist internationalism, that one's daily life and social relations should reflect the unity of heaven and earth.

Conclusion

It is time we rid ourselves of the metaphor that China is open or closed in relation to historically changing worlds. This would include the Chinese phrases *duiwai kaifang* (opening to the outside world) and *yu shijie jiegui* (getting on track with the world). The open/closed metaphor performs distortions of history that echo colonial relations of power. China has long been an active creator of various worlding projects, from dynastic tianxia to anticolonial nationalism, to socialist internationalism, to the contemporary worlding project of global capitalism. The current invocation of the metaphor ineluctably leads us to forget about one of those historical periods in particular: socialist internationalism. It creates a sense of inevitability, moreover, about the need to accept global capitalism, as if there were no other worlding projects for us to imagine.

To remember the period of socialist internationalism is not to romanticize it. As Lin Chun has argued so eloquently, the socialist era in China was rife with contradictions.[60] Alongside the redistribution of wealth was the division between rural and urban that exploited the countryside to feed rapid industrial development in the cities; alongside informal modes of democratic participation in which peasants and workers truly could have a voice in politics—that is, in local decisions about how to redistribute wealth and later, how to challenge corruption and the emergence of new privileges—were political campaigns to stifle democracy and target individual citizens. There were plenty of abuses of power and disastrous policies. Indeed, these policies were entangled in and developed through China's conflicts in the international arena. And the wreckage of international communism was of its own making.

Nonetheless, for too long evaluations of socialist internationalism have emphasized degradations of power, as if no one believed in anything in the socialist era. Moreover, we have forgotten China's active participation in that worlding project as well as the project of third world liberation. We have accepted the revisionist idea that China was entirely closed in on itself until it allowed capitalism through its doors. As Foucault taught some time ago, all historical periods combine imagination with power.[61] Socialist internationalism imagined a world rid of capitalist exploitation, a world that enabled national economic stability and growth. China shared this world vision with other socialist states in an actual world riven by powerful inequalities among and within those states. Utopias can lead people to the most violent actions in the fervent belief in their ultimate dream.[62] Global capitalism, another type of utopia, dreams of freedom, but of one kind only: the market. With global capitalism we are allowed to dream only about the endless, ceaseless pursuit of profit, to come up with the most creative ways to exploit natural resources as well as human beings.

It is time to develop more nuanced insights, not merely to have an accurate history but also to imagine a more just future. If we hope that China will lead the way to a world of greater social justice, then it is imperative not to succumb to historical amnesia. The concept of tianxia helps in this endeavor. It enables us to rethink what it would mean to live in a world that sees itself as universal in its value but can accept and incorporate difference.

Coda

I cannot help but tell one last story to underscore the irony of my argument in this chapter. It also helps to show how tianxia can be revived, though in revisionist guise. Recently, I had the pleasure of visiting for the first time Xian, the capital of Shaanxi Province in northwestern China. Xian is no longer a major cultural or political center of China, but from the Zhou dynasty (1029–256 BCE) through the Tang dynasty (618–907) it was both the political and cultural capital of the Middle Kingdom. I had the opportunity to visit Xian's famous Shaanxi History Museum, which tells a story of the development of China's civilization through history, as marked conventionally by dynastic periods.[63] I had expected to see a story about China's civilizational richness that led China to become a major empire. I was familiar with that narrative and its emphasis on the Chinese aspect of its civilization building, and it was in line with twentieth-century nationalism. I was surprised, then, by the story I found instead: that China has always been a country open to the rest of the world and that its strength is founded on this openness.

This story is told repeatedly through the three main exhibition halls. The first hall moves through archaeological findings of human evolution to the founding of the Zhou and Qin dynasties, both considered to be the beginnings of the Chinese empire. The glory of the Qin dynasty is emphasized through objects from the famous tomb of the emperor Qin Shihuang, most notably his terra cotta warriors. The unification of the warring states under Qin Shihuang is framed in terms of a multinational (*duo minzu*) state. As the English description of the Qin dynasty states: "In the year 221 B.C., Emperor Qin Shihuang unified China, and established the first unified, multi-nationalities and centralized country in Chinese history. Its politics, economic and military institutions set examples for the later generations."

The second exhibition hall, focused on the ensuing Han dynasty (206 BCE–220 CE) continues this story of openness. The explanatory placard states: "The Han dynasty reached the first peak in the social development of ancient China. Its social economy and culture embraced a full development. Its open policy and contacts with the outside world made it one of the most prosperous countries in the world." The story of China opening up to the world is mostly told through the figure of Zhang Qian, an imperial envoy sent twice to the western regions of Central and Western Asia. He is credited with initiating the Silk Road, through which "the East and the West [came to] depend on one another."

The final exhibition hall, about the Sui (581–618) and Tang (618–907) dynasties, displays Xian (then known as Chang'an) as a fully international city, with foreigners from all over the world coming to live, trade, and make obeisance to the Chinese emperor. Calling Chang'an a "real international metropolis," one video shows a reenactment of history, with the emperor receiving foreign emissaries, played by foreign actors in different costumes, all bearing tribute. Another room displays images of foreign dancers and musicians; coins from the Turgash Kingdom, the eastern Roman Empire, the Uighur Khaganate, the Arab world, Persia, and Japan; and porcelain figures of foreigners, including civil officers and riders. The section on the Tang dynasty concludes with another diorama of the Silk Road, but this model includes Europe, Africa, and South and Southeast Asia instead of focusing only on Central Asia.

That this museum is not an exceptional reflection of current official discourse is underscored by Ana Maria Candela's insightful analysis of two projects that emphasize China's historical openness to "the world."[64] These projects are located in southeastern China. Sponsored by UNESCO, one examines the Maritime Silk Route expedition, highlighting the roles of Guangzhou and Quanzhou as Silk Road ports. The other is an Overseas Chinese Museum, highlighting the role of *qiaoxiang*, or sojourner villages, in China's development. Candela argues that the first project "fostered a re-orientation of local historical narratives away from a nation-centered framework and towards a maritime history of Asian globality," while the second attempts to draw the Chinese diaspora back to their native places.[65] Both projects, she concludes, do the work of building a new structure of feeling that fashions local place-based imaginaries in the southeastern province of Guangdong in relation to China's current insertion into a capitalist global economy. Both projects grapple with the experiences of social contradictions engendered by the contemporary transformations of southern China.

One can readily discern the tianxia concept invigorating these various exhibitions. Yet it is tianxia in the context of a postsocialist worlding project. These exhibits revive the idea of Chinese history as one of universality and difference, but they also implicitly speak to the open/closed metaphor used to interpret it. Hence their emphasis is not on what Chinese civilization brought to other places but on what those other places brought to China.

The irony of the convergence of my argument with official Chinese discourse reinforces the point that historical context in the telling of historical stories is everything. A history of the present is always embedded in genealogies of the past.

Notes

I would like to thank Wang Ban and Li Haiyan for organizing a workshop on tianxia at Stanford University, which gave me the opportunity to write this chapter. I would also like to thank Jeremy Tai for his thorough research assistance, Elena Glasberg for being my writing angel, and the two anonymous reviewers for their insightful suggestions for revision.

1. Said, *Orientalism*.
2. Cheah, "What Is a World?"; Zhan, *Other-Worldly*.
3. Cheah, "What Is a World?," 26, 30.
4. Zhan, *Other-Worldly*, 7.
5. Zhan, *Other-Worldly*, 24.
6. Perdue, "A Frontier View of Chineseness."
7. Benjamin, "Theses on the Philosophy of History."
8. Chen, "Nationalism, Internationalism and Chinese Foreign Policy," 41. For a more recent incarnation of this utopian goal, see Hardt and Negri, *Empire*.
9. Dai, "*Hero* and the Invisible *Tianxia*."
10. Dittmer, *Sino-Soviet Normalization*, 99.
11. Goldstein, "Nationalism and Internationalism," 228.
12. Goldstein, "Nationalism and Internationalism," 229.
13. Perdue, "A Frontier View of Chineseness."
14. Kirby, "China and the Socialist World Economy."
15. Kirby, "China and the Socialist World Economy."
16. Volland, "Translating the Socialist State."
17. Volland, "Translating the Socialist State," 53.
18. Volland, "Translating the Socialist State," 53. According to Kirby ("China and the Socialist World Economy," 67), 100 million volumes of Soviet books were translated, 747 Soviet films were shown in China, and 102 Chinese films were shown in Russia.
19. Volland, "Translating the Socialist State," 63.
20. Volland, "Translating the Socialist State," 55, 57. Volland argues that it is important to remember that these exchanges also revealed the unequal distribution of power in this socialist world and the tensions that would later break open.
21. Kirby, "China and the Socialist World Economy," 61.
22. Dittmer, *Sino-Soviet Normalization*, 18.
23. Dittmer, *Sino-Soviet Normalization*, 19–20.
24. Dernberger, "Economic Development and Modernization," 197, as quoted in Dittmer, *Sino-Soviet Normalization*.
25. Dittmer, *Sino-Soviet Normalization*.
26. Kirby, "China and the Socialist World Economy," 63.
27. Kirby, "China and the Socialist World Economy," 66.
28. Wallerstein, *Utopistics*, 66–70.
29. For a thorough review of the literature on the causes of the dispute, see Dittmer, *Sino-Soviet Normalization*.
30. Shen Zhihua, "The Rupture of the Sino-Soviet Alliance."
31. Goldstein, "Nationalism and Internationalism," 227.
32. Shen Zhihua, "The Rupture of the Sino-Soviet Alliance," 288.

33. Chen, "Nationalism, Internationalism and Chinese Foreign Policy," 43.

34. Snow, "China and Africa," 318.

35. Dittmer, *Sino-Soviet Normalization*, 122. However, Philip Snow, "China and Africa," argues that China has always inserted its presence into Africa in terms of its own strategic interests, variously opposing the United States, the Soviet Union, and Taiwan's activities there and focusing on certain key zones and trying to enlist African support for its own campaigns, though without much success.

36. Dittmer, *Sino-Soviet Normalization*, 129.

37. Snow, "China and Africa," 287.

38. Snow, "China and Africa," 288.

39. Zhan, *Other-Worldly*, 34.

40. Zhan, "Does It Take a Miracle?," 463.

41. Zhan, *Other-Worldly*, 39.

42. Snow, "China and Africa."

43. Zhan, *Other-Worldly*.

44. Hardt and Negri, *Multitude*; Hardt and Negri, *Empire*.

45. At least at that time, the reigning ideology was that national economies and thus the international economy thrive best under peaceful conditions—despite the fact that, of course, profit seekers have always taken advantage of war. That idea is now defunct. See Ferguson, *Global Shadows*.

46. For an elaboration of this argument, see Rofel, "Desiring China."

47. My analysis here is inspired by Mei Zhan's "Civet Cats, Fried Grasshoppers, and David Beckham's Pajamas."

48. See Han, *Peng Zhuang*, for this argument.

49. Gallagher, *Contagious Capitalism*, 34.

50. Lee, "Raw Encounters"; Sautman and Yan, "Friends and Interests."

51. Zhang, *In Search of Paradise*; Wang, *The Qiangs between the Hans and the Tibetans*.

52. Lee, "Buying Stability in China."

53. This is not the first time by any means that Chinese have formed a wide-ranging diaspora, as indicated earlier in this chapter. See also Kuhn, *Chinese among Others*; Ong and Nonini, *Ungrounded Empires*; and Ma and Cartier, *The Chinese Diaspora*.

54. The United States serves as a contradictory site of identification and competition for China. In the initial years of economic reform, it provided a source of critique for those in China opposed to the Communist Party and a source of dreams about democracy. But as the years wore on, the following events exposed deep contradictions in what America signifies to Chinese citizens: American government involvement in rejecting China's first bid for the Olympics, the translation into Chinese of Samuel Huntington's *Clash of Civilizations*, the U.S. bombing of the Chinese embassy in Belgrade during the Kosovo war, a U.S. spy plane flying over Chinese airspace, the Wen Ho Lee case, and finally, the appearance of U.S. military bases in former Soviet countries. That means China is now completely surrounded by the U.S. military.

55. Hockx and Strauss, *Culture in the Contemporary PRC*.

56. Wasserstrom, *Global Shanghai*, 13.

57. Connery, "Waves."

58. Rofel, *Desiring China.*

59. Pun, *Made in China*; Yan, *New Master, New Servants.*

60. Lin, *The Transformation of Chinese Socialism.*

61. Foucault, *The Order of Things.*

62. See Wallerstein, *Utopistics,* for an elaboration of this argument.

63. After I returned from the conference in Xian, I realized I wanted to write about the Shaanxi History Museum but did not have my ethnographer's hat on when I went through the exhibits. I thank Jeremy Tai for taking detailed notes for me that have enabled me to write this coda.

64. Candela, "*Qiaoxiang* on the Silk Road."

65. Candela, "*Qiaoxiang* on the Silk Road," 1.

PART IV.

TIANXIA AND ITS

DISCONTENTS

*

10

THE SOFT POWER OF THE
CONSTANT SOLDIER

or, Why We Should Stop Worrying
and Learn to Love the PLA

Haiyan Lee

*

Both within China and globally, a veritable chorus has emerged to greet the imminent arrival of China as a soft power giant poised to remake the world in its own image. If we regard soft power as an extension of the concept of hegemony to the realm of international relations and, as such, necessarily derivative of hard power, it is safe to say that there is a significant gap between China's economic and military clout and its cultural sway. This is most acutely manifested in divergent perceptions of the People's Liberation Army (PLA) domestically and abroad. In international media, reporting on the PLA is invariably framed by skepticism about China's peaceful rise. Domestically, however, the PLA has always been instrumental to the Communist Party's regime of charismatic power. A recent hit television serial, *Soldiers Sortie* (*Shibing tuji*, 士兵突击, 2007), can help us reevaluate the PLA's special place in the dialectics of hard and soft power.

In this chapter, I try to make sense of the appeal of this all-male soap opera about scores of servicemen training hard, bonding hard, and never thinking of women. I seek to bring together the usually separate questions of domestic hegemony and international influence. The fact that a huge hit like *Soldiers Sortie* is unlikely to be marketable to foreign audiences (other than military analysts) raises the following questions: Can soft power be assessed merely on the basis of the outward image projected by a country and apart from its living culture? Can the military-industrial-entertainment complex, of which the PLA is an indispensable part, cross borders and conquer hearts and minds without Orientalizing itself? I argue that we need to know what excites the Chinese before we can discuss how China will excite the world. To do so, we need to come to terms with a collective self-image that is increasingly the contingent product of negotiations among an overweening state, a digitally active population, and a mass media tacking between official mandates and market imperatives.

Introduction

In 2007 and 2008, a thirty-part television serial drama titled *Soldiers Sortie* became the most talked-about show in China. This is surprising because it lacks the usual selling points of popular soaps: courtship, marriage, extramarital affairs, divorce, teenage rebellion, urban adventure, crime detection, official corruption, imperial nostalgia, martial arts, espionage, warfare, and so on.[1] Instead, it features scores of servicemen in the PLA training hard, bonding hard, and shedding bucketfuls of sweat and tears. And yet its all-male cast of characters, played by then relatively obscure actors, is adored and feted by fans, including legions of female fans who regard them as heartthrobs and highly desirable mates. Its central Forrest Gump–like character, a new recruit named Xu Sanduo (许三多) who joins the army to escape a tyrannical father, is universally beloved and admired as the ultimate embodiment of the soldierly spirit. Perhaps most surprising of all is the fact that a drama about soldiery set entirely in peacetime is able to elicit such overwhelming audience enthusiasm.

The serial is the brainchild of scriptwriter Lan Xiaolong (兰小龙), who graduated from the Central Drama Academy and is a staff writer of the PLA Beijing Division's drama troupe. After embedding himself for nearly a year in an army unit, Lan scripted a serialized television drama, only to have it roundly rejected by the stations he approached.[2] To fulfill a writing quota from his work unit, he adapted it into a stage play that went on to win the Lao She Literature Prize and the Cao Yu Drama Prize. He then readapted the play for the small screen and, after overcoming much skepticism about its viability, managed to gain the backing of the PLA's August First Film Studio and the collaboration of a fairly successful director and a team of producers and publicists. The serial was first quietly broadcast in Shaanxi in late 2006 and then in Guangdong,

Sichuan, and Shandong in early 2007; soon word began to spread on the Internet, and the show got its big break when the Beijing Satellite Station aired it in 2007 with record ratings. Other regional satellite stations quickly followed suit, some airing it repeatedly and further boosting its popularity.[3] Tabloid stories, commentaries, and blogs blanketed cyberspace; mainstream media outlets and entertainment venues gave the show extensive coverage; awards and accolades piled on, especially on the actor Wang Baoqiang (王宝强), who played Xu Sanduo; and tie-in products such as a video game, a novel, and inspirational manuals cropped up quickly.[4] While not quite conquering overseas markets, the serial received the best foreign drama award at the inaugural Tokyo Television Drama Festival in 2008. Reportedly, military analysts in the Pentagon have scrutinized the show for revealing information on the state of Chinese military technology, operational concepts, logistics, and personnel training.[5]

Attending the low-key award ceremony at the Tokyo festival were the head of the August First studio, Ming Zhenjiang (明振江), and the lead actor, Wang Baoqiang. Ming gloated to Chinese reporters about Soldiers Sortie being the first army-themed television drama to receive recognition overseas: "It means that foreigners are beginning to appreciate the glamor [fengcai 风采] of Chinese soldiers." He added that he was in the process of negotiating the broadcast rights, possibly without any cuts or edits, with two Japanese television stations. Wang Baoqiang, on his part, mentioned that he had received numerous calls from the Chinese diaspora in the United States praising the show: "The show's spirit of 'never letting go, never giving up' should have a worldwide appeal."[6] The absence of any follow-up reporting on the show's overseas distribution makes it reasonable to assume that the negotiations did not go through.[7] This is not surprising given that Chinese television programs, with a few exceptions, have yet to cross borders (zouchu guomen 走出国门) in the same way that Hong Kong, Japanese, and Korean programs have done for decades, not to mention the enormous popularity of American soap operas throughout Asia and the world.[8] Chinese film and literature fare slightly better, but the so-called cultural trade deficit (wenhua maoyi nicha 文化贸易逆差) between China and major exporters of cultural products such as the United States and Japan is glaring and unlikely to be reversed anytime soon.

Nonetheless, both within China and globally, China is seen as an emerging soft power giant eager to remake the world in its own image. If soft power is an extension of the Marxist concept of hegemony to the realm of international relations and derivative of hard power, there is a significant gap between China's economic and military strength and its cultural influence. How might we account for this? Why has a huge hit like Soldiers Sortie gained little traction in overseas markets, apart from the diaspora and a few military analysts? Can China project soft power if it cannot excite the world with what excites the Chinese? The misalignment of attraction is most acutely manifested in the divergent perceptions of the PLA domestically and abroad. In international media, reporting on the PLA is invariably framed by concerns about regional security and skepticism about China's self-proclaimed peaceful rise (*heping jueqi* 和平崛起). Domestically, however, the PLA has always been instrumental not only to the party's grip on power, but also to its political hegemony and legitimacy. In the reform era, the worker and the peasant of the socialist holy trinity, *gongnongbing* (工农兵), have lost their ideological halo, leaving the soldier to shoulder the burden of exemplifying what it means to be Chinese. More often than not, the PLA is portrayed in a symbolic or beneficent light that obscures its role as an instrument of violence. Military-themed film and television dramas constitute an important official, or "main-melody," genre that offers a steady diet of nationalism, heroism, and action to domestic audiences.

Under what conditions can the PLA, as an instrument of domestic hegemony, also become a source of soft power that can be projected globally in tandem with China's rising GDP? Can the military-industrial-entertainment complex of which the PLA is an indispensable part anchor the "socialist spiritual civilization" with harmony at its core? Can such a civilization cross borders and conquer hearts and minds without Orientalizing itself, that is, without kung fu, Peking opera, or Cold War melodrama about tyranny and liberty? How will China reconcile the intimacy of national culture and its staunch defense of national sovereignty with its global ambitions, officially enunciated in the annual Party Central Committee plenum meeting and unofficially articulated as a restorationist project centered on the atavistic keyword tianxia (天下)?[9] This chapter first examines the broader question of soft power and then turns to *Soldiers Sortie* to assess the universalizing potential of a national obsession.

The Will to (Soft) Power

Since Joseph Nye first introduced the term in 1990, "soft power" has become a ubiquitous buzzword in intellectual circles as well as diplomatic arenas, and increasingly so among the Chinese intelligentsia and China specialists.[10] An anthology by a group of political scientists and international relations scholars explores the concept's relevance to China's ascension to global prominence.[11] They generally agree that, notwithstanding conscious efforts on the part of the Chinese state, it is premature to boast of or to be alarmed by the extent to which China's soft power is "transforming the world," as Joshua Kurlantzick claims in the subtitle of his book *Charm Offensive*. Nye coined the term at the end of the Cold War period to urge America, the sole superpower, to reconceptualize its global leadership role by tapping into its enormous reservoirs of goodwill in the world.[12] America alone, it seemed, had the wherewithal to get what it wanted through attraction rather than coercion or inducement. All the more reason it should utilize culture, political values, and public diplomacy to maintain world order: "When you get others to admire your ideals and to want what you want, you do not have to spend as much on sticks and carrots to move them in your direction."[13]

Soft power is essentially an ideologically neutral and geopolitically decentered way of identifying the hegemonic sway that a powerful nation wields in the international arena.[14] As Mingjiang Li points out, it does not inhere in any power resource per se but is rather an effect of the deliberate cultivation of attraction, persuasion, co-optation, and emulation. Nor is it necessarily the intrinsic property of a particular culture, ideology, or institution, which can under certain circumstances "result in resentment, repulsion, hostility and even conflict."[15] Both the state and civil society can generate soft power, sometimes working in concert and sometimes at odds with each other. Geraldo Zahran and Leonardo Ramos note that corporations, sports idols, pop stars, and civic groups all can become potent sources of soft power that the state cannot fully control but can try to reinforce or exploit as part of its agenda of global hegemony.[16] That said, soft power is rarely independent of economic, technological, or military (hard) power, and for that reason is typically associated with advanced industrialized nations, particularly the United States. In other words, soft power accrues mostly to the wealthy and powerful players in the international arena, and it becomes an issue with regard to a developing nation only when the latter is perceived to be well on its way to joining the ranks of global economic powerhouses. Just as Japan not so long ago wrung its hands about the efficacy of its soft power, now China is undergoing a similar bout of self-doubt as to whether it is loved and admired more than it is feared and resented.

The soft power discourse has found a receptive audience among Chinese intellectuals for at least two reasons. One, it implies that China, a pariah state only a few decades ago, has finally arrived in the global capitalist order. Talking about China's soft power, even in the future tense, can be taken as an implicit form of recognition. Two, the idea of getting what one wants by means of moral suasion and cultural attraction resonates deeply with the traditional Confucian conception of power. The most fundamental article of faith in Confucian political philosophy is government by moral example, or the rule of virtue. Winning hearts and minds through the charisma of *de* (德, virtue, which is homophonous with *de* 得, to gain or obtain) guarantees legitimacy and perpetual peace, whereas dominion achieved by force can never be truly secure or free of enemies. Consider the following advice from Mencius: "There is a way to win the empire. Win the people and you win the empire. There is a way to win the people. Win their hearts and you will win the people."[17] The rule of virtue is said to be the Kingly Way (*wangdao* 王道), which would eventually bring about universal harmony and unity for all under heaven, or *tianxia datong* (天下大同). Historically, "all under heaven" was a project of moral hegemony that remained in tension with the fact that every new dynasty was founded by the sword and that no imperial regime could dispense with harsh penal codes or fend off external threats through moral charisma alone.[18] Prasenjit Duara maintains that "the universalistic claims of Chinese imperial culture constantly bumped up against, and adapted to, alternative views of the world order."[19] In other words, tianxia was necessarily supplemented by a more bounded conception of community, which could be drawn along either cultural or ethnic lines depending on the nature of the threat in a given crisis. However, the "ideological defensiveness in the face of the relativization of the conception of the universal empire (*tianxia*)" tends to be overlooked by historians who are wont to "accept Chinese declarations of universalism at face value."[20] And this includes contemporary Chinese intellectuals reaching back into the classical tradition for moral resources and theoretical inspiration in order to articulate a uniquely Chinese vision of world order.

In the past decade, a contingent of Chinese intellectuals has rallied behind Zhao Tingyang's (赵汀阳) effort to promote tianxia as an alternative to the modern world system of nation-states. Zhao propounds that "the concept of All-under-Heaven is meant to be an empire of world-ness responsible for the common happiness of all peoples."[21] In his vision, tianxia would be the signature Chinese political principle that could not only help China make others want what it wants but also underwrite a very different model of world governance, one that would, on the basis of a "reciprocity of hearts" rather than of interests, place cooperation above competition and harmony above conflict.[22] It would achieve this by reverting to a neofeudalistic way of ordering regions and economies that subordinates national sovereignty and special interests to an empirelike world institution administered by the elite. Zhao's rhetoric is deliberately evocative of Confucianism, yet has interesting echoes of the discourse of American exceptionalism, or the idea that the United States is an empire that is uniquely innocent of the vices of empire—territorial conquest, colonial rule, and so on. George Bush père may well have been ventriloquizing Zhao's custodial elite in his avowal of hegemonic benevolence: "The world trusts us with power—and the world is right. They trust us to be fair and restrained; they trust us to be on the side of decency. They trust us to do what's right."[23]

Nevertheless, tianxia is believed to be a radical departure from, and hence the very antithesis of, the none-so-benevolent Pax Americana. Yan Xuetong prophesies in the *New York Times* that China will be able to defeat America on the strength of its moral leadership: "The key to international influence was political power, and the central attribute of political power was morally informed leadership.... And, as China's ancient philosophers predicted, the country that displays more humane authority will win."[24] For Zhao, since tianxia is grounded in people's hearts rather than divine will, its legitimacy is beyond dispute. As to how to decipher people's hearts, Zhao proposes an elitist solution: "Most people do not really know what is best for them, but ... the elite do, so the elite ought genuinely to decide for the people." The people, on their part, have the "autonomy" to follow or not to follow. Democracy, therefore, would be superseded by "demo-allegiance."[25]

If tianxia advocates are like Isaiah Berlin's "hedgehogs" who are devoted to one big idea, there are also more foxlike or pragmatic intellectuals who steer clear of the fuzzily utopian discourse of tianxia and set their sights on short-to-medium-range goals that seek to enlarge China's share of soft power in the existing world order: an active role in multilateral trade cooperation, leadership in global institutions, and predominance in the transnational circuits of art and entertainment.[26] They acknowledge the status quo of American dominance and see greater possibility in a war of positions than in a war of movement, to adapt Antonio Gramsci's terminology. Recognizing that, in the words of Arif Dirlik, "China [is] able to claim a place for itself among the ranking powers of the world—not by virtue of ideological priority as a socialist state but as a country on which capital globally [has] come to depend," they search for a way to leverage that dependency.[27] Without completely ruling out the eventuality of edging out a Pax Americana with a Pax Sinica, some of them are drawn to the challenge of theorizing and propagating the so-called Chinese model of development (*Zhongguo moshi*) or Beijing Consensus (*Beijing gongshi*) to offset American hegemony. The Beijing Consensus is commonly understood as a mutually beneficial alliance of authoritarian governance and market capitalism, along the line of the Singaporean model. It is believed to be more conducive to stability and sustainable growth than the Washington Consensus, or the neoliberal formula of political democracy and laissez-faire capitalism, now discredited in the eyes of many in the developing world after the financial meltdown of 2008.[28]

However, the appeal of the Beijing Consensus has two limitations: one, it is attendant on growth rates (with built-in volatility) and per capita income levels (which will remain low given the size of the population); two, its endorsement of authoritarianism makes it a tough pill to swallow in parts of the world where democracy is still a noble ideal and inviolable principle, however people might fight over their discrepant understandings and practices thereof. So if a tianxia world order might be too utopian and the Beijing Consensus too unpalatable, in what can China ground its soft power? The report prepared by the National Soft Power Project Committee (*Guojia ruanshili ketizu* 国家软实力课题组) based at Beijing University concedes that in the foreseeable future, China's soft power offensive will be limited to the diplomatic arena.[29] Still, the state has not stinted when it comes to investing in the weak link of its soft power regime: cultural attraction.

Zhao Qizheng, former director of the State Council Information Office, had this to say about China's lackluster presence in the global marketplace for cultural and entertainment products: "If China can only export TV receivers but not attractive TV programs, it means that China cannot export its own ideas and we will become 'a hardware factory.'"[30] So far, statistics have borne out Zhao's fear: for example, in the publication trade, which encompasses books, newspapers, periodicals, and audio-video wares, China imported 12,386 copyrighted titles in 2006 while exporting only 2,057, with the caveat that overseas consumers of Chinese publications are usually concentrated in the Sinophone communities of Hong Kong, Taiwan, Southeast Asia, and North America, which constitute what Ying Zhu calls "the Greater China cultural-linguistic market."[31] In response, the PRC unveiled a five-year cultural development plan to expand channels of cross-cultural exchange, enhance Chinese media presence abroad, and boost the global competitiveness and influence of Chinese cultural products.[32] More specifically, the plan includes one thousand or so Confucius Institutes and Confucius Classrooms to promote Chinese language instruction and cultural literacy in partnership with foreign educational institutions, the Xinhua twenty-four-hour English-language news network modeled on CNN to shape world public opinion, and the China Book International program to subsidize translation and publication of Chinese books.

With keen appreciation for the centrality of audio and visual media in our hypermediated world, the five-year plan sets up a particularly ambitious goal for the film, radio, and television industries, which is to

> get China's voice heard in every part of the world. Within five years (2001–2006), our country's radio, TV, film industries should have a

major development or breakthrough in reaching out to viewers or listeners in every country in the world, especially in North America and Western Europe, and let these audience[s] have a better understanding of the "real China." Efforts should be made to let foreign audience[s] know China's position and perspective on all major international issues. In the next ten years our radio, film and TV industries should be strong enough to compete with major Western media companies.[33]

A more recent initiative aimed to win over millions globally by 2016 through a network of six CCTV hubs and eighty bureaus constituting China's "cultural aircraft carrier."[34] Behind all this is an awareness that soft power, unlike the premodern notion of moral charisma, requires active reaching out and prevailing against indifferent, resistant, or even hostile publics, or else a plethora of misperceptions about China will rule the international airwaves and cyberspace. In other words, soft power must become positively missionary, despite the warning of cultural imperialism from Zhao Tingyang, who maintains that "an empire of All-under-Heaven could only be an exemplar passively *in situ*."[35] Indeed, the imperative to present the "real" China to the world infuses a sense of moral mission into the various programs put in place to reverse China's cultural trade deficit. Underlying this crusade is dismay and frustration over the disjunction between Chinese self-perception and alleged foreign misunderstanding and distortion, between what appeals to domestic audiences and what sells in overseas markets.

In 2005, Joseph Nye opined in the *Wall Street Journal Asia* that "China's soft power still has a long way to go" despite the gains it had made in East and Southeast Asia, Africa, and Latin America: "China does not have cultural industries like Hollywood, and its universities are far from the equal of America's. It lacks the many non-governmental organizations that generate much of America's soft power. Politically, China suffers from corruption, inequality, and a lack of democracy, human rights and the rule of law. While that may make the 'Beijing consensus' attractive in authoritarian and semi-authoritarian developing countries, it undercuts China's soft power in the West."[36] The point is clear: soft power is a matter not only of source but of target. And for Nye, the target that truly matters is the West, a reluctant audience/witness/judge increasingly caught among hubris, insecurity, and begrudging acknowledgment of a multipolar world. Underlying this mixed attitude is the assumption that soft power is a zero-sum game and that China's influence, precisely because it needs to win recognition and respect from the West, can only truly grow at the expense of the latter, an assumption professedly shared by Yan Xuetong.[37] Thus China's quest for soft power is often perceived as trying to cash in on "the decline of America," which Kurlantzick dates to the Clinton years; he blames George Bush fils for the further downward spiral, "as cuts in American public diplomacy, scandals in American corporations, new restrictions on entering the United States, misguided trade policies, a retreat from multilateral institutions, and human rights abuses in Iraq, Guantánamo Bay, and other places have combined to undermine the allure of America's ideas, values, and models."[38] Once upon a time, everyone dreamed of becoming an American, but now that dream seems to be dying. For many, the election of 2016 was the final nail in the coffin.

The fading of the American dream, however, has not been accompanied by a global embrace of the China Dream. The West still exercises tremendous discursive hegemony, or what the Chinese call *huayuquan* (话语权), on the global commons, to the resentment of many non-Western states. It may be said that so long as the referee is the West, China's charm offensives will always have a whiff of wishful thinking to them. For a long time, the Chinese have blamed Western bias and ill intentions (to stymie China's rise and contain China's influence), imagining that if only Westerners could take off their ideologically tinted glasses and get to know the "real" China, all cross-cultural misunderstandings would be cleared up. Sleeping in this line of thinking is a positivist assumption that there is only one kind of national reality (*guoqing* 国情) that is self-evident to all Chinese but somehow remains stubbornly opaque to non-Chinese.

The West, for its part, is prone to conjure up the bogeyman of communism as the true obstacle that is preventing the Chinese people from embracing universal Enlightenment values and partaking of the bonanza of consumer capitalism. In this logic, if a work of art or literature were banned in China, it would be deliberately promoted as worthy of attention among conscientious Western publics as a gesture not only of protest against the Chinese government's willful abrogation of artistic freedom but also of surrogate enjoyment, for, it is imagined, ordinary Chinese are all dying to get hold of the work in question but are unable to, thanks to the curmudgeonly nanny state. When a particular work of an edgy artist unexpectedly passes censorship or even wins official endorsement, Western critics habitually go into overdrive to tease out subversive messages that must have been cleverly woven into the work in question and thus have eluded the not-so-bright party hacks. The assumption is that the artificial barriers in the global cultural commons will automatically vanish as soon as the government relinquishes its choking grip on people's freedom to create, consume, and share. In this light, the state is the cause of China's soft power deficiency, so it should be the last agent to promote Chinese culture abroad. Its patronage of culture is tantamount to a kiss of death.

The truth arguably lies somewhere in between. On the one hand, the Chinese government has been quite successful in getting the world to sign on to its signature soft power offensive, the Confucius Institutes; on the other hand, it is unable to compel foreign consumers to warm to officially packaged and overly scrubbed Chinese cultural exports, or what Dirlik calls "the song-and-dance version of Chinese culture."[39] In one way or another, this dilemma confronts all latecomers trying to reverse the prevailing tide of cultural flows from the metropolitan West to the rest. It is thus instructive to look at how Japan has coped with its soft power challenge during the era of "Japan as number one." In her article about the attraction of J-pop among American youth, Anne Allison relates how the Japanese government made news headlines trying actively to capitalize on its GNC (gross national cool), which Allison glosses as "the global prominence of Japanese creative or fantasy goods—comic books (*manga*), animation (anime), video and electronic games, youth fashion, Hello Kitty, and Pokémon collectible card games."[40] Ironically, Japan's GNC owes little to direct government sponsorship and much to the vitality of its commercial sphere and civil society. Allison quotes the inventor of the Sony Walkman, Kuroki Yasuo, lamenting that few customers outside of Japan ever play Japanese music on their Walkmans, a situation that is partly due to the practice of *mukokuseki*, the erasing or "deodorizing" of national identity from Japanese cultural products marketed abroad. As a result, "the globalization of Japanese pop culture does not equate to Japanese soft power."[41] To me, this assessment does not do justice to the leap Japan has made from exporting hardware only to commanding legions of worldwide devotees avidly consuming J-pop on (mostly) Chinese-made electronics. The discomfort about the conscious fading out of Japanese elements is probably a combined effect of the departure from an earlier, self-Orientalizing era and disorientation from plunging into the global melting pot of pop culture. While J-pop and K-pop are culturally and stylistically distinctive, few can deny that their principal appeal has less to do with their national branding than with their creative, free-wheeling blending of pop cultural memes.

Unlike Japan and South Korea, which have managed their entry into the global marketplace of pop culture fairly unproblematically (despite the above-noted disquiet) thanks in large part to their prior incorporation into the global capitalist and liberal democratic order, China faces a much higher threshold even if it is content with joining the gold rush of multiculturalism with a deodorized C-pop, or continuing to purvey a self-Orientalizing song-and-dance version of Chinese culture. But it is not. Instead, it wants to unseat the West from its monopoly of universalism in every sense of the word, cultural, moral, and political. To do this, according to Suisheng Zhao, China needs a compelling moral vision, which has so far been slow in coming into focus:

> The future growth of China's soft power, however, is seriously restrained by the fact that pragmatic political values behind China's rapid economic growth are attractive mostly to authoritarian elites. In addition, China's view of a world order derived from either the old Sinocentric hierarchy or the realist tradition with an emphasis on absolute national sovereignty is hardly compatible with evolving transnational norms. In spite of its initial success, China's current approach to soft power lacks a contemporary moral appeal and therefore is hardly sustainable in the competition with the United States to inspire the vision of building a free and prosperous world.[42]

Thus the same question returns: If the Chinese model of development appeals only to authoritarian rulers and requires continual, unsustainable high-level growth, and if a Sinocentric tianxia world order is difficult to reconcile with China's consecration of the Westphalian principle of national sovereignty, how can Chinese culture achieve transnational fungibility without the foundation of three centuries of colonialism, imperialism, and capitalism that undergirded the West's claim to be the arbiter of universalism?

During the "culture fever" of the 1980s, a seemingly paradoxical formulation—"The more Chinese something is, the more worldly/universal it will become" (*Yue shi minzu de, jiu yue shi shijie de* 越是民族的，就越是世界的)—lent justification to the roots-searching (*xungen* 寻根) fervor among writers, filmmakers, and artists, as well as the ardent embrace of classical learning (*guoxue*) among scholars. For them, China's place in the world cannot be secured with sanitized official culture but requires a robust living culture, warts and all. Arguably, it is their creative and critical endeavors that have done much to win China growing goodwill around the world. Strangely, the literature on soft power has been relatively reticent on their efforts. For example, although most of the contributors to the volume on soft power and China follow Nye's threefold definition of soft power as consisting of culture, political values, and diplomacy, they tend to concentrate on the last category, whereby they can speak of concrete initiatives, events, and statistics. Some rightly question Nye's untenable exclusion of carrots and sticks from the playing field of soft power, and insist on bringing investment, trade, foreign aid, and technology transfer into the mix. Still, besides some sociological discussions of education reforms and the cultural trade deficit problem, the volume largely steers clear of the terrain of culture or values. The international media, on the other hand, focus almost exclusively on large-scale events and programs such as the 2008 Beijing Olympics, the 2010 Shanghai Exposition, and the Confucius Institutes. These splashy but tightly scripted megaevents are quite good at packaging a hip version of Chinese culture replete with iconic Chinese elements (*Zhongguo yuansu* 中国元素) such as quotations from the classics, kung fu, and Peking opera. The image of China projected is mellow, ideologically neutral, and culturally colorful. But to the extent to which these productions reify Chinese culture and are quite remote from daily life, their soft power potential remains debatable. The gulf between lavish investments in megaevents and uncertain, even diminishing returns is perhaps the biggest drawback of any official campaign-style effort to woo global affection. Attraction, after all, rarely obliges the intention of the suitor. And for every successful charm offensive it pulls off, the government can cancel it out several times over by jailing a dissident, suppressing a mass protest, or sickening foreigners' poodles with melamine-laced pet food. That is to say, when its domestic policies or jittery concerns about legitimacy contravene what Suisheng Zhao calls "transnational norms," the damage to soft power can be heavy.

If there must be a moral vision behind the song-and-dance version of Chinese culture, both the party and many intellectuals seem to prefer Confucianism to Marxism or socialism, as is evident in their shared enthusiasm for tianxia. Aside from the problems of utopianism and elitism noted earlier, the officially sponsored Confucian revival proceeds from the assumption that a set of classical ideals can constitute a soft power source apart from the entwined operations of coercion and consent, that Confucianism has continuously and substantially underwritten China's experience of modernity, and that a century of revolutions and reforms has left no moral or spiritual imprint in Chinese society. If Nye is correct in locating the genuine source of soft power in civil society, then we need to look beyond official public relations campaigns and ask whether contemporary social and cultural life—comprising the dreams and lived experiences of ordinary Chinese, whose cultural diet surely is not limited to Confucian chicken soup for the soul—can indeed be a resource for China's bid for global cultural hegemony.

Herein lies the crux of the dialectic of soft and hard power. As Yan Xuetong clearly recognizes: "How, then, can China win people's hearts across the world? According to ancient Chinese philosophers, it must start at home. Humane authority begins by creating a desirable model at home that inspires people abroad."[43] In this we hear echoes of a passage from the 1964 American Council of Learned Societies report on the role of the humanities in America's global leadership: "World leadership of the kind which has come upon the United

States cannot rest solely upon superior force, vast wealth, or preponderant technology. Only the elevation of its goals and the excellence of its conduct entitle one nation to ask others to follow its lead. These are things of the spirit."[44] In the Chinese case, a moral vision that can guide a nation through the thicket of frenzied development may ultimately do more for China's global stature than highly orchestrated megaevents with their stilted messages and showy gimmicks. Evidence suggests that the outside world is less and less easily satisfied with fortune cookie–style Chinese culture and more and more eager to find out what excites the Chinese, what they cherish as things of the spirit.

Examining a surprise hit program about the PLA, externally the shorthand for the China threat and internally the officially anointed bearer of the core values of "the socialist spiritual civilization," can therefore help us understand the dialectics of hard and soft power. In the remaining space of this chapter, I use *Soldiers Sortie* as a case study to flesh out the moral spirit the PLA is supposed to represent: the spirit of constancy. I argue that its universalizing potential is enhanced by the enchantment of modern military technology and the bonds of manhood, both tropes freely borrowed from Hollywood. In conclusion, I ponder, with reference to *Forrest Gump*, the universal appeal of such a proto-C-pop specimen that leans on official culture but gestures toward the global cool.

Soldiers Sortie: The Soft Power of Constancy

At the most basic level, the serial is a bildungsroman about the growth and maturation of the main character, Xu Sanduo, from a country bumpkin to a prized member of a PLA elite unit.[45] In the first episode, Sanduo is a timid and inarticulate rural youth who cowers before his blisteringly domineering father and is wantonly bullied by village toughs. His father desperately wants him to join the army, hoping that the army can make a man of him and pave his path out of rural poverty. Under the father's shameless cajoling and out of pity for Sanduo, the recruiting officer, Shi Jin (史今), takes Sanduo under his wing. The village head's son Cheng Cai (成才), Sanduo's bully-in-chief, is also recruited in the same round. At the new recruits' boot camp, Cheng Cai excels in all skills, particularly marksmanship, while Sanduo withers in clumsiness and becomes the butt of collective derision. For his subpar performance, Sanduo is packed off to a tiny, godforsaken prairie outpost whose sole charge is the maintenance of the PLA's fuel pipes. It is here that Sanduo's sterling qualities begin to shine: he refuses to recognize his assignment as a punishment for his ineptitude or sink to the same listlessness that keeps the other four members of the unit at the card table from dawn to dusk, to the neglect of drill, duty, and personal hygiene. Instead, he rises each day before dawn, scrupulously makes his own bunk bed as well as those of his comrades, and discharges his sentry duty with solemnity. In response to a jesting order from the squad leader, he sets out to construct a pebble road that connects the barracks to the lookout post all by himself, undeterred by jeers and sabotage from his fellow soldiers.

When word about Sanduo's road accidentally reaches the ear of the regimental commander, who has a weakness for headstrong soldiers, Sanduo is reassigned to the famed Iron Seventh Company, in which Cheng Cai has been serving as a sharpshooter since leaving boot camp. Nearly everyone in the company, particularly the commander, Gao Cheng (高城), and deputy squad leader, Wu Liuyi (伍六一), resents Sanduo's coming, fearing that his conspicuous incompetence will drag the company down.[46] The exception is squad leader Shi Jin, who essentially becomes Sanduo's surrogate parent, shielding him from insults and patiently imparting to him the ways of soldiery. For example, Shi Jin encourages Sanduo to practice the backward flip on the single bar in order to overcome his motion sickness, a damning condition given that the Seventh Company is a mechanized reconnaissance unit. Nourished by Shi Jin's tear-soaked tenderness, Sanduo blossoms into a crack soldier, breaking records in endurance training and scoring huge points for his unit in a simulated military campaign by capturing a colonel from a rival regiment. Meanwhile, Cheng Cai shocks the whole company by announcing that he has requested to be transferred to a different unit where his matchless marksmanship is more valued. Much to his dismay, however, he is dispatched to Sanduo's old unit on the prairie, apparently as a retaliatory measure against anyone who is too full of himself.

Sometime later, Lieutenant Colonel Yuan Lang (袁朗), who was Sanduo's captive in the simulation and instinctively recognized Sanduo's worth, returns to recruit the latter for his elite unit, known only by its code name, A Team. Sanduo and anyone else who wishes to join the A Team must take part in a grueling cross-country trekking/combat exercise, and only the top three finishers will gain admission. In the final leg of the competition in which Sanduo, Cheng Cai, and Wu Liuyi are a few paces ahead of several others, Wu suffers a strained tendon and is unable to go on. Sanduo, himself barely able to walk, insists on carrying Wu to the finish line, forcing Wu to ignite his smoke signal to announce his formal withdrawal from the competition. During their tug-of-war, Cheng Cai lets go of them both and narrowly beats another soldier to the finish. At A Team's training camp, Sanduo has the most alienating experience of his military career: the officers are diabolically mean and the fellow trainees are fiercely competitive. Sanduo's only consolation is Cheng Cai's company, and yet it is soon taken away from him when the latter's failure to persevere under adverse circumstances precipitates his disqualification.

During a live-fire mission to help the armed police force intercept a narcotic-smuggling operation across the Yunnan border, Sanduo comes face to face with a gun-toting smuggler and is forced to kill him in an act of self-defense. Profoundly shaken by this experience, Sanduo becomes disillusioned with the soldier's calling. The far-sighted Yuan Lang takes the unprecedented step of granting him an extended furlough so that he can work through his psychic trauma. Sanduo visits his old unit and reconnects with his old comrades. Gradually, wholesome camaraderie heals Sanduo's psychic wound, and he returns to A Team more gung ho than ever. The serial ends with Sanduo's extraordinary performance in an elaborate military drill in which he also helps Cheng Cai redeem himself and win readmission to A Team.

The frequency of military exercises in which a full panoply of state-of-the-art weaponry is mobilized and in which firefights, explosions, and mayhem occur regularly should be enough to quell any doubts about the viability of a military-themed show set entirely in peacetime. The PLA has not seen full-scale combat since the Sino-Vietnamese Border War of 1979, largely forgotten in the popular imagination. But *Soldiers Sortie* does not disappoint even where the video game generation is concerned: there is plenty of (simulated) action and the troops are smartly attired, armed to the teeth, and digitally wired, just like American GIs in the televised wars of the past decade and a half. The hawkishly patriotic youth born in the 1980s and 1990s can find much excitement in seeing the hardware and warcraft that they read about in military history and technology magazines and websites put to live use. Small wonder that a video game has spun off from the show to satisfy this niche crowd and to capitalize on their collective techno-fantasy and what Jia Leilei calls "war complex" (*zhanzheng qingjie* 战争情结).[47]

The show thus departs radically from historically based military dramas in which PLA troops are barely distinguishable from their peasant base that is supposed to be, along with Mao Zedong thought and party leadership, the source of their mighty strength and invincibility, notwithstanding their crude rifles and ragged uniforms.[48] Their decisive victories against the Japanese and the Nationalists always redound to the true superiority of the people's war. Not only do these period dramas come off as technologically primitive, their collectivist ethos may also fail to excite in the age of consumer individualism and the absence of any present and clear danger to the motherland. The runaway success of *Soldiers Sortie* would not be possible without the thrills afforded by the foregrounding of military hardware. The makers are clearly confident that today's youth are far more likely to be enchanted by technological wizardry than by the (unfamiliar) strength of collective action.[49] In a way, the latest emphasis on technology signals the entrenchment of the military-industrial-entertainment complex in which the PLA has been a central player. Throughout PRC cinematic history, PLA soldiers have routinely filled in as extras in war epics and historical sagas that feature large crowd scenes. As late as 2008 they supplied the principal manpower to Zhang Yimou's body-intensive opening and closing ceremonies of the Beijing Olympics. With *Soldiers Sortie*, the PLA is now able to deliver (simulated) war as a spectator sport and corner a slice of the mass entertainment market after it was ordered to withdraw from sundry lucrative industries in the late 1990s.[50]

Running parallel to the enchantment of technology is the show's emphatic portrayal of manliness. Again, this is a show that boldly claims audience attention with an all-male cast. What it offers in abundance, in lieu of romance and sex, is masculine rivalry and homosocial bonding that are evocative of many Hollywood classics. Crucially, loyalty to comrades has replaced patriotism as the first principle. Sanduo does not join the army for the usual lofty reasons that even a minimally educated rural youth like him should be able to parrot: to defend the motherland, to protect her territorial integrity, and to safeguard state property and the people's livelihood. Instead, he is driven into the army by an opportunistic father who practically stuffs him down the throat of the recruiting officer. Once inducted, Sanduo strives hard only in order to reciprocate Shi Jin's saintly kindness and to win the acceptance of those who disparage his abilities (or lack thereof) and who make light of Shi's blind faith in him. A nonsmoker himself but eager to please his chain-smoking mates, he keeps a pack of cigarettes always on him, so that he can peripherally partake of the male ritual of sharing a smoke.[51] Eventually, he wins the trust and affection of all his comrades, including the haughty Gao Cheng, who has zero tolerance for incompetence, and the sniping Wu Liuyi, who is jealous of his best buddy Shi Jin's willingness to cut him slack repeatedly and give him a second chance. Others who have made sport of his rustic gaucheness come to admire his simple virtues and bond with him unconditionally.

In his awkward taciturnity, Sanduo serves as a placid mirror in which the whole spectrum of masculine splendor is reflected: from the regiment commander's avuncular leadership to the commissar's paternal magnanimity, the lieutenant colonel's raffish swagger, the company leader's imperious demand for perfection, the squad leader's gentle mentorship, and the deputy squad leader's warmth beneath a stony exterior, and fellow soldiers' teasing jocularity. As is commonly pointed out, each of these servicemen sports a distinctive personality from which is derived much of the show's attraction and dramatic tension. Xueping Zhong locates the show's appeal in its attempt to bring back idealism, albeit in a different key, by making the personality quirks of the soldiers the focus of narrative representation.[52] Instead of larger-than-life heroes like Lei Feng (雷锋) or cynical antiheroes common in youth dramas, the soldiers are both robustly human and eminently elevated. The vast majority of fan commentary is devoted to spelling out their subtle differences of temperament and to rating them for likeability or, for female fans, marriageability. These characters have thus come a long way from the bland uniformity that typically characterizes PLA screen images. As one commentator puts it: "Among the countless army-themed domestic productions, this is probably the first time when PLA servicemen are treated as individualized beings, each with his own soul and value. They are no longer conflated with the 'people' or weighted down by the freight of country or nation. In other words, the 'people' are no longer the default backdrop of war, for on the battleground there are no people, only comrades."[53] The men in the show are first and foremost comrades to each other. Country, party, and people come second, if at all. There is a distinct sense that they are not nameless automatons at the beck and call of some greater authority and ready to charge at equally nameless enemies, even if as PLA troops they must play that role. In this show at least, they rather resemble the warriors in *Romance of the Three Kingdoms*, who place personal loyalty and male bonding above all else (certainly wives, children, and personal well-being), or the band of strongmen who congregate on Mount Liang to revel in their sworn brotherhood and enforce their own brand of justice, as memorably portrayed in *Outlaws of the Marsh*. Though quite free of the mystical trappings of kung fu or swordplay drama, the show is a contemporary update of the knight-errantry genre, thereby tapping into a deep cultural reservoir of meaning and winning audiences almost in spite of itself. The soldiers occasionally evince an awareness of the larger causes they serve, but there is never any doubt that their allegiance is overwhelmingly to their immediate commanders and closest comrades. Even the officers betray very little careerism or care much for military glory: as Yuan Lang puts it, "I wrack my brains in devising strategies and tactics, and yet I dare not speak casually of victory. My only goal is to lose fewer soldiers in the battlefield."[54] One need only recall Mao's declaration that China was prepared to sacrifice half of its population in a nuclear showdown with the Soviet and American superpowers in order to appreciate the radicalness of such rumination. There is a palpable sense that every soldier is to be genuinely treasured and no one will be cavalierly let go as mere cannon fodder.

The enchantment of technology and the bonds of manhood, however, are common attractions in war stories. What makes *Soldiers Sortie* stand out and gives it soulful resonance across a broad spectrum of viewers is its consecration of the principle of constancy. In the Aristotelian as well as Confucian traditions, constancy is the ur-virtue that presupposes the wholeness of a human life unified by a singleness of purpose.[55] In our fragmented modern world where the individual is practically immobilized by an abundance of choice, the army furnishes the best possible context for conceiving of one's life as dedicated to an overarching purpose. When Sanduo is reassigned to the Iron Seventh Company, he is made to swear a six-character oath in a ceremony unique to that company: "Never let go, never give up" (*Bu paoqi, bu fangqi* 不抛弃，不放弃). Behind this oath is the company's peculiar way of reckoning its membership and its history. Sanduo is told that he is the company's 4,956th member since its founding. Of the 4,955 soldiers, 1,104 have laid down their lives for the country. During the Korean War, the company suffered near total annihilation and came close to being disbanded. But three soldiers miraculously made it to base camp alive and brought back the will of the 107 martyrs: to rebuild the Iron Seventh Company. "From then on," roars the inducting officer, "the Seventh Company has kept alive the memory of the martyrs and thrived on their hope and honor." Sanduo then joins the entire group in "singing" the tuneless company anthem—tuneless because those who knew the tune are all dead.

While such talk of martyrdom may seem typical of the PLA, what is new is that the feeling of belonging and the sense of mission are overwhelmingly cathected to a single unit. Indeed, the words "motherland" and "party" are scarcely uttered. Cheng Cai's voluntary withdrawal from the Seventh Company is unmistakably construed as an act of betrayal that indelibly marks him as a lesser man, though one could make the argument that he might serve the army and country better in another unit. In this regard, the Seventh Company is no different from any football team in America, toward which local loyalty can be so ardent as to blot out any sense of a national community.

Underlying the company's intense local pride is the spirit of constancy as encapsulated in the six-character oath. Other units, we are told, may take pride in having produced a decorated war hero or having a general rise through their ranks, but the Seventh Company's greatest glory is its members' adherence to the iron principle of constancy. Again and again, the six-character slogan is recited as an incantation to rally morale, boost performance, and enforce cohesion. Taking the slogan to heart is what turns Sanduo into a man and soldier, and taking it all too casually is what renders Cheng Cai the only character in the show whose manliness is found wanting. During routine training as well as simulated war exercises, Sanduo excels not only because he never hesitates to put his body and spirit through harrowing tests, but also because he never wavers in his faith in the goodness of his comrades or in his willingness and determination to give them all he has.

Building a road single-handedly and training to overcome his motion sickness are only the two most dramatic instances of Sanduo's spirit of constancy. In fact, just about everything he undertakes, mostly mundane, instantiates this virtue. For example, after the Seventh Company is dissolved during a major personnel reform, Sanduo and company leader Gao Cheng are the only two left in the empty barracks for a stretch of several months.[56] Gao sinks into a state of despondency, but Sanduo acts as if nothing unusual had transpired: he goes about his goody-two-shoes ways as if all his comrades were right there beside him. His unflappability utterly exasperates Gao, who screams and flails wildly in front of him, to little effect. A scene like this—in which an officer egregiously abuses an underling for simply doing his duty—is unthinkable in the older mode of portraying the PLA and army life. Yet here, it endears both characters to the audience by accentuating Gao's manly impetuosity as well as Sanduo's generosity of spirit.

For the sake of drama, Sanduo's constancy is conveyed in qualities that are normally deprecated as blockheadedness, obstinacy, tunnel vision, or, to use a Chinese expression, *yigenjin* (一根筋, having only a single tendon, or being mulish and clueless). One can argue that Sanduo is set up in the tradition of the idiot savant whose profound inner wisdom is incompatible with ordinary lingua franca and is therefore perceived by lesser intellects as stupidity, a tradition summed up in the Chinese idiom *dazhi ruo yu* (大智若愚). Or as Gao Cheng puts it, Sanduo is "a brave man born with the face of a coward." His lack of easy charm would also make him quite at home in a Jane Austen novel, in the company of such Austenian heroines of constancy as Fanny Price (*Mansfield Park*) and Anne Elliot (*Persuasion*). "Charm," as Alasdair MacIntyre explains, "is the characteristically modern quality which those who lack or simulate the virtues use to get by in the situations of characteristically modern social life." Compared with Elizabeth Bennet or Emma Woodhouse, "Fanny is charmless; she has only the virtues, the genuine virtues, to protect her. . . . She pursues virtue for the sake of a certain kind of happiness and not for its utility."[57] Likewise, Sanduo has no other purpose in life than to do his job well and thereupon suture his self into a larger unity. He does not turn against anyone, or give up on anything until he reaches perfection or wins approval.

In his unbending steadfastness, Sanduo is also a figure of innocence, standing aloof from the world of calculation, opportunism, vainglory, and ressentiment. For this reason, he has been likened to Forrest Gump, the fictional half-wit American GI from Alabama whose life intersects with nearly all the momentous events of postwar U.S. history and who comes out of each a triumphant hero without, however, losing an ounce of his insouciant innocence. Critics have denounced the film as a right-wing farcical rendition of the progressive movements that have so profoundly transformed American society: the civil rights movement, the feminist movement, the antiwar movement, the gay liberation movement, the countercultural movement, and so on. Stephen Brockmann calls Gump a "Teflon character" who goes through this turbulent history without having his feathers ruffled or his single-minded commitment to goodness soiled by war, ideology, cynicism, or racism.[58] He is in American history but not of it. A fatherless child, he lives by his mother's folksy motto: "Life is like a box of chocolates. You never know what you're gonna get." In an era in which a smorgasbord of emerging groups clamors for rights, recognition, and entitlement, Gump alone makes no claim on society or the government. Rather, he takes what he is given and gives back plenty more. In an era of sexual permissiveness, Gump has just one sexual encounter, with his childhood sweetheart Jenny, who only at the very end, dying of AIDS, requites his lifelong chaste love. While serving in Vietnam, Gump has no notion of the horrors of war and manages to win a medal of honor by saving his comrades under enemy fire without having to kill anyone himself. For Brockmann, Gump glides through this period of generalized loss of innocence in American history with his virginal innocence completely intact.[59]

There are many parallels between Gump and Sanduo. Sanduo never entertains thoughts about money, women, or sex (the only time money troubles his head is when he tries to help his father repay a ruinous debt). A motherless child, he lives by his father's tautological motto: "What is meaningful is a well-lived life; to live a good life is to do meaningful things." Again, this translates into just one thing for Sanduo: to do what he is told and to do it well. Meaning, in fact, is the last thing that worries him. Xueping Zhong reads this circular maxim as betokening the moral and ideological void in contemporary Chinese society: "While there is a desire for meaning that is more than material success and possessions, the society as a whole is unsure about what should constitute that meaning."[60] I would add that the show fills the void with the prosaic, even vacuous virtue of constancy without probing too deeply into the substantive question of meaning and value—as a way of skirting ideological commitment. In other words, Sanduo does not stand for any specific principle or creed whose validity or desirability might be subject to debate; instead, he is a cipher for the universal virtue of perseverance and diligence. Every human enterprise could surely use a few Sanduos.

Blessedly free of prejudice and paranoia, Sanduo never imagines that others could harm him or that being a soldier might require him to harm or kill others. In all his strivings in the army, "doing meaningful things" has meant no more than winning approval from his commanders and acceptance from his comrades, never maiming or killing. Hence the only time Sanduo's innocence is deeply threatened is when he comes face to face with the menacing drug trafficker. His first and only act of killing nearly unravels him. But like Gump's sole sexual experience that comes to him unbidden and is symbolically purified through fertility (it is the only sex act in the film that is reproductive, leading to the birth of his son), Sanduo's act of killing is easily forgivable: the enemy is a despicable criminal who holds a female accomplice hostage and nearly stabs Sanduo fatally when Sanduo tackles him.

Still, for the first time Sanduo begins to have doubts about the meaning of military service and contemplates giving up a promising career. During his furlough, he briefly wanders into a nearby city, changes into civilian clothes, and window-shops on a bustling street. But very quickly he grows restless and beats a hasty retreat to the barracks. When news about his father's botched business venture and ensuing debts reaches him, he returns to the village ready to take charge and help his father and brother to their feet with the funds that Yuan Lang has raised on his behalf. Here the show diverges quite significantly from *Forrest Gump*. Although Gump has never had entrepreneurial ambitions, after his best buddy nicknamed Bubba, a black GI from Florida, dies of a combat wound, he buys a shrimping boat as a way of vicariously fulfilling Bubba's life-long wish to go into the shrimp business. Almost miraculously, his business takes off and he finds himself willy-nilly a rich man. Gump's innocence is thus handsomely rewarded, and his success reenacts the American dream and reaffirms the fundamental American faith in the fairness of free market capitalism. When Sanduo turns over the money pooled from his comrades to his father—to bail him out of jail and repay his debts—the PLA is essentially playing a therapeutic role of healing the self-inflicted wounds of reckless entrepreneurship. It is the stolid pillar of constancy in a society giddily caught up in the maelstrom of capitalist profit seeking.

In my article on how the official iconography of Tiananmen Square relies on PLA martyrology and pageantry to animate the charisma of power, I borrow Prasenjit Duara's notion of the "regime of authenticity" to highlight the symbolic status of the PLA in the Chinese social imaginary.[61] I argue that the PLA is a vehicle of unchanging authenticity that anchors the ceaseless and turbulent transformations of contemporary China. In *Soldiers Sortie*, the principle of constancy reinforces the symbolic role of the PLA as the authentic core of Chinese society. Li Yang, one of the producers of the serial, puts it this way: "*Soldiers Sortie* is not a work of 'creation' [*chuangxin* 创新], but one of 'return' [*huigui* 回归]. It's about returning to the traditional authenticity of military culture, to its enduring spirit, which our nation and people can never afford to lose. . . . We have striven hard and wandered about for 30 years while chanting the slogan of 'marching to the world' [*zouxiang shijie* 走向世界]. Now it's time to go home for a visit."[62] If army barracks are our true home, then PLA soldiers are our true selves. *Soldiers Sortie* invites its audiences on a homecoming journey to reconnect with their true selves, and viewers have fervently signed on, gushing endlessly about the show's nobility of spirit and profundity of message.

Unlike the military parades periodically staged in Tiananmen Square, the serial gives greater weight to individual innocence and probity than to collective discipline and integrity. Its viral popularity indicates that the soldiers as quirky individuals in *Soldiers Sortie* are far more capable of winning audiences than those faceless bodies moving in lockstep, however breathtaking they may be as a human machine. The limited overseas coverage of the sixtieth anniversary celebration of the founding of the People's Republic on October 1, 2009, largely focused on the unprecedented display of advanced weaponry in the military parade. Keen observers were left wondering how this new emphasis on military hardware and striking capability could be squared with the official cant of China's peaceful rise and the government's soft power agendas. While the parade was certainly intended to awe domestic and international spectators alike, particularly those who might challenge China's sovereignty claims, I argue that displays of military might cannot be separated from the PLA's place in the larger political culture, and that a technologically enhanced PLA, showcased much more fully and dynamically in programs like *Soldiers Sortie* than in Tiananmen Square, can be as much a source of enchantment as an instrument of aggression or domination.

Conclusion

I hope to have convinced my readers that one can learn much about what kind of soft power giant China is likely to become from scrutinizing a television program not expressly intended for foreign viewers that allows a revealing glimpse into potentially deeper sources of soft power: the elevated goals and exemplary conduct that make up a nation's ethico-political capital. The unforgiving reality of the cultural trade deficit, particularly the inability of Chinese television programs—perhaps the best barometer of the national psyche—to cross borders, reminds us that China is far from ready to parlay that capital into moral suasion in the global arena. The world's love affair with China is still largely fixated on economic numbers rather than on things of the spirit. At some level, this sits quite well with China, as it first and foremost wants to be strong and powerful, so as permanently to forestall any future replay of the century of humiliation (*bainian guochi* 百年国耻). Yet it also wants to be admired and loved. Above all, it wants to be regarded as an unstoppable rising power that has something valuable and healing to offer a world buffeted by terrorism, financial crises, and climate change. Straining to shed the image of a "fragile superpower" struggling with a troubled past and an uncertain future,[63] it seeks to project the image of "a trustworthy, cooperative, peace-loving, developing country that takes good care of its enormous population"[64] and will gladly extend that paternal care to the rest of the world, because it has both the wherewithal and the goodwill to do so.

Anyone who claims that China is poised to remake the world in its image needs first of all to spell out how China sees itself, or rather, how the Chinese see themselves. It is a tall order, as the Chinese self-image is increasingly a contingent, pluralized product of contentious negotiations between an overweening state and a restless population, and it may or may not resonate with the kitschy, Orientalized, and slickly harmonious image deliberately projected outward. It is for this reason that we turn to a popular television serial that seems to have ignited a national effervescence and been embraced at the grassroots level as an idealized collective self-portrait. In Ming Zhenjiang's assessment, the appeal of *Soldiers Sortie* can be summed up in three words: sincerity (*zhencheng* 真诚), truthfulness (*zhenshi* 真实), and passion (*zhenqing* 真情).[65] Another commentator notes that the story feels authentic and true to life precisely because it refrains from haranguing the viewer or loading up on "MSG and pepper powder," that is, the kind of spices that the inclusion of, say, a general's daughter or a female journalist can add to bland army life. The resulting work is sunnier and more uplifting than many main-melody offerings: there are no dark secrets or unwritten rules at play. With the minor exception of Cheng Cai (who has a mild case of individualism but is reintegrated into the brotherhood at the end), everyone is admirably upright and transparent. Thus "it is truly a realm of purity [*jingtu* 净土, a Buddhist term]," opines the same commentator.[66]

In particular, Sanduo presents the cleanest slate, completely free of psychic demons and personal guilt. He is as much a Pollyannaish yet ultimately loveable chap to his comrades as a lean and mean fighting machine for the state.

He may be a simpleton, the show suggests, but only a man of constancy like him can truly anchor the nation in the vertigo of frenzied growth and development. He may not be as recognizably Chinese as Confucius or the panda, but his improbable chemistry with Chinese audiences suggests that the moral appeal of which Suisheng Zhao speaks may well be grounded in his artless combination of strength and innocence, even if his mindless conformity evokes uncomfortable associations for some viewers. That the Chinese should choose to attach the ideal of innocence to a PLA soldier may also strike an international observer as eerily sinister in view of the PLA's role in the 1989 Tiananmen massacre. And yet in post-Mao political culture, innocence and goodwill seem perversely bound up with dazzling demonstrations of muscle power in a way reminiscent of the pre-Vietnam American imaginary of the world wars. Not only must Sanduo and his comrades accomplish kung fu–esque feats of valor and engage in genuine derring-do during drills, the show also has to roll out state-of-the-art military technologies and campaign maneuvers—at least the nonsecret kind. In other words, the soldiers' attraction does not rest with their nice guy image alone.[67] Likewise, Forrest Gump possesses preternatural physical gifts (in running and playing ping pong) that he is able to translate into entrepreneurial advantages and winds up a wealthy businessman without having to exploit or harm anyone or anything. He is perhaps the most morally impeccable capitalist ever to have graced the silver screen. Wealth, like power, enchants, and the kind of innocence that can ride mammon fascinates far more than the kind that is chained to penury. Whereas the latter is oftentimes a virtue made out of necessity, the former requires zenlike detachment or Daoist going with the flow— "You never know what you're gonna get." Indeed, what could better legitimize capitalism than a noble fool like Gump who sits atop a pile of money and yet is endlessly fascinated by a feather fluttering in the wind?

Only a couple of decades ago Chinese filmgoers enthusiastically embraced *Forrest Gump*, having resolved to put history (Maoism and 1989, among other things) behind and become a nation of "no-nonsense" (*bu zheteng* 不折腾) capitalist roaders.[68] They seemed eager to prove the producer, Steve Tisch, right when he claimed, somewhat disingenuously, that "all over the political map, people have been calling Forrest their own. But, *Forrest Gump* isn't about politics or conservative values. It's about humanity, it's about respect, tolerance and unconditional love."[69] Such claims of moral universality have long been vital to American soft power, so much so that a conservative "emptying out of [progressive] history" can masquerade as a paean to unconditional love.[70] If Gump once made Pax Americana palatable to many, perhaps deceptively so, can Sanduo or some later avatar become the human face of the Beijing Consensus and supply the moral gravitas to a Pax Sinica? The prominent economist Lang Xianping (朗咸平) seems to think so, lauding Sanduo for exemplifying the traditional Chinese virtues of sincerity, loyalty, and unquestioning dedication to duty on the one hand, and the quintessential capitalist spirit of trust and responsibility on the other. Lang also prefers Sanduo to Lei Feng on consideration of the former's bottom-up emergence as a popularly acclaimed hero, however homely and obtuse, as opposed to a top-down, officially manufactured flawless paragon: "Today we don't need the government to tell us what to do, because truth and justice are lodged in our own hearts. . . . The spirit of Xu Sanduo is the reverberation of the inner voices of the common people."[71] If, as Zhao Tingyang tells us, tianxia is rooted in people's hearts, then Sanduo may well be its image ambassador (*xingxiang dashi* 形象大使). The brave new empire presupposes a benevolent arbiter, but the show leaves who that might be out of the picture and urges us to stop worrying and learn to love the PLA as the constant guardian of world peace.

NOTES

1. See surveys by Ying Zhu (*Television in Post-reform China*) and Xueping Zhong (*Mainstream Culture Refocused*) of the major subgenres of Chinese television drama, including dynasty or emperor drama, anticorruption drama, youth drama, and family-marriage drama. Zhong discusses *Soldiers Sortie* (which she translates as *Soldiers, Be Ready*) as a youth drama, though it is more commonly referred to in Chinese media as a *junlüpian* (军旅片, army life or barracks drama), which is a relatively marginal subgenre.

2. Qi Zhenxin, "*Shibing tuji.*"

3. *Bu paoqi, bu fangqi*, 196–197. Subsequent references to this compilation of reviews, blogs, and reminiscences use the abbreviation ss for *Soldiers Sortie*.

4. SS, 175. Many have pointed out that Wang Baoqiang's own background bears some resemblance to the role he plays. In 2007, at the height of the show's popularity, on a popular website Wang Baoqiang was voted the most influential young Chinese born after 1980, beating out such youth idols as Yao Ming and Han Han, who essentially lost the top spot to a fictional character. See Zhong, *Mainstream Culture Refocused*, 119; and "Dreams Do Come True."

5. SS, 176, 184; see also Wood, "The Spirit of Xu Sanduo."

6. Luo Junpeng, "*Shibing tuji* Riben duode 'Haiwai youxiu dianshiju' jiang."

7. It is difficult to imagine how the general audience in Japan might respond to *Soldiers Sortie*, given the overall dearth of military-themed film or television programming in an avowedly pacifist society. See Frühstück, *Uneasy Warriors*. In a talk at Stanford University, Frühstück points out that the Japanese video game industry has been able to circumvent the domestic ambivalence toward war and the military engendered by the contradiction between Article 9 of the Constitution and having one of the world's top ten ranked mili-

tary forces, by collaborating with the U.S.-based military-industrial complex to provide violent, often reality-based war games to both teenage gamers and military recruits. Perhaps *Soldiers Sortie* would have been viewed as a kind of surrogate virtual war game. But the fact that the deal did not go through may have something to do with the unease that a militarily strong China might arouse in a Japanese audience.

8. See Keane, "From National Preoccupation to Overseas Aspiration," on the Chinese television industry's effort to achieve export status. So far, its most successful exports are costume dramas adapted from beloved traditional novels or set in ascendant periods of dynastic history. Surprisingly, a few military-historical-themed dramas have done well in the Korean market, but Keane does not elaborate on this (152). Also see Zhu, *Television in Post-reform China*, 101–125, for a survey of the three Chinese-language television genres that have dominated "the Chinese cultural-linguistic market": the PRC's dynasty dramas, Taiwan's youth idol dramas, and Hong Kong's martial arts and social mobility dramas.

9. Wines, "China Tries to Add Cultural Clout."

10. Nye, *Bound to Lead*.

11. Li, *Soft Power*.

12. Nye, *Bound to Lead*; Nye, *Soft Power*.

13. Nye, *Soft Power*, x–xi.

14. For a perceptive analysis of the relevance of the Gramscian notion of hegemony to the study of international relations and the discourse of soft power, see Zahran and Ramos, "From Hegemony to Soft Power." See Fraser, *Weapons of Mass Distraction*, 18–33, for a discussion of why "soft power" more aptly captures the decentralized processes of globalization than does "cultural imperialism."

15. Li, *Soft Power*, 3–4.

16. Zahran and Ramos, "From Hegemony to Soft Power," 20.

17. Chan, *A Source Book in Chinese Philosophy*, 74.

18. Dreyer, "The 'Tianxia Trope.'"

19. Duara, "De-constructing the Chinese Nation," 33.

20. Duara, "De-constructing the Chinese Nation," 33.

21. Zhao Tingyang, "Rethinking Empire from a Chinese Concept," 34.

22. Zhao Tingyang, "Rethinking Empire from a Chinese Concept," 35.

23. George H. W. Bush, quoted in Layne, "The Unbearable Lightness of Soft Power," 60.

24. Yan Xuetong, "How China Can Defeat America."

25. Zhao Tingyang, "Rethinking Empire from a Chinese Concept 'All-under-Heaven' (Tian-xia)," 31, 32. Callahan (*China Dreams*; *China*) finds Zhao's tianxia project problematic on two fronts: the decontextualized and ahistorical appropriation of the Chinese classics and the superficial critique of the West and lack of engagement with progressive Western social theory. In Callahan's view, a tianxia world order that has no "outside" and possesses "a view from everywhere" smacks of utopianism and elitism, ignoring the history of punitive campaigns and conquests on the frontiers of the Chinese empire and substituting hierarchical assimilation of difference (*hua*) for genuine regard for alterity. In essence, tianxia is "a patriotic form of cosmopolitanism" (*China*, 209) that has resonance domestically rather than a viable planetary program of perpetual peace. In Zhao's defense,

he has always seen tianxia as unabashedly utopian: "It refers to a theoretical or *conceptual* empire that has never really existed" ("Rethinking Empire from a Chinese Concept 'All-under-Heaven' (Tian-xia)," 34, emphasis in original). The elitism charge too may not bother Zhao, who deems "demo-allegiance" vastly superior to democracy, whereby "the masses always make the wrong choices for themselves" (32). The barely disguised hubris does little to appeal to a Western academe highly sensitized against imperialist pretensions. June Dreyer ("The 'Tianxia Trope,' " 1031), for example, is blunt in her critique: "Supporters of the revival of *tianxia* as a model for today's world are essentially misrepresenting the past to talk about the present 以古为今, distorting it in order to advance an equally distorted political agenda . . . [and] selectively comparing the theories of one system with the practices of the other, essentially rewriting history in a manner that is at best disingenuous and at worst dangerous."

26. Berlin, *The Hedgehog and the Fox.*

27. Dirlik, "June Fourth at 25," 306.

28. Kennedy, "The Myth of the Beijing Consensus."

29. See Wu Nong, "Zhongguo de ruanshili zai nali?"

30. Zhao Qizheng, quoted in Li, *Soft Power*, 145.

31. Li, *Soft Power*, 150; Zhu, *Television in Post-reform China*, 107.

32. Li, *Soft Power*, 146.

33. Quoted in Li, *Soft Power*, 152.

34. Branigan, "Chinese State TV Unveils Global Expansion Plan."

35. Zhao Tingyang, "Rethinking Empire from a Chinese Concept 'All-under-Heaven' (Tian-xia)," 36.

36. Nye, "The Rise of China's Soft Power."

37. Yan Xuetong, "How China Can Defeat America."

38. Kurlantzick, *Charm Offensive*, 10, see also ch. 9.

39. Jensen, "Culture Industry, Power"; Dirlik, "June Fourth at 25," 315.

40. Allison, "The Attractions of the J-Wave," 100.

41. Allison, "The Attractions of the J-Wave," 104, 105.

42. Li, *Soft Power*, 247.

43. Yan Xuetong, "How China Can Defeat America."

44. ACLS, *Report of the Commission on the Humanities*, 5.

45. The meaning of Sanduo's name is ambiguous. Xueping Zhong believes it means "the third who is one too many" (as Sanduo is his father's third son) (*Mainstream Culture Refocused*, 117). I prefer "triple plentiful" on the assumption that there can never be too many sons for a rural Chinese family, even a poor family.

46. The serial identifies the officers sometimes by rank and sometimes by position. The English equivalents used here are at best approximations.

47. Jia Leilei in *SS*, 185.

48. *SS*, 184.

49. *SS*, 185.

50. In November 2011, a twelve-part reality show also called *Soldiers Sortie* aired on the Yunnan Satellite Station, featuring ninety PLA soldiers competing for the title of "soldier king" (*bingwang*) by running the gauntlet of nearly forty "devil's tests." At the

end of the program, the top sixteen contenders would be recruited into a special force unit of the People's Armed Police. According to *Southern Weekly*, this was the first time that the PLA participated in a television reality show, following precariously on the heels of a restraining order on mindless entertainment from the State Administration on Radio, Film, and Television. Li Yilan, "*Shibing tuji*: Shouge budui canyu de xuanxiu jiemu," *Nanfang zhoumo*, December 1, 2011, http://www.infzm.com/content/65112. Earlier in the year, a twenty-four-part serial titled *I Belong to the Special Force Unit* (*Wo shi tezhongbing*), adapted from a popular online novel, *Save the Last Bullet for Me* (*Zuihou yi ke zidan liugei wo*), aired on China Central Television Station and pushed audience enthusiasm for techno-machismo to new heights.

51. Kohrman, "Depoliticizing Tobacco's Exceptionality."

52. Zhong, *Mainstream Culture Refocused*, 121.

53. *SS*, 5.

54. *SS*, 3.

55. MacIntyre, *After Virtue*, 203.

56. The reform was part of Jiang Zemin's military modernization drive of the 1990s, aimed at transforming the PLA into a streamlined high-tech fighting force. According to Xiaobing Li, PLA personnel were reduced by nearly half, from 4.24 million in 1985 to 2.5 million in 1997 (*A History of the Modern Chinese Army*, 276).

57. MacIntyre, *After Virtue*, 242.

58. Brockmann, "Virgin Father and Prodigal Son," 353.

59. Brockmann, "Virgin Father and Prodigal Son," 356.

60. Zhong, *Mainstream Culture Refocused*, 121.

61. Lee, "The Charisma of Power."

62. *SS*, 199.

63. Shirk, *China*.

64. d'Hooghe, "Public Diplomacy in the People's Republic of China," 88

65. Ming Zhenjiang, in *SS*, 179.

66. Ming Zhenjiang, in *SS*, 149.

67. A counterexample would be *A World without Thieves* (*Tianxia wu zei* 天下无贼, dir. Feng Xiaogang, 2005), which casts Wang Baoqiang as a migrant worker named Shagen (傻根, country rube) who refuses to believe that anyone could be so evil as to rob him of his hard-earned cash on his train ride back home. His self-willed vulnerability poses an ethical challenge to his would-be robbers, and the railway journey is turned into a moving stage for a high-octane martial arts showdown between the cabal that tries to rob him and the one that tries to protect him. The drama and enchantment are concentrated on the master thief (played by the Hong Kong superstar Andy Lau) and his nemesis (played by the mainland superstar Ge You), not Shagen, the passive cipher of guileless naïveté. In the international arena, Kurlantzick points to America's military power when assessing its soft power advantages over China, for military power can complement soft power, especially when deployed for humanitarian missions (*Charm Offensive*, 227). Domestically the PLA has always been at the forefront of disaster relief, which has, in the post-Tiananmen era, greatly restored its image. As China begins to participate in international peacekeeping and humanitarian missions, the PLA will likely be able to contribute more directly to

China's soft power. See Bell's reflection ("War, Peace, and China's Soft Power") on how the Mencian theory of just and unjust war can provide the moral foundation for China's role in international conflict and help check the temptation for imperial ventures.

68. At a conference held in 2008 to commemorate thirty years of reform and opening up, then president Hu Jintao made the following remarks: "As long as we don't waver, don't slack off and don't *zheteng* [折腾], and as long as we firmly push forward reform and opening up . . . we are certain to be able to successfully realize this grand blueprint and achieve the goals we are striving for." The colloquial expression *bu zheteng* elicited chuckles from the audience. Yet at a subsequent press conference, the official interpreter left it untranslated, leaving many overseas Chinese and foreign reporters baffled. China's netizens took up the challenge, offering up a number of possible renditions, including "don't flip-flop," "don't get sidetracked," "don't sway back and forth," "no dithering," and "no major changes." I prefer to be descriptive: "no more pointless expenditure of time and energy." Various opinion pieces seem to have converged on an interpretation of steadfast pragmatism and repudiation of the ideologically driven campaigns and political movements that have supposedly derailed China's developmental path in the past. These moments of zheteng would include not only Mao's class struggles but also the 1989 protests. See "Hu Jintao's '*Bu Zheteng*' Baffles Foreign Media"; Peh Shing Huei, "What Is That Again, Mr Hu?"

69. Steve Tisch, quoted in Byers, "History Re-membered," 420.

70. Byers, "History Re-membered," 421.

71. Lang Xianping, "*Shibing tuji* de jingjixue."

11

TRACKING TIANXIA

On Intellectual Self-Positioning

Chishen Chang and Kuan-Hsing Chen

*

For the past two decades, China's rising economic and political power in the international arena has triggered rounds of intellectual debate. For those of us living outside mainland China, these debates have exerted an impact on our domestic intellectual life as interaction across the strait becomes more and more intensified. As the regional economy becomes more integrated and politics more entangled, critical intellectual work in Taiwan can no longer be isolated from mainland China, as it has been since 1949. Twenty years ago, it was easy to take a political and theoretical position in support of the June Fourth student movement in Tiananmen without any sense of internal political dynamics. Now an event like Liu Xiaobo winning the Nobel Peace Prize produces an emotional split in the expatriate circle of thought. Whether we like it or not, mainland China's problem has become our own. Having said that, we also have to admit that, lacking a sense of the postwar lived history of mainland China, not to mention the long-lost ability to speak to mainland China as a whole, it is difficult for us to enter the debates.

Nevertheless, a different trajectory of historical experiences and practices may provide a more open-ended anchoring point, and we do believe that a transitory speaking position can perhaps contribute something meaningful to the debates. The recent debate focuses on the contrast between the first thirty years of the People's Republic after 1949 and the thirty years of Deng's reform.[1] One major concern is with contemporary crises: increasing cleavages in society, widening inequality, and rural-urban polarization in a growing economy. The issue resonates with the problematic of the early subaltern studies articulated by Indian scholars: Why was the peasantry sidelined by the postcolonial Indian state in the wake of the people's successful mobilization and empowerment in the anticolonial struggle? China's situation is different. For the first thirty years of the People's Republic, the peasantry and urban working class were hailed as the subjects of the communist nation and masters of a new socialist society. In the reform era, however, they have become the victims of capitalist market development. The massive flow of labor from rural areas to urban centers in search of low-paying jobs is a sure sign that the Chinese peasantry is devalued and the village community is being eroded. Meanwhile, a substantial number of workers in state-owned industries lost their jobs during the liberalization process. Can one attribute China's phenomenal growth to its recent integration with the global market? Did the Mao era's infrastructure pave the way for Deng's reforms and later changes? Is there a pure rupture between the two periods? Is the market turn to capitalism a transitional stage toward socialism? Does one see the sixty years of PRC history as one single process? As the debate rages on, one thing is certain: its context can no longer be confined within the national boundaries. China is fully integrated into the global economic and political system, and the country's domestic contradictions have to be explained in relation to local as well as regional and world history.

In this context, the burgeoning works on the classical notion of tianxia serve to mediate both the inside and outside, internal and external. In November 2009, Beijing Library Publisher released an eleven-volume series under the title *Tianxia*.[2] The term has become a framing device across the fields of literature, philosophy, anthropology, and political science.[3] This trend reflects an internal demand and anxiety about providing a properly Chinese vision of the world. It remains unclear, however, whether tianxia discourse is an adequate response to changing global conditions. The underlying thrust of the tianxia discussion is to find ways to locate viable intellectual resources of the Chinese tradition in order to move beyond the Western paradigm of modernity anchored to nation-state, global capitalism, and imperialism. As the Stanford workshop (in which the current chapter was first written) statement suggests: "The Chinese

Revolution, the socialist experiments, cultural transformations, persistent communitarian ethics, Marxist internationalism, anti-hegemonic struggles and the self-reliant agenda to find its own modern path constitute China's drive to be part of world history." These historical practices may or may not easily be subsumed under the umbrella of tianxia.

In response to the current invocation of tianxia as an alternative to the Euro-American understanding of world order, this chapter undertakes a theoretical exercise to fill the gap by tracking the notion of tianxia in Chinese history from the Western Zhou to the Warring States period. Our assumption is that tianxia has its own genealogical trajectory and cannot be instrumentally deployed as a new political imaginary. We go on to examine the viability of adopting tianxia in the contemporary global context. We then initiate a self-critique to locate the conditions of Chinese intellectuals' anxiety and argue that rather than falling back on the imperial worldview, they need to renew and reformulate critical sources of internationalism, third worldism, and Asianism for self-positioning in the emerging climate of the rise of China.

Drawing on Chisen Chang's works and Kuan-Hsing Chen's *Asia as Method: Towards Deimperialization*, we trace the origin of the term "tianxia" in Chinese intellectual history and describe the nature of the political world captured by it.[4] We then analyze the connotations of tianxia from the Spring and Autumn period to the Warring States period, and discuss various aspects of the conceptual order in tianxia, concluding with a reference to the research by Mark Edward Lewis and Hsieh Mei-yu in this volume. In the second section we engage the philosopher Zhao Tingyang's influential account of tianxia. The third section comments on possible directions for positioning ourselves as critical Chinese intellectuals in the present conjuncture of history.[5]

The Earliest Uses of the Term "Tianxia"

Pioneering studies of the concept of tianxia were published by Tong and Gu, Joseph Levenson, Takeo Abe, Hsing, Luo, and Watanabe.[6] This section attempts to supplement these works.

Although the term "tianxia" was not found among the excavated Shang oracle inscriptions, Hsing I-tien thinks that the idea of tianxia (i.e., the Shang king as the center ruled the peoples in the four cardinal directions) might have already existed during the Shang period.[7] In the written records of the Western Zhou, the term had already appeared, though only seldom.[8] However, the recently found inscription of tianxia on the Western Zhou *Sui gong xu* (䢵（遂）公盨) provides solid evidence of the term's early use.[9] Literally, "tianxia" is composed of *tian* (heaven) and *xia* (down, under); thus its literal meaning might be simply "that which is under heaven." But its use in the Western Zhou texts obviously may have had further connotations. In the reliable parts of *The Book of Zhou*, the term was generally used in connection with certain active and interfering deeds or character of heaven (such as the decree of heaven, the dreaded majesty of heaven, or the punishment of heaven) toward the human world, hence denoting a political world ruled by heaven via its agents under its mandates.[10]

If tianxia referred to a political world in the Western Zhou period, the essence of that world consisted in *fengjian*, a term often translated as "feudalism." *Feng* means "bestowing a name," and *jian* means "to establish." According to research, fengjian was a mechanism by which the Zhou people projected their political power over an expanse of land and its residents.[11] In other words, tianxia during the Western Zhou might have mainly referred to the polities and peoples subject to the Zhou king through the mechanism of fengjian.

Tianxia in the Spring and Autumn Period

From the Spring and Autumn on, tianxia appeared more frequently in written records. It continued to refer to the political world ruled by the Zhou king through the colonies or vassal polities subject to him, collectively called *zhuxia*. Tianxia thus connoted the political-geographical terrain occupied by zhuxia.[12] In some cases, it denoted a larger political world that included both zhuxia and non-zhuxia people or polities.[13] During this period, tianxia, in most cases, simply denoted a political world or a geographical space as an object of political dominance or other political actions. Examples of political dominance can be found in the expression *de tianxia* (to get tianxia).[14] Another expression is *yuo tianxia* (to have or obtain tianxia).[15] Tianxia can also be *qu* (taken), as King Ling of Ts'oo (Chu) vowed that he would take tianxia for himself. Examples of tianxia as an object of political action can be found in the expression *huai rou tianxia* (to treat tianxia with benevolent caring as a way to win support from those peoples), which is rendered by Legge as the founders of Zhou "cherishing with gentle indulgence all under heaven."[16]

Another key term also emerged in this period, namely *zhongguo*. Although zhongguo had already appeared in the Western Zhou period, its earliest use might have referred to either the former domain of the Shang polity or to *luoyi* (also known as Chengzhou). Thus zhongguo was understood as "the Central State."[17] It might also have meant "the city that was located in the middle of the peoples or polities, with medium distance to them from all directions."[18] During the Spring and Autumn period, zhongguo had around six meanings: (1) the domain of the king of Zhou; (2) zhuxia; (3) the political-geographical domain of zhuxia; (4) the area inside the city walls of a polity's capital; (5) the domain of a polity; and (6) the civilization.[19] The second and third meanings of zhongguo coincided with the two aforementioned connotations of tianxia in this period. Although the two terms were equivalent, when zhuxia and its political-geographical domain were referred to, tianxia was used more often than zhongguo.

Jiuzhou, Sihai, Zhongguo, and Tianxia during the Warring States Period

Four terms were interrelated in the Warring States texts: tianxia, zhongguo, jiuzhou, and sihai. Clarifying their meanings is necessary for accurate understanding of the connotations of tianxia in this period.

Jiuzhou (nine counties) had geopolitical connotations. It had several conceptual origins as well as textual versions.[20] According to the most famous version, "The Tribute of Yu," jiuzhou was created by the god-sage Yu.[21] According to legend, he terminated the Great Flood (a metaphor for chaos and disorder) by launching a huge hydroengineering work, akin to creating a new political order. Having achieved that, Yu divided the land into nine counties (jiuzhou). Many scholars have pointed out that the locations of these counties reflected geopolitical conditions from the late Spring and Autumn period to the Warring States period. In this context, jiuzhou might be viewed as the further expansion of Spring and Autumn tianxia (zhongguo). According to some earlier statements, the terrain of jiuzhou was estimated as a square with the length of each side being three thousand li.[22]

Sihai (four seas) was a term affiliated with jiuzhou. In the Warring States texts, jiuzhou was understood as being surrounded by sihai. Thus jiuzhou was also called hainei (that which is surrounded by hai) or sihai. Although the term "sihai" is composed of four (si) and sea (hai), it sometimes meant the lands where the different ethnic groups man, yi, rong, and di lived rather than seas.[23]

In the Warring States texts, "zhongguo" had developed at least eight meanings: (1) zhuxia; (2) the Central Plain; (3) jiuzhou; (4) the area of the Three Jins; (5) the capital of legendary sage-kings; (6) the area within the bounds of a state or one's homeland; (7) a medium-sized state; or (8) a cultural community that symbolized human civilization.[24] The third meaning of zhongguo was equivalent to jiuzhou, sihai, or hainei, and they all referred to a geopolitical land mass estimated to be three thousand square li.

With these terms as context, now we can try to determine the primary meaning of tianxia in the Warring States texts, where it appeared hundreds of times.[25] Although a comprehensive study of its meanings in this period has not yet been carried out, we can be quite certain that one of its primary meanings was jiuzhou. Thus tianxia in this sense is equivalent to jiuzhou, sihai, hainei, and zhongguo. Since this meaning is limited, it can be understood as tianxia in its narrow sense.

Another concept of tianxia in these texts denoted an overarching scope that includes both jiuzhou and the area of sihai outside it and therefore can be understood as tianxia in its broad sense. In some cases, the space farther outside sihai was also included.[26] In other words, during the Warring States period there were at least three conceptions of tianxia, denoting the narrow, broad, and broadest senses.

The primary meaning of tianxia in its narrow sense referred to the political-geographical area (jiuzhou) that forms the core of what is now known as China. During the Warring States period, there emerged a notion that people of tianxia in the above sense shared a common culture. This common culture included culinary style (cooked food and grain eating), costume style, language, and the rules, norms, and rites that regulated human relations between kin as well as between subjects and kings.[27] Moreover, this common culture was understood as being shared only by people living within the bounds of tianxia or jiuzhou, and markedly different from the less civilized cultures of peoples outside jiuzhou.

Although tianxia in this period denotes a clearly bounded political-geographical area with a shared common culture, we must not hasten to assume that the term was used in the Warring States texts to refer to a cultural community. In fact, it appears that most of the usages in these texts refer only to the geographical-political world symbolized by jiuzhou, whereas the cases of its use referring to a cultural community are extremely rare, if any can be found. In other words, Joseph Levenson's claim that, in premodern Chinese history, tianxia referred to a universal world of civilization could find little evidence in the Warring States texts.[28] If such a cultural community was articulated, it called zhongguo instead.[29]

Tianxia as a World Order

Having examined the narrow sense of tianxia, we now turn to its broad sense, which denoted a space that included both jiuzhou and sihai—China and its neighboring peoples. It implied a world order in which the king of China ruled jiuzhou (China) directly and subdued sihai (neighboring regions of China, where the man, yi, rong, and di—collectively called *siyi*, "four yi"—resided) indirectly. This represents the earliest known theoretical design by the Warring States thinkers regarding the relationship between China and its neighbors.

The most concrete expression of this world order was described by the renowned scholar Gu Jiegang as the *jifu* (畿服) system.[30] According to various descriptions of this system, certain rules were designed to maintain siyi's inferior and subordinate status. One rule dictated that the rulers of siyi must rank no higher than the lowest of Chinese feudal lords, however large or powerful the rulers' polities might have been. Other descriptions listed the obligations of siyi to the ruler of China, the ritual of offering tribute or paying homage. Since siyi were not directly governed by China's ruler, the amount of tribute and the frequency of homage visits prescribed for them were not as onerous as those for the vassals within China and were supposed to be merely symbolic.[31]

According to this world order, China does not actually rule siyi, and the relation of the former to the latter is simply a symbolic bond between a nominal lord and his nominal subjects rather than the actual bond between a ruler and his domestic subjects. The idea was that the polities of siyi would have the option to participate or not in this world order, as the ruler of China could not force them to be part of it. But if they chose to participate, they had to accept their status as nominal subjects of their Chinese lord.

Tianxia thus had the following characteristics in the Warring States texts. In terms of integrating China and neighboring polities, it was more inclusive than the term's narrow sense. Nevertheless, tianxia's scope was still limited, extending to five thousand square li at most.[32] In other words, even this more inclusive tianxia was not all inclusive. Second, this tianxia was definitely not a "world government," as Zhao Tingyang claims, since people like siyi were not actually governed by China.[33] Third, considering that siyi could choose whether to be part of this world order or not, tianxia appears to have been highly tolerant. Fourth, if siyi wanted to be part of this world order, they had to accept an inferior and subordinate status as the nominal subjects of their Chinese lord. In this light, the tianxia order seems highly discriminative. Finally, this world order did not rule out the possibility that a ruler of siyi could become the lord of China and thus reverse siyi's previously inferior status. In later historical periods, for instance the Manchurian Qing, such a possibility did become a reality. A world order like this, which allowed foreigners to be the legitimate rulers of China, is utterly inconceivable to the Chinese today. Moreover, tianxia as a world order during the Warring States was still limited. Although it was simultaneously tolerant and discriminative, tianxia was not analogous to a world government. In the contemporary context, tianxia as an open system does not sit well with China's nationalist passion.

In sum, in its formative moment in the Western Zhou period, tianxia referred to the political world under Zhou's dominance. From the Spring and Autumn to the Warring States periods, the primary meaning of tianxia included the areas of jiuzhou. In its broad sense, tianxia implied a world order that was still limited in scope, and was simultaneously tolerant, discriminative, and openly accessible in either its membership or its lordship. Largely unaware of these characteristics, Zhao Tingyang takes the term in its literal sense and uses it as the foundation for articulating a utopian world order marked with "the exclusion of nothing and nobody" or "the inclusion of all peoples and all lands."[34] This utopian world order seems to be at odds with the historical concepts of tianxia in many ways.

To conclude this section, we offer some remarks on chapter 1 in this volume, by Lewis and Hsieh. They begin by reviewing the connotations of tianxia from the Spring and Autumn to the Warring States periods. Where their presentation differs from ours is that they focus on Levenson's thesis and draw a broad picture of how politics and culture interplay in the discourses of tianxia. Our goal is to clarify the meanings and interrelations of tianxia, zhongguo, jiouzhou, and sihai. One might say that their presentation is oriented more toward intellectual history, and ours is more philologically oriented. Bearing this in mind, readers may benefit from both of the two studies. Here we simply add a few notes to their presentation.

Regarding the interplay of politics and culture in the discourses of tianxia, as noted, in the Warring States texts, it was extremely rare for "tianxia" to denote culture, civilization, or a cultural community. If those things were intended, the term "zhongguo" was used instead. In other words, tianxia might have pointed to a political world sharing a common culture, but this connection was established via the concept of jiuzhou, a geopolitical world with a shared culture.

Mozi's contribution to the concept of tianxia as a new world order has been pointed out by Abe.[35] Lewis and Hsieh suggest that the principle of giving priority to insiders and marginalizing outsiders, articulated repeatedly in the *Gongyang zhuan*, appeared after Mozi's universalism. This point might need more evidence, since this principle bears marks of Spring and Autumn zhuxia thinking.

Zhao Tingyang's *Tianxia tixi*

Now we turn to Zhao Tingyang's discourse of tianxia tixi (the system of all under heaven). Since the publication of Zhao's book *Tianxia tixi*, scholars and critics have commented on and criticized the work.[36]

Zhao contends that the tianxia system is a political, philosophical proposal aimed at a novel theorization of world politics. Since it is purely philosophical and utopian in nature, its deviation from historical fact is not his concern, and the proposal itself should not be criticized from a historiographical point of view. Such a methodological abstraction allows Zhao to freely employ the concept of tianxia without being constrained by both the actual, historical mutations of the concept itself and its practice in Chinese history. Zhao is solely concerned with working out its theoretical possibility: "The analysis of the possible connotations of the Chinese ideas overtakes the representation of China's actual performance in history as well as the original features of various concepts. . . . Philosophy is interested in the best theoretical possibility rather than historical fact."[37]

Zhao sets out to construct tianxia as a theoretically fruitful concept by leaving Chinese history out of his horizon. Yet he constantly cites examples from Chinese history as illustrations of tianxia in actual practice. He claims, for instance, that the tianxia system had already become a reality during the Western Zhou period.[38] Similar methodological deviations also appear in his discussion of the deficiencies inherent in Western political philosophy. If he follows his methodological principle closely enough, he is supposed to explore the purely theoretical possibilities of some key concepts in Western thought that he confronts throughout his discourse (e.g., individuality, right, freedom) while leaving their actual practice aside. But he constantly cites certain aspects of the current world order or Western political practices as evidence of their fundamental flaws. From the very beginning, Zhao's theoretical venture has encountered the difficulty of sticking consistently to his own methodological principle.

Zhao's proposal of tianxia as a new political philosophy consists of three cardinal points. He privileges tianxia as an alternative over the international interstate system, valorizes *minxin* (people's heart) as an alternative to democracy, and upholds family and kinship ties over individuality.

Zhao begins with a globalized world in which peoples of different states form humankind by binding their fates together. This newly formed entity, however, has no place in the current world order, which has been organized in a system in which the decisive unit is the nation-state. The nation-state system recognizes entities no greater than the state; hence there is no room for the world as an integrated whole. The problem of the world therefore can only be dealt with by nations or states rather than by a world polity with a worldwide view, "seeing the affairs and problems of the world by the worldly standards."[39] Zhao complains, "Our supposed world is still a non-world."[40]

Since this system of nation-states recognizes no entities larger than the state, the world is regarded as a space between states and understood as international. Since there is no world polity to take overall responsibility for global problems and welfare, the world space is left for exploitation by the states: "Today, a 'world' in the political sense, endowed with its own institution, management and order, has not yet existed. Thus the world in the physical or geographical sense has become a wasteland for which no one takes responsibility, and in which public resources and assets can be plundered and fought for at will, a battlefield for conquest."[41]

In the nation-state system, each state acts in its own national interest. Due to the absence of a world polity, the international order can only be organized by the mightiest states to suit their own interests. Such an order lacks legitimacy. The dominant powers claim that their values are universal and not only impose these values upon other nations but also label certain nations negatively: "In fact, the world nowadays is led by certain American-made prejudicial discourses—such as 'clash of civilization,' 'rogue state,' 'failed state'—in a wrong direction. In an illegitimate way, these discourses legitimize the erroneous leadership and unjust rule of the American empire."[42]

The political philosophy rooted in the nation-state is to Zhao a philosophy of the world rather than a philosophy for the world. The distinction is clear: the former does not treat the world as a substantial entity higher than the state but simply regards it as an international space, whereas the latter aims to replace the international with a larger vision transcending the nation-state. He thus proposes his theory of tianxia tixi as an example of a philosophy for the world. Citing a passage from the Chinese classic *Laozi*, Zhao argues that it is characteristic of Chinese political philosophy to treat the world as a substantial entity higher than the state, and this world is understood as tianxia: "Viewing the world as a whole is an epistemological principle first used by Laozi (580–500 B.C.). He says: 'the best way to understand everything is to view a person from the viewpoint of a person, a family from the viewpoint of a family, a village from the viewpoint of a village, a state from the viewpoint of a state, and all-under-heaven from the viewpoint of all-under-heaven.'"[43]

Regarding the world as a substantial entity rather than an international space, adopting a worldwide stance rather than insisting on the nation-state—these are the characteristics of tianxia as a philosophy for the world. Notably, for tianxia to work successfully, the nation-state has to withdraw.[44] Thus once the world has become a tianxia, all the current nation-states would have to be transformed into local administrative units.

To what extent would the tianxia world differ from international space? Higher than nations, this order is to be governed by representatives of the world's peoples through minxin rather than *minzhu* (a common Chinese translation of "democracy"):

> Being the core concept, "*tianxia*" has three connotations at the same time: 1) the land of the whole world. . . . Evidently, the rivers, lakes, and seas that are located on the same surface as the land also belong to the concept of land. Land is collectively owned by all peoples of the world. . . . [It] is public property; 2) all the peoples of the world. . . . More precisely, it means the preference of the heart of all peoples, namely *minxin* in totality (general heart), somewhat similar to *gongyi* (general will). . . . The land of *tianxia* is merely the physical expression of *tianxia*, and it is the *minxin* of *tianxia* that makes up the latter's spiritual meaning; 3) a world institution . . . it means the way the world is governed or the condition of existence for the current world to become the world.[45]

> The key Chinese term "all under heaven" is a dense concept meaning "world." It has three meanings: 1) the Earth or all lands under the sky; 2) a common choice made by all peoples in the world, or a universal agreement in the "hearts" of all peoples; 3) a political system for the world with a global institution to ensure universal order. . . . A humanized world *is . . . defined* as political by a worldwide institution reflecting the universally accepted feelings of all peoples. . . . With the all under heaven concept the world is understood as consisting of the physical world (land), the psychological world (the general sentiment of peoples), and the institutional world (a world institution).[46]

In short, the tianxia world is governed by a world government, supported by all peoples of the world through their general will or feelings in pursuit of the well-being of humankind. Since it is an international body that is not led and dominated by powerful states, it would have more legitimacy. Since its governance aims to enhance the well-being of all peoples rather than protecting the national interests of the great powers, such governance would be just and fair.

In addition to the above features, Zhao maintains that world government must not favor or adhere to any particular culture, religion, or ideology, so that no culture, state, or people would be excluded or discriminatively labeled. Therefore, tianxia is characterized by its inclusiveness and the absence of externality, something utterly alien to Western culture. Two characteristics of Western thought, individualism and paganism, tend to create externality to be overcome or to struggle against. Under the influence of individualism, one thinks in a self-centered way, treating other individuals and the world as outside oneself.[47] External to oneself are only other individuals and an interindividual space. There is no other substantial being higher than the individual. Western political philosophy is therefore incapable of developing a philosophy of an integrated world:

> The fundamental assumption presupposed by the most influential political world outlook in modern times might be Hobbes' "jungle assumption." According to this assumption, the political problem is understood as how to reach agreement so as to avoid the peril of the lawless "jungle." Furthermore, it is about how to protect the rights of a given political entity (ranging from the individual's rights as the smallest unit up to state sovereignty) to the greatest extent, and how to maximize self-interest under a given order. Accordingly, the political problem is further pointedly presented as what Carl Schmitt called the problem of "friends and enemies." In appearance, Western political philosophy has its own persuasive logic. Its starting point is largely correct. . . . The following steps seem to be all right, thus it develops theories of individual's rights, state sovereignty, democracy, and rule of law. But when the scope of the political problem has eventually reached the stage in which the world has to be considered as a political unit . . . such political logic can no longer hold true. It can advance no more. Obviously, the world cannot but be one world. It is an institutional existence that has to be shared by all, an entire political space recalcitrant to the divisive mode of understanding. The world has become a common task, and the logic of existence it requires has fundamentally changed. . . . It no longer sets up its opposite or needs an enemy. . . . Regarding the problem of the world, the political institution envisioned by Western political philosophy loses its explanatory power. . . . Western political philosophy is erroneous from its root. Its fundamental methodology is problematical in the first place.[48]

As for the connection of the concept of paganism to externality, Zhao argues that Christianity regards God and pagans as transcendent beings, which can never be assimilated by any means. Such transcendence is the origin of externality:

> Chinese thought does not recognize the transcendent as the absolutely outside, namely, the kind of being that cannot be "transformed" by any means. Accordingly, China can have neither religion nor the categori-

cally untransformable enemy. All the religions in the rigorous sense, such as Christianity, have to assume an absolute being, i.e., God, and concomitantly the pagan as its irreconcilable enemy. . . . God is appointed as the origin of everything, and the other people—the pagans in particular—are regarded as the irreconcilable enemy. . . . The consequences of recognizing the transcendent are religion and the political theory that creates enemies. This is the veiled truth of Western thought. From individualism and paganism to the jungle assumption and the nation/state-oriented theories of international politics, etc.—these ideas that led the world into conflict and chaos all have to do with the recognition of the transcendent.[49]

In contrast to Western thought, which by nature has to create externality, Chinese tianxia is different. Another characteristic of tianxia is *wuwai* (literally, excluding nothing as the external or outside), recognizing no externality or untransformable being. This characteristic leads to the absence of the irreconcilable enemy or other people: "The unity of the world promised by the concept of *tianxia* is the a priori given wholeness, and the presumed unity of the world constitutes the recognition of the internal diversity of the world. . . . It [i.e., the concept of tianxia] rejects dangerous thinking such as 'heretic,' 'war,' 'conflict.' "[50]

In Zhao, tianxia is not merely a theoretical concept to replace the international. It also symbolizes the essence of Chinese thought, which is nonexclusive and unimposing by nature, thus more appealing than its Western counterpart as a leading worldwide value system.[51]

The Heart of the People as Alternative to Democracy

Zhao maintains that tianxia as a world government has to be supported by minxin (people's heart) rather than democracy. The rationale is that democracy is an institution in which the less virtuous people make up the majority, and the decisions made by such a majority can never serve the true common good, and thus fall short of legitimacy:

> We have no confidence in thinking that the virtuous people are more numerous than the less virtuous ones. On the contrary, many signs show that the latter are more in number. Psychology, crowd psychology in particular, points out that the blind followers, the selfish, the irresponsible, the foolish, the mediocre ones apparently constitute the majority. . . . Accordingly, democracy in its modern form is founded on those whose

sense of responsibility is rather dubious. . . . A society that benefits the liars, the less virtuous, the bad, the mediocre, and rogues will not hold and will lack legitimacy.[52]

Legitimacy derived from democracy is not only dubious but also suffers from another fatal deficiency that disqualifies it from being the political model at the national or world levels. The preferences of the people in democratic elections are inauthentic, as they have been distorted by all kinds of factors such as money, media, and strategic voting. In short, "what democracy expresses is that which the people do not really want but are misled to think they do."[53]

The remedy for the ills of democracy is to replace it with minxin, winning the hearts of the people. Zhao argues that minxin is far superior to democracy in providing impeccable legitimacy. It is the judgments made by the majority under the influence of the virtuous ones: "From the ancient time onward, qualities such as diligence, wisdom, bravery, and righteousness have been regarded everywhere as the highest form of humanity. Whoever has these virtues is the 'elite' (the 'elite' here are defined by admirable virtues and have nothing to do with social status, occupation, and wealth). An institution disapproved by the elite must be a bad one. Therefore . . . an institution is legitimate if and only if it is agreed by the majority of people, which must include the majority of the elite."[54] In short, if the legitimacy derived from democracy springs from the less virtuous majority, the legitimacy formed via minxin has a much sounder base.

In contrast to the public versions of democracy plagued by manipulation and distortion, minxin can better reflect authentic popular preferences. Minxin is the judgments made by the elite for the sake of the true common good of the people. Zhao argues that the elites, among the rulers and the ruled, know better than the ordinary masses about what the common good is and how to pursue it. The former rule for the people and the latter make judgments (on behalf of minxin) on their governance: "*Minxin* is not identical with the desire of the masses, but is the thought based on the general heart and for the general interest. Those ideas that are thought 'for the sake of the general interest' do not belong to certain people exclusively but to mankind instead. Although they are figured out and uttered by the elites, the latter do so not for themselves but for the common well-being of mankind."[55]

And how do the elites among the ruled express their judgments regarding the rulers' governance? Zhao claims that they do this in an implicit way in the social atmosphere indicative of popular sentiments or feelings. Such a social atmosphere would be created by the elites and the less virtuous people working together collectively, from the manipulation or distortion prevalent in democracy. Zhao claims that in Chinese history minxin normally existed in the form of *minqing* (people's sentiments and feelings): "*Minqing* always expresses itself as the social atmosphere that can be intuited or felt directly. Moreover, the people's intuition of *minqing* and perception of social atmosphere seem to be never mistaken."[56]

In other words, the elites among the ruled implicitly indicate their judgments, which eventually become certain general feelings or a social atmosphere and loom as minxin. The ruling elites carefully and sincerely observe the trends of minxin to detect the true preferences of the people and govern the people accordingly.[57] Such is the way the world government would rule humankind with tianxia as an alternative to democracy.

The Family as an Alternative to Individuality

Zhao criticizes Western thought for giving priority to individualism, which is responsible for the ills of the current world order. The tianxia model, in contrast, must adopt the family as the baseline of a whole political order. Clearly, Zhao employs family ties as the theoretical foundation and pillar of his tianxia system, just as individualism plays the pivotal role in the Western system of political order.

In Zhao's analysis, the family seems to proceed along two fronts. On the one hand, the core structure of the traditional Chinese political order works like a family. In contrast, the Western sociopolitical order is based on individuality. This distinction allows Zhao to argue that the traditional Chinese system is superior to its Western counterpart. On the other hand, he contends that a family can do better than an individual in achieving the primary goal of individualism—the maximization of individual self-interest. Replacing individualism with family relations is logical or even necessary.

Zhao asserts that a good political order must satisfy the criteria of consistency and transitivity: there must be homology and a continuum between each level of the system. By homology he means that the same political order has to be universally applicable to every level of the system. "Continuum" denotes the relationship of mutual presupposition. On this view the Western system fails to meet the criterion, as democracy is applicable only to the nation-state but not the world. In the Chinese system, by contrast, the family writ large as a political order is applicable to the levels of the family, the state, and the world, meeting the criterion of consistency. This system scores better than the Western one in the sense that through fulfilling the ethical obligations of family, the Chinese system achieves political governance of the state like a family unit. This can be true of the world envisaged as a family of nations. Political governance at the higher level presupposes ethical functions at the lower levels. Zhao designates this process as political transposition. To reverse the direction, the fulfillment of family obligations justifies the governance of the state, and the same justification may be expanded to states in the world. The ethical function at the lower levels provides legitimacy for political governance at the higher levels, and this relationship is deemed ethical transposition. The two forms of transposition mutually support each other. By contrast, the Western system sees political transposition only between the state and the individual, not between the world and the state. It thus fails to meet the criterion of transitivity and is inferior to its Chinese counterpart.[58]

For Zhao the family is ontologically prior to the individual. Rather than individuals forming the family via mutual agreement, individuals must be established and nurtured within the family. The family is a community in which the maximization of love and obligation toward other people happens to align with the maximization of the individual's self-interest. Therefore, the family can better maximize individual self-interest than the individual alone. The competitive situation inevitably diminishes each individual's chance to realize a productive self. Since the family is superior to individuality, Zhao argues, a political system modeled on family relations would be more capable of maximizing each individual's self-interest than one based on the ideology of individualism. With family membership as the core principle, tianxia would be organized as a family in which harmony and mutual benefit prevail.[59]

Some Critical Observations

As mentioned earlier, the concept of tianxia in Chinese intellectual history is not exempt from the presupposition of an externality, namely, *yidi* (barbarian). Wang Mingke has pointed out that an ethnic name, Qiang, was used by Chinese from the Shang period on as a floating and mobile ethnic boundary between themselves and other peoples in western China. Its use excluded certain people from *huaxia*.[60] Chang made similar observations in a detailed study of the meanings of man, yi, rong, and di from the Western Zhou to the Spring and Autumn period, arguing that the primary meaning refers to outsiders or zhuxia; the terms also operate as marks of exclusion.[61]

Whether yidi are a transformable externality is another interesting question. Chinese ethnic thought historically held two different beliefs on this issue. One claimed that yidi could be transformed via cultural conversion. The other argued that they are untransformable, although this view contains rather complicated dimensions. If yidi are untransformable, it is unnecessary to transform them, as they, as well as the people of zhongguo, are made out of their unique essence respectively, and the way of politics is not to eliminate such differences but rather to organize them into a fruitful and productive harmony. This view bears a good deal of similarity to cultural pluralism in our age.[62] However, the notion that yidi are untransformable is the rationale for the separation and exclusion of yidi from China. After centuries of development, by the seventeenth century this view had evolved into a strand of ethnic thought that bears striking similarities to nationalism.[63] In short, tianxia as a world order in Chinese history also presupposes an externality. When this externality has to be included according to the principle of wuwai, this is always achieved by integrating the externality into a discriminative hierarchical order.

Our second criticism also addresses the issue of externality. For the individual's interest to be maximized within the family presupposes an external society consisting of strangers. It is precisely due to the need to distinguish itself from such an externality that the family is constructed in the same way as a community, for the maximization of individual interest in accordance with the common good. However, once tianxia is constructed as a family, there would no longer be strangers, neither would there be any boundaries. Without externality, it is highly dubious that the family could still function as such a harmonious community, especially if Zhou's distrust of the quality of the masses is also taken into account.

We have demonstrated the main themes and arguments of Zhao's discourse of the tianxia system and its inadequacy with respect to theoretical coherence. Leaving the interpretation of Zhao's arguments to the reader, we would like to ask one further question: Is there any positive potential in elaborating the concept of tianxia?

In the contemporary world, it is true that certain values such as democracy, freedom, and human rights have been abused by the Western powers as the means to pressure non-Western sovereign nations to accept the rules of the game set up by the West. But one must not forget that the major forces of repression and domination today consist of both capitalism and authoritarian regimes. These two institutions have one thing in common: both tend to divide humankind into insignificant individuals isolated and alienated from each other, so that people cannot forge a unified power to challenge the established order. If the concept of tianxia has any positive value, it lies in a new emphasis on a long-forgotten ideal, namely, the unity and solidarity of humankind. This ideal was the driving force behind the historical movements of Marxism and anarchism and has been forgotten in recent decades. To propose the concept of tianxia as a solution to contemporary problems reminds us once again of the ideal drowned out by the triumph of the pseudo-Hegelian end of history.

Nevertheless, if solutions to contemporary problems have to confront contemporary conditions, then tianxia seems to have little to offer. Unlike theories such as Marxism, which look for solutions in actual practice, Zhao's tianxia system sees no connection whatsoever between the ideal of tianxia and current problems. While urging us to remember the lost ideal once again, he offers no concrete analysis of the possible means to fulfill that ideal.

We may delve into the current Chinese context undergirding the discourse of tianxia. Such a discourse helps to construct a Chinese view of political order and may be directed more at domestic than international audiences. Although it has received critical and popular acclaim in China, Zhao's book aroused little interest internationally. This indicates that tianxia is more attractive to the Chinese than to outsiders. Rather than a critique of the Westphalian nation-state system, the tianxia discourse is deployed as an ideological instrument to facilitate the consolidation of national identity in China. Becoming the prevalent standpoint in Chinese domestic politics, tianxia provides more grounds for rejecting norms such as nation-state sovereignty, democracy, and individualism upheld by the West and presumed to guide Chinese domestic politics and foreign policy. Zhao's argument that minxin is superior to democracy aims to supply a badly needed theoretical justification for the reign of the Chinese Communist Party. Finally, his proposal to replace individuality with the family framework might serve as a solution to the problem of independence movements in Tibet, Xinjiang, and Taiwan. To counter these movements bent on independence and sovereignty, the tianxia system proposes that giving up individuality (i.e., sovereignty) and joining the family of China would be more profitable for pro-independence people.

Self-Positioning

Rather than arguing that there is nothing valid in the notion of tianxia, we question the metaphysical fantasy in Zhao's formulation. What is disturbing is an unspoken Sinocentrism in the guise of critiquing Euro-American-centrism. The struggle over which version of universalism is more productive is a familiar story of postcolonial resentment. And how intellectuals from the Global South would respond to the notion of tianxia is an urgent and pertinent question. Would they feel this is the next wave of neoimperialist ideology for expansionism, since externality disappears and the world is one? Is this the discourse of an emerging power pitted against existing global power, just as the United

States was set against Europe in the early twentieth century? We are cautious that the subject position behind tianxia may be a contemporary recuperation of the imperial order of the past, and worse, that it defines itself by its rivals.

If the rise of China marks a sense of urgency for Chinese intellectuals to articulate a new political vision, one necessary task is self-critique from which to arrive at solidarity with others. *Respect and Farewell—to Japan*, a book published in 2009 by the leading writer Zhang Chengzhi, exemplifies this self-critique and launches an interrogation of imperial Sinocentrism. With strong intellectual relations with Japan, where he studied in 1983 and taught in 1993, and with some of his major works translated into Japanese, Zhang develops his analyses of contemporary Japan on the level of a set of intellectual sentiments. Japan's dream of being a strong nation in the nineteenth century ran amok to the point of forgetting self-respect and respect for others, leading to imperialist conquest and colonial expansion. Mediating through concrete historical events and trajectories of action and thought, Zhang invites his reader to unpack the changing conditions for shaping the social psyche. Nuclear bombs made Nagasaki not only a pacifist city committed to the cause of abolishing nuclear weapons but also a monument questioning the brutality of Western powers; the internationalist spirit of the Red Army in solidarity with the Palestinian struggle for autonomy has produced a next generation of revolutionaries to work for the underdogs; the continuing popularity of the story of the "forty-seven warriors," evocative of the classical spirit of the samurai fight to fulfill promise and loyalty, reveals the deep-seated subjectivity of what it means to be Japanese; moving personal encounters with the folksinger Okabayashi Nobuyasu (岡林信康) over thirty years is a case of heartfelt brotherhood across nationalities. On the other hand, works by prominent intellectuals like Sato Haruo (佐籐春夫), Dazai Osamu (太宰治), Hotta Yoshie (堀田善衞), and Takeuchi Yoshimi (竹内好), sympathetic and appreciative in nature, ultimately fail to deliver a critique of embedded national arrogance; Asianism, running across a different political spectrum in Japan's modern history, gave rise to both imperialist conquest and to genuine solidarity for prewar Indian revolutionary support as well as postwar support for Muslim schooling in Qinghai, China. These are the central themes of Zhang's book, which is unique in its deeper critique of China by way of critical reflections on Japan. Here are passages from the concluding chapter:

> While sorting out things Japanese, I have China in mind. Perhaps it is time for China, indulging now in the excitement of dreaming about rising as a powerful country, to think about Japan's road to modernity.

Yesterday, embracing the dream to be a powerful country, they [the Japanese] fell into insanity and pushed nationalism to a dead end only in the early evening of the same day. Without criticizing and abandoning the dangerous idea of big-country chauvinism; without respecting the right of others and neighbors to survive; without pursuing a nation's existential sense of beauty, its people would fall into insanity and the country ultimately could not be powerful.

We need to get rid of ideas such as "the whole world's submission to us" (*sihai chenfu* 四海臣服), "tributes from all directions" (*sifang laichao* 四方來朝), and "vassals and barbarians" (*fanshu siyi* 藩屬四夷). Otherwise, distrust will accumulate day by day, not only from Japan but also from neighboring Asia and the third world. We have started to be aware that before the country attains material wealth, it is more important to pursue richness in thought. What we are after is not a new Chinese empire—no, neither a wealthy country, nor a powerful (military) force. What we are eager to reach is dignity, tolerance, and good will, aspiring to a friendly coexistence of all nations, which can be recognized as a nation of beauty.[64]

Zhang goes on:

From Japanese stories, we understand more deeply another critical conviction: fanatic and selfish nationalism is the most terrifying poison. We have begun to examine in detail the long-lasting chauvinist Chinese nationalism, of which we used to be so proud from childhood.

If it cannot settle accounts with its repeated invasions of others while on the way to be a powerful country, Japan will prove unworthy of the elegance of its own classical learning and culture. Since the bandits of the Yuan time, through the Sino-Japanese War to the Russo-Japanese War, arrogant victories generated an outrageous devil face; in this "country of beauty," fearful ugliness overshadowed.

This paradox sends a warning to China. Indeed, hiding inside the island country's disgust toward China is a jealousy of the mainland empire, coupled with a seething wariness about the menace from it.

Like it or not, we have to repeat over and again: "victory" is necessary but also dangerous for a nation. On its way to becoming a powerful country, sooner or late it will sink into the swamp if it fails to purge itself of archaic, groundless nationalism. If we want to criticize Japan's aggression, we need to examine the historical gene of aggression against others in our own body.

When the old show has not yet come to an end, Japan has started a new round of "leaving Asia for Europe."

China is also now busy preparing to rise as a powerful country, moving closer to the tribunal of history.

Between our countries, China and Japan, what story will take place? Which direction to choose? What trend to follow? Will the two move toward war or peace?

Insh Allah. Only Allah would know.

But even if each is to follow the existing path, it does not mean that no effort can be made. Countless predecessors have, for the sake of peace among neighbors, overcome all the difficulties to carve out a wide avenue to peace. Today, we will join them.

We do not have any extra intellectual ammunition. Situated on shaky ground in the whirlwind of ideas, we both confront the most powerful imperialism ever in history and take on the critique of narrow-minded nationalism. We must endure this split, which is painful. Only in the midst of the immense pain can we pursue radical humanism, turning around the edge of the knife to examine ourselves and thrusting at the hugely self-important Chinese psyche with that sharp critique. This is for no other reason than that self-critique is the sole weapon we have.

Indeed, this strong self-pride in Chinese thought, deeply entrenched in my heart—isn't this something more in need of a headlong challenge? Is it necessary to first step over pretentious national self-importance so that we can achieve the spiritual progress of our motherland? Red leaves are silent. Watching them quietly, I think—we will have to practice the much touted proposition: "The toughest thing is to anatomize oneself."[65]

We cite Zhang's work at length to highlight this sober strain of the critical intellectual. In questioning the reactive and reactionary triumphalism of nationalism, Zhang is working out an alternative intellectual self-positioning that refuses to place a country among the nation-states scrambling for power in the contemporary capitalist order. With self-critique, he insists on examining the taboo subject of Chinese chauvinism embedded in the country's own past dynastic worldview.[66] As a symptomatic return of the repressed, China's current triumphalism needs to be challenged and critiqued. Zhang's thinking embodies diverse critical intellectual sources in modern China, including the sharp critique of Han nationalism in Lu Xun.[67] Sympathy and penetrating analysis of Japan continues the long tradition of the Chinese version of Asianism.[68] As a horizon of solidarity from the Bandung era of the 1950s, the third world was aligned with the spirit of socialist internationalism practiced in the Chinese Revolution.[69] More importantly, Zhang's Muslim background well positions him to critically access these sources of modern thought. More than anything else, the notion of the third world is the key to self-positioning. Sidelined and discredited these days, the third world concept is challenged by the internal divisions produced by the different speeds of economic development. Moreover, China, formerly an active ally, has become a core member of the celebrated BRICS (Brazil, Russia, India, China, and South Africa)—the engines of the world economy. These former third world countries seem to have emerged as the leading edge of global capitalism. Nevertheless, third world solidarity for a generation of postwar Chinese intellectuals is still the most significant source of self-positioning in the world today.

Taiwan writer Chen Yingzhen, in his critical and literary work since the 1970s, has expanded the notion of the third world beyond political economy to the area of cultural-mental life.[70] For Chen, the third world points to the postcolonial world of Asia, Africa, and Latin America, where former colonies and semicolonies, emerging from the postwar anticolonial struggle and civil wars, found themselves involved in a new battle between capitalism and socialism. The Cold War system transformed the world into a neocolonial structure and aggravated national divisions in certain places. This structural condition suppressed and suspended critical reflection in former colonies like Taiwan. Rather than a homogeneous entity, the third world is composed of radically diverse local histories. Visions of the third world can be actively mobilized as alternative systems of reference from which to understand and transform oneself through the analysis of others, as in Zhang Chengzhi's analysis of Japan. Moreover, having a common historical agenda, the third world engaged in the project of anti-imperialism and antifeudalism, which remains an unfinished enterprise. But it is at risk of being taken over by the neoliberal rhetoric of globalization. Nevertheless, today the third world remains a symbolic site to articulate solidarity and alliance beyond the nation-states, and continues to inspire movements to break down the old world of empire cum empire in search of alternative world visions.

Writing in 2015 in the context of the sixtieth anniversary of the Bandung Conference, we need to be reminded of the ongoing intellectual project for more systematic interactions among circles of thought in Asia, Africa, Latin America, and the Caribbean in order to generate alternative modes of knowledge. In our view, works such as Vijay Prashad's *The Darker Nations: A People's History of the Third World* and Pankaj Mishra's *From the Ruins of the Empire: The Revolt against the West and the Remaking of Asia* exemplify such important moves. Placing Jamal al-Din al-Afghani, Liang Qichao, and Rabindranath Tagore on the same plane of analysis, Mishra is able to show us not only that early modern intellectuals living in the Islamic, Han Chinese, and Indic civilizations shared the same structure of sentiment and anxiety but also that we have not yet moved very far beyond the problems facing our predecessors 100 to 150 years ago. Only by redirecting our desire and placing our eyes on ourselves as the double or mirror image can we begin to take each other seriously, and to internalize al-Afghani, Tagore, and Liang within ourselves. Sixty years ago, the Bandung Conference was a collective gesture of decolonization by the newly independent states. In retrospect, this symbol calls on us to take further steps not just to divest our world of the nation-state form as an invention of the European empires but also to continue the intellectual deimperialization of mind and knowledge. It behooves Chinese and third world intellectuals to continue to work on this. To be able to articulate an alternative vision of the future world, we can no longer simply indulge ourselves with wisdom inherited from the classical Han Chinese tradition. Like Zhang Chengzhi's penetrating analysis of modern Japan from inside out, we will need to seriously study and engage with critical intellectual works developed in other parts of the third world to properly understand the conditions of popular life and thought before we can propose any viable visions for change.

NOTES

1. For an account of the relations between Mao's period and the post-Mao period, see Qian, *Mao's Time and the Post-Mao Time*.

2. http://wenku.baidu.com/view/6b5de9272af90242a895e55b.html, accessed January 16, 2017. This publication is a reissue of *Tianxia* magazine, retrospectively edited by known scholars like Wu Jingxong, Lin Yutang, and others. The publisher's statement indicates that *Tianxia* is an English publication of literary and cultural materials, created by Chinese intellectuals who studied in Europe and America to "explain Chinese culture to the West," rather than "introducing Western culture to China," therefore "promoting international cultural exchange."

3. Han, *Tianxia*; Zhao Tingyang, *Tianxia tixi*; Wang Mingming, "Tianxia as World Map"; Shi Zhiyu, "Three Way Crossroads."

4. Chang's major scholarship is his PhD dissertation, "The Concept of 'Zhongguo' and the Distinction of 'Hua' 'Yi.'" A revised version is being published by Linking Press in Taiwan.

5. The historical trajectory of the connotations of tianxia presented in the following sections is based on the first part of Chang, "Tianxia System on a Snail's Horns," but presented here in a rewritten form.

6. Tong and Gu, "Ideas about the World"; Levenson, "T'ien-hsia and Kuo"; Levenson, *Confucian China and Its Modern Fate* (we are indebted to Lewis and Hsieh, chapter 1, this volume, for this reference); Abe, "The Idea of *Tianxia* of the Chinese People"; Hsing, "All under Heaven as One Family"; Hsing, "The Symbolic Meaning of the Great Wall"; Luo, "The Five-*Fu* System of the Pre-Qin Period"; and Watanabe, *The Imperial Power and the Order of All under Heaven*. More relevant studies are found in Hsu and Linduff, *Western Chou Civilization*.

7. Hsing I-tien, "All under Heaven as One Family," 439–440.

8. For a comprehensive list and detailed analysis of its appearance in the Western Zhou materials, see You, "The Four Corners, All under Heaven," 41–44; Chang, "The Formation of Two Key Concepts."

9. Zhou, *Collected Annotations of Recently Found Western Zhou Bronze Inscriptions*, 177.

10. Legge, *The Chinese Classics*, vol. 3, 429–430, 610.

11. Hsu and Linduff, *Western Chou Civilization*, 150–158; Du, *Society and State in Ancient Time*, 333–394.

12. Chang, "A New Study on the Chinese Ethnic Thought."

13. Chang, "The Formation of Two Key Concepts," 193–198.

14. Legge, *The Chinese Classics*, vol. 3, 616, 649, 675.

15. Legge used this term to mean that King Woo of Chow "obtained" grand "possession of all the land" (*The Chinese Classics*, vol. 3, 727).

16. Legge, *The Chinese Classics*, vol. 3, 192. For all of the examples of tianxia treated as an object of either dominance or other political actions, see Chang, "The Formation of Two Key Concepts," 193n44, 198.

17. Hsu and Linduff, *Western Chou Civilization*, 96.

18. Chang listed three meanings of zhongguo during the Western Zhou period: luoyi; one of Zhou's capitals; and central state (Shang polity). Chang, "The Formation of Two Key Concepts," 172–184.

19. Chang, "The Formation of Two Key Concepts," 185–190.

20. Chang, "The Formation of Two Key Concepts," 200–205.

21. See Legge, *The Chinese Classics*, vol. 3.

22. Legge, *The Chinese Classics*, vol. 3, 200–206, 213–215.

23. Watanabe argues that, from the mid–Warring States period to the Western Han period, sihai basically meant "four seas" or boundaries. It was not until the Eastern Han period, due to the influence of the Old Text School, that the term obtained the connotation of the lands inhabited by man, yi, rong, and di. Watanabe, *The Imperial Power and the Order of All under Heaven*, 55–57. However, the use of the term "hai" in the Spring and Autumn texts and the Warring States texts indicates that hai already had the connotation of land areas in these texts. See Chang, "The Formation of Two Key Concepts," 206–212.

24. For a somewhat comprehensive list of all the entries in the Warring States texts in which zhongguo was used (there are 108), see Chang, "The Formation of Two Key Concepts," 219–233. For the cultural and quasi-ethnic connotations of the concept of China during the Warring States period, see Chang, "The Concept of 'Zhongguo,'" 166–180.

25. For the frequency of its use in each of the Warring States texts, see Abe, "The Idea of *Tianxia* of the Chinese People," 451. You Yi-fei, "The Four Corners, All under Heaven,"

56. Statistics vary among scholars due to their respective views regarding the authenticity of the texts.

26. Chang, "The Formation of Two Key Concepts," 216–218.

27. Chang, "The Concept of 'Zhongguo,'" appendix, 13.

28. Levenson, *Confucian China and Its Modern Fate*, 99–103.

29. Chang, "The Formation of Two Key Concepts," 222–229.

30. Gu, *Shi lin za shi chu bian*, 19.

31. Chang, "The Concept of 'Zhongguo,'" 195.

32. Gu, *Shi lin za shi chu bian*, 15; Watanabe, *The Imperial Power and the Order of All under Heaven*, 45–72.

33. Zhao Tingyang, "A Political World Philosophy," 5–18.

34. Zhao Tingyang, "A Political World Philosophy," 10.

35. Abe, "The Idea of *Tianxia* of the Chinese People," 462–482.

36. See Zhang, "Theory of Tianxia and World Institution," 18–30; Callahan, "Chinese Visions of World Order," 749–761; Bell, "War, Peace, and China's Soft Power," 26–40; Zhou, "The Two Methodological Principles of *Tianxia Tixi*"; Zhou, "The Most Fashionable and the Most Relevant"; Zhang Feng, "The Tianxia System"; Gan, "Tianxia, a Reform by the Authority." For a summary of these criticisms, see Chang, "Tianxia System on a Snail's Horns."

37. Zhao Tingyang, *Tianxia tixi*, 16.

38. Zhao Tingyang, "A Political World Philosophy," 7–8.

39. Zhao, "Rethinking Empire from a Chinese Concept," 30.

40. Zhao Tingyang, "A Political World Philosophy," 6.

41. Zhao Tingyang, *Tianxi tixi*, 18.

42. Zhao Tingyang, *Tianxi tixi*, 117.

43. Zhao Tingyang, "A Political World Philosophy," 9–10. Some cautious remarks may be salutary here: there is little reliable biographical data about Laozi, and the relationship between Laozi and *Dao De Jing* (also known as *Laozi*) remains controversial.

44. He criticizes the supranational organizations or governments such as the UN and EU as insufficient compared to tianxia, since they still have nations and states as their foundation, and thus are incapable of prioritizing a common interest over the interest of each member state. See Zhao Tingyang, "Rethinking Empire from a Chinese Concept," 37–38.

45. Zhao Tingyang, *Tianxia tixi*, 124. In Chinese, *gong* is usually understood as "public" and *yi* as "will" or "intention"; thus the literal translation of "gongyi" in Chinese is "public will." Lu Ding—the translator of Zhao's third essay (2009) into Chinese—uses "gongyi" as the Chinese translation of the English term "general will."

46. Zhao Tingyang, "A Political World Philosophy," 9.

47. "Briefly, the Western metaphysical presupposition of the absolute individual inevitably results in conflict (imagined by Hobbes) between each and every person. This logically leads to Carl Schmitt's concept of politics as being between enemies, a very honest representation of Western political thinking." Zhao Tingyang, "A Political World Philosophy," 14.

48. Zhao Tingyang, *Tianxia tixi*, 21–22.

49. Zhao Tingyang, *Tianxia tixi*, 14–15.

50. Zhao Tingyang, *Tianxia tixi*, 100.

51. Zhao also contends that Chinese thought upholds the principle of nonimposing, which can be found in an expression from the ancient texts—*li bu wan jiao* (do not teach formal rituals without being requested). He maintains that this makes his theory of tianxia a kind of "cultural liberalism." Zhao Tingyang, *Tianxia tixi*, 33.

52. Zhao Tingyang, *Tianxia tixi*, 27.

53. Zhao Tingyang, *Tianxia tixi*, 28.

54. Zhao Tingyang, *Tianxia tixi*, 27–28. Considering the frustrating lack of virtues in the majority of the people, how the virtuous ones would lead them to form collective judgments or sentiments that would be against the majority's basic inclinations is a mystery unexplained in Zhao's argumentation.

55. Zhao Tingyang, *Tianxia tixi*, 29.

56. Zhao Tingyang, *Tianxia tixi*, 57.

57. Zhao maintains that the ruling elite's knowledge of minxin comes from "observation of social trends or preferences." It is his belief that such knowledge can better reveal the true preference of the people: "In fact, careful and sincere observations can better detect truth and come to a better reflection of public choice than do democratic elections, which become spoilt by money, misled by media and distorted by strategic voting" ("Rethinking Empire from a Chinese Concept," 31).

58. Zhao Tingyang, *Tianxia tixi*, 140–148; Zhao Tingyang, "A Political World Philosophy," 12–13.

59. Zhao Tingyang, *Tianxia tixi*, 69–70.

60. Wang, *The Peripheries of Huaxia*; Wang, *The Qiangs between the Hans and the Tibetans*.

61. Chang, "A New Study on the Chinese Ethnic Thought."

62. Chang, "The Concept of 'Zhongguo,'" 203–205.

63. Chang, "The Concept of 'Zhongguo,'" 242–324.

64. Zhang, *Respect and Farewell*, 277–278.

65. Zhang, *Respect and Farewell*, 278–280.

66. See also Kuan-Hsing Chen, *Asia as Method*, 257–268.

67. Zhang is not alone in his critique. Qian Liqun, a representative Lu Xun scholar, has also tackled problems of Sinocentrism and the chauvinism of great nations in the Mao and post-Mao eras. See Qian, *Mao's Time and the Post-Mao Time*.

68. See Wang, "The Concept of Asia in Modern China," 197–201.

69. See Qian, "The Way Our Generation Imagined the World," 523–534; Chen, "What the 'Third World' Means to Me."

70. See Chen, "Chen Yingzhen's Third World."

Bibliography

Abe, Takeo 安部健夫. "The Idea of *Tianxia* of the Chinese People" 中國人の天下觀念. In *Historical Studies on the Yüan Period* 元代史の之研究, 425–526. 1954. Reprint, Tokyo: Sobunsha 創文社, 1972.

ACLS. *Report of the Commission on the Humanities*. New York: American Council of Learned Societies, 1964.

Aguiar, Carolina Moulin. "Cosmopolitanism." In *Globalization and Autonomy Glossary*, Carolina Mulin-Academia.edu, uploaded September 28, 2006.

Ahmad, Aijaz. *In Theory: Classes, Nations, Literatures*. London: Verso, 2008.

Allison, Anne. "The Attractions of the J-Wave for American Youth." In *Soft Power Superpowers: Cultural and National Assets of Japan and the United States*, edited by Yasushi Watanabe and David L. McConnell, 99–110. Armonk, NY: M. E. Sharpe, 2008.

Amin, Samir. "China 2013: Is China Capitalist or Socialist?" *Monthly Review* 64, no. 10 (2013): 14–33.

Anagnost, Ann. *National Past-Times: Narrative, Representation, and Power in Modern China*. Durham, NC: Duke University Press, 1997.

Anderson, Kevin. *Marx at the Margins: On Nationalism, Ethnicity and the Non-Western Societies*. Chicago: University of Chicago Press, 2010.

Anderson, Perry. "Internationalism: A Breviary" (editorial). *New Left Review* 14 (March–April 2002): 5–25.

———. "Modernity and Revolution." *New Left Review* 144 (March–April 1984): 96–113.

———. *Spectrum*. London: Verso, 2005.

Angel, Stephen C. *Contemporary Confucian Political Philosophy*. Cambridge: Polity, 2012.

An Yanming. "Liang Shuming: Eastern and Western Cultures and Confucianism." In *Contemporary Chinese Philosophy*, edited by Chun-Ying Cheng and Nicholas Bunnin, 147–163. London and Oxford: Blackwell, 2002.

Apter, David E., and Tony Saich. *Revolutionary Discourse in Mao's Republic*. Cambridge, MA: Harvard University Press, 1994.

Arrighi, Giovanni. *The Long Twentieth Century*. London: Verso, 1994.

Baba, Kumihiko. *Sengo nihon no chūgoku zō: Nihon no haisen kara—bunkadai kakumei/ nichū fukkō made* [The image of China in postwar Japan: From Japan's defeat in the war to the Cultural Revolution and the restoration of diplomatic relations between China and Japan]. Tokyo: Shinyakusha, 2010.

Bai Bide 白璧德 (Irving Babbitt). "Bai Bide zhongxi renwen jiaoyu shuo" 白璧德中西人文教育說 [Babbitt on humanistic education in China and the West]. In *Guogu xinzhi lun* [Discussions of national traditions and new learning], edited by Sun Shangyang and Guo Lanfang, 39–48. Beijing: Zhongguo guangbo dianshi chubanshe, 1995.

Bai Tongdong. "A Mencian Version of Limited Democracy." *Res Publica* 14, no. 1 (2008): 19–34.

Ban Gu 班固. *Han shu* 漢書. Beijing: Zhonghua, 1962.

Bao Maohong. "Environmental NGOs in Transforming China." *Nature and Culture* 4, no. 1 (2009): 1–16.

Barfield, Thomas. *The Perilous Frontier: Nomadic Empires and China*. Oxford: Basil Blackwell, 1989.

Barkey, Elaine. *Empire of Difference: The Ottomans in Comparative Perspective*. Cambridge: Cambridge University Press, 2008.

Bell, Daniel A. *Beyond Liberal Democracy: Political Thinking for an East Asian Context*. Princeton, NJ: Princeton University Press, 2006.

———. *The China Model: Political Meritocracy and the Limits of Democracy*. Princeton, NJ: Princeton University Press, 2016.

———. *China's New Confucianism: Politics and Everyday Life in a Changing Society*. Princeton, NJ: Princeton University Press, 2010.

———. "War, Peace, and China's Soft Power: A Confucian Approach." *Diogenes* 221 (2009): 26–40.

Bell, Daniel A., and Avner de-Shalit. *The Spirit of Cities: Why the Identity of a City Matters in a Global Age*. Princeton, NJ: Princeton University Press, 2013.

Bell, Daniel A., and Yingchuan Mo. "Harmony in the World 2013: The Ideal and the Reality." *Social Indicators Research* 118, no. 2 (2014): 797–818.

Benjamin, Walter. *Selected Writings*. Edited by Michael Williams Jennings, Howard Eiland, and Gary Smith. Translated by Rodney Livingstone. 4 vols. Cambridge, MA: Belknap, 1996–2003.

———. "Theses on the Philosophy of History." In *Illuminations: Essays and Reflections*, 253–264. 1955. Reprint, New York: Schocken, 1968.

Berger, Mark, and Heloise Weber. *Rethinking the Third World: International Development and World Politics*. London: Palgrave, 2014.

Berlin, Isaiah. *The Hedgehog and the Fox: An Essay on Tolstoy's View of History*. New York: Simon and Schuster, 1953.

Berman, Harold J. *Law and Revolution: The Formation of the Western Legal Tradition*. Cambridge, MA: Harvard University Press, 1983.

Billioud, Sébastien, and Joël Thoraval. *The Sage and the People: The Confucian Revival in China*. Oxford: Oxford University Press, 2015.

Bol, Peter. "Government, Society and State: On the Political Visions of Ssu-ma Kuang and Wang An-shih." In *Ordering the World: Approaches to State and Society in Sung Dynasty China*, edited by Robert Hymes and Conrad Schirokauer. Berkeley: University of California Press, 1993.

Brandt, Conrad. *Stalin's Failure in China*. Cambridge, MA: Harvard University Press, 1959.

Brandt, Conrad, Benjamin Schwartz, and J. K. Fairbank, eds. *A Documentary History of Chinese Communism*. New York: Atheneum, 1967.

Branigan, Tania. "Chinese State TV Unveils Global Expansion Plan." *Guardian*, December 8, 2011, http://www.guardian.co.uk/world/2011/dec/08/china-state-television-global-expansion.

Brockmann, Stephen. "Virgin Father and Prodigal Son." *Philosophy and Literature* 27, no. 2 (2003): 341–362.

Bu paoqi, bu fangqi: Shibing tuji xianxiang 不抛弃，不放弃：士兵突击现象 [Never let go, never give up: The phenomenon of *Soldiers Sortie*]. Beijing: Haiyang chubanshe, 2008.

Burbank, Jane, and Frederick Cooper. *Empires in World History: Power and the Politics of Difference*. Princeton, NJ: Princeton University Press, 2010.

Byers, Thomas B. "History Re-membered: *Forrest Gump*, Postfeminist Masculinity, and the Burial of the Counterculture." *Modern Fiction Studies* 42, no. 2 (1996): 419–444.

Cai Jingquan 蔡靖泉. *Chu wenhua liubian shi* 楚文化流變史 [A history of the development of Chu culture]. Wuhan: Hubei renmin chubanshe, 2001.

Callahan, William A. *China: The Pessoptimist Nation*. Oxford: Oxford University Press, 2010.

———. *China Dreams: 20 Visions of the Future*. Oxford: Oxford University Press, 2013.

———. "Chinese Visions of World Order: Post-hegemonic or a New Hegemony?" *International Studies Review* 10 (2008): 749–761.

Candela, Ana Maria. "*Qiaoxiang* on the Silk Road: Cultural Imaginaries as Structures of Feeling in the Making of a Global China." Paper presented at the Shifting Geopolitical Ecologies and New Spatial Imaginaries Workshop of the Conference on Inter-Asian Connections III, Hong Kong, June 6–8, 2012.

Carlson, Allen. "Moving beyond Sovereignty? A Brief Consideration of Recent Changes in China's Approach to International Order and the Emergence of the *Tianxia* Concept." *Journal of Contemporary China* 20, no. 68 (2011).

———. "Reimagining the Frontier: Patterns of Sinicization and the Emergence of New Thinking about China's Territorial Periphery." Paper presented at the Civilizations and Sinicization Workshop, Beijing University, March 25–26, 2011.

Chan, Alan. "Harmony as a Contested Metaphor and Conceptions of Rightness (*Yi*) in Early Confucian Ethics." In *How Should One Live? Comparing Ethics in Ancient China and Greco-Roman Antiquity*, edited by Richard King and Dennis Schilling. Berlin: De Gruyter Verlag, 2011.

Chan, Joseph. "Democracy and Meritocracy: Toward a Confucian Perspective." *Journal of Chinese Philosophy* 34, no. 2 (June 2007).

———. "Territorial Boundaries and Confucianism." In *Boundaries, Ownership, and Autonomy*, edited by David Miller and Sohail H. Hashmi. Princeton, NJ: Princeton University Press, 2001.

Chan, Wing-tsit. *A Source Book in Chinese Philosophy*. Princeton, NJ: Princeton University Press, 1963.

Chang, Chishen 張其賢. "The Concept of 'Zhongguo' and the Distinction of 'Hua' 'Yi'—a Historical Survey" 「中國」概念與「華夷」之辨的歷史探討. PhD diss., National Taiwan University 國立台灣大學政治學系博士論文, 2009.

———. "The Formation of Two Key Concepts: Zhongguo and Tianxia" 「中國」與「天下」概念探源. *Soochow Journal of Political Science* 東吳政治學報 27, no. 3 (2009): 169–256.

———. "A New Study on the Chinese Ethnic Thought during the Spring and Autumn Period" 春秋時期族群概念新探. *Taiwanese Journal of Political Science* 政治科學論叢 39 (2009): 85–158.

———. "Tianxia System on a Snail's Horns." *Inter-Asia Cultural Studies* 12, no. 1 (March 2011): 28–42.

Chauhan, Shivdan Singh. *Nationalities Question in USA and USSR*. New Delhi: Sterling, 1976.

Cheah, Pheng. *Inhuman Conditions*. Cambridge, MA: Harvard University Press, 2006.

———. *Spectral Nationality: Passages of Freedom from Kant to Postcolonial Literatures of Liberation*. New York: Columbia University Press, 2003.

———. "What Is a World? On World Literature as World-Making Activity." *Daedalus* 137, no. 3 (2008): 26–39.

Chen, Kuan-Hsing. *Asia as Method: Toward Deimperialization*. Durham, NC: Duke University Press, 2010.

———. "Chen Yingzhen's Third World" 陳映真的第三世界. *Taiwan: Radical Quarterly in Social Studies* 台灣社會研究季刊 78 (2010): 215–268.

Chen, Yingzhen. "What the 'Third World' Means to Me." Translated by Petrus Liu. *Inter-Asia Cultural Studies* 6, no. 4 (2005): 535–540.

Chen, Zhimin. "Nationalism, Internationalism and Chinese Foreign Policy." *Journal of Contemporary China* 14, no. 42 (2005): 35–53.

Chen Duxiu 陳獨秀. "Bo Kang Youwei zhi zongtong zongli shu" 駁康有爲致總統總理書 [A refutation of Kang Youwei's letter to the president and the prime minister]. In *Duxiu wencun* 獨秀文存 [Extant writings of Chen Duxiu], 68–72. Hefei: Anhui renmin chubanshe, 1987.

Chen Guanzhong 陳冠中. "中國天朝主義與香港" (Zhongguo tianchaozhuyi yu xianggang) [China's tributary system and Hong Kong]. In 《香港：都市想像與文化記憶》(*Xianggang: Dushi xiangxiang yu wenhua jiyi*) [Hong Kong: Imagining the city and cultural memory], 國際學術研討會 (Guoji wenshu taohui) [International Academic Symposium], Hong Kong, December 17, 2011.

Chen Guying 陳鼓應, ed. *Zhuangzi jinzhu jinyi* 莊子今注今譯. Beijing: Zhonghua, 1994.

Chen Qiyou 陳奇猷, ed. *Lü shi chun qiu jiao shi* 呂氏春校釋. Shanghai: Xuelin, 1984.

Chen Shuyu 陳漱渝. "Sibada zhihun yu Liang Qichao" 斯巴達之魂與梁啟超 ["The Soul of Sparta" and Liang Qichao]. *Lu Xun yanjiu yuekan* 魯迅研究月刊 [Lu Xun Studies Monthly] 10 (1993): 62.

Chen Xujing 陳序經. *Chen Xujing xueshu lunzhu* 陳序經學術論著 [Academic writings of Chen Xujing]. Edited by Qiu Zhihua 邱志華. Hangzhou: Zhejiang renmin chubanshe, 1998.

Chen Zehuan. "Individuals, Nation States, and the World: A Study of Liang Qichao's Views on Human Rights." Paper presented at Chinese Academy of Social Sciences, Beijing, 2010.

Chernilo, Daniel. "Cosmopolitanism and the Question of Universalism." In *Handbook of Cosmopolitan Studies*, edited by G. Delanty, 47–59. Oxon: Routledge, 2012.

"China's ENGOs Increase by Almost 8000." *People's Daily* (English edition), March 5, 2013.

Chunqiu Gongyang zhuan zhushu 春秋公羊傳注疏. In *Shisan jing zhushu* 十三經注疏, vol. 7. Taipei: Yiwen, 1976.

Cohen, Paul. *Discovering History in China: American Historical Writing on the Recent Chinese Past*. New York: Columbia University Press, 1984.

Connery, Chris. "Waves." In *Ten Thousand Waves*, edited by Isaac Julien, Chris Connery, Andrew Maerkle, and Gao Shiming, 10–18. London: Victoria Miro Gallery, 2010.

Connor, Walter. *The National Question in Marxist-Leninist Theory and Strategy*. Princeton, NJ: Princeton University Press, 1984.

Curtius, Ernst Robert. *European Literature and the Latin Middle Ages*. Translated by Willard R. Trask. 1948. Reprint, Princeton, NJ: Princeton University Press, 1953.

Dai, Jinhua. "*Hero* and the Invisible *Tianxia*." Translated by Yajun Mo. In *The Post-Post Cold War*, edited by Lisa Rofel. Durham, NC: Duke University Press, forthcoming.

Day, Alexander. "The End of the Peasant? New Rural Reconstruction in China." *boundary 2* 35, no. 2 (2008): 49–73.

de Bary, Theodore, and Irene Bloom, eds. *Sources of Chinese Tradition*. 2nd ed. New York: Columbia University Press, 1999.

Deng Shi 鄧實. "Guxue fuxing lun" 古學復興論 [On the revival of traditional learning]. *Guocui xuebao* 國粹學報 [National Essence Journal] 9 (1905): 1023–1030.

Deng Xiaoping. *Selected Writings of Deng*, vols. 2 and 3. Beijing: People's Publishing House, 1993, 1995.

Dernberger, Robert F. "Economic Development and Modernization in Contemporary China." In *Technology and Communist Culture: The Socio-cultural Impact of Technology under Socialism*, edited by Frederic J. Fleron Jr., 201–248. New York: Praeger, 1977.

d'Hooghe, Ingrid. "Public Diplomacy in the People's Republic of China." In *The New Public Diplomacy: Soft Power in International Relations*, edited by Jan Melissen, 88–105. Hampshire, UK: Palgrave Macmillan, 2005.

Di Cosmo, Nicola. *Ancient China and Its Enemies: The Rise of Nomadic Power in East Asian History*. Cambridge: Cambridge University Press, 2002.

Dikotter, Frank. *The Discourse of Race in Modern China.* Hong Kong: Hurst, 1992.

Dimberg, Ronald G. *The Sage and Society: The Life and Thought of Ho Hsin-yin.* Monographs of the Society for Asian and Comparative Philosophy, no. 1. Honolulu: University of Hawai'i Press, 1974.

Dirlik, Arif. "June Fourth at 25: Forget Tiananmen, You Don't Want to Hurt the Chinese People's Feelings—and Miss Out on the Business of the New 'New China'!" *International Journal of China Studies* 5, no. 2 (2014): 295–329.

Dittmer, Lowell. *Sino-Soviet Normalization and Its International Implications, 1945–1990.* Seattle: University of Washington Press, 1992.

Doyle, Michael. "Kant, Liberal Legacies and Foreign Affairs." *Philosophy and Public Affairs* 1–2, no. 12 (1983).

"Dreams Do Come True." *Beijing Review*, February 15, 2008, http://www.bjreview.com .cn/culture/txt/2008-02/15/content_99534.htm.

Dreyer, June Teufel. "The 'Tianxia Trope': Will China Change the International System?" *Journal of Contemporary China* 24, no. 96 (2015): 1015–1031.

Du, Zhenshen. *Society and State in Ancient Time* 古代社會與國家. Taipei: Linking, 2000.

Duan Huaiqing 段懷清. *Bai Bide yu Zhongguo wenhua* 白璧德與中國文化 [Babbitt and Chinese culture]. Beijing: Shoudu shifan daxue chubanshe, 2006.

Duara, Prasenjit. *The Crisis of Global Modernity: Asian Traditions and a Sustainable Future.* Cambridge: Cambridge University Press, 2015.

———. "De-constructing the Chinese Nation." In *Chinese Nationalism*, edited by Jonathan Unger, 31–55. Armonk, NY: M. E. Sharpe, 1996.

———. *Rescuing History from the Nation: Questioning Narratives of Modern China.* Chicago: University of Chicago Press, 1997.

———. *Sovereignty and Authenticity: Manchukuo and the East Asian Modern.* Lanham, MD: Rowman and Littlefield, 2004.

Duverger, Maurice, ed. *Le Concept d'empire.* Paris: Presses Universitaires de France, 1980.

Du Yaquan 杜亞泉. *Du Yaquan wenxuan* 杜亞泉文選 [Selected writings of Du Yaquan]. Shanghai: Huadong shifan daxue chubanshe, 1993.

Eagleton, Terry. *The Ideology of the Aesthetic.* New York: Blackwell, 1990.

Elvin, Mark. *The Retreat of the Elephants: An Environmental History of China.* New Haven, CT: Yale University Press, 2006.

Erfid, Robert. "Learning by Heart: An Anthropological Perspective on Environmental Learning in Lijiang." In *Environmental Anthropology Today*, edited by Helen Kopnina and Leanor Shoreman-Oiumet, 254–266. New York: Routledge, 2011.

———. "Learning the Land beneath Our Feet: NGO 'Local Learning Materials' and Environmental Education in Yunnan Province." Unpublished essay.

Ertman, Thomas. *Birth of the Leviathan: Building States and Regimes in Medieval and Early Modern Europe.* Cambridge: Cambridge University Press, 1997.

Fairbank, John K., ed. *The Chinese World Order: Traditional China's Foreign Relations.* Cambridge, MA: Harvard University Press, 1968.

Falkenhausen, Lothar von. "On the Typology of Chu Bronzes." *Beiträge zur allgemeinen und vergleichenden Archäologie* 11 (1991): 57–113.

Fan Ye 范曄 et al. *Hou Han shu* 後漢書. Beijing: Zhonghua, 1965.

Fei Xiaotong. "Xiangtu bense." In *Xiangtu Zhongguo* [Rural China], 1–7. Shanghai: Guanchashe, 1947.

Feng Youlan (Fung Yu-lan). *A Short History of Chinese Philosophy.* New York: Free Press, 1948.

Ferguson, James. *Global Shadows: Africa in the Neoliberal World Order.* Durham, NC: Duke University Press, 2006.

Feuerwerker, Yi-tsi Mei. "Reconsidering *Xueheng*: Neo-conservatism in Early Republican China." In *Literary Societies of Republican China*, edited by Kirk A. Denton and Michel Hockx, 137–169. Lanham, MD: Lexington, 2008.

Fletcher, Joseph. "Integrative History: Parallels and Interconnections in the Early Modern Period, 1500–1800." *Journal of Turkish Studies* 9 (1985): 37–57.

Fogel, Joshua. *Politics and Sinology: The Case of Naitō Konan.* Cambridge, MA: Harvard University Press, 1984.

Foucault, Michel. *The Order of Things: An Archaeology of the Human Sciences.* New York: Pantheon, 1970.

Frank, Andre Gunder. *ReOrient: Global Economy in the Asian Age.* Berkeley: University of California Press, 1998.

Fraser, Matthew. *Weapons of Mass Distraction: Soft Power and American Empire.* New York: Thomas Dunne, 2005.

Frühstück, Sabine. *Uneasy Warriors: Gender, Memory, and Popular Culture in the Japanese Army.* Berkeley: University of California Press, 2007.

Fukuyama, Francis. *The Origin of Political Order: From Prehuman Times to the French Revolution.* New York: Farrar, Straus and Giroux, 2011.

Fukuzawa Yukichi. *An Outline of the Theory of Civilization.* Translated by David Dilworth and G. Cameron Hurst III. New York: Columbia University Press, 2008.

Furth, Charlotte. "Intellectual Change: From the Reform Movement to the May Fourth Movement, 1895–1920." In *An Intellectual History of Modern China*, edited by Merle Goldman and Leo Ou-fan Lee. New York: Cambridge University Press, 2002.

Gallagher, Mary Elizabeth. *Contagious Capitalism: Globalization and the Politics of Labor in China.* Princeton, NJ: Princeton University Press, 2005.

Gallahan, William. "Chinese Visions of World Order: Post-hegemonic or a New Hegemony?" *International Studies Review* 10 (2008): 749–761.

Gan, Chuen-song 干春松. "Tianxia, a Reform by the Authority of the Ancient in an Age of Globalization" 天下，全球化時代的托古改制. *China Book Review* 中國書評 5 (2006): 31–40.

Gan Chunsong 干春松. *Chonghui wangdao: Rujia yu shijie zhixu* 重回王道：儒家與世界秩序 [A return to the Kingly Way: Confucianism and the world order]. Shanghai: Huadong shifan daxue chubanshe, 2012.

———. 儒学概论 (*Rujia gailun*) [An introduction to Confucian studies]. Beijing: Zhongguo renmin daxue chubanshe, 2009.

———. "王者无外"与"夷夏之防": 公羊三世说与夷夏观念的冲突与协调 (Wangzhi wuwai yu yixia zhi fang: Gongyang san shi shuo yu yixia guannian de chongtu yu xietiao) [The Kingly Way without outsiders and protection against barbarians: The conflict and compromise between the *Gongyang shishuo* and the concept of barbarians]. Paper presented at People's University, October 24, 2010.

Gan Yang 甘陽. *Gujin zhongxi zhi zheng* 古今中西之爭 [Contention: Tradition and modernity, China and the West]. Beijing: Sanlian, 2006.

———. *Jiangcuo jiucuo* 將錯就錯 [Live with errors]. Beijing: Sanlian, 2002.

———. *Tong santong* 通三統 [Traversing three traditions]. Beijing: Sanlian, 2007.

———. *Wenming guojia daxue* 文明・國家・大學 [Civilizations, nation-states, universities]. Beijing: Sanlian, 2011.

———. "Zhongguo daolu: Sanshinian he liushinian" 中國道路: 三十年和六十年 [China's path: Thirty years and sixty years]. *Dushu* 讀書 [Reading] 6 (2007): 1–6.

———. "Zhongguo jiandanhua xuexi xifang de shidai yijing jieshu le" 中國簡單化學習西方的時代已經結束了 [The age in which China simplistically learned from the West is over]. *Kaifang shidai* 開放時代 [Open Times] 1 (2009), www.opentimes.cn.

Gellner, Ernest. *Nations and Nationalism.* Oxford: Blackwell, 1983.

Ge Zhaozhao 葛兆兆. 宋代《中国》意识的凸显—关于近世民族主义思想的一个远源 (Songdai [Zhongguo]—Yishi de tuxian—Guanyu jin shi minzuzhuyi sixiang de yi ge yuanyuan) [The prominence of "China" consciousness in the Song dynasty: A distant source of nationalist thought in modern times]. *Journal of History, Literature, and Philosophy* 1 (2004).

Gill, Bates, and Yanzhong Huang. "Sources and Limits of China's Soft Power." *Survival* (summer 2006).

Gittings, John. *Survey of the Sino-Soviet Dispute: A Commentary and Extracts from Recent Polemics, 1963–67.* Oxford: Oxford University Press, 1968.

Glanville, Luke. "Retaining the Mandate of Heaven: Sovereign Accountability in Ancient China." *Millennium* 39, no. 2 (2010).

Gleijeses, Piero. *Conflicting Missions: Havana, Washington and Africa, 1959–1976.* Chapel Hill: University of North Carolina Press, 2002.

Goldstein, Steven M. "Nationalism and Internationalism: Sino-Soviet Relations." In *Chinese Foreign Policy: Theory and Practice*, edited by Thomas W. Robinson and David Shambaught, 224–265. Oxford: Clarendon, 1994.

Goossaert, Vincent, and David Palmer. *The Religious Question in Modern China.* Chicago: University of Chicago Press, 2011.

Gottlieb, Roger S. "The Transcendence of Justice and the Justice of Transcendence: Mysticism, Deep Ecology, and Political Life." *Journal of the American Academy of Religion* 67, no. 1 (March 1999): 149–166.

Graff, David A. *Medieval Chinese Warfare, 300–900.* London: Routledge, 2002.

Grieder, Jerome B. *Hu Shih and the Chinese Renaissance: Liberalism in the Chinese Revolution, 1917–1937.* Cambridge, MA: Harvard University Press, 1970.

Gu, Jiegang 顧頡剛. *Shi lin za shi chu bian* 史林雜識初編 [Personal notes of a gleaner in the forest of history: The preliminary collection]. 1963. Reprint, Beijing: Zhonghua, 2005.

Guevara, Che. "At the Afro-Asian Conference in Algeria" (February 24, 1965). In *Che Guevara Reader*, edited by David Deutschmann. Minneapolis: Ocean, 2005, https://www.marxists.org/archive/guevara/1965/02/24.htm.

———. *Che Guevara Reader: Writings on Politics and Revolution*. Edited by David Deutschmann. Los Angeles: Ocean Press, 1997.

Guex, Samuel. *Entre nonchalance et désespoir: Les intellectuels japonais face à la guerre* [Between nonchalance and despair: Japanese intellectuals facing war]. Berne: Peter Lang, 2005.

Gupta, Uma Das, ed. *The Oxford India Tagore: Selected Writings on Education and Nationalism*. Delhi: Oxford University Press, 2009.

Gu Zhun 顾准. *Gu Zhun wenji* 顾准文集 [Collected writings of Gu Zhun]. Guiyang: Guizhou renmin chubanshe, 1994.

———. *Xila chengbang zhidu* 希腊城邦制度 [The Greek system of city-states]. Beijing: Zhongguo shehui kexue chubanshe, 1982.

Habermas, Jürgen. *Time of Transitions*. Edited and translated by Ciaran Cronin and Max Pensky. Cambridge: Polity, 2006.

Hadot, Pierre. *Philosophy as a Way of Life: Spiritual Exercises from Socrates to Foucault*. Edited by Arnold I. Davidson. Translated by Michael Chase. Malden, MA: Blackwell, 1995.

Halliday, Fred. "Marxist Analysis and Post-revolutionary China." *New Left Review* 100 (November–December 1976).

Hammerschlag, Susan. *The Figural Jew: Politics and Identity in Postwar French Thought*. Chicago: University of Chicago Press, 2010.

Hampshire, Stuart. *Innocence and Experience*. Cambridge, MA: Harvard University Press, 1989.

Han, Deqiang. *Peng Zhuang: Quanqiu Hua Xianjing yu Zhongguo Xianshi Xuanze* [Collision: The pitfalls of globalization and China's realistic choices]. Beijing: Jingji Guanli Press, 2000.

Han, Yuhai 韓毓海. *Tianxia: China Contains All Foreigners* 天下：包納四夷的中國. Beijing: Jiuzhou, 2011.

Hardt, Michael, and Antonio Negri. *Empire*. 2000. Reprint, Cambridge, MA: Harvard University Press, 2011.

———. *Multitude: War and Democracy in the Age of Empire*. New York: Penguin, 2004.

Harootunian, Harry. "Who Needs Postcoloniality? A Reply to Linder." *Radical Philosophy* 164 (November–December 2010): 38–44.

Harvey, David. *A Brief History of Neoliberalism*. Oxford: Oxford University Press, 2005.

———. *The Enigma of Capital and the Crises of Capitalism*. Oxford: Oxford University Press, 2010.

Hayot, Eric. *The Hypothetical Mandarin: Sympathy, Modernity, and Chinese Pain*. Oxford: Oxford University Press, 2009.

Heberer, Thomas. "Some Considerations on China's Minorities in the 21st Century: Conflict or Conciliation." *Duisburg Working Papers on East Asian Studies* 31 (2000): 4–25.

Heinzig, Dieter. *The Soviet Union and Communist China 1945–50: The Arduous Road to the Alliance.* Armonk, NY: M. E. Sharpe, 2015.

He Zhaotian 賀照田, ed. *Xifang xiandaixing de quzhe yu zhankai* 西方现代性的曲折与展开 [The circuitousness and unfolding of Western modernity]. Changchun: Jilin renmin chubanshe, 2002.

Ho, Ping-Ti. "In Defense of Sinicization: A Rebuttal of Evelyn Rawski's 'Reenvisioning the Qing.'" *Journal of Asian Studies* 57, no. 1 (February 1998): 123–155.

Hockx, Michel, and Julia Strauss, eds. *Culture in the Contemporary PRC.* Cambridge: Cambridge University Press, 2005.

Holzman, Donald. "Confucius and Ancient Chinese Literary Criticism." In *Chinese Approaches to Literature, from Confucius to Liang Ch'i ch'ao,* edited by Adele Austin Rickett, 21–48. Princeton, NJ: Princeton University Press, 1978.

Hon, Tze-ki. "National Essence, National Learning, and Culture: Historical Writings in *Guocui xuebao, Xueheng,* and *Guoxue jikan.*" *Historiography East and West* 1, no. 2 (2003): 242–286.

Hoselitz, Berthold. *The Progress of Underdeveloped Areas.* Chicago: University of Chicago Press, 1952.

Hsiao, Kung-chuan. *A Modern China and a New World: K'ang Yu-Wei, Reformer and Utopian, 1858–1927.* Seattle: University of Washington Press, 1975.

Hsieh, Meiyu. "Viewing the Han Empire from the Edge." PhD diss., Stanford University, 2011.

Hsing, I-tien 邢義田. "All under Heaven as One Family—Chinese View of Tianxia" 天下一家—中國人的天下觀. In *The Ever-Flowing Great River* 永恆的巨流, edited by Liu Dai and Hsing I-tien, 433–478. Taipei: Linking, 1981.

———. "Dong Han de Hu bing" 東漢的胡兵 [Eastern Han barbarian soldiers]. *Zhengzhi Daxue xuebao* 12 (1973): 143–166.

———. "Han dai de yi Yi zhi Yi lun" 漢代的以夷治夷論 [The Han-period theory of using barbarians to control barbarians]. *Shi yuan* 史苑 5 (1974): 9–53.

———. "The Symbolic Meaning of the Great Wall during the Qin-Han Periods Interpreted from the Ancient Idea of Tianxia" 從古代天下觀看秦漢長城的意義. In *All under Heaven as One Family: Emperor, Officials, and Society* 天下一家：皇帝, 官僚與社會, edited by Hsing I-tien, 84–135. 2002. Reprint, Beijing: Zhonghua, 2008.

Hsiung, James. *China into Its Second Rise.* London: World Scientific, 2012.

Hsu, Cho-yun, and Katheryn M. Linduff. *Western Chou Civilization.* New Haven, CT: Yale University Press, 1988.

Huang Jie 黃節. "Huangshi lisu shu" 黃史禮俗書 ["Yellow history": Rites and customs]. *Guocui xuebao* 國粹學報 [National Essence Journal] 3 (1905): 299–312.

Huang Kewu 黃克武. *Yige bei fangqi de xuanze: Liang Qichao tiaoshi sixiang zhi yanjiu* 一個被放棄的選擇: 梁啟超調適思想之研究 [A rejected option: A study of Liang Qichao's eclecticism]. Taipei: Zhongyang yanjiuyuan jindaishi yanjiusuo, 1994.

Hu Fengxiang 胡逢祥. *Shehui biange yu wenhua chuantong: Zhongguo jindai wenhua baoshou zhuyi sichao yanjiu* 社會變革與文化傳統: 中國近代文化保守主義思潮研究 [Societal change and cultural tradition: A study of conservative thought in modern China]. Shanghai: Shanghai renmin chubanshe, 2000.

"Hu Jintao's 'Bu Zheteng' Baffles Foreign Media." *People's Daily Online*, January 8, 2009, http://en.people.cn/90001/90782/90873/6570469.html.

Huntington, Samuel P. *The Clash of Civilizations and the Remaking of World Order.* New York: Simon and Schuster, 1997.

Hu Shi 胡適. *Hu Shi zizhuan* 胡適自傳 [Hu Shi's autobiography]. Edited by Cao Boyan 曹伯言. Hefei: Huangshan shushe, 1986.

———. "Xinxin yu fanxing" 信心與反省 [Confidence and introspection]. *Duli pinglun* 獨立評論 103 (June 3, 1934).

Hymes, Robert, and Conrad Schirokauer, ed. *Ordering the World: Approaches to State and Society in Sung Dynasty China.* Berkeley: University of California Press, 1993.

Ivy, Marlyn. *Discourses of the Vanishing: Modernity, Phantasm, Japan.* Chicago: University of Chicago Press, 1995.

Jacques, Martin. *When China Rules the World: The Rise of the Middle Kingdom and the End of the Western World.* London: Penguin, 2009.

Jensen, Lionel M. "Culture Industry, Power, and the Spectacle of China's 'Confucius Institutes.'" In *China in and beyond the Headlines*, edited by Timothy B. Weston and Lionel M. Jensen, 271–299. Lanham, MD: Rowman and Littlefield, 2012.

Jiang Lihong 蔣禮鴻, ed. *Shang Jun shu zhuizhi* 商君書錐知. Beijing: Zhonghua, 1996.

Jiang Qing. *A Confucian Constitutional Order: How China's Past Can Shape Its Political Future.* Translated by Edmund Ryden. Edited by Daniel A. Bell and Fan Ruiping. Princeton, NJ: Princeton University Press, 2012.

———. 生命信仰与王道政治:儒家文化的现代价值 (*Shenming xinyang yu wangdao zhengzhi: Rujia wenhua de xiandai jiazhi*) [A faith in life and the Kingly Way of politics: The modern value of Confucian culture]. Taipei: Yang Zheng Tang, 2004.

Jiang Shigong. *Zhongguo Xianggang: Wenhua yu zhengzhi de shiye* [China's Hong Kong: The establishment of culture and institutions]. Hong Kong: Oxford University Press, 2008.

Jiang Xianbin 蔣賢斌. "Ba Gu Zhun huangei lishi: Gu Zhun de dansheng yu zhenglun" 把顧准還給歷史: 顧准的誕生與爭論 [Return Gu Zhun to history: Controversies over the birth of "Gu Zhun"]. *Xueshu lunheng* 學術論衡 [Scholarly Review] 6 (2006): 19–28.

Johnston, Alasdair Ian. *Cultural Realism: Strategic Culture and Grand Strategy in Chinese History.* Princeton, NJ: Princeton University Press, 1995.

Kang, David. *East Asia before the West: Five Centuries of Trade and Tribute.* New York: Columbia University Press, 2011.

Kang Youwei. *Datong shu* 大同書 [Book of the great community]. Shenyang: Liangning renmin, 1994.

———. "Gongmin zizhi pian" 公民自治篇 [Essay on citizens' self-rule]. *Xinmin congbao* 新民叢報 5 (April 1902).

———. *Kang Youwei quanji* 康有為全集 [Complete works]. Vols. 2 and 3. Shanghai: Shanghai guji, 1992.

———. *Kang Youwei zhenglun ji* 康有為政論集 [Collected political commentaries of Kang Youwei]. Beijing: Zhonghua shuju, 1981.

———. *Ta T'ung Shu: The One-World Philosophy of K'ang Yu-wei*. Translated by Laurence Thompson. London: Routledge, 2011.

Kant, Immanuel. *Critique of the Power of Judgment*. Translated by Paul Guyer and Eric Mathews. Cambridge: Cambridge University Press, 2000.

———. "Idea for a Universal History from a Cosmopolitan Point of View." In *On History*, edited by Lewis White Beck. Indianapolis: Library of Liberal Arts, 1963.

———. "Idea for a Universal History with a Cosmopolitan Purpose." In *Kant: Political Writings*, edited by H. S. Reiss. Cambridge: Cambridge University Press, 1991.

———. *Political Writings*. Translated by H. B. Nisbet. Cambridge: Cambridge University Press, 1991.

Karl, Rebecca. *Staging the World: Chinese Nationalism at the Turn of the Twentieth Century*. Durham, NC: Duke University Press, 2002.

Keane, Michael. "From National Preoccupation to Overseas Aspiration." In *TV Drama in China*, edited by Ying Zhu, Michael Keane, and Ruoyun Bai, 145–156. Hong Kong: Hong Kong University Press, 2008.

Kennedy, Scott. "The Myth of the Beijing Consensus." *Journal of Contemporary China* 19, no. 65 (2010): 461–477.

Kern, Martin. *The Stele Inscriptions of Ch'in Shih-huang: Text and Ritual in Early Chinese Imperial Representation*. New Haven, CT: American Oriental Society, 2000.

Kim, Youngmin. "Political Unity in Neo-Confucianism: The Debate between Wang Yangming and Zhan Ruoshui." *Philosophy East and West* 62, no. 2 (2012): 246–263.

Kirby, William C. "China and the Socialist World Economy." In *Global Conjectures: China in Transnational Perspective*, edited by William C. Kirby, Mechthild Leutner, and Klaus Mühlhahn, 56–72. Berlin: Lit Verlag, 2006.

Kohrman, Matthew. "Depoliticizing Tobacco's Exceptionality: Male Sociality, Death, and Memory-Making among Chinese Cigarette Smokers." *China Journal* 58 (2007): 85–109.

Kopnina, Helen, and Leanor Shoreman-Oiumet, eds. *Environmental Anthropology Today*. New York: Routledge, 2011.

Kuhn, Philip A. *Chinese among Others: Emigration in Modern Times*. New York: Rowman and Littlefield, 2008.

Kurlantzick, Joshua. *Charm Offensive: How China's Soft Power Is Transforming the World*. New Haven, CT: Yale University Press, 2007.

Lang Xianping 郎咸平. "*Shibing tuji* de jingjixue" 《士兵突击》的经济学 [The economics of *Soldiers Sortie*]. *Wuye lanhua shouzha* 午夜兰花手札 (Xyzlove.com), n.d. (accessed March 16, 2011).

Lattimore, Owen. *Inner Asian Frontiers of China*. 1940. Reprint, Boston: Beacon, 1967.

Layne, Christopher. "The Unbearable Lightness of Soft Power." In *Soft Power and US Foreign Policy: Theoretical, Historical and Contemporary Perspectives*, edited by Inderjeet Parmar and Michael Cox, 51–82. London: Routledge, 2010.

Lee, Ching Kwan. "Buying Stability in China: Markets, Protests, and Authoritarianism." Lecture at University of California, Santa Cruz, February 9, 2015.

———. "Raw Encounters: Chinese Managers, African Workers and the Politics of Casualization in Africa's Chinese Enclaves." *China Quarterly* 199 (2009): 647–666.

Lee, Haiyan. "The Charisma of Power and the Military Sublime in Tiananmen Square." *Journal of Asian Studies* 70, no. 2 (2011): 397–424.

Legge, James. *The Chinese Classics*, vol. 3: *The Shoo King, or The Book of Historical Documents*. 1935. Reprint, Taipei: SMC, 2000.

———. *The Chinese Classics*, vol. 5: *The Ch'un Ts'ew, with the Tso Chuen*. 1935. Reprint, Taipei: SMC, 2000.

———, trans. and ed. *The Works of Mencius*. New York: Dover, 1970.

Lenin, Vladimir. *Collected Works of Lenin*. Vol. 20. Moscow: Progressive, 1972.

Levenson, Joseph R. *Confucian China and Its Modern Fate: A Trilogy*, vol. 1: *The Problem of Intellectual Continuity*. 1958. Reprint, Berkeley: University of California Press, 1968.

———. *Revolution and Cosmopolitanism: The Western Stage and the Chinese Stages*. Berkeley: University of California Press, 1971.

———. "T'ien-hsia and Kuo, and the 'Transvaluation of Values.'" *Far Eastern Quarterly* 11, no. 4 (1952): 447–451.

Levine, Steve. "China Is Building the Most Extensive Global Commercial-Military Empire in History." *Quartz*, June 9, 2015, http://qz.com/415649/china-is-building-the-most-extensive-global-commercial-military-empire-in-history/.

Lewis, Mark E. *China between Empires*. Cambridge, MA: Harvard University Press, 2009.

———. *China's Cosmopolitan Empire: The Tang Dynasty*. Cambridge, MA: Harvard University Press, 2009.

———. *The Construction of Space in Early China*. Albany: State University of New York Press, 2006.

———. *The Early Chinese Empires*. Cambridge, MA: Harvard University Press, 2010.

———. "The Han Abolition of Universal Military Service." In *Warfare in Chinese History*, edited by Hans van de Ven, 57–60. Leiden: Brill, 2000.

———. *Writing and Authority in Early China*. Albany: State University of New York Press, 1999.

Li, Chenyang. "The Confucian Ideal of Harmony." *Philosophy East and West* 56, no. 4 (October 2006): 583–603.

———. *The Confucian Philosophy of Harmony*. London: Routledge, 2014.

———. "The Ideal of Harmony in Ancient Chinese and Greek Philosophy." *Dao: A Journal of Comparative Philosophy* 7, no. 1 (February 2008): 81–98.

———. "Where Does Virtuous Leadership Stand?" *Philosophy East and West* 59, no. 4 (2009).

Li, Mingjiang, ed. *Soft Power: China's Emerging Strategy in International Politics*. Lanham, MD: Lexington, 2009.

Li, Xiaobing. *A History of the Modern Chinese Army*. Lexington: University Press of Kentucky, 2007.

Liang Qichao. *Liang Qichao quanji* 梁啓超全集 [Complete works of Liang Qichao]. Beijing: Beijing chubanshe, 1999.

———. *Yinbing shi heji* 飲冰室合集 [An anthology of the writings of the Yinbing Studio]. Beijing: Zhonghua shuju, 1989.

Liang Shuming 梁漱溟. *Dong Xi wenhua ji qi zhexue* 東西文化及其哲學 [The cultures and philosophies of the East and the West]. In *Zhongguo xiandai xueshu jingdian: Liang Shuming juan* 中國現代學術經典: 梁漱溟卷 [Classics of modern Chinese scholarship: Liang Shuming]. Shijiazhuang: Hebei jiaoyu chubanshe, 1996.

Li Fang 李方. "试论唐朝的 '中国' 与 '天下'" (Shilun Tangchao de "Zhongguo" yu "Tianxia") [An analysis of "China" and "tianxia" in the Tang dynasty]. 中国边疆史地研究 (*Zhongguo bianjiang shi di yanjiu*) [Research on the History and Geography of China's Borderlands] 17, no. 2 (June 2007).

Li ji zhushu 禮記注疏. In *Shisan jing zhushu*, vol. 5. Taipei: Yiwen, 1976.

Lilla, Mark. "Reading Strauss in Beijing." *New Republic*, December 8, 2010.

Lin, Chun. *China and Global Capitalism: Reflections on Marxism, History and Contemporary Politics*. London: Palgrave, 2013.

———. "Modernity and the Violence of Global Accumulation: The Case of the Ethnic Question in China." In *Global Modernity and Social Contestation*, edited by Breno Bringel and Jose Mauricio Domingues, 51–70. London: Sage, 2015.

———. *The Transformation of Chinese Socialism*. Durham, NC: Duke University Press, 2006.

Linklater, Andrew. *Men and Citizens in the Theory of International Relations*. 2nd ed. London: Macmillan, 1990.

Lin Shaoyang. "Romanticism and Aestheticized Politics: Yasuda Yojurō and the Discourse of 'Overcoming the Modern' in Wartime Japan." *Shisōshi kenkyū* 13 (2011): 173–214.

Liu, James J. Y. *The Art of Chinese Poetry*. Chicago: University of Chicago Press, 1962.

Liu Chenglin 劉成林. *Jitan yu jingjichang: Yishu wangguo li de Huaxia yu gu Xila* 祭壇與競技場: 藝術王國裏的華夏與古希臘 [The altar and the arena: Ancient China and Greece in the kingdom of art]. Beijing: Shehui Kexue wenxian chubanshe, 2003.

Liu Junping 刘军平. "'天下' 宇宙观的演变及其哲学意蕴" ("'Tianxia' yuzhouguan de yanbian yu qi zhexue yiyun) [The development and philosophical meaning of tianxia cosmology]. *Journal of Literature, History and Philosophy* 6 (Serial No. 285) (2004).

Liu Xiaofeng 劉小楓. *Chongqi gudian shixue* 重啓古典詩學 [Poetica classica retractata]. Beijing: Huaxia chubanshe, 2010.

———. *Ciwei de wenshun* 刺猬的溫順 [The docility of the hedgehog]. Shanghai: Shanghai wenyi chubanshe, 2002.

———. *Rujiao yu minzu guojia* 儒教與民族國家 [Confucianism and the nation-state]. Beijing: Huaxia chubanshe, 2007.

———. "Shitelaosi de lubiao" 施特勞斯的路標. In *Xifang xiandaixing de quzhe yu zhankai* 西方現代性的曲折與展開 [The circuitousness and unfolding of Western modernity], edited by He Zhaotian 賀照田, 3–85. Changchun: Jilin renmin chubanshe.

———. "Shitelaosi yu Zhongguo: Gudian xinxing de xiangfeng" 施特劳斯與中國: 古典心性的相逢 [Strauss and China: The meeting of classical minds]. *Sixiang zhanxian* 思想戰綫 [Frontiers of Thought] 2 (2009): 59–65.

Li Yangfan 李扬帆. "天下观念" ("Tianxia" guannian) [On the concept of "tianxia"]. 国际政治研究 (*Guoji zhengzhi yanjiu*) [Research in International Politics] 1 (2002).

Li Yujie 李玉潔. *Zhongguo zaoqi guojia xingzhi: Zhongguo gudai wangquan he zhuanzhi zhuyi yanjiu* 中國早期國家性質: 中國古代王權和專制主義研究 [The nature of the early Chinese state: A study of monarchy and autocracy in ancient China]. Kaifeng: Henan Daxue chubanshe, 1999.

Lu, Di. "Has China's 'Going Out' Squeezed World Development?" *Guanchazhe*, December 22, 2016, http://www.guancha.cn/ludi/2016_12_22_385467_s.shtml.

Luo, Zhitian 羅志田. "The Five-*Fu* System of the Pre-Qin Period and the Ancient Ideas of *Tianxia* and *Zhongguo*" 先秦的五服制與古代的天下中國觀. In *Nationalism and Modern Chinese Thought* 民族主義與近代中國思想, 2nd ed. 1996. Reprint, Taipei: San Min Book 三民書局, 2011.

———. "From '*Tianxia*' (All under Heaven) to 'the World': Changes in the Late Qing Intellectuals' Conceptions of Human Society." *Social Sciences in China* 29, no. 2 (May 2008).

———. "Lixiang yu xianshi: Qingji minchu shijie zhuyi yu minzu zhuyi de guanlian yu hudong" 理想與現實: 清季民初世界主義與民族主義的關聯與互動 [Ideal and reality: Relation and interaction between cosmopolitanism and nationalism during the Qing and early Republican eras]. In *Xiandai Zhongguo sixiang de hexin guannian* 現代中國思想的核心概念 [Key concepts in modern Chinese thought], edited by Xu Jilin and Song Hong. Shanghai: Shanghai renmin chubanshe, 2011.

———. *Minzu zhuyi yu jindai Zhongguo sixiang* 民族主義與近代中國思想 [Nationalism and modern Chinese thought]. Taipei: Dongda tushu gongsi, 1998.

Luo Junpeng 骆俊澎. "*Shibing tuji* Riben duode 'Haiwai youxiu dianshiju' jiang" 《士兵突擊》日本奪得'海外优秀电视剧'奖 [*Soldiers Sortie* won Best Foreign Television Drama Prize in Japan]. *Junshi wenyi wang* 军事文艺网 [Military Arts and Entertainment], n.d., http://shibing.milblog.com.cn/20081027/143234.html (accessed March 16, 2011).

Lv, Xinyu. "The Narrative of the Images of Ethnic Minorities in New China: History and Politics." Unpublished manuscript.

Lynch, Michael. *Mao.* London: Routledge, 2004.

Ma, Laurence J. C., and Carolyn Cartier. *The Chinese Diaspora: Space, Place, Mobility, and Identity.* Lanham, MD: Rowman and Littlefield, 2003.

MacIntyre, Alasdair. *After Virtue.* 2nd ed. Notre Dame, IN: University of Notre Dame Press, 1984.

Makeham, John. *Lost Soul: "Confucianism" in Contemporary Chinese Academic Discourse.* Cambridge, MA: Harvard-Yenching Institute, 2008.

Mao Zedong. *The Chronology of Mao*, vol. 7. Beijing: Central Documentary Press, 2014.

———. "Meeting with Friends from Africa." August 8, 1963. In *Quotations from Mao.* Beijing: Foreign Language Press, 1966.

———. *Selected Works of Mao Tse-tung*, vol. 2. Beijing: Foreign Language Press, 1965.

———. *Selected Writings of Mao*, vol. 8. Beijing: People's Publishing House, 1999.

———. "Weixin lishiguan de pochan" [The bankruptcy of the idealist perspective of history]. In *Mao Zedong xuanji* [Selected works of Mao Zedong], 4:1509–1517. Beijing: Remin, 1960.

Ma Rong. *Social Development and Ethnic Relations in Chinese Minority Regions*. Beijing: Social Science Academic, 2012.

Marx, Karl. *Capital*, vol. 1. London: Penguin, 1990.

Marx, Karl, and Friedrich Engels. *Collected Works of Marx and Engels*, vol. 40. New York: International Publishers, 1983.

———. *The Communist Manifesto*. London: Verso, 1998.

———. *Critique of the Gotha Program*. Beijing: Beijing Foreign Language Press, 1972.

———. *The German Ideology*. Edited by C. J. Arthur. New York: International Publishers, 1970.

Mearsheimer, John. *The Tragedy of Great Power Politics*. New York: Norton, 2001.

Mei Guangdi 梅光迪. "Lun jinri wuguo xueshujie zhi xuyao" 論今日吾國學術界之需要 [What is needed in our country's academia nowadays]. In *Guogu xinzhi lun* [Discussions of national traditions and new learning], edited by Sun Shangyang and Guo Lanfang, 138–144. Beijing: Zhongguo guangbo dianshi chubanshe, 1995.

———. "Ping tichang xinwenhua zhe" 評提倡新文化者 [Comments on advocates of New Culture]. In *Guogu xinzhi lun*, edited by Sun Shangyang and Guo Lanfang, 71–77. Beijing: Zhongguo guangbo dianshi chubanshe, 1995.

———. "Xianjin xiyang renwen zhuyi" 現今西洋人文主義 [Humanism in the contemporary West]. In *Guogu xinzhi lun*, edited by Sun Shangyang and Guo Lanfang, 34–38. Beijing: Zhongguo guangbo dianshi chubanshe, 1995.

Miliband, Ralph. *Class War Conservatism*. London: Verso, 2015.

Mishra, Pankaj. *From the Ruins of the Empire: The Revolt against the West and the Remaking of Asia*. London: Penguin, 2012.

Mizoguchi Yuzo. *Chūgoku zenkindai shisō no kussetsu to tenkai* [The development and refraction of premodern Chinese thought]. Tokyo: Tokyodaigaku shuppankai, 1980.

———. *Hōhō to shite no chūgoku*. Tokyo: Tokyodaigaku shuppankai, 1989.

———. "'Ten' to 'jinmin' ni tsuite" [On heaven and human beings]. In *Nishi Junzō chosaku shū: Bekken hito to gakumon*, 160–173. Tokyo: Uchiyama shoten, 1995.

Mou Zhongjian 牟钟鉴. "She tianxia yi jia haishi ruorouqiangshi" 是天下一家还是弱肉强食. 本刊特稿 (*Benkan tegao*) [Special issue, *Benkan*] 1 (2007).

Moyo, Sam, Paris Yeros, and Praveen Jha. "Imperialism and Primitive Accumulation: Notes on the New Scramble for Africa." *Agrarian South: Journal of Political Economy* 1, no. 2 (2012): 181–203.

Murthy, Viren. "The 1911 Revolution and the Politics of Failure: Takeuchi Yoshimi and Global Capitalist Modernity." *Frontiers of History in Modern China* 6, no. 1 (2012): 19–38.

Muthu, Sankar. *Enlightenment against Empire*. Princeton, NJ: Princeton University Press, 2003.

Needham, Joseph. *Science and Civilization in China*, vol. 2. Cambridge: Cambridge University Press, 1956.

———. *Science and Civilization in China*, vol. 3. Cambridge: Cambridge University Press, 1959.

Nehamas, Alexander. *The Art of Living: Socratic Reflections from Plato to Foucault.* Berkeley: University of California Press, 1998.

Nishi Junzō. "Chūgoku shisō no naka no jinmin gainen." *Nishi* 2 (1995): 202–218.

———. "Mu kara no keisei." *Nishi* 3 (1995): 14–36.

———. *Nishi Junzō chosaku shū*, vols. 1–3. Tokyo: Uchiyama shoten, 1995.

Nishi Shinichirō and Koito Natsujirō. *Ri no igi to kōzō* [The meaning and structure of rituals]. Tokyo: Kokumin seishin kenkyujo, 1937.

Nolan, Peter. "Imperial Archipelagos: China, Western Colonialism, and the Law of the Sea." *New Left Review* 80 (March–April 2013): 77–95, http://newleftreview.org/II /80/peter-nolan-imperial-archipelagos.

———. "The Silk Road by Land and Sea." Paper presented at the China Development Forum, March 2014. Unpublished manuscript.

Nussbaum, Martha. "Comparing Virtues," review of *Mencius and Aquinas: Theories of Virtue and Conceptions of Courage*, by Lee H. Yearley. *Journal of Religious Ethics* 21, no. 2 (fall 1993): 345–367.

Nye, Joseph S. *Bound to Lead: The Changing Nature of American Power.* New York: Basic Books, 1990.

———. "The Rise of China's Soft Power." *Wall Street Journal Asia*, December 29, 2005, http://belfercenter.hks.harvard.edu/publication/1499/rise_of_chinas_soft_power.html.

———. *Soft Power: The Means to Success in World Politics.* New York: Public Affairs, 2004.

Ogden, Schubert M. *The Point of Christology.* San Francisco: Harper and Row, 1982.

Olsen, Lawrence. *Ambivalent Moderns: Portraits of Japanese Cultural Identity.* Lanham, MD: Rowman and Littlefield, 1992.

O'Neill, Onora. *Constructions of Reason: Explorations of Kant's Practical Philosophy.* Cambridge: Cambridge University Press, 1989.

Ong, Aihwa, and Donald Macon Nonini. *Ungrounded Empires: The Cultural Politics of Modern Chinese Transnationalism.* New York: Routledge, 1997.

Ouyang Zhesheng 歐陽哲生. "Zhongguo de wenyi fuxing: Hu Shi yi Zhongguo wenhua wei ticai de yingwen zuopin jiexi" 中國的文藝復興：胡適以中國文化為題材的英文作品解析 [China's renaissance: Analyses of Hu Shi's English writings on Chinese culture]. *Jindaishi yanjiu* 中國近代史研究 [Studies on Early Modern History] 4 (2009): 22–40.

Owen, Stephen. *Mi-Lou, Poetry, and the Labyrinth of Desire.* Cambridge, MA: Harvard University Press, 1989.

Palmquist, Stephen. "'The Kingdom of God Is at Hand!' (Did Kant Really Say That?)" *History of Philosophy Quarterly* 11, no. 4 (October 1994): 421–437.

Peh Shing Huei. "What Is That Again, Mr Hu?" *Straits Times* [blog], December 2008, http://blogs.straitstimes.com/2008/12/31/what-is-that-again-mr-hu.

Perdue, Peter. "A Frontier View of Chineseness." In *The Resurgence of East Asia: 500, 150 and 50-Year Perspectives*, edited by Giovanni Arrighi, Takeshi Hamashita, and Mark Selden, 51–77. New York: Routledge, 2003.

———. "History without Borders: China and Global History." *YaleGlobal online*, February 24, 2015, http://yaleglobal.yale.edu/content/history-without-borders.

Pines, Yuri. "Beasts or Humans: Pre-imperial Origins of the Sino-Barbarian Dichotomy." In *Mongols, Turks and Others*, edited by Reuven Amitai and Michal Biran, 59–102. Leiden: Brill, 2005.

———. "Changing Views of *Tianxia* in Pre-imperial Discourse." *Oriens Extremus* 43, nos. 1–2 (2002): 101–116.

———. "Disputers of the Li: Breakthroughs in the Concept of Ritual in Pre-imperial China." *Asia Major* (3rd ser.) 13, no. 1 (2000): 1–41.

———. *Envisioning the Eternal Empire: Chinese Political Thought of the Warring States Era*. Honolulu: University of Hawai'i Press, 2009.

———. "'The One That Pervades All' in Ancient Chinese Political Thought: Origins of the 'Great Unity Paradigm.'" *T'oung Pao* 86, nos. 4–5 (2000): 280–324.

———. "The Question of Interpretation: Qin History in the Light of New Epigraphic Sources." *Early China* 29 (2004): 1–44.

Pomeranz, Kenneth. *The Great Divergence: Europe, China, and the Making of the Modern World Economy*. Princeton, NJ: Princeton University Press, 2000.

Postone, Moishe. *Time, Labor and Social Domination: A Reinterpretation of Marx's Critical Theory*. Cambridge: Cambridge University Press, 1993.

Prashad, Vijay. *The Darker Nations: A People's History of the Third World*. New York: New Press, 2007.

Pun, Ngai. *Made in China: Women Factory Workers in a Global Workplace*. Durham, NC: Duke University Press, 2005.

Qian, Kun. *Imperial-Time Order: Literature, Intellectual History, and China's Road to Empire*. Leiden: Brill, 2016.

Qian, Liqun 錢理群. *Mao's Time and the Post-Mao Time (1949–2009): An Alternative Historical Writing* 毛澤東時代與后毛澤東時代：另一種歷史書寫. Taipei: Linking 台北：聯經, 2012.

———. "The Way Our Generation Imagined the World." Translated by Zhang Jingyuan. *Inter-Asia Cultural Studies* 6, no. 4 (2005): 523–534.

Qi Zhenxin 祁振欣. "*Shibing tuji*: San ge nanren yi tai xi"《士兵突击》三个男人一台戏 [*Soldiers Sortie*: Three men on one stage]. *Junshi wenyi wang* 军事文艺网 [Military Arts and Entertainment], March 11, 2008, http://shibing.milblog.com.cn/20080311/110352.html.

Rawski, Evelyn. "Reenvisioning the Qing: The Significance of the Qing Period in Chinese History." *Journal of Asian Studies* 55, no. 4 (November 1996): 829–850.

Ricoeur, Paul. *Figuring the Sacred: Religion, Narrative and the Imagination*. Translated by David Pellauer. Edited by Mark I. Wallace. Minneapolis: Fortress, 1995.

Rofel, Lisa. "Desiring China: China's Entry into the WTO." In *Desiring China: Experiments in Neoliberalism, Sexuality and Public Culture*, 157–196. Durham, NC: Duke University Press, 2007.

———. *Desiring China: Experiments in Neoliberalism, Sexuality and Public Culture*. Durham, NC: Duke University Press, 2007.

Rossabi, Morris, ed. "Introduction." In *China among Equals: The Middle Kingdom and Its Neighbors*. Berkeley: University of California Press, 1983.

Said, Edward. *Orientalism*. New York: Pantheon, 1978.

Sakamoto Hiroko. "Nishi Junzō." In *Nishi Junzō chosaku shū: Bekken hito to gakumon*. Tokyo: Uchiyama shoten, 1995.

Saussy, Haun. "Contestatory Classics in 1920s China." In *Classics and National Cultures*, edited by Susan A. Stephens and Phiroze Vasunia, 258–266. New York: Oxford University Press, 2010.

Sautman, Barry, and Hairong Yan. "Friends and Interests: China's Distinctive Links with Africa." *African Studies Review* 50, no. 3 (2007): 75–114.

Schram, Stuart. *Mao Tse-Tung*. Baltimore, MD: Penguin, 1966.

Schwartz, Benjamin. "The Chinese Perceptions of World Order, Past and Present." In *The Chinese World Order*, edited by John K. Fairbank, 276–288. Cambridge, MA: Harvard University Press, 1968.

———. *The World of Thought in Ancient China*. Cambridge, MA: Harvard University Press, 1985.

Schweickart, David. *After Capitalism*. Lanham, MD: Rowman and Littlefield, 2011.

Sen, Nabaneeta Dev. "Crisis in Civilization, and a Poet's Alternatives: Education as One Alternative Weapon," paper presented at "Tagore's Philosophy of Education," a conference dedicated to the memory of Amita Sen, Kolkata, March 29–30, 2006.

Shen Zhihua. "The Rupture of the Sino-Soviet Alliance: An Assessment of the National Intelligence Evaluation." In *Challenges to Chinese Foreign Policy: Diplomacy, Globalization, and the Next World Power*, edited by Yufan Hao, C. X. George Wei, and Lowell Dittmer, 275–294. Lexington: University Press of Kentucky, 2009.

Shirk, Susan L. *China: Fragile Superpower*. Oxford: Oxford University Press, 2007.

Shi Zhiyu 石之瑜. "Three Way Crossroads—Challenges for Contemporary China Studies from 'Tianxia' and 'Asia'" 三叉路口——"天下"与"亚洲"对当代中国研究的挑战. In *Lectures on Advanced Studies of China* 中国深度研究高级讲演录, vol. 1, edited by Deng Zhenglai, 1–26. Shanghai: Shangwu, 2010.

Sima Qian 司馬遷 et al. *Shi ji* 史記. Beijing: Zhonghua, 1959.

Sivji, Issa. "Preface." In *The Agrarian Question in the Neoliberal Era: Primitive Accumulation and the Peasantry*, edited by Utsa Patnaik and Sam Moyo, 1–6. Oxford: Pambazuka, 2011.

Smith, John. *Imperialism in the 21st Century: Globalization, Super-exploitation, and Capitalism's Final Crisis*. New York: Monthly Review Press, 2016.

Snow, Philip. "China and Africa: Consensus and Camouflage." In *Chinese Foreign Policy: Theory and Practice*, edited by Thomas W. Robinson and David Shambaugh, 283–321. Oxford: Clarendon, 2004.

Spence, Jonathan. *The Gate of Heavenly Peace*. New York: Penguin, 1981.

Sun Shangyang 孫尚揚 and Guo Lanfang 郭蘭芳, eds. *Guogu xinzhi lun: Xueheng pai wenhua lunzhu jiyao* 國故新知論: 學衡派文化論著輯要 [Discussions of national traditions and new learning: Essential writings on culture by the Critical Review Group]. Beijing: Zhongguo guangbo dianshi chubanshe, 1995.

Su Xiaokang 蘇曉康 and Wang Luxiang 王魯湘. *He shang* 河殤 [River elegy]. Hong Kong: Zhongguo tushu kanxingshe, 1988.

Takeuchi Yoshimi. "Chūgoku no kindai to nihon no kindai: Rojin wo tegakari to shite" [Chinese modernity and Japanese modernity: Taking Lu Xun as a clue]. (This essay is also known as "What Is Modernity?," in Takeuchi Yoshimi, *Nihon to ajia* [Japan and Asia]. Tokyo: Chikuma gakugei bunko, 1993.)

———. *Rojin*. Tokyo: Noma Sawako, 2003.

———. "Watashi to shuyi no chugoku bungaku." In *Takeuchi Zenshū*, 67–73. Tokyo: Chikuma shobo, 1981.

———. *What Is Modernity? Writings of Takeuchi Yoshimi*. Translated by Richard Calichman. New York: Columbia University Press, 2004.

Tan, Sor Hoon. "Secular Religiosity in Chinese Politics: A Confucian Perspective." In *State and Secularism*, edited by C. L. Ten and Michael S. K. Heng, 95–122. Singapore: World Scientific, 2010.

Tanaka, Stefan. *Japan's Orient: Rendering Pasts into History*. Berkeley: University of California Press, 1995.

Tang Yongtong 湯用彤. "Ping jinren zhi wenhua yanjiu" 評近人之文化研究 [Comments on recent studies of culture]. In *Guogu xinzhi lun* [Discussions of national traditions and new learning], edited by Sun Shangyang and Guo Lanfang, 97–100. Beijing: Zhongguo guangbo dianshi chubanshe, 1995.

Tang Zhijun 湯志鈞. *Kang Youwei zhuan* 康有為傳 [Biography of Kang Youwei]. Taipei: Taiwan shangwu, 1997.

Taylor, Charles. *Sources of the Self*. Cambridge, MA: Harvard University Press, 1992.

Thompson, Laurence. *Ta T'ung Shu: The One-World Philosophy of K'ang Yu-wei*. London: Routledge, 2011.

Tilly, Charles. *Coercion, Capital, and European States: A.D. 990–1992*. Oxford: Blackwell, 1992.

Tocqueville, Alexis de. *The Old Regime and the Revolution*. Translated by John Bonner. New York: Harper and Brothers, 1856.

Tohti, Ilham. "Why Have the Uyghurs Felt Defeated?" VOA Interview, July 6, 2013, Urghyur American Association website, uploaded January 12, 2016.

Tong, Shuye, and Gu Xiegang 童書業、顧頡剛. "Ideas about the World and Stories of Overseas Connections in the Pre-Han Period" 漢代以前中國人的世界觀念與域外交通的故事. In *Historical and Geographical Essays* 童書業歷史地理論集, edited by Tong Shuye, 130–168. 1936. Reprint, Beijing: Zhonghua, 2004.

Toshikuni Hihara 日原利國. *Shunjū Kuyōden no kenkyū* 春秋公羊傳の研究. Tokyo: Sobunshō, 1976.

Travel, Taylor. "Regime Insecurity and International Cooperation: Explaining China's Compromises in Territorial Disputes." *International Security* 2, no. 30 (fall 2005).

Uhl, Christian. *Wer war Takeuchis Lu Xun: Ein Annäherungsversuch an ein Monument der japanischen Sinologie* [Who was Takeuchi's Lu Xun? An attempt to approximate a monument in Japanese sinology]. Munich: Iudicum, 2003.

Volland, Nicolai. "Translating the Socialist State: Cultural Exchange, National Identity, and the Socialist World of the Early PRC." *Twentieth-Century China* 33, no. 2 (2008): 51–72.

Wallerstein, Immanuel. *The End of the World as We Know It: Social Science for the 21st Century*. Minneapolis: University of Minnesota Press, 1999.

———. "The Taiwan Question in the Great Change of Contemporary Chinese History: An Analysis Beginning with the 2014 Sunflower Movement." *Cultural Review* 1 (2015): 54–71.

———. *Utopistics: Or, Historical Choices of the Twenty-First Century*. New York: New Press, 1998.

———. "What Cold War in Asia? An Interpretative Essay." In *The Cold War in Asia: The Battle for Hearts and Minds*, edited by Zheng Yangwen, Hong Liu, and Michael Szonyi, 15–24. Leiden: Brill, 2010.

Wang, Ban. "Discovering Enlightenment in Chinese History." *boundary 2* 34, no. 2 (2007): 217–238.

Wang, Mingke 王明珂. *The Peripheries of Huaxia—Historical Memories and Ethnic Identities* 華夏邊緣—歷史記憶與族群認同. Taipei: Yunchen Culture 允晨文化, 1997.

———. *The Qiangs between the Hans and the Tibetans* 羌在漢藏之間. Taipei: Linking, 2003.

Wang, Xiaoming. "The Concept of Asia in Modern China." Translated by Petrus Liu. *Inter-Asia Cultural Studies* 11, no. 2 (2010): 197–201.

Wang Dasan 王达三. "儒家天下觀念與世界秩序重建" (Rujia tianxia guannian yu shijie chengxu zhongjian) [The Confucian concept of tianxia and the construction of the global order]. Confucianism website (儒家網), uploaded November 11, 2010.

Wang Hui. "Gongli, shishi yu yuejie de zhishi" 公理、時勢與越界知識 [Knowledge concerning public principle, judgment of times, and crossing boundaries]. https://wen.org.cn (accessed December 26, 2013).

———. "The Korean War in the 20th-Century Chinese Historical Perspective." *Cultural Review* 6 (2013): 78–100.

———. *The Politics of Imagining Asia*. Cambridge, MA: Harvard University Press, 2011.

———. "The Politics of Imagining Asia: A Genealogical Analysis." *Inter-Asia Cultural Studies* 8, no. 1 (2007): 1–33.

———. "The Taiwan Question in the Great Change of Contemporary Chinese History: An Analysis Beginning with the 2014 Sunflower Movement." *Cultural Review* 1 (2015): 54–71.

———. *Xiandai Zhongguo sixiang de xingqi* 現代中國思想的興起 [The rise of modern Chinese thought]. Beijing: Sanlian shudian, 2004.

Wang Mingming. "'All under Heaven' (*Tianxia*): Cosmological Perspectives and Political Ontologies in Pre-modern China." *Hau: Journal of Ethnographic Theory* 2, no. 1 (2012): 337–383.

———. "Tianxia as World Map" 作為世界圖示的天下. In *Yearbook of Scholarship* 年度学术, edited by Zhao Tingyang, 45–60. Beijing: Zhongguo renmin daxue chubanshe, 2004.

Wang Xianqian 王先謙, ed. *Xunzi jijie* 荀子集解. Beijing: Zhonghua, 1992.

Wang Yougui 王友貴. *Fanyijia Zhou Zuoren* 翻譯家周作人 [Zhou Zuoren the translator]. Chengdu: Sichuan renmin chubanshe, 2001.

Wasserstrom, Jeffrey N. *Global Shanghai, 1850–2010*. New York: Routledge, 2009.

Watanabe, Shinichiro 渡辺信一郎. *The Imperial Power and the Order of All under Heaven in Pre-modern China* 中國古代的王權與天下秩序：從日中比較史的視角出發 (中国古代の王権と天下秩序―日中比較史の視点から). 徐沖. Translated by Xu Chong. Beijing: Zhonghua, 2008.

Weber, Max. *The Religion of China*. Translated and edited by Hans Gerth. 1951. Reprint, New York: Free Press, 1964.

Weber, Samuel. *Benjamin's -Abilities*. Cambridge, MA: Harvard University Press, 2008.

Weinstein, Franklin. "The 2nd Asian-African Conference: Preliminary Bouts." *Asia Survey* 5, no. 7 (July 1965): 359–373.

Wei Tsai-ying 魏綵瑩. "Liao Ping lun *Chunqiu* bozheng xia de shijie zhixu yu Zhongguo" 廖平論《春秋》撥正下的世界秩序與中國 [Liao Ping's view of China's role in the world order]. *Intellectual History* (Sixiang shi) 2 (2014): 54–119.

Westad, Odd Arne. *The Global Cold War: Third World Interventions and the Making of Our Times*. Cambridge: Cambridge University Press, 2007.

Williams, Bernard. *Ethics and the Limits of Philosophy*. Cambridge, MA: Harvard University Press, 1985.

———. *Shame and Necessity*. Berkeley: University of California Press, 1993.

———. *Truth and Truthfulness: An Essay in Genealogy*. Princeton, NJ: Princeton University Press, 2002.

Williams, Charles Kenneth. *Poetry and Consciousness*. Ann Arbor: University of Michigan Press, 1998.

Wines, Michael. "China Tries to Add Cultural Clout to Economic Muscle." *New York Times*, November 8, 2011, http://www.nytimes.com/2011/11/08/world/asia/china-seeks-cultural-influence-to-match-economic-muscle.html.

Womack, Brantley. *China among Unequals: Asymmetrical Foreign Relations in Asia*. London: World Scientific, 2010.

Wood, Ellen. "A Manifesto for Global Capitalism?" In *Debating Empire*, edited by Gopal Balakrishnan, 61–82. London: Verso, 2003.

Wood, Peter. "The Spirit of Xu Sanduo: The Influence of China's Favorite Soldier." *China Brief* 13, no. 15 (2013).

Wu Lengxi. *Ten Years of Debate, 1956–66: Memoir of the Sino-Soviet Relationship*. Beijing: Central Documentary Press, 2013.

Wu Mi 吳宓. "Lun xinwenhua yundong" 論新文化運動 [On the new culture movement]. In *Guogu xinzhi Lun* [Discussions of national traditions and new learning], edited by Sun Shangyang and Guo Lanfang, 78–96. Beijing: Zhongguo guangbo dianshi chubanshe, 1995.

Wu Nong 吳儂. "Zhongguo de ruanshili zai nali?" 中国的软实力在哪里 [Whence China's soft power?]. *Nanfang zhoumo*, September 14, 2012, http://www.infzm.com/content/80833.

Wu Yujiang 吳毓江, ed. *Mozi jiaozhu* 墨子校注. Beijing: Zhonghua, 1994.

Xiang Shiling. "A Study on the Theory of 'Returning to the Original' and 'Recovering Nature' in Chinese Philosophy." *Frontiers of Philosophy in China* 3, no. 4 (2008): 502–519.

Yan, Hairong. *New Master, New Servants: Migration, Development and Women Workers in China.* Durham, NC: Duke University Press, 2008.

Yang Bojun 楊伯峻, ed. *Mengzi yi zhu* 孟子譯注. Beijing: Zhonghua, 1992.

Yang Guobin and Craig Calhoun. "Media, Civil Society and the Rise of a Green Public Sphere in China." *China Information* 21 (2007): 211–234.

Yang Shiqun 楊師群. *Dong Zhou Qin Han shehui zhuanxing yanjiu* 東周秦漢社會轉型研究 [Studies on societal changes in the eastern Zhou, Qin, and Han]. Shanghai: Guji chubanshe, 2003.

Yan Xuetong. *Ancient Chinese Thought, Modern Chinese Power.* Edited by Daniel A. Bell and Sun Zhe. Translated by Edmund Ryden. Princeton, NJ: Princeton University Press, 2011.

———. "How Assertive Should a Power Be?" *New York Times*, March 31, 2011.

———. "How China Can Defeat America." *New York Times*, November 21, 2011, http://www.nytimes.com/2011/11/21/opinion/how-china-can-defeat-america.html.

Yearley, Lee H. "The Author Replies [to Nussbaum, Van Norden, and Jenkins]." *Journal of Religious Ethics* 21, no. 2 (fall 1993): 385–395.

———. "Conflicts among Ideals of Human Flourishing." In *Prospects for a Common Morality*, edited by Gene H. Outka and John P. Reeder, 233–253. Princeton, NJ: Princeton University Press, 1993.

———. "An Existentialist Reading of Book Four of the *Analects*." In *Confucius and the Analects, New Essays*, edited by Bryan Van Norden, 237–274. New York: Oxford University Press, 2002.

———. "Freud and China: The Pursuit of the Self and Other Fugitive Notions." In *China and Freud*, edited by Tao Jiang and P. J. Ivanhoe, 169–195. New York: Routledge, 2012.

———. "Freud and Zhuangzi: Resonances and Contrasts in Their Pursuit of the Self and Other Fugitive Notions." In *China and Freud*, edited by Tao Jiang and P. J. Ivanhoe, 219–251. New York: Routledge, 2012.

———. *Mencius and Aquinas: Theories of Virtue and Conceptions of Courage.* Albany: State University of New York Press, 1990. [Chinese translation: *Mengzi yu Akuina: Meide lilun yu yonggan gainian.* Translated by Shi Zhonglian. Beijing: Zhongguo shehui kexue chubanshe, 2011.]

———. "Poetic Language: Zhuangzi and Du Fu's Poetic Ideals." In *Ethics in Early China: An Anthology*, edited by Chris Fraser, Timothy O'Leary, and Dan Robins, 209–228. Hong Kong: University of Hong Kong Press, 2011.

———. "Selves, Virtues, Odd Genres, and Alien Guides: An Approach to Religious Ethics." *Journal of Religious Ethics* (25th anniversary suppl.) 25, no. 3 (September 1997): 127–155.

———. "Virtue Ethics in Ancient China: Light Shed and Shadows Cast." In *How Should One Live? Comparing Ethics in Ancient China and Greco-Roman Antiquity*, edited by R. King and D. Schilling, 121–151. Berlin: De Gruyter Verlag, 2011.

———. "Virtues and Religious Virtues in the Confucian Tradition." In *Confucian Spirituality*, edited by Tu Weiming and Evelyn Tucker, 134–162. New York: Crossroads, 2003–2004. [Chinese translation: "Rujia chuantong zhong de daode he zongjiao daode." Translated by Dongfang Shuo, http://www.chinakongzi.org/rjwh/ddmj /dongfs/200705/t20070523_2176643.htm.]

———. "Xunzi: Ritualization as Humanization." In *Ritual and Religion in the Xunzi*, edited by T. C. Kline and Justin Tiwald, 81–106. Albany: State University of New York Press, 2014.

Yin, Zhiguang. "De-frontiers: The Global Order, the Caliphate Empire and the Xinjiang Question under the Crisis of Ideology." *Sociology of Ethnicity* 187 (July 2015): 1–18.

Yoshimi Shunya. "Rekishi ha doko he iku no ka" [Where is history going?]. In *Nihon no kingendaishi wo dō miru no ka.* Tokyo: Iwanami shinso, 2010.

You, Yi-Fei 游逸飛. "The Four Corners, All under Heaven, Commanderies and Kingdoms: Transformation and Development of Views of Tianxia in Ancient China" 四方、天下、郡國—周秦漢天下觀的變革與發展. Master's thesis, National Taiwan University 國立台灣大學歷史學系碩士論文, 2009.

Young, Louise. *Japan's Total Empire: Manchuria and the Culture of Wartime Imperialism.* Berkeley: University of California Press, 1998.

Yu, Geore. "China's Failure in Africa." *Asian Survey* 6, no. 8 (August 1966): 461–468.

Zahran, Geraldo, and Leonardo Ramos. "From Hegemony to Soft Power: Implications of a Conceptual Change." In *Soft Power and U.S. Foreign Policy*, edited by Inderjeet Parmar and Michael Cox, 12–31. London: Routledge, 2010.

Zhan, Mei. "Civet Cats, Fried Grasshoppers, and David Beckham's Pajamas: Unruly Bodies after SARS." *American Anthropologist* 107, no. 1 (2005): 31–42.

———. "Does It Take a Miracle? Negotiating Knowledges, Identities and Communities of Traditional Chinese Medicine." *Cultural Anthropology* 6, no. 4 (2001): 453–480.

———. *Other-Worldly: Making Chinese Medicine through Transnational Frames.* Durham, NC: Duke University Press, 2009.

Zhang, Chengzhi 張承志. *Respect and Farewell—to Japan* 敬重與惜別一致日本. Beijing: Zhongguo youyi chuban gongsi, 2009.

Zhang, Li. *In Search of Paradise: Middle-Class Living in a Chinese Metropolis.* Ithaca, NY: Cornell University Press, 2010.

Zhang, Longxi. *Mighty Opposites: From Dichotomies to Difference in the Comparative Study of China.* Stanford, CA: Stanford University Press, 1998.

Zhang, Shuguang 張曙光. "Theory of Tianxia and World Institution: Learning from Mr. Zhao Tingyang by Asking Questions on *Tianxia* System" 天下理論和世界制度—就《天下體系》問學於趙汀陽先生. *China Book Review* 中國書評 5 (2006): 18–30.

Zhang, Xin. "One Belt One Road in the Perspective of State Capitalism." *Cultural Review* 6 (2015): 30–35.

Zhang Feng. "Regionalization in the *Tianxia*: Continuity and Change in China's Foreign Policy." Paper presented at the China-West Intellectual Summit, Paris, February 23–24, 2009.

———. "Rethinking the 'Tribute System': Broadening the Conception Horizon of Historical East Asian Politics." *Chinese Journal of International Politics* 2 (2009).

———. "The *Tianxia* System: World Order in a Chinese Utopia." *Chinese Heritage Quarterly* 21 (March 2010).

———. "The Tianxia System: World Order in a Chinese Utopia." *Globalasia* 4, no. 4 (2010), http://www.globalasia.org/V4N4_Winter_2010/Feng_Zhang.html.

Zhang Taiyan. "Da Tie Zheng" [Letter to Tie Zheng]. In *Zhang Taiyan quanji* [The complete works of Zhang Taiyan], 4: 368–375. Shanghai: Shanghai renmin chubanshe, 1985.

Zhan guo ce 戰國策. Annotated by Fan Xiangyong 范祥雍. Shanghai: Shanghai Guji, 2006.

Zhang Yulin. "'Tiandi yibian' yu Zhongguo nongcun yanjiu" ["Upheaval on heaven and earth" and research on Chinese villages]. *Zhongguo yanjiu*, spring 2009, 1–17.

Zhao, Dingxin. *The Power of Tiananmen: State-Society Relations and the 1989 Beijing Student Movement*. Chicago: University of Chicago Press, 2001.

Zhao Tingyang. "All-under-Heaven and Methodological Relationism: An Old Story and New World Peace." In *Contemporary Chinese Political Thought: Debates and Perspectives*, edited by Fred Dallmayr and Zhao Tingyang. Lexington: University Press of Kentucky, 2012.

———. "Cong shijie kaishi de *tianxia* zhengzhi" 從世界開始的天下政治 [Tianxia politics with the world as point of departure]. In *Dongya zhixu* 東亞秩序 [Asia order], edited by Zhou Fangying and Gao Cheng, 44–84. Beijing: Shehui kexue wenxian chubanshe, 2012.

———. "A Political World Philosophy in Terms of All-under-Heaven (*Tian-xia*)." *Diogenes* 56, no. 5 (2009): 5–18.

———. "Rethinking Empire from a Chinese Concept 'All-under-Heaven' (*Tian-xia*)." *Social Identities: Journal for the Study of Race, Nation and Culture* 12, no. 1 (2006): 29–41.

———. *Tianxia tixi* 天下體系 [The tianxia system]. Nanjing: Jiangsu jiaoyu, 2005.

———. *Tianxia Tixi: An Introduction to a Philosophy of World Institution* 天下體系：世界制度哲學導論. Nanking: Jiang su jiao yu chubanshe, 2005.

Zheng Shiqu 鄭師渠. *Wan Qing guocuipai wenhua sixiang yanjiu* 晚清國粹派文化思想研究 [The cultural thought of the National Essence Group in the late Qing]. Beijing: Beijing shifan daxue chubanshe, 1997.

Zhong, Xueping. *Mainstream Culture Refocused: Television Drama, Society, and the Production of Meaning in Reform-Era China*. Honolulu: University of Hawai'i Press, 2010.

Zhou, Baohong 周寶宏. *Collected Annotations of Recently Found Western Zhou Bronze Inscriptions* 近出西周金文集釋. Tianjin: Tianjin gu ji chubanshe, 2005.

Zhou, Lian. "The Most Fashionable and the Most Relevant: A Review of Contemporary Chinese Political Philosophy." *Diogenes* 221 (2009): 128–137.

———. "The Two Methodological Principles of *Tianxia Tixi*" 《天下體系》的兩條方法論原則. *China Book Review* 中國書評 5 (2006): 5–17.

Zhou, Taomo. "Ambivalent Alliance: Chinese Policy towards Indonesia, 1960–1965." *China Quarterly* 221 (March 2015): 208–228.

Zhou Enlai. "Ethnic-Regional Autonomy Enhances Solidarity of Nationalities and Common Progress." In *Selected Writings of Zhou Enlai on the United Front*, 334–346. Beijing: People's Publishing House, 1984.

———. "On a Few Questions Concerning Our Nationality Policy." In *Selected Writings of Zhou Enlai on the United Front*, 369–377. Beijing: People's Publishing House, 1984.

Zhou Zuoren. *Zhou Zuoren wen leibian* 周作人文類編 [A thematic anthology of Zhou Zuoren's writings]. 10 vols. Edited by Zhong Shuhe 鈡叔河. Changsha: Hunan wenyi chubanshe, 1998.

Zhu, Ying. *Television in Post-reform China: Serial Dramas, Confucian Leadership and the Global Television Market.* London: Routledge, 2008.

Zhuang Guotu 庄国土. "略论朝贡制度的虚幻：以古代中国与东南亚的朝贡关系为例" (Luelun chaogong zhidu de xuhuan: Yi gudai zhongguo yu dongya de chaogong guanxi yi li) [An account of the illusion of the tributary system: An example of the relationships in the tributary system in ancient China and East Asia]. *Research on Nanyang* 南洋問題研究 3 (2005).

Zhu Renqiu. "The Formation, Development, and Evolution of Neo-Confucianism with a Focus on the Doctrine of 'Stilling the Nature' in the Song Period." *Frontiers of Philosophy in China* 4, no. 3 (2009): 322–342.

Contributors

DANIEL A. BELL (chapter 6) is dean of the Faculty of Politics and Public Administration at Shandong University (Qingdao) and professor at Tsinghua University (Beijing). His latest book is *The China Model: Political Meritocracy and the Limits of Democracy* (Princeton University Press, 2016) and he is the editor of the Princeton-China series. He writes frequently for leading media outlets in China and the West.

CHISHEN CHANG (chapter 11) is assistant professor in the Department of Political Science, National Chengchi University, Taiwan. His PhD thesis, which has been substantially revised for publication, was about the connotations of Chineseness in history, and the formation of the ethnocentric strand in Chinese ethnic thought before the eighteenth century. He has published journal articles on Chinese ethnic thought and other issues such as the discourse of the tianxia system. His research interests also include Chinese political thought of the pre-Qin period.

KUAN-HSING CHEN (chapter 11) is professor in the Graduate Institute for Social Research and Cultural Studies, Chiao Tung University, Taiwan, and is the founding chair of the board of trustees for the Inter-Asia School and its current executive director. He has been a visiting professor at UC-Berkeley; Tokyo, Toshisha, and Ritsumenken Universities; Yonsei University in Korea; Shanghai University; Nanjing University; Xiamen University; Lingnan University in Hong Kong; National University of Singapore; Makerere University in Uganda; University of Addis Ababa in Ethiopia; Duke University; and UC-Santa Cruz. His publications include *Asia as Method: Towards Deimperialization* (Duke University Press, 2010). He has edited *Stuart Hall: Critical Dialogues in Cultural Studies* (Routledge, 1996), *Trajectories: Inter-Asia Cultural Studies* (Routledge, 1998), and *Inter-Asia Cultural Studies Reader* (Routledge, 2007). His edited Chinese volumes include *Cultural Studies in Taiwan* (2000), *The Partha Chatterjee Seminar: Locating Political Society* (2000), *Chinese Revolution Reconsidered: Mizoguchi's Mode of Thought* (2010), *Paik Naik-chung: Division System and National Literature* (2010), and *Chen Yingzhen: Thought and Literature* (2011). Recently he has been involved in the West Heavens (India-China Social Thought) Project and in establishing the Inter-Asia School to launch the Modern Asian

Thought project (2010–), Asian Circle of Thought Shanghai Summit (2012), Inter-Asia Biennale Forum (2014), and Bandung/Third World 60 Years Series (2015). Under the umbrella name Decolonizing the Earth, he is setting up the Council for Social Research in Asia, and the Bandung Institute for Africa-Asia-America-Caribbean on Hangzhou's China Academy of Art campus. A core member of *Taiwan: A Radical Quarterly in Social Studies*, he is a coeditor of the journal *Inter-Asia Cultural Studies: Movements* (2000–) and *Renjian Thought Review*.

PRASENJIT DUARA (chapter 3) is the Oscar Tang Chair of East Asian Studies at Duke University. Born and educated in India, he received his PhD in Chinese history from Harvard University. He was professor of history and East Asian studies at the University of Chicago (1991–2008) and Raffles Professor and Director of the Asia Research Institute at the National University of Singapore (2008–2015). His books include *Culture, Power and the State: Rural North China, 1900–1942* (Stanford University Press, 1988), winner of Fairbank Prize of the AHA and Levenson Prize of the AAS; *Rescuing History from the Nation* (University of Chicago Press, 1995), *Sovereignty and Authenticity: Manchukuo and the East Asian Modern* (Rowman, 2003), and *The Crisis of Global Modernity: Asian Traditions and a Sustainable Future* (Cambridge University Press, 2014).

MEI-YU HSIEH (chapter 1) is assistant professor of world history at the Marion campus of Ohio State University. Her research interests include preimperial and early imperial Chinese history, historical archaeology of East Eurasia, Chinese paleography, and the sociology of power relations and state institutions, with a special focus on the correlations between communication and empire building. She is currently completing a book manuscript titled *The Making of Imperial East Eurasia: A Multipolar Perspective*, which explores the tensions and compromises between the imperial metropole, government bureaucrats, and local populations as the Han dynasties extended their political influence westward from East to Central Asia between the first centuries BCE and CE.

HAIYAN LEE (chapter 10) is professor of Chinese literature at Stanford University. She was educated at Beijing University, the University of Chicago, and Cornell University. She is the author of *The Stranger and the Chinese Moral Imagination* (Stanford University Press, 2014) and *Revolution of the Heart: A Genealogy of Love in China, 1900–1950* (Stanford University Press, 2007), which won the 2009 Joseph Levenson Prize (post-1900 China) from the Association for Asian Studies. She is also the guest editor of "Taking It to Heart: Emotion, Modernity, Asia," a special issue of *positions: east asia cultures critique* (2008). Her scholarly articles have appeared in *PMLA*, *Telos*, *Public Culture*, *Journal of Asian Studies*, *positions*, *Modern China*, *Twentieth-Century China*, and elsewhere.

MARK EDWARD LEWIS (chapter 1) is Kwoh-Ting Li Professor in Chinese history in the Department of History at Stanford. He received his PhD from the University of Chicago and studied Chinese at Stanford. He researches many aspects of Chinese civilization in the late preimperial, early imperial, and middle periods (contemporary with the centuries in the West from classical Greece through the early Middle Ages), and investigates empire as a political and social form. He is the author of *Sanctioned Violence in Early China*, *Writing and Authority in Early China*, and *The Construction of Space in Early China*, with the companion volume *The Flood Myths of Early China*. Lewis has written the first three volumes of a six-volume survey of the entire history of imperial China: *The Early Chinese Empires: Qin and Han*; *China between Empires: The Northern and Southern Dynasties*; and *China's Cosmopolitan Empire: The Tang Dynasty*.

LIN CHUN (chapter 8) has a doctorate from Cambridge University in history and political science and teaches at the London School of Economics. Lin is the author of *The British New Left* (1993), *The Transformation of Chinese Socialism* (2006), and *China and Global Capitalism* (2013). She is also the editor of *China I, II, and III* (2000) and coeditor with Gregor Benton of *Is Mao Really a Monster?* (2009). Her articles appear in various journals and languages. Among her books in Chinese are *Reflections on China's Reform Trajectory* (2008) and (coedited) *Women: The Longest Revolution* (1997). She sits on the executive committee of *China Quarterly* and coedits Palgrave's China in Transformation book series.

VIREN MURTHY (chapter 7) is associate professor of history at the University of Wisconsin–Madison and researches Chinese and Japanese intellectual history. He is the author of *The Political Philosophy of Zhang Taiyan* (Brill, 2011). He is coeditor with Axel Schneider of *The Challenge of Linear Time: Nationhood and the Politics of History in East Asia* (Brill, 2013), coeditor with Prasenjit Duara and Andrew Sartori of *A Companion to Global Historical Thought* (Blackwell, 2014), coeditor with Joyce Liu of *East-Asian Marxisms and Their Trajectories* (Routledge, 2017), and coeditor with Max Ward and Fabian Schaefer of *Confronting Capital: Rethinking the Kyoto School* (Brill, forthcoming 2017). He has published articles in *Critical Historical Studies*, *Modern Intellectual History*, *Modern China*, *Inter-Asia Cultural Studies*, *Frontiers of History in China*, and *positions: asia critique* and is currently working on a project tentatively titled *Pan-Asianism and the Conundrums of Postcolonial Modernity*.

LISA ROFEL (chapter 9) is professor of anthropology and director of the Center for Emerging Worlds Anthropology at University of California, Santa Cruz. She has written and coedited five books and numerous articles on China, including *Other Modernities: Gendered Yearnings in China after Socialism* and *Desiring China: Experiments in Neo-liberalism, Sexuality and Public Culture*. She has completed a coauthored book (with Sylvia Yanagisako) titled *Made in Translation: A Collaborative Ethnography of Italian-Chinese Global Fashion* (Duke University Press); has edited a book of translated essays by the renowned Chinese cultural studies scholar Dai Jinhua, titled *After the Post–Cold War* (Duke University Press, forthcoming); and is editing a translated collection of short stories by the queer experimental filmmaker and writer Cui Z'en titled *Silver Bible of the W.C.*

BAN WANG (editor, introduction, chapter 4) is the William Haas Professor in Chinese Studies at Stanford University. He teaches in the departments of East Asian Languages and Comparative Literature. His major publications include *The Sublime Figure of History: Aesthetics and Politics in Twentieth-Century China, Illuminations from the Past*, and *History and Memory*. He edited and coedited *Trauma and Cinema, The Image of China in the American Classroom, China and New Left Visions, Debating the Socialist Legacy and Capitalist Globalization in China*, and *Words and Their Stories: Essays on the Language of the Chinese Revolution*. He was a research fellow with the National Endowment for the Humanities in 2000 and the Institute for Advanced Study at Princeton in 2007. He has taught in Beijing Foreign Studies University, SUNY-Stony Brook, Rutgers University, Harvard University, East China Normal University, and Seoul National University in Korea.

WANG HUI (chapter 2) is professor of literature and history at Tsinghua University and director of the Institute for Advanced Study in Humanities and Social Sciences at Tsinghua University. Wang studied under the guidance of Professor Tang Tao, a famous literary historian and one of Lu Xun's students, on Lu Xun and literary history and achieved his PhD at the Chinese Academy of Social Sciences in 1988. In 2002, he moved from CASS to Tsinghua University. From 1996 to 2007, he organized a series of intellectual discussions in China as the chief editor of *Dushu Magazine*, a highly influential intellectual journal. He has published extensively on Chinese intellectual history and literature, and engaged in debates on historical and contemporary issues. Many of his books have been translated into English, Italian, Spanish, Japanese, Korean, German, Slovenian, and so on, including the English translations *China from China's Twentieth Century* (2015), *Empire to Nation-State* (2014), *The Politics of Imagining Asia* (2010), *The End of Revolution* (2009), and *China's New Order* (2003). His four-volume work *The Rise of Modern Chinese Thought* (2004) is considered one of the most important contributions to the Chinese academic world in the last twenty years. Wang Hui has received several awards, including the 2013 Luca Pacioli Prize, which he shared with Jürgen Habermas.

YIQUN ZHOU (chapter 5) is associate professor in the Department of East Asian Languages and Cultures, Stanford University. Her major research interests include Chinese and comparative women's history, early Chinese history and literature, late imperial Chinese fiction, China-Greece comparative studies, and the reception of antiquity in the modern age. She is the author of *Festivals, Feasts, and Gender Relations in Ancient China and Greece* (Cambridge University Press, 2010).

Index

class nation, 14, 17, 177, 181–184, 188, 193, 197–198, 204, 205n12

Cold War, 13, 66, 87, 135, 155, 187–189, 195–196, 200, 205n11, 207n28, 207n31, 216, 224, 240–241, 288; post-, 74, 214–215, 219, 223, 227

colonialism, 5, 7, 13–15, 20, 93, 156, 168, 182, 248; Japanese, 166; Portuguese, 194

Comintern, 191, 216

communist cosmopolitanism, 14

competition, 1, 19, 28, 31, 33–34, 56, 66, 89, 93, 107, 121, 126n21, 138, 180, 191, 199, 224–225, 233n54, 242, 248, 251

conceptual empire, 264

Confucianism, 2, 6, 9, 14, 93, 99, 100, 113, 118–120, 122, 131, 141, 146n52, 153, 158–160, 170, 202, 242, 249; Kang Youwei and, 49–57, 61–64, 101, 104, 133. *See also* Neo-Confucianism; New Text Confucianism; Song Confucianism

Confucian universalism, 7, 8, 10, 50, 57, 60–62, 89

Confucius Institute, 244, 247, 249

consumption, 18, 74, 227–228

cosmology, 8, 70–72, 201

cosmopolitan ethos, 2, 9–10

cosmopolitanism, 2, 5, 9–10, 12, 14, 19, 81n2, 87–88, 106, 108, 124, 199, 215, 226–227, 263; capitalist, 18; Kang Youwei and, 100; Kant and, 67, 89, 92; Tagore and, 76

cosmopolitan empire, 30, 44

cosmopolitan state, 6, 41

cosmopolitan tianxia, 39, 42

Critical Review, 118–119, 122–123, 126n29, 126n32

Critique of the Power of Judgment, 105n9, 105n10

cultural community, 117, 271–272, 274

cultural empire, 70

Cultural Revolution, 113, 166, 188, 190, 196, 215, 221

Dao, 70, 76, 101

Daoism, 50–51, 75–76, 261

datong, 15, 54, 61–63, 71, 99, 102. *See also* great unity

Datong shu. See Book of the Great Community

decolonization, 13, 17–18, 188, 195, 289

de minxin, 2

democracy, 4, 13, 60–61, 70, 80, 100, 103–104, 113–114, 118, 121, 126n34, 137, 140, 142, 145n36, 160, 169, 195, 198, 202, 206n14, 211n73, 229, 233n54, 243–245, 264n25, 275, 277–281, 283–284

de Tocqueville, Alexis, 61–62, 103–104

Deng Xiaoping, 14, 166, 209n52, 210n58, 268

development, 1, 17–18, 61, 66, 77, 112, 145, 151–152, 161, 165, 172, 180–183, 188–190, 195, 198–199, 203, 205n9, 205–206, 207n31, 208n36, 209n56, 211–212, 217, 219, 220–221, 229, 231, 243, 248, 250, 261, 266n68, 268, 288; cultural, 140, 244; human, 186; national, 18, 181, 201

developmentalism, 197, 200, 207n30, 213

developmental state, 181

Di people, 26, 29, 43, 271–272, 282

diplomacy, 1, 8, 190, 241, 246, 248

disinterestedness, 98

diversity, 17, 46, 50, 53, 60, 71, 112, 184–185, 279

Dong Zhongshu, 54, 57, 99, 102

dual state, 42, 44, 48n42

Du Yaquan, 115–116, 118, 125n14, 126n21, 126n23

Eagleton, Terry, 91, 96, 98

Eastern Han, 31, 40–44, 290n23

East-West cultural debate, 109, 126n23

ecology, 75

empathy, 91–92, 95, 97

Emperor Wu, 36–37, 40, 51

empire, 4, 7–9, 13, 16, 29–34, 37, 40–42, 45–46, 47n11, 50, 56–63, 70–71, 89, 93, 97, 100, 103, 114, 124, 128n47, 132, 138, 143n3, 171, 178–180, 182, 205n7, 206n14, 230–231, 242, 245, 262, 263n25, 286, 288; American, 276; European, 289; Greco-Roman, 62; oriental, 49; Soviet, 130; steppe, 33, 40, 44; Tsarist, 186; Umayyad, 138

enlightenment, 10, 12

unity, 4, 8–10, 15, 17, 20, 28, 50–56, 58–60, 71, 101, 103, 157, 160, 179, 185, 189, 194, 206n20, 209n49, 228, 242, 256, 279, 283

universalism, 7, 8, 10–11, 18, 50, 57, 60–61, 65, 67, 69, 71–74, 79, 80, 81n2, 89, 202, 242, 247–248, 274, 284; Christian, 62; Kantian, 67, 70; Mozi and, 284; socialist, 215

universal state, 47n12, 57

unsocial sociability, 11, 69, 90–92, 95, 98

utopia, 60–61, 66, 69, 70–71, 80, 90, 106, 117, 121, 139, 160, 164–165, 174, 215, 229, 232n8, 243–244, 249, 263n25, 264n25, 274–275

Wallerstein, Immanuel, 205n10, 209n47, 219

wang, 27, 32, 43

wangdao. *See* Kingly Way

Wang Yangming, 73

Warring States period, 19, 26–29, 46n6, 47n13, 50–54, 93, 95, 112, 131, 140, 180, 269, 271–274, 290n23, 290n24, 290n25

Warsaw Pact, 135, 190, 208n38, 216

Washington Consensus, 243

Weber, Max, 179, 180, 82n11

Westphalian system, 20, 87, 93, 101, 130, 134, 143n2, 203, 248, 284

Wight, Martin, 88

worlding, 18, 213–215, 217–218, 222–225, 227, 229, 231

world politics, 19, 201, 275

WTO (World Trade Organization), 2, 224–226

Vietnam, 187, 188, 192, 194–196, 209n52, 210n57, 218, 252, 257, 261

Xia, 28–29, 47n10; central realm of China, 58; civilized, 201; dynasty, 53

Xianbei, 40, 42–44

xiaokang, 63–64, 100, 102

Xinjiang, 37, 44, 186, 197, 201, 206n21, 219, 284

Xiongnu, 8, 30–44, 47n22

Xunzi, The, 27, 47n11, 134, 138, 144n23, 144n28

Yangtze River, 31–32, 34

Yellow River, 31–38, 40, 43–44, 126n21, 178

Yen, Y. C. James "Jimmy," 76

yi, 29, 47n10, 58, 201, 271–273, 282, 289n4, 290n23

yidi, 29, 282–283

Zhang Chengzhi, 20, 285–289, 292n67

Zhang Taiyan, 104, 114, 150, 160, 162–163, 170

Zhao, Tingyang, 2–4, 19–20, 70–72, 132–134, 137–138, 139, 144n18, 145n41, 242–245, 248–249, 262, 263n25, 269, 273–284, 292n51, 292n54, 292n57

zhi, 27, 53. *See also* order

Zhongguo, 7, 25, 28, 59, 77, 93, 109, 132, 243, 249, 270–274, 283, 290n18, 290n24

zhongyong, 117

Zhou dynasty, 2, 19, 26–29, 46n8, 47n13, 50, 70–72, 82n15, 99–100, 132, 145n41, 230, 269–270, 274–275, 282, 290n8, 290n18

Zhou Enlai, 143n6, 186, 189, 194, 206n21

Zhou Zuoren, 76, 116–118, 126n25

Zuo Commentary, 11, 21n23, 26–27, 101, 140

Zuo Zhuan. *See Zuo Commentary*

Zuozhuan. *See Zuo Commentary*

www.ingramcontent.com/pod-product-compliance
Lightning Source LLC
Chambersburg PA
CBHW070710280326
41926CB00089B/3445